The Political Psychology of Terrorism Fears

THE POLITICAL PSYCHOLOGY OF TERRORISM FEARS

Edited by
Samuel Justin Sinclair

and

Daniel Antonius

OXFORD
UNIVERSITY PRESS

Oxford University Press is a department of the University of Oxford.
It furthers the University's objective of excellence in research, scholarship,
and education by publishing worldwide.

Oxford   New York
Auckland   Cape Town   Dar es Salaam   Hong Kong   Karachi
Kuala Lumpur   Madrid   Melbourne   Mexico City   Nairobi
New Delhi   Shanghai   Taipei   Toronto

With offices in
Argentina   Austria   Brazil   Chile   Czech Republic   France   Greece
Guatemala   Hungary   Italy   Japan   Poland   Portugal   Singapore
South Korea   Switzerland   Thailand   Turkey   Ukraine   Vietnam

Oxford is a registered trademark of Oxford University Press in the UK and certain other
countries.

Published in the United States of America by
Oxford University Press
198 Madison Avenue, New York, NY 10016

© Oxford University Press 2013

All rights reserved. No part of this publication may be reproduced, stored in a
retrieval system, or transmitted, in any form or by any means, without the prior
permission in writing of Oxford University Press, or as expressly permitted by law,
by license, or under terms agreed with the appropriate reproduction rights organization.
Inquiries concerning reproduction outside the scope of the above should be sent to the
Rights Department, Oxford University Press, at the address above.

You must not circulate this work in any other form
and you must impose this same condition on any acquirer.

Library of Congress Cataloging-in-Publication Data
The political psychology of terrorism fears / edited by Samuel Justin Sinclair and Daniel Antonius.
pages cm
Includes bibliographical references.
ISBN 978-0-19-992592-6
1. Terrorism—Psychological aspects.   2. Terrorism—Political aspects.   I. Sinclair, Samuel J., 1975–
II. Antonius, Daniel.
HV6431.P6185 2013
363.32501'9–dc23
2013001914

9 8 7 6 5 4 3 2 1
Printed in the United States of America
on acid-free paper

Samuel Justin Sinclair:
This book is dedicated to my mentor and friend, Dr. Kimberly Bistis. You have taught me a lot about being a better psychologist, thinker, and person.

Daniel Antonius:
To "farfar," who at the young age of 94 continues to be inspirational in everything I do.

CONTENTS

Dedication   v
Acknowledgments   ix
Contributors   xi
Introduction   xv
   Samuel Justin Sinclair and Daniel Antonius

PART ONE
1. Trust in the U.S. Government and Antiterrorism Policies After 9/11: Are We All in This Together?   3
   Virginia A. Chanley
2. Perceptions of Threat, Trust in Government, and Policy Support for the War in Iraq   20
   George Shambaugh
3. Negative Emotions and Political Engagement   51
   Michael J. Stevens
4. Beyond the Water's Edge: Threat, Partisanship, and Media   67
   Shana Kushner Gadarian
5. The War/Crime Narrative and Fear Content in Leader Rhetoric About Terrorism   85
   Krista De Castella and Craig McGarty
6. Fear of Suicide Terrorism: Consequences for Individuals and Politics   107
   C. Dominik Güss, Alexandra Foust, and Dietrich Dörner
7. Policy Preference in Response to Terrorism: The Role of Emotions, Attributions, and Appraisals   125
   Geoffrey Wetherell, Bradley M. Weisz, Ryan M. Stolier, Adam J. Beavers, and Melody S. Sadler

PART TWO
8. The Legacy of Fear in Northern Ireland   139
   Rachel Monaghan
9. A New Normal? Australian Responses to Terrorism and Their Impacts   156
   Anne Aly

10. Psychological Determinants of the Threat of Terrorism and Preferred Approaches to Counterterrorism: The Case of Poland   171
   Katarzyna Jaśko, Małgorzata Kossowska, and Maciej Sekerdej
11. An Exposure Effect? Evidence from a Rigorous Study on the Psychopolitical Outcomes of Terrorism   193
   Daphna Canetti, Carmit Rapaport, Carly Wayne, Brian J. Hall, and Stevan E. Hobfoll
12. Political Psychology of the Death Terror   213
   Abdolhossein Abdollahi
13. Risk Perception, Fear, and Its Consequences Following the 2004 Madrid and 2005 London Bombings   227
   Marie-Helen Maras
14. Rallying Without Fear: Political Consequences of Terror in a High-Trust Society   246
   Dag Wollebæk, Kari Steen-Johnsen, Bernard Enjolras, and Guro Ødegård

PART THREE

15. The Politics of Terrorism Fears   267
   Richard Jackson
16. Constructing Psychological Terror Post 9/11   283
   David L. Altheide
17. Why Is It So Difficult to Evaluate the Political Impact of Terrorism?   299
   Ami-Jacques Rapin

Notes on Contributors   313
Index   321

ACKNOWLEDGMENTS

We would like to express our profound appreciation to the distinguished group of scholars who contributed to this volume and who gave their valuable time, expertise, and resources in helping us put together what we believe is an important body of work. The strength of the volume is reflected in the eminent group of professionals who contributed, and we are profoundly grateful and honored to have gotten the chance to work with you.

We would also like to express our sincere gratitude to Abby Gross at Oxford University Press, who encouraged us to publish this book and helped evolve our thinking along the way. This is the second time we have been privileged to work with you, and your professionalism, support, and kindness are unparalleled. We hope to have this opportunity many more times! Thank you.

This book would also not have been possible without the support of our respective institutions, and we feel it is important to take a moment to express our appreciation. SJS would like to thank his colleagues and friends at the Massachusetts General Hospital and Harvard Medical School, and specifically at the Psychological Evaluation and Research Laboratory (*The PEaRL*). More specifically, thank you to Drs. Mark Blais, Kimberly Bistis, Michelle Stein, Jenelle Slavin-Mulford, and Sheila O'Keefe. DA would like to thank his colleagues and friends at University at Buffalo, New York University, and Erie County Forensic Mental Health Services. We feel very lucky to have such an amazing group of friends and colleagues with whom to share this work.

Finally, and perhaps most importantly, we'd like to thank our respective families for the constant support and love we feel, even when our work carries us away for a while. SJS would like to say thank you to his crew: Tatum, Cole, Reese, Ma, Q, Lucy, and Maggie Muffin—I love you guys. DA would like to thank his family in Denmark, Norway, and the United States—Thank you for everything!

CONTRIBUTORS

Samuel Justin Sinclair
Department of Psychiatry
Massachusetts General Hospital &
 Harvard Medical School
Boston, Massachusetts

Daniel Antonius
Department of Psychiatry
University at Buffalo School of Medicine
 and Biomedical Sciences
Buffalo, New York

Abdolhossein Abdollahi
Department of Psychology
University of Limerick
Limerick, Ireland

David Altheide
School of Social Transformation
Arizona State University
Phoenix, Arizona

Anne (Azza) Aly
Department of Social Science and
 International Relations
Curtin University
Perth, Australia

Adam Beavers
Department of Psychology
San Diego State University
San Diego, California

Daphna Canetti
School of Political Science
University of Haifa
Haifa, Israel

Virginia Chanley
George Mason University
Fairfax, Virginia

Krista De Castella
Department of Psychology
Stanford University
Stanford, California

Dietrich Dörner
Institute for Theoretical Psychology
Otto-Friedrich Universität
Bamberg, Germany

Bernard Enjolras
Institute for Social Research
Oslo, Norway

Alexandra N. Foust
Vanderbilt University
Nashville, Tennessee

Shana Kushner Gadarian
Department of Political Science
Maxwell School of Citizenship and
 Public Affairs
Syracuse University
Syracuse, New York

C. Dominik Güss
Department of Psychology
University of North Florida
Jacksonville, Florida

Brian J. Hall
Bloomberg School of Public Health
Johns Hopkins University
Baltimore, Maryland

Stevan Hobfoll
Department of Behavioral Sciences
Rush Medical College
Chicago, Illinois

Richard Jackson
National Centre for Peace and
    Conflict Studies
University of Otago
North Dunedin, New Zealand

Katarzyna Jasko
Institute of Psychology
Jagiellonian University
Kraków, Poland

Malgorzata Kossowska
Institute of Psychology
Jagiellonian University
Kraków, Poland

Marie-Helen Maras
Department of Criminal Justice
State University of New York at
    Farmingdale

Craig McGarty
School of Psychology
Murdoch University
Perth, Australia

Rachel Monaghan
School of Criminology, Politics, and
    Social Policy
University of Ulster
Newtonabbey, United Kingdom

Guro Odegaard
Institute for Social Research
Oslo, Norway

Carmit Rapaport
School of Political Science
University of Haifa
Haifa, Israel

Ami-Jacques Rapin
Department of History
University of Lausanne
Lausanne, Switzerland

Melody Sadler
Department of Psychology
San Diego State University
San Diego, California

Maciek Sekerdej
Institute of Psychology
Jagiellonian University
Kraków, Poland

George E. Shambaugh
School of Foreign Service and
    Department of Government
Georgetown University
Washington, DC

Kari Steen-Johnsen
Institute for Social Research
Oslo, Norway

Michael J. Stevens
Department of Psychology
Illinois State University
Normal, Illinois

Ryan Stolier
Department of Psychology
San Diego State University
San Diego, California

Carly Wayne
IDC Herzliya
Herzliya, Israel

Bradley M. Weisz
Department of Psychology
San Diego State University
San Diego, California

Geoffrey Wetherell
Department of Psychology
DePaul University
Chicago, Illinois

Dag Wollebaek
Institute for Social Research
Oslo, Norway

INTRODUCTION

SAMUEL JUSTIN SINCLAIR AND DANIEL ANTONIUS

The last decade has seen a dramatic shift in how governments across the globe understand and prioritize issues of national security, with terrorism emerging as one of the single most critical threats with which to contend. Since the attacks of September 11, 2001, over a trillion dollars has been spent by the United States in the "War on Terror" (Mueller & Stewart, 2011), and the sociopolitical landscape has changed dramatically with two new wars in Afghanistan and Iraq also bearing significantly on international resources. Some have argued that we have evolved into a "securitized" culture constructed to combat these threats, while other priorities such as education, poverty, social security, social programs designed to help the disadvantaged, and maintaining our basic infrastructure (e.g., roads, bridges, police and fire, etc.) all have taken a backseat to the complex and ever-expanding national security priorities that have ensued. These issues have been further complicated by the evolving dynamic in the Middle East, with new worries about a nuclear arms race and potential for these weapons to fall into the hands of terrorists.

In light of this change in zeitgeist, issues of terrorism and political violence have become hotly debated topics in the political sphere around the globe. The events of September 11, 2001 in particular have completely reshaped the landscape in which we as citizens engage the political process. Policies about security and safety have topped the agendas of government administrations over the last decade, particularly within the United States. However, despite the fact that 9/11 occurred on U.S. soil, one could easily argue that the fallout has been experienced internationally. For example, some have argued that the 2004 Spanish General election was impacted significantly by the terrorist attacks on Madrid in March, 2004. Others have suggested that worries about terrorism have affected governmental decision-making on issues such as whether and how to supply military assistance to the ongoing NATO efforts in Iraq and Afghanistan.

Fears of terrorism have continued over the last decade, and most recently have become a central issue in the 2012 U.S. presidential debates, following on the September 11 anniversary attacks on the U.S. embassy in Libya, which resulted in the assassination of Ambassador Stevens. As recently as last year, terrorism alerts were issued across Europe as evidence emerged that countries such as Germany and France were specific targets. Following on this, cargo planes were intercepted in the United States with packages containing bombs that were being sent to synagogues in Chicago. Although we find ourselves a decade past 9/11, the reverberations of this event continue to be felt.

As a means of further unpacking the psychology of terrorism, we (the Editors) recently completed a volume exploring the phenomenon of terrorism fears specifically, seeking to root these dynamics within known theoretical and empirical frameworks (Sinclair & Antonius, 2012). Our central thesis was that despite normalizing rates of psychopathology within the United States and beyond, people continue to fear terrorism in meaningful ways. We further argued that existing frameworks for understanding how people are affected psychologically by terrorism are inadequate, often relying on specific clinical criteria for making a psychiatric diagnosis of some kind. In short, we made the case that while many may not meet these specific *clinical* criteria, there is evidence to suggest that people remain fearful about terrorism, and that fear varies widely across time and context. These fears affect how people make decisions in their lives, including where and what they do for work, as well as patterns of socializing and traveling. These fears have also been shown more recently to impact how people make decisions about political process, including the candidates they endorse for public office and policies they support for legislation. For example, Toner and Elder (2001) reported that in a December 2001 *New York Times/CBS News* poll, roughly two-thirds of Americans surveyed after the 9/11 attacks said they were in favor of granting the president additional powers to change the constitution as a means of keeping the nation safe, and approximately the same number thought the government should be allowed to monitor conversations between suspects and their lawyers. Roughly 80 percent of those queried also supported the indefinite detention of terror suspects.

This pattern of data reflects the tendency of people to place more trust in their governments to keep them safe from future violence following large-scale terrorist attacks, as has been noted elsewhere in the literature (Chanley, 2002; Chanley, Rudolph, & Rahn 2000; Sinclair & LoCicero, 2010). For example, Chanley et al. (2000) noted that trust in government had declined considerably prior to the 9/11 attacks, but that following the attacks trust in government "… rose to a level not seen since the mid-1960s" (Chanley, 2002, p. 469). Sinclair and LoCicero (2010) sought to empirically test this phenomenon more recently, and demonstrated that fears of terrorism and the impact of changes in the governments' color-coded alert system were found to be significant predictors of trust in government for protection. Attachment theory and evolutionary psychology were then used as frameworks for understanding these effects, where people are driven to seek safety and security from an authority figure when a significant threat is present.

Fears of terrorism following a terrorist attack have also been shown to affect the economy, which itself is a prominent political issue. For example, in the years following the 9/11 attacks the U.S. airline industry suffered billions of dollars in losses, and were forced to lay off tens of thousands of employees. The U.S.

Congress was forced to pass a $15 billion bailout package for the industry. Two airlines (US Airways and United) were subsequently forced to file for bankruptcy in 2002 as a function of plummeting revenues and fewer people flying. The stock markets have also been found to be sensitive to terrorism fears. For example, Lim (2004) reported that immediately following the location of a bomb beneath the train tracks in Paris in 2004, the Dow Jones Industrial average declined 80 points. Granted, this event occurred after the Madrid bombings, which also likely played a role in people's fears, but it demonstrated the economic impact that terrorism fears have as well.

As a means of further understanding how different types of emotional responses to terrorism impact support for different governmental policies, Lerner and colleagues (2003) evaluated whether fear versus anger reactions had different effects in terms of people's perceptions of risk and policy preferences. As expected, Lerner et al. (2003) reported that fear was associated with greater perceived risk than anger, and was more predictive of precautionary, conciliatory measures aimed at reducing external threat. They also noted that people exhibited greater optimism in the context of increased anger, and greater pessimism in the context of fear. The authors explain these findings in part by noting that anger, unlike fear, may lead people to experience a greater sense of control over their environment, whereas fear may lead people to experience a loss of control.

Some have suggested at various points over the last decade that fear has been used as a political strategy to enlist support for both political candidates and specific governmental policies. For example, in 2009 Former Secretary of Homeland Security, Tom Ridge, published a book in which he reported that he felt some pressure to raise the U.S. terror alert level in the context of the 2004 Presidential elections, leading some to speculate that this was done for political purposes (Charles, 2009). Despite these claims, which have been made with increasing frequency in more recent years, there has been very little systematic and scientific evaluation of the impact of terrorism fears on political process. Instead, people have been left to speculate as to who this benefits and how.

The purpose of this volume is to present an interdisciplinary and integrated body of work, which explores how terrorism fears impact the political process in a number of contexts. The volume contains multiple empirical studies examining how emotions more globally, and fear specifically, are associated with political decision-making and behavior. Further, it also contains a number of chapters presenting various theoretical frameworks, such as probability neglect, terror management theory, and other cognitive heuristics, which function as models for determining how and why these dynamics manifest. Finally, given that this is an issue of international significance, the current volume also contains a number of chapters examining how fear and other emotions related to terrorism have impacted the political process in nations around the globe, including: Northern Ireland, the Israeli-Palestinian context, Poland, Iran, Australia, Norway, England, and Spain. In doing so, we hope to demonstrate the complexity of these issues across cultures and time, and provide some insight into how terrorism fears vary markedly as a function of context and exert differing levels of influence on the political dynamic.

In our earlier work, we sought to present a new framework for understanding the psychological impact of terrorism from a behavioral sciences perspective (Sinclair & Antonius, 2012). In this former volume, we presented preliminary data in support of the presence of fear as separate from discrete forms of psychopathology, and began to discuss the impact of these fears on real-world functioning. The primary aim of the current volume is to extend this work by presenting new research investigating how and why terrorism, and fears about terrorism specifically, affect political decision-making and engagement in the political process. The implications of these findings are then presented.

OVERVIEW OF THE VOLUME

The volume is organized into three main sections. The first section presents a number of empirical and theoretical studies examining how perceived threat and emotional responses to terrorism have been found to be associated with trust in government more globally, as well as support for more discrete policies related to security and defense. In the first chapter, Dr. Chanley presents research on how trust in government has varied considerably in the last decade, spiking immediately following the 9/11 attacks and then dissipating over time. She then presents research discussing how differences in reactions to terrorism have been found to be associated with different types of approach-avoidant behaviors as it relates to subsequent decision-making about policy. She discusses these trends within the context of Evolutionary Theory, where different responses to a perceived threat may lead to different patterns of behaviors (for example, supporting aggressive retaliation versus pulling back and avoiding conflict)—all aimed at protecting a given population.

In chapter 2, Dr. Shambaugh extends this work in several important ways. First, he discusses how varying levels of trust in government during the last three years of the George W. Bush Administration impacted threat perception and policy support for the war in Iraq. Further, he demonstrates how these effects varied as a function of how trust in government is defined (for example, whether it depended on how trustworthy the information is, the integrity of public officials, or effectiveness of governmental policy). One interesting finding he discusses, which is perhaps explained in part by the evolutionary model presented above, is that higher trust in the integrity of public figures was found to be associated with lower perceived threat, while those with lower trust have a higher level of perceived threat. Additionally, Dr. Shambaugh discusses the distinction between perceiving threat to one's self versus the larger nation, and the varying impact of this on policy support.

Dr. Stevens expands this discussion in chapter 3 to explore how different kinds of emotions (fear versus anger, for example) potentiate different types of reactions, and how this may vary depending on context. For example, he discusses research on how people become more unforgiving and less tolerant in the context of persistent and repeated acts of terrorism over time, which in turn may increase support for government retaliation and a more general "hostile-world effect." Dr. Stevens presents a body of research showing how these reactions may be moderated by emotional response, where fear and anxiety are associated with more avoidant behavior, less support for military intervention, and greater preference for isolationist policies—all as a means of mitigating threat. Conversely, emotions such as anger are associated with more aggressive and retaliatory policies, and higher level of engagement and approach behavior. Dr. Stevens then discusses certain heuristics which describe how emotions may impact the processing of information, and lead to overestimating versus underestimating threat information.

Following earlier chapters focused on issues of governmental trust, Dr. Gadarian presents her own experimental research demonstrating the effect of partisanship on threat perception in a politicized context in chapter 4. Specifically, her findings suggest that following 9/11, Democrats who perceive threat information as being manipulated in some way (and therefore less trustworthy) are *less* likely to accept the information and more prone to resist it. That is, as issues related to terrorism are perceived as being politicized in some way, it is more likely to be rejected by Democrats, suggesting that political ideology also plays a meaningful role in risk perception and subsequent emotional response.

Because the media and political elites alike have the ability to control the flow of threat information, which raises questions about the potential for this information to be used for political purposes, it is also important to understand how political leaders communicate with the public they are elected to represent. In chapter 5, De Castella and McGarty present a very interesting narrative analysis of various speeches made by George W. Bush, Tony Blair, and Osama bin Laden. Based on these analyses, they note that fear content in these communications vary markedly across time, context, and speaker—all of which has implications for how the public would be expected to support different policies (e.g., going to war with Iraq). They conclude their chapter with a call for both politicians and the public alike to consider the manner in which these types of narratives perpetuate certain political dynamics, and to move towards a more rational and evenly considered narrative approach as a means of reducing fear and worry, and moving away from the War/ Crime discourse of terrorism.

In chapter 6, Güss, Foust, and Dörner seek to present a more integrated approach to understanding the psychological mechanisms (e.g., motivational, emotional, cognitive) underlying how people respond to acts of suicide terrorism, and how this in turn impacts political attitudes both at the level of the general population and political leader. These dynamics are considered across various contexts, including in the aftermath of terrorist attacks and in contexts where terrorism is more common. The fear response is considered more specifically in terms of how it impacts decision-making as it relates to terrorism, and motivates people to seek out specific needs.

Finally, Section One concludes with a chapter by Wetherell, Weisz, Stolier, Beavers, and Sadler (chapter 7). These authors present two theoretical models (Attribution Theory and Appraisal Theory) as a means of examining how different emotional and cognitive factors may play a role in policy making and support for antiterrorism policies. Further, they convincingly argue that government officials and media outlets have the power to influence, or even elicit, specific emotional reactions in the public, which subsequently may have a significant impact on public opinion and decision-making when it comes to the development and implementation of terrorism policies.

Section Two presents a series of studies examining the impact of fear and other emotional reactions on political process across a number of international contexts. In chapter 8, Dr. Monaghan presents the case of Northern Ireland and ways in which the "legacy of fear" has contributed to various counter-terrorism measures resulting in further segmentation of society and creation of "suspect communities." In doing so, these policies have perpetuated greater societal division and in ways fueled an underlying sense of fear of "the other", and inhibited the overall peace process and integration of society.

Following on this, Dr. Aly provides an in-depth analysis of how Australians construct media and political images of terrorism, and makes a convincing argument for how fears of terrorism are more closely associated with the political and social responses to terrorism than to the threat of a terrorist attack itself (chapter 9). Aly then discusses various factors that contribute to terrorism fears, and how these factors have subsequently perpetuated the post 9/11 state of insecurity—which in essence creates a cycle of fear.

In chapter 10, Jaśko, Kossowska, and Sekerdej discuss how terrorism risk perception varies across Europe more generally, and Poland specifically, as a function of multiple variables including context, proximity to terrorism, and perception of different risk factors—including how terrorists are themselves perceived. With respect to this latter point, the authors present research suggesting that when terrorists are perceived as being more unpredictable and uncontrollable, fear is accentuated—perhaps due to the pereived loss of control in managing this threat. In contrast, when terrorists are perceived as rational and fighting on behalf of a cause, fear tends to be reduced and there is a greater amenability for diplomatic actions. Based on these subtle but important distinctions in terms of how terrorists are perceived, meaningful differences were found in a variety of political attitudes, including support for a national missile defense system in Poland. Other factors such as religion and nationalism were also found to moderate the effect of emotion on support for different policies.

In chapter 11, Canetti and colleagues present a stress-based model to elucidate how emotions such as fear and worry contribute to different kinds of political outcomes in contexts where there is protracted conflict, such as the Israeli-Palestinian situation. More specifically, the chapter examines how people on both sides of this conlict experience high levels of trauma and anxiety, which in turn impact perception of threat and support for governmental policies designed to mitigate threat. The end result is a similar chain of events on both sides of the conflict, which perpetuate conflict and continued aggression directed at the other. Canetti and colleagues also discuss factors which may promote resiliency in these contexts, as well as theoretical models such as *Conservation of Resources Theory* which help to explain these dynamics. The authors conclude their chapter with a call for more research in active conflict zones as a means of understanding not only the psychological implications, but also the political consequences and ways in which these dynamics fuel discord.

In chapter 12, Dr. Abdollahi presents Terror Management Theory (TMT) as a framework for understanding how terrorism fears manifest, as well as factors that may buffer against fear and promote resiliency. Using an experimental design in an Iranian undergraduate sample, he demonstrates how priming reminders of death (as opposed to dental pain) is associated with support for pro-martyrdom operations against the West. Dr. Abdollahi also discusses a parallel study conducted in the United States, in which college students who were primed with reminders of death and identified themselves as conservative in terms of ideology tended to support more aggressive measures against perceived enemies in the Middle East. However, consistent with the findings by Dr. Gadarian, these patterns did not hold for students identifying themselves as liberal, suggesting again that political ideology may be another factor moderating these relationships.

In chapter 13, Dr. Maras discusses the dynamics of fear in Europe following the 2004 Madrid and 2005 London terrorist attacks, and ways in which increased fear reduced resistance to more restrictive security practices that ensued (e.g., measures requiring the preventive detention, mass registration, and mass surveillance of citizens). The chapter then presents a number of theoretical models based in cognitive psychology that are useful in understanding these patterns, including availability heuristic, probability neglect, and prospect theory.

In chapter 14, Wollebæk and colleagues present a unique perspective of fear and political process in Norway following the July 22, 2012, terrorist attack by a right-wing extremist seeking to retaliate against the government for supporting multicultural policies. In contrast to many other studies presented in this volume, these researchers found that high levels of initial trust in government and societal cohesion "served as a prophylactic that stymied fear" in a large multiwave national study of Norwegian citizens. The authors discuss how "high-trust" societies, such as Norway may in fact respond differently to terrorism, as a result of low levels of fear. These findings follow nicely on the work of Dr. Abdollahi (chapter 12), who used TMT as a model for understanding how connection to culture buffers against fear and anxiety.

Section 3 concludes the volume by presenting a number of papers which discuss the larger societal implications of terrorism fears, and ways in which many cultures have become more securitized as a result. In chapter 15, Dr. Jackson discusses the more recent concept of terrorism fears in a larger historical/cultural context that has perpetuated fear in other meaningful ways over the last few decades, including with respect to drugs, gangs, violent crime, pedophiles, etc. In rooting terrorism fears this way, Jackson argues that society has slowly evolved into becoming more fearful, and that terrorism is simply the most recent manifestation of this phenomenon.

Dr. Jackson goes on to discuss the implications of fear being normalized in our society, where issues of security and terrorism are embedded in our consciousness, leading to uncritical support of a massive terrorism industry that has developed in the last decade. Given this dynamic, the implications are that fear can now be manipulated and politicized as a means of maintaining this industry.

In a similar vein, Dr. Altheide roots the issue of terrorism specifically in a larger culture of fear that has developed in the United States in chapter 16. The result has been a discourse of fear that has embued itself in all aspects of society, and is manifest in a myriad of ways in popular culture, from the television shows and movies we watch to the video games our children play. Similar to the argument made by Dr. Jackson in chapter 15, Dr. Altheide discusses the implications of fear being used in political process as an instrument for affecting some political or social reality.

In chapter 17, Dr. Rapin concludes the volume with a discussion of how terrorism is inherently ambiguous, and is often difficult to measure with adequate reliability—which in turn increases the potential for these data to be used on behalf of more specific political (or other social) agendas as a consequence of the assumptions that are made (e.g., what constitutes a terrorist attack). As a result, an interesting dynamic has emerged where a culture of fear has led to the development of an entirely new security industry (and political system) that is designed to address a phenomenon that is difficult to define and therefore measure reliably, open to interpretation, and fundamentally subjective. All of these factors may in fact contribute to fear as a function of the actual risk involved being confused, and governments tasked by their constituents to maintain their safety may be prone to overresponding as a means of mitigating this risk.

CONCLUSION

Although each of the chapters contained within this volume present important empirical and theoretical perspectives on how terrorism fears impact political process, as well as what the larger implications of this may be in terms of securitizing society and the potential for fear to be used as an instrument for affecting some political reality, there are a few more global themes that cut across these chapters that we would like to highlight here. First, as has been pointed out by numerous authors, high levels of emotionality and fear specifically impact how people engage their respective political systems—from the politicians they elect to office to the policies they support. However, not all emotions are created equal, and there have been numerous studies demonstrating the differential effects of fear and anger, for example, on trust in government and support for different security policies. Second, this dynamic is made even more complex by other factors, including political ideology, which may moderate these relationships in important ways. Although many of these studies were conducted at one point in time, following the 9/11 attacks and during the George W. Bush Administration, there is evidence to suggest that high levels of emotion primed in those identifying as Democrats/liberals during this period in the United States in fact leads to greater skepticism and reactance to more aggressive terrorism policies.

Another very important theme to have emerged in this body of work is how cultural context may in fact play an important role in terms of how people react to terrorism and then subsequently engage in political decision-making. That is, in some countries/cultures, such as Norway, which are identified as "high-trust" societies, the response to terrorism may be marked by low levels of fear, which in turn may have implications for how people respond in the political arena. These findings dovetail nicely with theoretical models including Terror Management Theory, as well as much of the trauma literature emerging after 9/11, which highlighted the importance of social connection and support as being significant in terms of its ability to mitigate fear and anxiety.

It is also important to consider the many ways that fear and anxiety, which has been embedded and reinforced in society over time, has the potential to shape culture longitudinally. This is particularly evident in more protracted conflict situations, such as Northern Ireland and the Israeli-Palestinian context, where chronic fear and anxiety has led to high levels of segregation and the creation of "suspect" communities that become the object of one's fears. In societies such as these, fear is a powerful motivating force for pursuing a perceived sense of safety and security, whether through increased aggression towards one's enemy or the complete alienation and isolation of the "other." These dynamics ironically perpetuate conflict, and impede the potential for peace.

One final theme that is important to consider in all of this is how current models for thinking about and understanding terrorism—including how we operationally define, measure, and evaluate issues related to terrorism—may in fact contribute to its prominence in our society. Several chapters contained herein discussed the problems with defining issues of terrorism, as well as measuring these variables in a reliable way across time, which in turn have serious implications for how these data are interpreted and by whom. We are now a decade past the devastating attacks of September 11, 2001, and society has changed in dramatic ways reflecting this new sense of insecurity and the potential threat that we face. Over a trillion dollars has been spent on constructing a security infrastructure to keep us safe from these ambiguous threats, at the expense of other important social and political initiatives. It is important to understand the complex array of factors that have contributed to this evolution, and to critically question these priorities moving forward. It is our hope that this volume contributes to this understanding, and informs both political figures and the public alike in terms of how they engage in political decision-making and priority setting. We again thank the contributors for their time, expertise, and professionalism, and hope you (the reader) find value in the volume.

Samuel Justin Sinclair, Ph.D.
Massachusetts General Hospital &
Harvard Medical School
Boston, MA
USA

Daniel Antonius, Ph.D.
University at Buffalo
School of Medicine and Biomedical Sciences
Buffalo, NY
USA

REFERENCES

Chanley, V. A. (2002). Trust in the government in the aftermath of 9/11: Determinants and consequences. *Political Psychology,* 23, 469–483.

Chanley, V. A., Rudolph, T. J., & Rahn, W. M. (2000) The origins and consequences of public trust in government: A time series analysis. *Public Opinion Quarterly,* 64, 239–256.

Charles, D. (2009). *Ridge says he was pushed to raise terror alert before election.* Reuters. Retrieved October 18, 2012 at: http://blogs.reuters.com/talesfromthetrail/2009/08/20/ridge-says-he-was-pushed-to-raise-terror-alert-before-election/.

Lerner, J. S., Gonzalez, R. M., Small, D. A., & Fischhoff, B. (2003). Effects of fear and anger on perceived risks of terrorism: A national field experiment. *Psychological Science,* 14, 144–150.

Lim, P. J. (2004). *Scared Street: Terrorism fears spook the stock market.* Retrieved December 2, 2008 from http://www.usnews.com

Mueller, J., & Stewart, M. J. (2011). Terror, security, and money: Balancing the risks, benefits, and costs of homeland security. Paper presentation at the Annual Convention of the Midwest Political Science Association Chicago, IL, April 1, 2011. Retrieved October 18, 2012 at http://politicalscience.osu.edu/faculty/jmueller//MID11TSM.PDF

Sinclair, S. J., & Antonius, D. (2012). *The psychology of terrorism fears.* Oxford, UK: Oxford University Press.

Sinclair, S. J., & LoCicero, A. (2010). Do fears of terrorism predict trust in government? *Journal of Aggression, Conflict and Peace Research,* 2, 57–68.

Toner, R., & Elder, J. (2001). Public is wary but supportive on rights curbs. *New York Times,* page 1.

PART ONE

CHAPTER 1

Trust in the U.S. Government and Antiterrorism Policies After 9/11

Are We All in This Together?

VIRGINIA A. CHANLEY

In the days after the September 11, 2001 (9/11) attacks on the World Trade Center and the Pentagon, U.S. public trust in the government in Washington rose to levels not seen since the 1960s. Since that time, trust in government has declined to among the lowest levels seen over the time period for which nationally representative data are available for the U.S. public. Given the theoretical importance of trust in government for maintaining the legitimacy of the political system, the issue is of long-standing interest to scholars of politics. Central to this study have been questions about the determinants and consequences of levels of trust in government. What are the factors that lead to changes in public trust, and to what extent does trust in government affect electoral and policy outcomes? In the context of 9/11 and its consequences, to what extent has trust in government been affected by fears of terrorism, and to what extent have trust in government and other factors influenced public support for policies purportedly designed to address the threat of terrorism?

The current chapter first reviews research on how and why public trust in the U.S. government has changed and the consequences of changes in trust in government, over the time period for which we have survey data from nationally representative samples. The chapter then focuses more specifically on changes in U.S. public trust in government since 9/11 and how responses to terrorism and other events have affected public opinion and subsequent public policies. In a step toward developing an understanding of public evaluations of government and policies to combat terrorism that is grounded in evolutionary theory, the chapter then explores how insight from evolutionary theory can contribute to an understanding of the causes and consequences of views of government and terrorism, and the implications for the policy choices made.

EXPLAINING CHANGES IN TRUST IN GOVERNMENT OVER TIME

Empirical research on the variables that affect trust in government has focused on what Nye (1997) identified as economic, sociocultural, or political factors. With respect to economic factors, scholars have examined how trust in government is affected by the performance of the national economy and by citizens' evaluations of the economy, finding that negative perceptions of the economy cause declines in trust (Chanley, 2002; Chanley, Rudolph, & Rahn, 2001; Citrin & Green, 1986; Citrin & Luks, 2001; Feldman, 1983; Hetherington, 1998; Hetherington & Rudolph, 2008; Miller & Borrelli, 1991). With respect to sociocultural factors, declines in trust have been found to occur as a result of rising crime (or public concern about crime) and declining social capital (Chanley, 2002; Chanley et al., 2000; Keele, 2007; Mansbridge, 1997; Pew Research Center, 1998). Changes in trust in government also have been linked to numerous political factors, including evaluations of political incumbents and institutions (Citrin & Green, 1986; Citrin & Luks, 2001; Craig, 1993, 1996; Erber & Lau, 1990; Feldman, 1983; Hetherington, 1998; Miller & Borrelli, 1991; Williams, 1985), the occurrence of political scandal and increased media focus on political corruption and scandal (Garment, 1991; Orren, 1997), and threats to national security, including concerns about terrorism, foreign policy, and national defense (Chanley, 2002; Chanley, Rudolph, & Rahn, 2001; Hetherington & Rudolph, 2008; Nye, 1997). Taken together, this research has found that trust in government suffers when the public is concerned about the effective performance of government and government accountability, as reflected in greater concern about the economy, crime, or political scandal and corruption. Conversely, trust in government rises with increased public attention to international concerns and threats to the nation.

Figure 1.1 presents data from the American National Election Studies (ANES) and provides the single longest time-series measure of U.S. public trust in government. These data are based on responses to the question, "How much of the time do you think you can trust the government in Washington to do what is right—just about always, most of the time, or only some of the time?" The ANES first asked this question in 1958, then at 2-year intervals from 1964 to 2004, and then most recently in 2008. The figure values represent the percentage of the public indicating they trust the government in Washington, DC, almost always or most of the time.

Based on the ANES data, U.S. public trust was at a high point of 76 percent in 1964, near the beginning of the time period for which data are available. From 1964 to 1982, trust almost consistently declined, falling to 25 percent in 1980. This decline coincided with growing public dissent for U.S. involvement in the conflict in Vietnam, followed by the Watergate scandal and resignation of President Nixon, and the Carter presidency. Trust rebounded somewhat during the Reagan presidency in the 1980s, reaching 44 percent in 1984 and remaining at 40 percent in 1988. Concurrent with the Iran-Contra scandal in Reagan's second term and the U.S. House of Representatives banking scandal in 1992, however, public trust was again on the wane. In 1990, trust had fallen to 28 percent and reached a low of

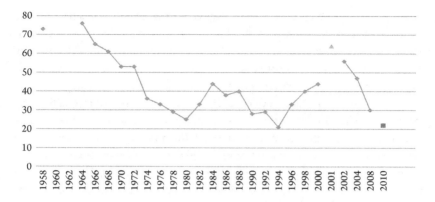

Figure 1.1:
Trust in the U.S. government: 1958–2010
Values are percentages responding "most of the time" or "just about always" to the question: "How much of the time do you think you can trust the government in Washington to do what is right—just about always, most of the time, or only some of the time?" From the American National Election Studies surveys, 1958–2008; *Washington Post* survey, September 2001; and Pew Research Center survey, March 2010.

21 percent in 1994. After this low point, coincident with the Republican takeover of the House of Representatives for the first time in 40 years and a period during which the federal government achieved the first federal budget surpluses since 1969, trust began to increase again slightly, rising to 44 percent in 2000.

As shown in the figure, in a *Washington Post* poll taken on September 27, 2001, just days after 9/11, the percentage of the public saying they trusted the government in Washington to do the right thing just about always or most of the time rose to 64 percent, the highest level observed since 1966. Consistent with the rally-round-the-flag effect seen during times of threat to the nation, first identified by Mueller (1973), the public shifted its focus from domestic to international concerns, and trust in government also rose. By October 2001, however, public concern about terrorism and issues of foreign policy began to dissipate, and trust in government also began to diminish (Chanley, 2002). Based on the ANES data, trust had declined to 47 percent in 2004, and then to 30 percent in 2008. Drawing on data from the ANES, Pew Research Center, ABC/*Washington Post*, CBS/*New York Times*, and CNN surveys, the Pew Research Center (2010) has developed a time-series measure of trust in government based on a three-survey moving average, showing trust in government to have been about 20 percent in 2010. With the economic crisis beginning in 2007 and the inability of President Obama and the U.S. Congress to agree on the best approach to responding to slow economic growth and ballooning federal debt, as of spring 2012, the prospects for increased trust appeared bleak.

FOCUSING ON THE DECLINE IN TRUST

Given the overall decline in trust in government since the 1960s, scholars of trust in government have sought to understand the factors that explain the decline and the extent to which the high level of trust observed at the time that data began being gathered was typical or exceptional. Alford (2001) examined changes in trust in government across different demographic and political groups from 1958 to 1996, finding a remarkably similar pattern in changes in trust in government among subgroups, regardless of race, education, age, income, partisanship, or ideology. Because changes in trust in government were consistent across groups that react differently to issues of policy, Alford reasoned that trust in government does not seem to be driven by the policy choices of government. Rather than looking to policy-specific explanations such as the Vietnam Conflict, civil rights legislation, or Great Society programs, on which different groups clearly held different views, Alford proposed the need for a broader perspective, designed to identify something affecting subgroups in largely the same way.

Alford (2001) first identified a general rise in cynicism, related to globalization and the general decline in social capital, as a potential explanation for the decline in trust. Lacking data for a time-series measure of broad cynicism, Alford used a measure based on an ANES question about respondents' beliefs that people are generally trustworthy, asked at regular intervals from 1964 to 1976. In contrast to trust in government in the same time period, however, public trust in other people varied relatively little. Specifically, the observed level of public trust in other people was about 2 percentage points lower in 1976 than in 1964, whereas trust in government declined by some 43 percentage points in the same time period. Alford also noted that trust in other people was about 20 percentage points lower than trust in government in 1964, whereas trust in other people was about 20 percentage points higher than trust in government in 1976. Given remarkably little change in trust in people but considerable change in trust in government, Alford was led to consider what might lead members of the public to trust the government so much more or less than their trust in other people. Noting that in 1976 it made sense that trust in government would be lower than trust in other people, Alford identified the high level of trust in government in 1964 as the more anomalous finding.

Alford (2001) proposed that distrust in government may be the natural state and that high levels of trust in large social institutions such as government may be short-lived and occur only periodically. Seeking to identify what could cause such a collective shift in trust in government, Alford focused on external threat and the rally-round-the-flag effect that occurs when the nation has been attacked or mobilizes to attack another nation. Lacking ANES data on public perceptions of threat to the nation over time, Alford relied on a measure of public identification of the most important problem facing the nation. Examining data from 1960 to 1996, Alford found that more than 60 percent of ANES respondents identified foreign policy or defense concerns as the number one problem facing the nation in 1960, whereas this percentage dropped below 10 percent from 1974 to 1978. In the 1980s, public concern about foreign policy and defense rose but not above 35 percent. There was a spike in public concern about foreign policy and defense in 1990, coinciding with the Iraqi invasion of Kuwait. By 1992, public concern about international affairs had again dropped to below 10 percent, where it remained through 1996.

Consistent with this explanation for high levels of trust, Chanley (2002) found an increase in both the percentage of the public identifying terrorism, foreign policy, and defense as the most important problems facing the nation and trust in the national government in the period immediately after the attacks of 9/11/2001. Analyzing quarterly time-series data from 1980 to the end of 2001 using multivariate regression models, Chanley found robust support over the entire time period for the effect of public focus on international concerns as a determinant of trust in government. Focusing more specifically on the effects of fears of terrorism and terrorism alerts on trust in government after 9/11, Sinclair and LoCicero (2010) found greater trust among individuals with higher fears of terrorism and terror alerts, based on analysis of individual-level data.

Hetherington and Nelson (2003), focusing on the causes and consequences of the rally effect after 9/11 and the subsequent beginning of the War on Terror, looked in more detail at how public trust in government was affected by U.S. involvement in the Gulf War in 1991 and the attacks of 9/11 and the start of the War on Terror. Before the beginning of Operation Desert Storm on January 17, 1991, public trust in government was less than 30 percentage points. By the end of the effort on February 28, 1991, trust had risen to almost 50 percentage points. Within 7 months, trust had declined to the level that preceded the war. After the attacks of 9/11 and the start of the "War on Terror," trust in government returned to pre-9/11 levels by July 2002, or within about 10 months.

To help explain why increases in trust in government at the time of events associated with external threat to the nation have been relatively short-lived, Hetherington and Nelson (2003) reported the results of a January 9, 2002, ABC News poll that asked the question about trust in government in two different ways. In one version of the question, respondents were asked, "When it comes to handling social issues like the economy, health care, Social Security, and education, how much do you trust the government in Washington to do the right thing?" In the second version of the question, respondents were asked, "When it comes to handling national security and the War on Terrorism, how much of the time do you trust the government in Washington to do the right thing?" When asked the question in the context of domestic issues, 38 percent of the public expressed a high level of trust, whereas when asked the question in the context of the War on Terrorism, 69 percent expressed a high level of trust. In other words, the effect of external threat on trust is associated with a difference in the criteria on which citizens are evaluating the government, and as threat recedes (or survey respondents are directed away from considering national threat in a survey question), the public is inclined to return to a focus on domestic concerns such the economy and education, issues on which there tends to be less trust in government action.

In a more comprehensive assessment of the effect of public focus on international concerns, Hetherington and Rudolph (2008) conducted a multivariate time-series analysis of the determinants of U.S. public trust in government using quarterly data from the beginning of 1976 through the first quarter of 2006. Like Alford (2001), seeking to explain why U.S. public trust in government has never returned to the relatively high levels of trust seen in the 1960s, Hetherington and Rudolph (2008) demonstrated that the effect of economic performance on trust is asymmetric, such that economic prosperity does not have as great a positive effect on trust as the negative effect associated with economic downturn. Consistent with earlier findings that increasing public focus on foreign policy, national defense, terrorism, and other international concerns also increases trust, Hetherington and Rudolph (2008) found greater trust in government when the percentage of the public identifying international concerns as the most important problem facing the nation increases. Although lacking quarterly time-series data on trust in government before 1976 and ANES trust data before 1958, Hetherington and Rudolph (2008) reported the results of 18 nationally representative Gallup surveys conducted in the 1950s asking respondents to identify the most important problem facing the nation. The median percentage of the U.S. public identifying an issue of international concern during the decade of the 1950s, a time when there was substantial public concern about the threat of nuclear war, was 53 percent. Moreover, in 12 of 15 Gallup surveys conducted from May 1960 to October 1962, 67 percent or more of the U.S. public identified international concerns as the most important problem facing the nation, comparable to the percentage of the public identifying terrorism and other international concerns as the most important national problem in the first poll taken after 9/11/2001. In other words, based on the available data from the late 1950s to the present, there is clear evidence that high levels of trust in the U.S. government coincide with high levels of public concern about threats to the security of the nation as a whole.

THE CONSEQUENCES OF U.S. PUBLIC TRUST IN GOVERNMENT

Although a substantial amount of empirical research on trust in the U.S. government has focused on causes of changes in public trust, the interest in understanding these causes is driven largely by the potential implications of low levels of trust. In democracies, citizen trust in government has been viewed as a prerequisite for making binding decisions and committing resources toward national goals (Gamson, 1968). Trust in government has also been identified as necessary to gain citizen compliance with the laws without coercion (Levi, 1997; Tyler, 1990), and research has found that trust in the government was more important for deterring cheating on tax returns than was fear of an Internal Revenue Service audit (Scholz & Lubell, 1998).

The questions of whether low levels of trust are a threat solely to incumbent politicians or, more seriously, to the system of government overall has been central to the study of the consequences of trust in government. Miller (1974a, 1974b) proposed that distrust in government could lead to public disaffection with the institutions of government, posing a threat to the system of government itself. Citrin (1974) took a more positive view, arguing that low levels of trust in government reflected dissatisfaction with the performance of incumbent policymakers and actually provided a necessary check on incumbent elected officials. If they do not change their behavior to restore trust, they may be voted out of office. Miller (1974a, 1974b) and Citrin (1974) each found empirical support in favor of their contrasting perspectives, although subsequent research may be seen as providing greater evidence in support of Citrin's views, at least in the context of U.S. public opinion.

Citrin and Green (1986) examined the relationship between approval of the incumbent president and trust in government and presented evidence that a lack of public confidence in President Carter had negative implications for trust in government, whereas greater public confidence in President Reagan had a positive effect on trust in government. Multivariate time-series analyses have indicated that confidence in both Congress and the executive branch tracks with trust in the national government, but changes in confidence in these institutions precede changes in trust (Chanley et al., 2001). In other words, negative evaluations of trust appear to be based more on evaluations of incumbent officials than on evaluations of the system overall. Although citizens may be unwilling to say they trust the government in Washington to do what is right just about always or most of the time, these same citizens often express pride and support when asked about their views of the "system of government" (Citrin, 1974; Lipset, 1995). Consistent with Easton's (1965) expectation that judgments about the system of government are more stable than views of incumbent politicians, shorter-term changes in policy or the state of the economy have a greater influence on evaluations of current office-holders than on support for the system of government overall (Norris, 1999).

The finding that low levels of trust do not correspond to a lack of support for the political system overall, however, does not mean that changing levels of trust do not have important implications. Declining trust has been identified as one of the factors increasing support for devolution of governmental action from the national to the local level (Hetherington & Nugent, 2001), and political distrust among whites leads to less support for programs targeted to benefit racial minorities (Hetherington & Globetti, 2002). Low levels of trust make it less likely for political leaders to succeed in implementing public policy (Hetherington, 1998), and declining trust leads to less public support for federal government spending in a range of areas, including education, the environment, and aid to cities (Chanley, 2002; Chanley et al., 2000, 2001). Distrustful voters are also more inclined to vote for third-party candidates and nonincumbents (Hetherington, 1999), as reflected in election outcomes in the 1980 election of Ronald Reagan, the 1994 Republican takeover of Congress, and the Democrats' loss of the House of Representatives in the 2010 midterm election.

After 9/11, the federal government directed substantial resources to help with the recovery in New York City, establish the Department of Homeland Security, and begin the international War on Terror. Based on theory and empirical evidence about the importance of trust in government for public support for government action, there were questions about whether citizen support for allocating the resources necessary to maintain the post-9/11 policy agenda could be maintained, unless a high level of trust could also be sustained (Chanley, 2002). As we have seen, trust in government has returned to pre-9/11 levels, but as of 2012, U.S. international and national policies continued to be influenced by concern about the threat of terrorism. Research on public reactions to 9/11 and the implications of distinct affective and cognitive responses helps provide an understanding of the dynamics of public opinion and policy after 9/11.

UNDERSTANDING THE EFFECTS OF 9/11 ON PUBLIC VIEWS OF POLICIES TO COMBAT TERRORISM

Huddy, Feldman, Taber, and Lahav (2005, p. 593) identified perceptions of threat and anxiety as distinct psychological reactions to acts of terrorism, noting that "[t]he distinction between perceived threat and anxiety is intimately tied to the major objectives of terrorists and governments in countries targeted by terrorism." In short, perceptions of external threat have been found to increase support for taking action in response to the threat, whereas anxiety has been found to increase the estimation of risk and risk-averse behavior. Terrorists, therefore, may be more likely to achieve their aims if they are able to inculcate anxiety among their targeted populace and create circumstances under which government officials are inclined to negotiate and make concessions to reduce the perceived risk of future attacks. Conversely, a populace that perceives a serious threat to national security, but among whom anxiety is tempered, is more likely to support strong punitive actions against the source of the threat. In other words, if a terrorist organization is able to produce a level of anxiety that is sufficiently greater than the perception of threat among the targets of their actions, they are more likely to avoid military retaliation.

Huddy and colleagues (2005) found that most members of the U.S. public expressed a high level of concern about terrorist threat, whereas a minority felt substantial anxiety in the aftermath of 9/11. Moreover, greater perception of threat led to greater support for President Bush and policies of the Bush administration, including overseas military action, restrictions on civil liberties, and increased surveillance and immigration limitations for Arabs. Conversely, individuals experiencing heightened anxiety were less likely to support a military response, expressed support for increased U.S. isolationism, and were more critical of President Bush's performance in response to 9/11. Huddy et al. (2005) noted that the Bush administration seemed aware of the link between perception of threat and support for military action. The administration issued a series of terrorist alerts in the months after 9/11, and the perceived risk of terrorism remained high at least into the early months of 2002.

Sinclair and LoCicero (2010) focused more specifically on whether fears of terrorism and terrorist alerts led to increased trust in government and identified attachment theory and evolutionary theory as providing theoretical explanations for the tendency of individuals to turn to those able to provide protection from the threat of harm. Consistent with their expectations, Sinclair and LoCicero (2010) found increased fears of terrorism to be associated with greater trust in government. Moreover, this finding remained robust in the presence of controls for political ideology, sense of patriotism, and feelings of anger.

Surveys looking at U.S. public evaluations of how well the government is doing at reducing the threat of terrorism and how specific actions have affected the likelihood of future terrorist attacks provide a mixed picture, with clear partisan differences in public views of government performance and a number of policy preferences. In Pew Research Center surveys of the U.S. public conducted immediately after 9/11, 1 year later in August 2002, 5 years later in August of 2006, and again 10 years later in August 2011, the percentage saying that the government was doing very or fairly well at reducing the threat of terrorism ranged from 88 percent in the period immediately after 9/11 to 74 or 76 percent in 2002, 2006, and 2001 (Pew Research Center, 2011). Examining partisan differences in evaluations of government actions to address terrorism, Pew Research Center analysts noted a gap throughout the period from 2001 to 2011. From 2001 to 2008, Republicans were more positive about government antiterrorism actions. In 2010, Democrats were more positive. In other words, the direction of the partisan gap switched with the change from a Republican to a Democratic president. This is not unlike the partisan gap that occurs in evaluations of trust in the government in Washington. Although changes in trust in government among Republicans and Democrats tend to move in tandem, Republicans become more trusting when a Republican is in the White House, whereas Democrats are more trusting when the president is a Democrat.

In a separate study of public reactions to 9/11 and other traumatic events up to February 2008, Shambaugh and colleagues (2010) reported less positive assessments than did the Pew Research Center of the overall performance of the U.S. government's response to 9/11. Specifically, in surveys of nationally representative samples of the U.S. adult population in both 2007 and 2008, only about 30 percent of the U.S. public said that they were satisfied with the way the national government responded to 9/11. Shambaugh et al. (2010) also noted the enduring effect of partisanship on public assessment of government response to such events, with Republicans consistently more supportive than Democrats of Bush administration actions. When asked about the likelihood of another terrorist attack within the United States in 2007, about one-third of the U.S. population said there was a greater than 50:50 likelihood of another attack within the next 2 years. When asked the same question in 2008, only about 20 percent indicated there was a greater than 50:50 likelihood of another attack.

The Pew Research Center (2011) also looked at public views of the consequences of U.S. government actions and expectations for future terrorist attacks in the United States. When asked (in August 2011) why they thought there had not been another terrorist attack in the United States since 2001, 43 percent said it was because "the government is doing a good job protecting the country," 16 percent said it was because "America is a difficult target for terrorists," 35 percent said it was because "America has been lucky so far," and about 7 percent were unsure. At the same time, in 2011, close to two-thirds of the U.S. public said that terrorists have the same (39 percent) or an even greater (23 percent) ability "to launch another major attack on the U.S.," whereas only about a third said that the ability is "less than it was at the time of the September 11th terrorist attacks." The public also expressed substantial concern about the rise of Islamic extremism. Thirty-seven percent indicated they were very concerned "about the rise of Islamic extremism around the world these days," and another 36 percent were somewhat concerned. Similarly, 36 percent indicated they were very concerned "about the possible rise of Islamic extremism in the U.S.," and another 31 percent said they were somewhat concerned. About a quarter of the public said that the wars in Iraq and Afghanistan have "lessened the chances of terrorist attacks in the U.S.," whereas about a third said that the wars "made no difference" (39 percent for Iraq and 34 percent for Afghanistan), and another third said the wars had "increased the chances of terrorist attacks in the U.S." (31 percent for Iraq and 37 percent for Afghanistan).

As of August 2011, the U.S. public also expressed mixed views on specific actions or policies designed to reduce the threat of terrorism. About 40 percent said that "it will be necessary for the average person to give up some civil liberties" to "curb terrorism in this country" compared with 55 percent who expressed this view immediately after 9/11. On balance, the public in 2011 was more inclined to favor (57 percent) than oppose (41 percent) "requiring all citizens to carry a national identify card at all times to show to a police officer on request." Fifty-three percent favored and 43 percent opposed "allowing airport personnel to do extra checks on passengers who appear to be of Middle-Eastern descent." Forty-two percent favored "the U.S. government monitoring credit card purchases," whereas 55 percent opposed this action. The public expressed less support for "the U.S. government monitoring personal telephone calls and emails," with 29 percent in favor of and 68 percent in opposition to this action.

Although it is often said that partisanship stops at the water's edge, partisan unity in times of crisis was fleeting in the decade after 9/11. By May 2002, congressional Democrats had begun to call for hearings to examine what President Bush had known about the potential for terrorist acts in advance of 9/11 (Chanley, 2002), and the initial period of bipartisanship after 9/11 did not last. Differences in the views of Republican and Democratic elected officials tended to be reflected in the views of Republican and Democratic citizens. In the Pew Research Center survey from 2011, for example, 29 percent of Republicans said that the war in Afghanistan had increased the likelihood of a future terrorist attack in the United States, compared to 42 percent of Democrats. When asked whether torture to gain information from suspected terrorists can be justified, 71 percent of Republicans said that torture can be justified either often or sometimes compared with 45 percent of Democrats. Not unlike Berinsky's (2007) findings from survey evidence and elite discourse surrounding U.S. involvement in World War II and the second Iraq war that followed the attacks of 9/11, when political elites differed in their views of intervention, the public was divided as well. Conversely, when political elites were in agreement, members of the public tended to follow suit.

As of June 2012, the Obama administration had continued or expanded on some of the antiterrorism activities of the Bush administration, while also beginning a drawdown of U.S. troops in Afghanistan. Although there has begun to be debate among elites about the wisdom of drone aircraft attacks against suspected terrorists in Pakistan, Yemen, and other areas, the public remains largely supportive of these attacks. As reported in a May 6, 2012, Op-Ed in the *Los Angeles Times* (McManus, 2012), an ABC News/*Washington Post* survey from February 2012 found that 83 percent of the U.S. public approved of the use of drone attacks against suspected terrorists overseas compared with 11 percent who disagreed and 6 percent who expressed no opinion. Moreover, 77 percent of liberal Democrats approved the use of drones. In the same survey, 56 percent of the public said they trusted President Obama to do a better job handling international affairs than candidate Mitt Romney, whereas 37 percent said they trusted Mitt Romney to do a better job (*Washington Post*, 2012). Similarly, 56 percent said they trusted President Obama to do a better job handling terrorism, whereas 36 percent said they trusted Mitt Romney to do a better job. Although the same survey did not measure trust in the government in Washington, a CNN/ORC International survey from September 2011 (*CNN Politics*, 2011) found that 15 percent of the U.S. public said they trusted the government to do what is right just about always or most of the time, the lowest point recorded in the time since this question has been asked of nationally representative samples of the U.S. public. Despite relatively high trust for President Obama's handling of international affairs and terrorism, it seems unlikely that trust in government overall had changed substantially from September 2011 to February 2012. In other words, in the decade after 9/11, high levels of trust in the U.S. government were not required for the enactment of new policies to combat terrorism and the outlay of substantial resources for homeland security and international antiterrorism efforts, including the wars in Afghanistan and Iraq.

As reflected in Sinclair and LoCicero's (2010) identification of evolutionary psychology as providing a theoretical explanation for the relationship between fears of terrorism and trust in government, scholars of political attitudes and behavior are increasingly turning to evolutionary theory for insight. To better understand the origins and consequences of public evaluations of government and policies such as those designed to combat terrorism and provide national security that is grounded in evolutionary theory, the chapter next considers how such insight may contribute.

WHAT HAVE WE LEARNED: TOWARD AN EVOLUTIONARY PERSPECTIVE ON UNDERSTANDING PUBLIC OPINION AND RESPONSES TO TERRORISM

The quality of citizens' judgments about politics and public policy has been central to the study of public opinion. Scholars have debated whether individual citizens respond rationally to events such as terrorist attacks and the threat of war, with "rationally" defined as assessing the costs and benefits of alternative courses of action and selecting the less costly alternative, or whether citizens evaluate information and make judgments on the basis of their political values and other predispositions (see, e.g., Zaller, 1992) or follow elite cues (e.g. Berinsky, 2007). Evolutionary psychology proceeds from the expectation that humans have evolved neurocomputational mechanisms for solving problems of survival and reproduction (Cosmides & Tooby, 2005). In this view, humans are expected to be adaptively rational, responding most effectively in the face of ecologically valid challenges comparable to the challenges our ancestors would have been likely to encounter (Haselton et al., 2009).

Throughout human history, our ancestors have faced threats from a variety of sources, including other humans (Alexander, 1987; Wilson, 2012). Violence that threatened intragroup cohesion could be tempered by support for a leader who could act as a peacekeeper within the group. Leaders could also be beneficial in facing threats posed by rival groups of humans. Individual humans who belonged to groups that were able to provide the security and means needed to outcompete other groups were more successful over evolutionary time than were individuals belonging to less successful groups (Wilson, 2012). Moreover, in some circumstances, groups composed of altruistic individuals were more successful than groups composed of selfish individuals. The ability to discern between individuals who can be trusted to reciprocate altruism and individuals who cannot be trusted to reciprocate has been central to human social evolution. Human social, cultural, and technological development, however, occurs more quickly than biological evolution, and humans evolved the emotive and cognitive architecture we currently have in far smaller groups than those represented by the nation state and with far less technological capability to target our enemies or wage war.

Although far more of human evolutionary history has been spent in tribes, rather than in nation states, in the modern world, a functioning national government may be necessary to provide protection from individuals, groups, and other nations that seek to do harm to the citizens of that government. As we have seen, high levels of trust in the U.S. national government are unlikely to be the norm, but the government continues to function and allocate resources with far-reaching consequences in the absence of high levels of trust. Consistent with expectations that threat to the group would cause individuals to place greater trust in leaders who could provide security, trust in the U.S. government has increased during times of high perception of threat to the nation. Conversely, when perceptions of threat to the nation recede, subnational group loyalties, such as those associated with partisanship, return to the fore.

Critics of an evolutionary perspective applied to human behavior might argue that there are other theories, such as group attachment theory, that make the same predictions as evolutionary theory. Proponents of evolutionary theory may counter, however, that such theories offer complementary rather than rival explanations (see, e.g., Alcock, 2009; Van Vugt, 2006). Moreover, if a current behavior is a byproduct of natural selection or is no longer adaptive, a full understanding of the behavior requires knowledge of why the neurocomputational mechanisms that underlay the behavior came to exist. From an adaptationist perspective, in other words, although other theoretical frameworks may provide accurate proximate explanations for a behavior or complex of behaviors, an explanation inconsistent with evolutionary theory needs to be reconciled with evolutionary theory.

The value of an evolutionary perspective may best be illustrated with reference to an example, in this case from the study of religion and terrorism. Scholars of the evolutionary study of religion have identified four cross-cultural characteristics of religion, proposing that this complex of characteristics developed to solve problems of group cooperation and commitment among human ancestral populations (Sosis & Alcorta, 2008). These traits are proposed to have contributed to maximizing the potential resource base for early human groups by encouraging cooperation and expanding the communication and collaboration among individuals, across both time and location. Contrary to the view that religion is the root cause of terrorist activity, such as the 9/11 attacks, Sosis and Alcorta (2008) identified religious beliefs, rituals, and institutions as useful mechanisms for increasing the likelihood of otherwise unlikely behavior. Framing terrorism in religious rather than political terms, for example, benefits terrorist groups that might alternatively be viewed as economically and politically self-serving. Religion serves to provide moral justification for the terrorist cause and facilitates the framing of conflict in terms of an absolute dichotomy, such as righteous versus evil. Religions may also offer benefits after death, which may help to motivate suicide terrorism or the willingness to put one's life in danger for the terrorist cause. The treatment of adolescence as the critical life phase for the transmission of religious values and belief is also central to the complex of characteristics proposed to have been selected for in early hominid populations, such that terrorist groups are more likely to successfully recruit adults whose early socialization occurred in a culture of martyrdom and sacrifice on behalf of religion.

On the basis of their analysis, Sosis and Alcorta (2008) identified policy implications that included proposals recommended by other researchers but consistent with an evolutionary perspective, as well as proposals derived from an adaptationist perspective that they had not previously seen. Framing conflict in terms of religion, for example, arouses public passion, and this may result in greater benefit to terrorist organizations than to governments who are seeking to reduce the potential for terrorist attacks. Furthermore, attempts to eliminate religious views are highly unlikely to be successful, as evidenced by a history of endurance of religious beliefs even in the face of persecution. A policy approach that encourages open expression of nonviolent religious beliefs and practices is more likely to succeed in countering terrorism than an approach that forbids such expression. Given the significant role of childhood socialization and exposure to religious beliefs and ritual, providing youths alternative forms of nonviolent religious expression based in religious tradition and alternatives to terrorist-funded schools are also policy options that may decrease the likelihood of religiously inspired terrorism.

An evolutionary understanding of human morality and other elements of our behavior are by no means complete, but knowledge of the evolutionary foundations of human behavior may make it easier to choose to behave in ways that counter our evolved impulses (Alcock, 2009; Alexander, 1987). In the context of actions designed to respond to the terrorist attacks of 9/11, the U.S. public has expressed strong support for actions taken by the Obama administration to markedly increase the use of drone attacks to target suspected terrorists. Although knowledge of how natural selection has shaped the human propensity to demonize and dehumanize enemies that pose real or imagined threats will not necessarily lead individuals to choose to react differently, it may make it less likely that we will act, and make choices that have implications for public policy, on the basis of our evolved nature without thinking more deeply about whether an alternative course of action would increase the likelihood of a more desirable outcome.

CONCLUSIONS

Despite concerns that low levels of trust in government may make it difficult to commit public resources to meet broad societal goals, the evidence from the context of U.S. politics and public policy indicates that change in governmental policies and commitment of significant public resources do not necessarily require sustained high levels of trust. In the decade since 9/11, the United States has committed substantial resources to full-scale wars in Afghanistan and Iraq and the broader War on Terror, while also creating the Department of Homeland Security and substantially increasing security and surveillance measures in areas ranging from transportation, communication, and domestic institutions such as museums, parks, and federal and state government offices. Technological advances in weaponry and killing, such as the use of drones to strategically target enemies, may make the use of violence seem to be more cost-effective. In reality, however, the net benefits may be negative, given the animosity and enmity aroused by perceptions of the loss of innocent life on the side of one's opponents, and the potential for a spiral of ever-increasing violence and cost in terms of both blood and treasure.

Theoretical explanations from the perspective of political or social cognition or social psychology may provide accurate proximate explanations for human political behavior and subsequent policy outcomes. To move beyond an effective theoretical expectation or prediction of behavior to consider how we may best effect change in human behavior and policy outcomes, however, it is important to consider why the neurocomputational mechanisms that make such behavior and outcomes probable came into being. Knowledge that natural selection has favored the demonization of enemies, real or imagined, and the selection of policy options that may benefit the few over the many, for example, does not ensure that individual citizens and policy makers will make improved policy choices. The absence of this knowledge, however, makes it impossible to consider whether alternative policy options that take advantage of knowledge of our evolving emotive and cognitive architecture might better serve the public good.

REFERENCES

Alcock, J. (2009). *Animal behavior: An evolutionary approach (9th ed.)*. Sunderland, MA: Sinauer.

Alexander, R. D. (1987). *The biology of moral systems*. London, UK: Aldine.

Alford, J. R. (2001). We're all in this together: The decline in trust in government, 1958–1996. In J. R. Hibbing & E. Theiss-Morse (Eds.), *What is it about government that Americans dislike?* (pp. 28–46). Cambridge, UK: Cambridge University Press.

Berinsky, A. (2007). Assuming the costs of war: Events, elites, and American support for military conflict. *Journal of Politics*, 69, 975–997.

Chanley, V. A. (2002). Trust in government in the aftermath of 9/11: Determinants and consequences. *Political Psychology*, 23, 469–483.

Chanley, V. A., Rudolph, T. J., & Rahn, W. M. (2000). The origins and consequences of public trust in government: A time series analysis. *Public Opinion Quarterly*, 64, 239–256.

Chanley, V. A., Rudolph, T. J., & Rahn, W. M. (2001). Public trust in government in the Reagan years and beyond. In J. R. Hibbing & E. Theiss-Morse (Eds.), *What is it about government that Americans dislike?* (pp. 59–78). Cambridge, UK: Cambridge University Press.

Citrin, J. (1974). Comment: The political relevance of trust in government. *American Political Science Review*, 16, 431–453.

Citrin, J., & Green, D. P. (1986). Presidential leadership and the resurgence of trust in government. *British Journal of Political Science*, 16, 431–453.

Citrin, J., & Luks, S. (2001). Political trust revisited: Deja vu all over again? In J. R. Hibbing & E. Theiss-Morse (Eds.), *What is it about government that Americans dislike?* (pp. 9–27). Cambridge, UK: Cambridge University Press.

CNN Politics. (2011). CNN poll: Trust in government at all-time low. Retrieved from: http://politicalticker.blogs.cnn.com/2011/09/28/cnn-poll-trust-in-government-at-all-time-low/.

Cosmides, L., & Tooby, J. (2005). Neurocognitive adaptations designed for social exchange. In D. M. Buss (Ed.), *The handbook of evolutionary psychology* (pp. 584–627). Hoboken, NJ: John Wiley & Sons.

Craig, S. C. (1993). *The malevolent leaders: Popular discontent in America*. Boulder, CO: Westview.

Craig, S. C. (1996). The angry voter: Politics and popular discontent in the 1990s. In S. C. Craig (Ed.), *Broken contract: Changing relationships between Americans and their government* (pp. 46–66). Boulder, CO: Westview.

Easton, D. (1965). *A systems analysis of political life*. New York, NY: Wiley.

Erber, R., & Lau, R. (1990). Political cynicism revisited: An information-processing reconciliation of policy-based and incumbency-based interpretations of changes in trust in government. *American Journal of Political Science, 34*, 236–253.

Feldman, S. (1983. The measure and meaning of trust in government. *Political Methodology, 9*, 341–354.

Garment, S. (1991). *Scandal: The culture of mistrust in American politics.* New York, NY: Times Books/Random House.

Gamson, W. A. (1968). *Power and discontent.* Homewood, IL: Dorsey.

Haselton, M., Bryant, G. A., Wilke, A., Frederick, D. A., Galperin, A., Frankenhuis, W. E., & Moore, T. (2009). Adaptive rationality: An evolutionary perspective on cognitive bias. *Social Cognition, 27*, 732–762.

Hetherington, M. J. (1998). The political relevance of political trust. *American Political Science Review, 92*, 791–808.

Hetherington, M. J. (1999). The effect of political trust on the presidential vote, 1968–96. *American Political Science Review, 93*, 311–326.

Hetherington, M. J., & Globetti, S. (2002). Political trust and racial policy preferences. *American Journal of Political Science, 46*, 253–275.

Hetherington, M. J., & Nelson, M. (2003). Anatomy of a rally effect: George W. Bush and the war on terrorism. *PS: Political Science and Politics, 36*, 37–42.

Hetherington, M. J., & Nugent, J. D. (2001). Explaining public support for devolution: The role of political trust. In J. R. Hibbing & E. Theiss-Morse (Eds.), *What is it about government that Americans dislike?* (pp. 134–151). Cambridge, UK: Cambridge University Press.

Hetherington, M. J., & Rudolph, T. J. (2008). Priming, performance, and the dynamics of political trust. *Journal of Politics, 70*, 498–512.

Huddy, L., Feldman, S., Taber, C., & Lahav, G. (2005). Threat, anxiety, and support for antiterrorism policies. *American Journal of Political Science, 49*(3), 593–608.

Keele, L. (2007). Social capital, government performance, and the dynamics of trust in government. *American Journal of Political Science, 51*, 241–254.

Levi, M. (1997). *Consent, dissent, and patriotism.* New York, NY: Cambridge University Press.

Lipset, S. M. (1995). Malaise and resiliency in America. *Journal of Democracy, 6*, 4–18.

Mansbridge, J. (1997). Social and cultural causes of dissatisfaction with U.S. government. In J. S. Nye, Jr., P. D. Zelikow, & D. C. King (Eds.), *Why people don't trust government* (pp. 133–154). Cambridge, MA: Harvard University Press.

McManus, D. (May 6, 2012). Coming clean on drones. *Los Angeles Times.*

Miller, A. H. (1974a). Political issues and trust in government: 1964–1970. *American Political Science Review, 68*, 951–972.

Miller, A. H. (1974b). Rejoinder to "Comment" by Jack Citrin: Political discontent or ritualism. *American Political Science Review, 68*, 989–1001.

Miller, A. H., & Borrelli, S. A. (1991). Confidence in government during the 1980s. *American Politics Quarterly, 19*, 147–173.

Mueller, J. (1973). *War, presidents, and public opinion.* New York, NY: Wiley.

Norris, P. (1999). The growth of critical citizens? In P. Norris (Ed.), *Critical citizens: Global support for Democratic citizens* (pp. 1–27). Oxford, UK: Oxford University Press.

Nye, J. S., Jr. (1997). Introduction: The decline of confidence in government. In J. S. Nye, Jr., P. D. Zelikow, & D. C. King (Eds.), *Why people don't trust government* (pp. 1–18). Cambridge, MA: Harvard University Press.

Orren, G. (1997). Fall from grace: The public's loss of faith in government. In J. S. Nye, Jr., P. D. Zelikow, & D. C. King (Eds.), *Why people don't trust government* (pp. 77–107). Cambridge, MA: Harvard University Press.

Pew Research Center. (1998). *Deconstructing trust: How Americans view government.* Washington, DC: Pew Research Center.

Pew Research Center. (2010). *Public trust in government: 1958–2010.* Washington, DC: Pew Research Center.

Pew Research Center. (2011). *Ten years after 9/11: United in remembrance, divided over policies.* Washington, DC: Pew Research Center.

Scholz, J. T., & Lubell, M.. (1998). Trust and taxpaying: Testing the heuristic approach to collective action. *American Journal of Political Science, 42,* 398–417.

Shambaugh G., Matthew R., Silver, R. C., McDonald, B., Poulin, M., & Blum S. (2010). Public perceptions of traumatic events and policy preferences during the George W. Bush administration: A portrait of America in turbulent times. *Studies in Conflict & Terrorism, 33,* 133–169.

Sinclair, S. J., & LoCicero, A. (2010). Do fears of terrorism predict trust in government? *Journal of Aggression, Conflict and Peace Research, 2,* 57–68.

Sosis, R., & Alcorta, C. S. (2008). Militants and martyrs: Evolutionary perspectives on religion and terrorism. In R. D. Sagarin & T. Taylor (Eds.), *Natural security: A Darwinian approach to a dangerous world* (pp. 105–124). Berkeley, CA: University of California Press.

Tyler, T. R. (1990). *Why people obey the law.* New Haven, CT: Yale University Press.

Van Vugt, M. (2006). Evolutionary origins of leadership and followership. *Personality and Social Psychology Review, 10,* 353–371.

Washington Post. (2012). Washington Post-ABC News Poll (conducted February 1 to February 4, 2012). Retrieved from http://www.washingtonpost.com/wp-rv/politics/polls/postabcpoll_020412.html

Williams, J. T. (1985). Systematic influences of political trust: The importance of institutional performance. *Political Methodology, 11,* 125–142.

Wilson, E. O. (2012). *The social conquest of Earth.* New York, NY: Liveright Publishing.

Zaller, J. R. (1992). *The nature and origins of mass opinion.* Cambridge, UK: Cambridge University Press.

CHAPTER 2

Perceptions of Threat, Trust in Government, and Policy Support for the War in Iraq

GEORGE SHAMBAUGH

Following the attacks of 9/11/2001, the George W. Bush Administration repeatedly used claims about the threat of terrorism to justify and bolster public support for the U.S. invasion of Iraq and other important policy initiatives. I analyze the effectiveness of this strategy using three-year panel surveys of randomly selected adults in the United States conducted between 2007 and 2009. These surveys were funded by a National Science Foundation Human and Social Dynamics grant with Roxane Silver, Richard Matthew, and George Shambaugh, co-principal investigators. The survey research team also included Scott Blum, Paloma Gonzalez, Bryan McDonald, and Michael Poulin. While the surveys were created jointly, I accept sole responsibility for the analysis presented in this chapter.

Our survey results suggest that during the last 3 years of the George W. Bush presidency, more than three-quarters of the American public believed that terrorism continued to pose a threat to national security and more than one third believed that it continued to pose a threat to their personal security. At the same time, the public increasingly questioned efforts to link the threat of terrorism to the war in Iraq—including repeated efforts by the Bush Administration to tie Saddam Hussein to the terrorist attacks on 9/11; Secretary Colin Powell's February 5, 2003, report to the United Nations regarding the presence of weapons of mass destruction in Iraq; and the repeated invocation of questionable claims regarding efforts by Iraq to secure yellowcake uranium ore from Niger. Our surveys indicate a decline in the public trust over time, with less than 15 percent of Americans surveyed at the end of this administration agreeing that government information about Iraq was objective and trustworthy. Meanwhile, more than half reported that national politicians were exploiting the war in Iraq for partisan or political advantage.

In this chapter, I evaluate the relationships among levels of trust in the national government, public perceptions of the threat from terrorism, and the degree of public support for U.S. government policy. While elite or partisan cues are important in promoting perceptions of threat and generating public support for counterthreat strategies, I argue that individuals are critical consumers of information. Thus, people interpret and respond to government signals about threats differently depending on the degree to which they trust the government on three different dimensions: the quality and objectivity of the information provided by the national government, the integrity of politicians not to exploit the information for political or partisan advantage, and the likelihood that the policies in question will be successful. See Figure 2.1.

The last 3 years of the George W. Bush Administration have several characteristics that make them ideal for analyzing the interactions among trust in government, perceptions of threat, and the level of public support. First, the administration repeatedly publically emphasized the persistence of a terrorist threat and explicitly used this threat to justify a wide range of counterterrorism policies at home and abroad, including the war in Iraq (Gershkoff & Kushner, 2005). Second, the level of public trust in the U.S. government varies on the three dimensions of interest: trust in the objectivity and truthfulness of information that the U.S. government provided about terrorism and about Iraq, trust in the integrity of politicians not to exploit this information for partisan or political advantage, and trust in the efficacy of U.S. counterterrorism and war-fighting policies. Third, the perceived level of threat from terrorism to national and personal security varies over time, as does the level of public support for the war in Iraq. Fourth, regardless of the media source through which it was reported, the U.S. government was one of the principal sources of public information about the threat of terrorism and the effectiveness of both counterterrorism policies and the war in Iraq. The lack of alternate authoritative

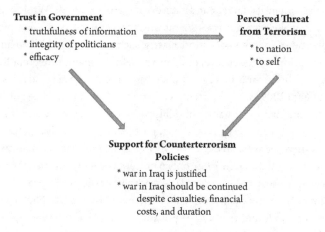

Figure 2.1:
Trust in government, perceived threat from terrorism, and support for counterterrorism policies.

sources made the information provided by the government particularly salient to the public's assessment of the threat of terrorism and success of counterterrorism policies.

THREAT AND TRUST IN GOVERNMENT

Theories about the causal linkages among the public's trust in the government, its perception of threat, and its support for governmental policies can be situated fruitfully within an ongoing debate between rationalist and elite-driven theories of public opinion. As articulated by Page and Shapiro (1992), scholars from the rationalist perspective argue that public opinion is coherent, stable, and responsive to shifts in international and domestic events. One of the most notable examples of research in this genre was pioneered by Mueller (1973), who analyzed public responsiveness to emergencies and dramatic events. He posited that the public would rally-around-the flag in support of the president and support for national policies would increase following events that were sharply focused, national in scope, and involved the president (Mueller, 1973). The public rally of support for President George W. Bush and his counterterrorism policies in the immediate aftermath of the 9/11 terrorist incidents reflects this dynamic (Hetherington & Nelson, 2003).

Others in the rationalist genre emphasize the public's ability to assess policies based on a cost-benefit calculation of objective information about the events at hand. Jentleson (1992) and Gelpi, Feaver, and Reifler (2005/2006) argue, for example, that public support for military operations, including its tolerance of war casualties and support for military intervention, reflects its assessment of the objectives and likelihood of success of the operation. Josiger (2009) and Nacos (2002, 2006) argue that public support for counterterrorism policies is similarly driven by the frequency, intensity, targets, and nature of terrorist incidents. While compelling, the ability to make accurate assessments presumes that the necessary information is available and widely shared. Unfortunately, such information is often limited and public perceptions of the nature, cost, and benefits of major foreign policy events are often inaccurate. In a survey of public assessments of war casualties, Bennett and Flickinger (2009) find, for example, that only a small percentage of the public predicts the number of casualties in military conflicts accurately and the majority of people overestimate the counts. They report that in 1945, only 8 percent of adult Americans surveyed were able to correctly assess the number of American servicemen killed during the war; in 1953, only 6 percent correctly assessed the number of those killed in Korea; and in 1966 only 17 percent of the public provided accurate assessments of U.S. servicemen killed in Vietnam (Bennett & Flickinger, 2009). The same surveys found that a large portion of people at the time overestimated the number of casualties. For example, 54 percent overestimated the number of U.S. servicemen killed in World War II, 47 percent overestimated the count in the Korea War, and 44 percent overestimated the count in Vietnam (Bennett & Flickinger, 2009).

Ironically, the public's tendency to overestimate casualties of war is matched by a comparable tendency to underestimate the causalities from terrorism. In our January 2009 survey, 86.3 percent of respondents indicated that 10 or fewer attacks against the United States or Western targets had taken place since 9/11, and 33.6 percent reported that no such terrorist incidents had occurred. The first estimate is close to the 13 reported by the International Terrorism Attributes of Terrorist Events database (ITERATE, 2009) to have taken place within the United States during the same period. This apparent accuracy diminishes dramatically, however, if the question is interpreted as referring to attacks against U.S. citizens overseas as well. Excluding incidents in Iraq and Afghanistan, ITERATE reports 281 attacks against U.S. targets. The inaccuracy of public perceptions regarding deaths in war and the number terrorist incidents suggests that the public often faces severe informational constraints that make objective assessments of ongoing threats and counterthreat policies difficult.

When faced with information constraints, individuals often compensate by seeking out other sources of information including cues from policy makers. Page and Shapiro (1992) argue that the public responds in rational ways to international and domestic events as they have been reported and interpreted by the mass media, policymakers, opinion leaders, and other elites. Thus, public perceptions of threat are likely to be driven both by their own interpretation of events (Josiger, 2009; Shambaugh & Josiger, 2004) and by interpretive signals received from the government, the media, and other sources (Mutz, 1998; Nacos, 2002, 2006).

Scholars of electoral politics have argued that if the information provider or the content of the signal it provides is known to be perfectly credible, then otherwise uninformed voters can use the content of the signal to make predictions about the consequences of electoral outcomes that match those of more informed individuals (Lupia, 1994; Sniderman, Brody, & Tetlock, 1991; Sobel, 1985). Thus, if the information provided by the government about threats of terrorism and the efficacy of counterterrorism policies are presumed to be credible, then the public could respond "as if" it had all the necessary information to support those counterterrorism policies that best reflect its preferences.

The problem is that the degree to which information is perceived to be credible is subjective and, thus, challenging to measure. Absent objective measures of credibility, scholars have analyzed a variety of factors that might increase the credibility of the information source (Druckman & Lupia, 2000; Groeling & Baum, 2008; Lupia & McCubbins, 1998). These include trustworthiness (Popkin, 1994), accuracy and objectivity (Iyengar & Kinder, 1985), and expert status (Page, Shapiro, & Dempsey, 1987). To assess perceived credibility, respondents are asked the extent to which they agree that, "Information provided to the public by the national government about Iraq is objective and can be trusted."

Shapiro and Page (1988, p. 223) argue that "it is difficult to distinguish leadership or education of the public from manipulation or deception through misleading, incomplete or inaccurate information." While recognizing this difficulty, I posit that individuals are likely make judgments about the degree to which politicians manipulate, deceive, or otherwise exploit information and that these judgments affect the degree to which they will accept the signals sent and the policies they are used to justify. Therefore, I hypothesize that higher levels of trust in the credibility of information provided by the government are likely to be associated with greater public acceptance of the government's interpretation of the issue at hand and greater public support for related policies. If true, then higher levels of trust in the information provided by the Bush Administration about terrorism and the war in Iraq should be associated with the greater perceptions of the threat from terrorism and greater levels of public support for counterterrorism policies, including the war in Iraq.

If the credibility of the signal cannot be verified, individuals may compensate further in a variety of other ways. Scholars analyzing the impact of polarization among elites on public opinion argue that when elites act in consensus with one another, the public is likely to actively support or at least acquiesce to policy positions taken (Abramowitz & Saunders, 1998; Holsti, 2004; Powlick & Katz, 1998; Souva & Rohde, 2007). Baker and Oneal (2001) argue, for example, that rallies of public support are likely to persist when there is a high degree of bipartisan support, media coverage, and support from the president. Psychologists suggest that framing issues as national in scope can facilitate this dynamic by creating an extended nationally based group identity that dominates other sub-national group identities based on party affiliation, religious affiliation, socioeconomic status, etc. (Brewer & Brown, 1998; Kam & Ramos, 2008). Scholars also emphasize the tendency of individuals to discount their own personal contexts in favor of signals from others when information is limited (Ansolabehere, Meredith, Snowberg, & Synder, 2007; Huddy et al., 2002, 2005; Kinder & Kiewiet, 1979, 1981). Joslyn and Haider-Markel (2007) argue that this sociotropic tendency applies to issues of terrorism that are likely to be considered broad social or national problems with similar consequences. Collectively, these propositions suggest that the linkage between perceptions of threat and policy support will be stronger if the threat is framed in terms of national rather than personal security.

In parallel, researchers posit that the level of partisanship among the public is likely to increase when national political leaders become divided (Kam & Ramos, 2008). In such situations, the public tends to increasingly prefer information based on partisan assessments of their trustworthiness (Souva & Rohde, 2007; Zaller, 1991). Brady & Sniderman (1985), Brody & Shapiro (1989), Berinsky (2005, 2007), Brody (2002), Zaller (1992, 1994), and Delii Carpini and Keeter (1996) argue, further, that likeability, elite framing and partisan cues rather than cost-benefit calculations of objective knowledge often drive public opinion. Consequently, as perceptions of disunity or opportunism among elites increase, partisanship is likely to play a greater role in shaping the public's interpretation of government signals and its support for related policies. From this, I hypothesize that greater public perceptions of political opportunism among politicians will be associated with an increase in the importance of partisanship in the public's receptivity to cues from the national government and support for its policies. To evaluate public perceptions of partisanship and political opportunism among leaders, respondents are asked the extent to which they agree with the statement, "National politicians are exploiting the situation with Iraq for electoral or partisan advantage."

The responsiveness of public opinion to national signals is also often attributed to perceptions of the likelihood of success (Gelpi, Feaver, & Reifler, 2005/2006). Peter Feaver, one leading scholars in this genre, served as special advisor for strategic planning and institutional reform on the National Security Council for the Bush Administration. Based on this proposition, I hypothesize that increased perceptions of policy success will lead to greater public receptivity to government cues and higher levels of support for related policy initiatives. To assess policy efficacy, respondents are asked the extent to they agree that U.S. actions at home and abroad have decreased the threat of terrorism, and whether the United States is better able to defend itself against and respond to terrorist attacks than before 9/11.

THE SURVEY AND DESCRIPTIVE STATISTICS

Panel data are collected from surveys of nationally representative samples of U.S. adults who responded to annual electronic questionnaires in three periods: December 28, 2006, to January 18, 2007 ($N = 1613$, 73.5 percent response rate), December 28, 2007, through February 18, 2008 ($N = 1157$, 71.7 percent response rate), and December 30, 2008, through February 9, 2009 ($N = 975$, 84.3 percent response rate). The duration of each survey was allowed to vary in order to achieve an initial target of 1600 and a response rate of at least 70 percent. All participants in the second survey took part in the first, and all participants in the third survey took part in the first two. Thus, the survey tracks responses by 1157 individuals over 2 years and 975 from that group over 3 years. The surveys were administered by Knowledge Networks using online questionnaires. The survey questions are specified in Figure 2.2.

The surveys were funded by a National Science Foundation Human and Social Dynamics grant, entitled, "Societal Implications of Individual Differences in Response to Turbulence: The Case of Terrorism." As noted in the introduction, the research team included Drs. Roxane Silver, Richard Matthew and George Shambaugh, co-principal investigators, as well as Scott Blum, Paloma Gonzalez, Bryan McDonald, and Michael Poulin.

TRUST IN GOVERNMENT

Historically, one frequently asked question about trust is: "Do you trust in government to do the right thing either just about always or most of the time?" Reflecting

Question	Variable Statement	Value Labels
"To what extent do you agree or disagree with the following statements?"		
	Trust in Policy Efficacy	1 = strongly disagree,
	"The United States is better able to defend itself from terrorist attacks than before 9/11."	2 = moderately disagree, 3 = neither agree nor disagree,
	"The United States is better able to respond to terrorist attacks than before 9/11."	4 = moderately agree, 5 = strongly agree
	"US actions at home since 9/11 have decreased the threat of terrorism."	
	"US actions abroad since 9/11 have decreased the threat of terrorism."	
	Trust in the Objectivity and Truthfulness of Information Provided	
	"Information provided by the national government about the war in Iraq is objective and can be trusted."	
	Trust the Integrity of Politicians	
	"National politicians exploited the war in Iraq for electoral or partisan advantage."	
	Existence of Terrorist Threat	
	"Terrorism is a threat to national security."	
	"Terrorism is threat to my personal security."	
	"Policy Support"	
	"The United States was justified in attacking Iraq after 9/11."	
	"U.S. policy in Iraq should not be altered by rising numbers of casualties."	
	"U.S. policy in Iraq should not be altered due rising financial costs."	
	"U.S. policy in Iraq should not be altered due to the time it takes for the US to achieve its objectives."	
"Please read each of the following questions and share with us your opinions using the scale provided."		
	Level of Terrorist Threat	1 = very low, 2 = low, 3 = medium,
	"How great will the threat from terrorism be to the United States in the next decade?"	4 = high
	"How great will the threat from terrorism be to you or your family in the next decade?"	
"What do you think is the percent chance . . ."		
	There will be a terrorist attack on US soil in the next two years.	1 = 1 to 10%, 2 = 11 to 20%,
	Someone close to you will be hurt by terrorism in next two years.	3 = 21 to 30%, 4 = 31–40%, 5 = 41–50%, 6 = 51–60%, 7 = 61–70%, 8 = 71–80%, 9 = 81–90%, 10 = 91–100%

Figure 2.2:
Variable definitions.

Question	Variable	Statement	Value Labels
Personal characteristics			
	Education	"What is your highest educational degree?"	1 = less than high school, 2 = some high school, no diploma, 3 = graduated high school, diploma or equivalent, 4 = some college, no degree, 5 = associate degree, 6 = bachelor's degree, 7 = master's degree, 8 = professional degree, 9 = doctoral degree
	Age	"In what age group do you belong?"	1 = 18–24 years old, 2 = 25–34 years old, 3 = 35–44 years old, 4 = 45–54 years old, 5 = 55–64 years old, 6 = 64–74 years old, 7 = 75+ years old
	Gender	"What is your gender?"	1 = female, 0 = male
	Region	"In what region of the country do you live?"	Region is designated as 1 if the respondent lives in mid-Atlantic or North Eastern section of the United States, from Washington, DC to New England, and 0 if the respondent lives elsewhere.

Figure 2.2:
(Continued)

Mueller's (1973) rally-around-the-flag effect, this aspect of trust in the U.S. government soared from a long-time norm of 29 percent in March 2001 to 64 percent at the end of September 2011 (Chanley et al., 2002). Six years later, in the fall of 2008, the rally-around-the-flag effect had ended and the percentage of people who trusted the government to "do the right thing" had decreased to 22 percent, 5 points lower than it was before 9/11 (Chanley et al., 2002). Our survey shows a similar result with the finding that 22.7 percent of those surveyed in January of 2009 that agreed that "the country was on the right track."

While useful as a general measure, the meaning of "do the right thing" and being "on the right track" are ambiguous. To better understand trust in government, it is useful to specify public perceptions and expectations of the government more precisely (Orren 1997). To do this, respondents are asked the extent to which they agree with statements regarding the efficacy of government policy, the objectivity of the information it provides, and the integrity of their political leaders.

With regard to the efficacy of government policy, the U.S. public generally trusts government to "do the right thing" to win the Global War on Terror (Shambaugh, Matthew, & McDonald, 2008; Shambaugh, Matthew, Silver, McDonald, Poulin, & Blum, 2009). Almost half of those surveyed in 2009 agreed or strongly agreed with statements that the United States is better able to defend itself against (47.5 percent) or respond to (51.4 percent) terrorist attacks than before 9/11. These levels of support remained relatively stable between 2007, 2008, and 2009 ($\chi^2 > .05$, estimated using all five categories of responses shown in Figure 2.2).

Many also considered U.S. counterterrorism policies to have been successful. In 2007, 40.7 percent of respondents moderately or strongly agreed that, "U.S. actions at home since 9/11 have decreased the threat of terrorism." This positive assessment increased to 41.7 percent in 2008 and 45.7 percent in 2009. This 3-year improvement is statistically significant (sig. $\chi^2 < .05$). Similarly, the percentage of respondents who moderately or strongly agreed that "U.S. actions abroad have decreased the threat of terrorism" improved significantly from 30.7 percent in 2007, to 34.2 percent in 2008, to 36.7 percent in 2009 (sig. $\chi^2 < .05$).

With regard to objectivity and integrity, respondents to our surveys were less trustful of the quality of the information provided by the national government than they were of the success of its counterterrorism policies. Only 22.3 percent of those surveyed in January of 2007 moderately or strongly agreed with the statement, "Information provided by the national government about 9/11 is objective and can be trusted." In addition, half (47.9 percent) of those surveyed in 2007 moderately or strongly agreed that national politicians exploited 9/11 for political purposes.

The percentage of people who moderately or strongly agreed that the information provided by the national government about the war in Iraq was objective and trustworthy was low and decreased over time from 15.3 percent in 2007 to 14.7 percent in 2008 and 13.8 percent in 2009 (sig. $\chi^2 < .05$). Politicians can take a little consolation in the knowledge the media fared worse—only 10.9 percent of respondents moderately or strongly agreed that information provided by the media about Iraq was objective and trustworthy in 2007, and this decreased to 9.3 percent in 2008.

More than half of those surveyed moderately or strongly agreed that national politicians exploited the situation in Iraq for political advantage. Interestingly, this assessment improved slightly over time, with the number decreasing from 55.9 percent in 2007, to 55.4 percent in 2008, and 53.9 percent in 2009 (sig. $\chi^2 < .05$).

In sum, public perceptions of trust in the government vary depending on how trust is defined. If "doing the right thing" is based on an assessment of success, the Bush Administration receives high marks by about one third of those surveyed. In contrast, only about 15 percent of those surveyed agreed that the information about Iraq was objective and trustworthy, and more than 50 percent responding that politicians were exploiting the information for partisan or political advantage. Trust in the government was low, but different aspects of trust varied differently and, counter to popular commentaries at the time, none were in free fall during the last 3 years of the Bush Administration.

PUBLIC PERCEPTIONS OF THREAT

Public perceptions of the threat from terrorism vary depending on how the threat is framed (Boettcher & Cobb, 2006). Consistent with the unchanging national threat level of "Orange" during each of the survey periods, on average three quarters (76.6 percent) of our respondents moderately or strongly agreed that "terrorism is a threat to national security." The small variations in this indicator over time are not statistically significant ($\chi^2 > .05$).

In contrast, if the threat of terrorism is framed in more specific terms, such as the likelihood of an attack against the United States in the next 2 years, public perceptions of threat are lower and decline significantly over time. In 2007, about one third (31.3 percent) of those surveyed argued that there was a greater than 50–50 chance of a terrorist attack against the United States in the next 2 years; by 2008, only a fifth (20.9 percent) held that view. The public also grew increasingly optimistic about the intensity of the threat. The percentage of people who reported that the threat from terrorism to the United States would be medium or high in the next decade dropped from 81.0 percent in 2007, to 74.0 percent in 2009, to 66.9 percent in 2009 (sig. $\chi^2 < .05$).

Perceptions also vary depending on whether the threat from terrorism is defined as a threat to the nation or to the individual. Perceptions of terrorist threats to personal security are generally much lower than those to national security, but they, too, vary with greater specificity. Public recognition of the existence of a terrorist threat to personal security decreased from 35.8 percent in 2007 to 31.2 percent in 2008 before increasing slightly to 33.9 percent in 2009 (sig. $\chi^2 < .05$). At the same time, the proportion of people who agreed that there is a greater than 50–50 chance that "someone close to you will be hurt by a terrorist attack in the next 2 years" declined from 5.7 percent 2007, to 5.1 percent in 2008 and 2.9 percent in 2009 (sig. $\chi^2 < .05$). Similarly, while over one third (36 percent) of those surveyed in 2007 agreed that the threat of terrorism to personal security will be high in the next decade, that number dropped to 32.1 percent in 2008, and to one quarter (24.6 percent) in 2009 (sig. $\chi^2 < .05$).

POLICY SUPPORT FOR THE WAR IN IRAQ

To assess the degree to which respondents accepted the President's linkage between the events of 9/11 and the invasion of Iraq, respondents were asked the degree to which they agreed that, "The United States was justified in attacking Iraq after 9/11." To assess casualty sensitivity, their tolerance for high financial costs, and war weariness, they were asked the degree to which they agreed that, "U.S. policy in Iraq should not be altered by rising numbers of casualties," "U.S. policy in Iraq should not be altered due to rising financial costs," and "U.S. policy should not be altered due to the time it takes for the United States to achieve its objectives." All responses are measured on a 5-point scale as noted in Figure 2.2.

Our results suggest that the U.S. public remained divided over its support for U.S. actions in Iraq during the last 3 years of the Bush Administration. On average over this time period, about one third of respondents supported the war effort.

Furthermore, public support did not drop precipitously over time. Between 2007, 2008 and 2009, people continued to moderately or strongly agree to stay in Iraq despite higher casualties (27.2, 30.2, and 29.4 percent, respectively), greater financial burden (30.5, 32.8, and 29.4 percent), or the length of the conflict (29.0, 32.1, and 30.0 percent). The The changes over time are statistically significant in all three indicators (sig. $\chi^2 < .05$).

CONTROL VARIABLES

Given the highly partisan atmosphere of the late George W. Bush Administration, it is possible that self-identified Democrats may have been less willing than Republicans or Independents to accept the President's signals regarding the level of terrorist threats or support his counterterrorism and war fighting policies. To control for this possibility, each respondent is asked to self-identify their political party on a 7-point scale, from strong republican to strong democrat. This variable is recoded as a dummy variable reflecting membership in the Democratic Party (1 = Democrat, 0 = Other). The proportion of the respondents who were democratic grows slightly from 52.7 percent in 2007 to 56.0 percent in 2009, though this change is not statistically significant.

Living near the sites of the 9/11 terrorist incidents may affect perceptions of vulnerability and threat. To control for this effect, respondents are asked to identify where they live. This information was used to create a regional dummy variable that indicates whether individual respondents live on the east coast of the United States from the mid-Atlantic to New England. The analyses also control for education level, age, and gender.

TRUST IN GOVERNMENT AND PERCEPTIONS OF THE THREAT OF TERRORISM

The relationship between levels of trust in government and perceptions of the threat of terrorism are evaluated using two different specifications of the threat. These include the degree to which respondents agree that terrorism poses a threat and the likelihood that a terrorist attack is imminent. The first set of equations in Table 2.1 estimate the effects of several different aspects of trust on the degree to which respondents agree that "Terrorism is a threat to national security." The level of agreement is specified using a five-point scale from "Strongly Disagree" to "Strongly Agree." The second set of equations in Table 2.1 estimate the percentage chance that respondents assign to a terrorist attack "on U.S. soil" in the next 2 years. Equations are modified in Table 2.2 to reflect threats to personal rather than national security. The dependent variables are the level of agreement that "terrorism is a threat to your personal security" and the percentage chance that "someone close" will be hurt by an attack in the next 2 years.

TABLE 2.1. TERRORISM AS A THREAT TO NATIONAL SECURITY

Terrorism Is a Threat to National Security	(1)	(2)	Percentage Chance of Attack on U.S. soil in Next 2 Years	(1)	(2)
Lagged Dependent Variable	1.012***	1.003***		0.326***	0.330***
	(0.0696)	(0.0730)		(0.0321)	(0.0316)
Govt. Info Trustworthy	0.0725	0.0689		0.0325	–0.0166
	(0.0630)	(0.0671)		(0.0814)	(0.0847)
Politicians Exploit Info	0.257***	0.274***		0.215***	0.257***
	(0.0561)	(0.0609)		(0.0673)	(0.0706)
Home Actions Successful	0.173**	0.171**		–0.134*	–0.116
	(0.0673)	(0.0697)		(0.0779)	(0.0779)
Actions Abroad Successful	0.0983	0.0712		0.0964	0.0754
	(0.0602)	(0.0663)		(0.0798)	(0.0844)
Democrat		–0.164			–0.300*
		(0.120)			(0.160)
Education		–0.0521			–0.0559
		(0.0591)			(0.0694)
Age		0.0368			–0.114***
		(0.0367)			(0.0420)
Female		0.179			0.242*
		(0.113)			(0.136)
East Coast USA		–0.223			0.301
		(0.137)			(0.192)
Constant	6.815***	6.720***		6.308***	5.861***
	(0.396)	(0.458)		(0.460)	(0.555)
Pseudo R^2	.1237	.1241		.0545	.0609
Sig. χ^2	.0000	.0000		.0000	.0000
Observations	1954	1791		1124	1116

Ordered logistic regression, robust standard errors in parentheses.

***$p < .01$, **$p < .05$, *$p < .1$.

Each model is estimated first (in column 1) with each of the four variants of trust (the extent to which the respondents agree that information provided by the government about the war in Iraq is objective and trustworthy, that politicians are exploiting the information for political or partisan advantage, and that U.S. actions at home or U.S. abroad are decreasing the threat of terrorism), all of which are measured using the same 5-point scale ranging from "Strongly Disagree" to "Strongly

TABLE 2.2. TERRORISM AS A THREAT TO PERSONAL SECURITY

Terrorism Is a Threat to my Personal Security	(1)	(2)	Percentage Chance Someone Close Will be Hurt by an Attack in the Next 2 Years	(1)	(2)
Lagged Dependent Variable	0.808***	0.814***		0.460***	0.432***
	(0.0554)	(0.0582)		(0.0384)	(0.0395)
Govt. Info Trustworthy	0.192***	0.170***		0.0918	0.104
	(0.0603)	(0.0656)		(0.0692)	(0.0749)
Politicians Exploit Info	0.0839	0.150**		−0.0624	0.000940
	(0.0535)	(0.0599)		(0.0587)	(0.0665)
Home Actions Successful	−0.0156	−0.00302		−0.0681	−0.0816
	(0.0662)	(0.0672)		(0.0770)	(0.0785)
Actions Abroad Successful	0.0877	0.105		0.0108	0.0496
	(0.0619)	(0.0665)		(0.0801)	(0.0866)
Democrat		−0.0297			0.165
		(0.112)			(0.145)
Education		−0.106*			−0.110
		(0.0586)			(0.0677)
Age		−0.0154			−0.0770*
		(0.0337)			(0.0399)
Female		0.219**			0.465***
		(0.108)			(0.135)
East Coast USA		−0.0642			0.126
		(0.131)			(0.168)
Constant	6.328***	6.401***		6.902***	6.958***
	(0.369)	(0.455)		(0.518)	(0.593)
Pseudo R^2	.0827	.0872		.0624	.0716
Sig. χ^2	.0000	.0000		.0000	.0000
Observations	1950	1786		1964	1798

Ordered logistic regression, robust standard errors in parentheses.

***$p < .01$, **$p < .05$, *$p < .1$.

Agree." Each model is estimated a second time (column 2) with the addition of controls for political party affiliation, education level, age, gender, and whether one lives in the Washington, DC, to New York City corridor where the events of 9/11 were targeted. All of the models are estimated using ordered logistic regression, significant coefficients are starred, and robust standard errors are reported in the parentheses. Each includes a lagged dependent variable to control for autocorrelation.

Nonparametric correlations between all of the independent variables indicate that multicolinearity is not likely to be a problem (tau-b < .7).

TRUST AND PERCEPTIONS OF A TERRORIST THREAT TO NATIONAL SECURITY

The results indicate that the integrity of politicians matters when assessing the threat of terrorism to national security, while the trustworthiness of information provided by the government does not. Success at home matters, but success abroad does not. Similarly, neither the perceived trustworthiness of information provided by the government about Iraq nor the success of U.S. counterterrorism policies abroad have a significant impact on the anticipation of an attack on U.S. soil in the next 2 years.

In contrast, those who believe that politicians exploited information about Iraq for political or partisan advantage are more likely than others to agree that that terrorism is a threat to national security and that an attack on U.S. soil in the next 2 years is likely. These relationships remain significant when controlling for political party, education level, age, gender and whether one lives in the Washington, DC, to New England corridor.

The results suggest that the relationship between trust in government and perceptions of the threat of terrorism is more nuanced than is suggested by the literature presented above. For example, although Democrats were less likely than others to anticipate an attack, political party affiliation did not have a significant effect on a respondents' perceptions of terrorism as a national threat (Table 2.1, column 2). This suggests that increased partisanship among national leaders may make people more cognizant of a particular issue, but does not necessarily increase the level of partisanship among the public. That those who consider terrorism to be a national threat also consider U.S. actions at home to be successful creates a beneficial feedback loop by creating a perceived need to domestic counterterrorism policies while building confidence that the threat can be managed.

While none of the control variables have a significant impact on perceptions of terrorism as a national security threat, they do have significant effects on the perceived likelihood of an attack against the United States. In particular, young people and women are more likely than others to anticipate such an attack, while Democrats are less likely to do so. Education level and living in the Washington, DC, to New England corridor do not have significant effects.

TRUST AND PERCEPTIONS OF A TERRORIST THREAT TO PERSONAL SECURITY

The trustworthiness of government information matters when assessing whether terrorism poses a threat to one's personal security, the effect of political integrity is mixed, and perceptions of policy success are irrelevant. Respondents who believe the information provided by the national government is objective and truthful are more likely than others to believe that terrorism poses a threat to their personal security. This effect remains significant when controlling for political party, education level, age, gender, and whether one lives between in Washington, DC, to New England corridor. When these control variables are considered, the results suggest that those who believe that politicians exploit information about Iraq for political or partisan advantage are also more likely than others to agree that terrorism poses a personal threat. Interestingly, regardless of how it is operationalized, one's trust in government has no significant impact on the expectation that someone close will be hurt by a terrorist attack in the next 2 years.

The results provide several interesting findings with regard to the respondents' personal characteristics. In particular, women are more likely than others to believe that terrorism poses a threat to personal security and that someone close to them will be a victim of terrorism in the near future. Highly educated people are less likely than others to consider terrorism a threat to personal security and young people are more likely to anticipate that someone close will be hurt in the near future. Political party and region of habitation have no effect perceptions of terrorism as a threat to personal security or as an imminent danger.

Finally, comparing the results in Tables 2.1 and 2.2 suggests that the particular aspect of trust that affects public perceptions of terrorism varies depending on whether the threat is cast in national or personal terms. When framed in terms of national security or an attack against the United States, the trustworthiness of information provided by the government is not associated with the public's perception of threat or the likelihood of an attack, yet the integrity of politicians and the perceived success of counterterrorism actions at home affect both. In contrast, when framed in terms of a threat to personal security, the trustworthiness of information and integrity of politicians matter to varying degrees, while policy success does not.

TRUST IN GOVERNMENT, PERCEPTIONS OF THREAT, AND PUBLIC SUPPORT FOR THE WAR IN IRAQ

Support for war within democratic countries has long been a topic debate. Some argue that democracies are inherently peaceful in part because democratic populations are less likely than others to tolerate human and other costs of battle (Jentleson, 1992). Others argue that democratic constituents can be mobilized readily following traumatic events and are often willing to support aggressive and extraordinary policy actions for a short period of time (Matthew & Shambaugh, 2005). This section analyzes how the level of trust in government and perceptions of threat affect the degree to which respondents support the U.S. government's justification of the invasion of Iraq and continuing the war despite rising costs in terms of casualties, money, and time.

The relationship between of trust in government and public support for the war in Iraq can be summarized as follows:

- Trust in the objectivity of the information provided by the government matters. Those who consider government information to be trustworthy are more likely to support the war.
- The integrity of politicians only matters with regard to the duration of the war. Those who think politicians are exploiting the war for political or electoral purposes less likely than others to support a long war.
- The efficacy of foreign policy matters, but success at home is irrelevant. Those who consider U.S. counterterrorism actions abroad to be successful are more likely than others to support the war.
- Perceptions of threats from terrorism matter, but their impacts vary depending on the issue at hand and how threat is defined.

The analyses are presented in Tables 2.3 through 2.6. Each dependent variable is analyzed multiple times using the different specifications of threat and trust discussed above. Each table presents models that assess how the level of agreement that terrorism poses a threat to national security affects the level of support for U.S. policies in Iraq (without and with respondent-specific controls, columns 1 and 2, respectfully). Each then presents models that assess how the level of agreement that terrorism poses a threat to personal security affects policy support (without and with the control variables, columns 3 and 4, respectfully). Next, they present results for models that assess how the perceived likelihood of a terrorist attack on U.S. soil in the next 2 years (columns 5 and 6) and the perceived likelihood that someone one you know will be hurt by a terrorist attack in the next 2 years (columns 7 and 8) affect support for U.S. policies. As earlier, models are estimated using ordered logistic analysis, significant coefficients are starred, and robust standard errors reports in the parentheses. Each includes a lagged dependent variable to control for autocorrelation.

TRUST IN GOVERNMENT AND POLICY SUPPORT

Trust in the objectivity and truthfulness of the information provided by the national government about Iraq is positively associated with support for the war. This relationship is statistically significant in every model (sig. < .01), even when considering different specifications of threat and controlling for the political affiliation and other personal characteristics of the respondents.

In contrast, trust in the integrity of politicians not to exploit information about Iraq for partisan or political advantage had only limited effects on the level of policy support. Trust in the integrity of politicians did not have a significant effect on whether respondents agreed that the war was justified, nor did it have an effect on this willingness to support the war effort despite high casualties or financial costs.

TABLE 2.3. THE UNITED STATES WAS JUSTIFIED IN ATTACKING IRAQ AFTER 9/11

The United States Was Justified in Attacking Iraq After 9/11	(1)	(2)	(3)	(4)	(5)	(6)	(7)	(8)
Lagged Dependent Variable	1.294***	1.220***	1.290***	1.207***	1.308***	1.225***	1.241***	1.201***
	(0.0732)	(0.0788)	(0.0731)	(0.0783)	(0.0730)	(0.0785)	(0.0940)	(0.0968)
Threat to National Security	0.254***	0.249***						
	(0.0626)	(0.0666)						
Threat to Personal Security			0.153***	0.152***				
			(0.0534)	(0.0560)				
Prob. Attack Someone Close					0.0620	0.0559		
					(0.0436)	(0.0446)		
Prob. Attack against U.S.							0.00663	0.00804
							(0.0358)	(0.0362)
Govt. Info Trustworthy	0.479***	0.512***	0.442***	0.478***	0.446***	0.486***	0.441***	0.476***
	(0.0747)	(0.0790)	(0.0758)	(0.0794)	(0.0751)	(0.0788)	(0.0998)	(0.0987)
Politicians Exploit Info	-0.0817	-0.0609	-0.0434	-0.0340	-0.0345	-0.0203	-0.0447	0.00186
	(0.0583)	(0.0631)	(0.0580)	(0.0634)	(0.0584)	(0.0642)	(0.0757)	(0.0822)
Actions at Home Successful	-0.116	-0.125	-0.0666	-0.0803	-0.0624	-0.0801	-0.204*	-0.208**
	(0.0864)	(0.0896)	(0.0823)	(0.0858)	(0.0819)	(0.0857)	(0.106)	(0.106)
Actions Abroad Successful	0.376***	0.349***	0.392***	0.361***	0.389***	0.354***	0.463***	0.434***
	(0.0786)	(0.0834)	(0.0775)	(0.0825)	(0.0777)	(0.0826)	(0.101)	(0.101)
Democrat		-0.386***		-0.455***		-0.451***		-0.314*
		(0.134)		(0.134)		(0.133)		(0.171)

	(1)	(2)	(3)	(4)	(5)	(6)	(7)	(8)
Education		-0.163***		-0.156***		-0.146**		-0.166**
		(0.0599)		(0.0596)		(0.0591)		(0.0782)
Age		0.0581		0.0730**		0.0688*		0.0784*
		(0.0364)		(0.0363)		(0.0361)		(0.0449)
Female		0.0562		0.0716		0.0782		0.251*
		(0.112)		(0.113)		(0.111)		(0.142)
East Coast USA		-0.0970		-0.139		-0.160		-0.224
		(0.135)		(0.137)		(0.138)		(0.171)
Constant	9.254***	8.663***	8.905***	8.286***	8.666***	8.052***	7.929***	7.769***
	(0.449)	(0.517)	(0.440)	(0.505)	(0.436)	(0.502)	(0.520)	(0.624)
Pseudo R^2	.2888	.2924	.2855	.2902	.2846	.2887	.2672	.2761
Sig. χ^2	.0000	.0000	.0000	.0000	.0000	.0000	.0000	.0000
Observations	1945	1782	1945	1781	1948	1783	1122	1114

Ordered logistic regression, robust standard errors in parentheses.

***$p < .01$, **$p < .05$, *$p < .1$.

TABLE 2.4. U.S. POLICY IN IRAQ SHOULD NOT BE ALTERED BY RISING NUMBERS OF CASUALTIES

U.S. Policy in Iraq Should Not Be Altered by Rising Numbers of Casualties	(1)	(2)	(3)	(4)	(5)	(6)	(7)	(8)
Lagged Dependent Variable	0.739***	0.706***	0.752***	0.715***	0.751***	0.712***	0.695***	0.682***
	(0.0579)	(0.0617)	(0.0582)	(0.0619)	(0.0583)	(0.0622)	(0.0725)	(0.0738)
Threat to National Security	0.0951*	0.0558						
	(0.0560)	(0.0572)						
Threat to Personal Security			0.0978**	0.0537				
			(0.0474)	(0.0499)				
Prob. Attack Someone Close					0.0930***	0.0924***		
					(0.0333)	(0.0347)		
Prob. Attack against U.S.							0.0313	0.0233
							(0.0280)	(0.0284)
Govt. Info Trustworthy	0.459***	0.458***	0.428***	0.429***	0.435***	0.432***	0.441***	0.450***
	(0.0687)	(0.0722)	(0.0693)	(0.0721)	(0.0689)	(0.0721)	(0.0903)	(0.0885)
Politicians Exploit Info	-0.0580	-0.0337	-0.0484	-0.0355	-0.0397	-0.0290	-0.0848	-0.0503
	(0.0531)	(0.0587)	(0.0531)	(0.0584)	(0.0534)	(0.0588)	(0.0724)	(0.0751)
Actions at Home Successful	-0.00558	-0.0355	0.0116	-0.0257	0.0125	-0.0287	-0.0244	-0.0185
	(0.0737)	(0.0765)	(0.0715)	(0.0747)	(0.0713)	(0.0744)	(0.0898)	(0.0913)
Actions Abroad Successful	0.243***	0.196***	0.258***	0.211***	0.256***	0.203***	0.251***	0.187***
	(0.0679)	(0.0725)	(0.0679)	(0.0725)	(0.0676)	(0.0725)	(0.0841)	(0.0863)
Democrat		-0.396***		-0.417***		-0.439***		-0.387***
		(0.114)		(0.114)		(0.114)		(0.147)

	(1)	(2)	(3)	(4)	(5)
Education		-0.225***	-0.220***		-0.279***
		(0.0521)	(0.0520)		(0.0639)
Age		0.0958***	0.106***	0.108***	0.121***
		(0.0339)	(0.0338)	(0.0340)	(0.0442)
Female		-0.0368	-0.0298	-0.0535	0.0431
		(0.103)	(0.103)	(0.104)	(0.131)
East Coast USA		-0.0661	-0.0760	-0.101	-0.0669
		(0.121)	(0.122)	(0.123)	(0.152)
Constant	6.584***	5.709***	5.718***	5.731***	5.347***
	(0.394)	(0.464)	(0.466)	(0.444)	(0.563)
Pseudo R^2	.1408	.1469	.1484	.1493	.1426
Sig. χ^2	.0000	.0000	.0000	.0000	.0000
Observations	1941	1779	1778	1780	1109

	(1)	(2)	(3)	(4)	(5)
Education		-0.225***	-0.220***	-0.210***	-0.279***
		(0.0521)	(0.0520)	(0.0524)	(0.0639)
Age		0.0958***	0.106***	0.108***	0.121***
		(0.0339)	(0.0338)	(0.0340)	(0.0442)
Female		-0.0368	-0.0298	-0.0535	0.0431
		(0.103)	(0.103)	(0.104)	(0.131)
East Coast USA		-0.0661	-0.0760	-0.101	-0.0669
		(0.121)	(0.122)	(0.123)	(0.152)
Constant	6.584***	5.709***	5.718***	5.731***	5.347***
	(0.394)	(0.464)	(0.466)	(0.444)	(0.563)
Pseudo R^2	.1408	.1469	.1484	.1493	.1426
Sig. χ^2	.0000	.0000	.0000	.0000	.0000
Observations	1941	1779	1778	1780	1109

Ordered logistic regression, robust standard errors in parentheses.

***$p < .01$, **$p < .05$, *$p < .1$.

TABLE 2.5. U.S. POLICY IN IRAQ SHOULD NOT BE ALTERED BY RISING FINANCIAL COSTS

U.S. Policy in Iraq Should Not Be Altered by Rising Financial Costs	(1)	(2)	(3)	(4)	(5)	(6)	(7)	(8)
Lagged Dependent Variable	0.603***	0.581***	0.612***	0.585***	0.615***	0.587***	0.558***	0.548***
	(0.0549)	(0.0585)	(0.0551)	(0.0585)	(0.0551)	(0.0587)	(0.0697)	(0.0705)
Threat to National Security	0.161***	0.110*						
	(0.0553)	(0.0569)						
Threat to Personal Security			0.110**	0.0650				
			(0.0468)	(0.0483)				
Prob. Attack Someone Close					0.0936***	0.0931**		
					(0.0353)	(0.0369)		
Prob. Attack against U.S.							0.0185	0.0136
							(0.0261)	(0.0267)
Govt. Info Trustworthy	0.389***	0.403***	0.356***	0.375***	0.365***	0.378***	0.348***	0.350***
	(0.0704)	(0.0744)	(0.0718)	(0.0749)	(0.0713)	(0.0749)	(0.0902)	(0.0882)
Politicians Exploit Info	-0.0452	-0.0260	-0.0297	-0.0231	-0.0206	-0.0196	-0.0601	-0.0360
	(0.0542)	(0.0603)	(0.0535)	(0.0594)	(0.0543)	(0.0599)	(0.0726)	(0.0768)
Actions at Home Successful	-0.0751	-0.0956	-0.0403	-0.0695	-0.0351	-0.0678	-0.0801	-0.0840
	(0.0729)	(0.0754)	(0.0716)	(0.0740)	(0.0715)	(0.0741)	(0.0904)	(0.0916)
Actions Abroad Successful	0.294***	0.237***	0.307***	0.246***	0.303***	0.237***	0.324***	0.268***
	(0.0705)	(0.0755)	(0.0706)	(0.0755)	(0.0702)	(0.0755)	(0.0899)	(0.0924)
Democrat		-0.362***		-0.392***		-0.422***		-0.359**
		(0.113)		(0.113)		(0.114)		(0.144)

Education		−0.211***	−0.211***		−0.199***	−0.174***
		(0.0558)	(0.0558)		(0.0562)	(0.0660)
Age		0.127***	0.134***		0.141***	0.130***
		(0.0324)	(0.0324)		(0.0323)	(0.0414)
Female		0.0623	0.0670		0.0411	0.194
		(0.102)	(0.102)		(0.102)	(0.130)
East Coast USA		−0.150	−0.189		−0.195	−0.156
		(0.124)	(0.125)		(0.126)	(0.151)
Constant	6.095***	5.459***	5.274***	5.844***	5.293***	5.226***	5.004***
	(0.391)	(0.467)	(0.465)	(0.373)	(0.450)	(0.488)	(0.550)
Pseudo R^2	.1117	.1222	.1227	.1123	.1245	.0970	.1097
Sig. χ^2	.0000	.0000	.0000	.0000	.0000	.0000	.0000
Observations	1938	1776	1776	1942	1777	1115	1107

Ordered logistic regression, robust standard errors in parentheses.

***$p < .01$, **$p < .05$, *$p < .1$.

TABLE 2.6. U.S. POLICY IN IRAQ SHOULD NOT BE ALTERED BY THE LENGTH OF TIME IT TAKES TO ACHIEVE OUR OBJECTIVES

U.S. Policy in Iraq Should Not Be Altered Due to the Length Of Time It Takes to Achieve Our Objectives	(1)	(2)	(3)	(4)	(5)	(6)	(7)	(8)
Lagged Dependent Variable	0.743***	0.689***	0.748***	0.690***	0.752***	0.691***	0.701***	0.664***
	(0.0614)	(0.0660)	(0.0614)	(0.0659)	(0.0619)	(0.0663)	(0.0804)	(0.0811)
Threat to National Security	0.0662	0.0247						
	(0.0545)	(0.0565)						
Threat to Personal Security			0.127***	0.0734				
			(0.0482)	(0.0509)				
Prob. Attack Someone Close					0.0820**	0.0924***		
					(0.0339)	(0.0354)		
Prob. Attack against U.S.							0.0346	0.0290
							(0.0293)	(0.0300)
Govt. Info Trustworthy	0.419***	0.413***	0.380***	0.379***	0.396***	0.386***	0.461***	0.453***
	(0.0681)	(0.0723)	(0.0688)	(0.0721)	(0.0688)	(0.0727)	(0.0891)	(0.0878)
Politicians Exploit Info	−0.129**	−0.115*	−0.134**	−0.132**	−0.123**	−0.123*	−0.154**	−0.140*
	(0.0565)	(0.0648)	(0.0567)	(0.0648)	(0.0572)	(0.0652)	(0.0708)	(0.0768)
Actions at Home Successful	0.0732	0.0611	0.0887	0.0713	0.0876	0.0674	0.155*	0.140
	(0.0744)	(0.0759)	(0.0723)	(0.0739)	(0.0723)	(0.0738)	(0.0928)	(0.0919)
Actions Abroad Successful	0.244***	0.189**	0.254***	0.199***	0.253***	0.192***	0.188**	0.127
	(0.0684)	(0.0736)	(0.0682)	(0.0735)	(0.0682)	(0.0736)	(0.0888)	(0.0929)

Democrat	-0.504***		-0.523***	-0.554***	-0.615***
	(0.115)		(0.114)	(0.114)	(0.148)
Education	-0.200***		-0.198***	-0.189***	-0.139*
	(0.0566)		(0.0565)	(0.0565)	(0.0708)
Age	0.0738**		0.0768**	0.0836**	0.0994**
	(0.0342)		(0.0339)	(0.0339)	(0.0442)
Female	-0.0282		-0.0416	-0.0643	0.0789
	(0.106)		(0.106)	(0.107)	(0.134)
East Coast USA	-0.0600		-0.0818	-0.0840	-0.0193
	(0.129)		(0.131)	(0.130)	(0.170)
Constant	5.280***	6.386***	5.317***	5.325***	5.566***
	(0.470)	(0.395)	(0.464)	(0.459)	(0.558)
		6.292***		6.257***	6.150***
		(0.407)		(0.391)	(0.492)
Pseudo R^2	.1531	.1459	.1538	.1577	.1551
Sig. χ^2	.0000	.0000	.0000	.0000	.0000
Observations	1775	1937	1774	1776	1107
		1937	1941	1115	

Ordered logistic regression, robust standard errors in parentheses.

***$p < .01$, **$p < .05$, *$p < .1$.

The integrity of politicians did, however, have a significant and negative effect on the public's patience. Specifically, those who believed that politicians exploited information about the war for political or partisan purposes are significantly less likely than others to support granting additional time to fight in the name of accomplishing U.S. objectives. This effect persists when controlling for different specifications of threat, political affiliation, and other personal characteristics of the respondents.

The success of counterterrorism policies abroad also matter when assessing the war in Iraq, while the success of counterterrorism policies on the home front do not. This suggests that the public may compartmentalize U.S. policy initiatives, linking their support of foreign policy actions to success abroad independently from success or failures at home. Higher levels of agreement that U.S. policies abroad have decreased the threat of terrorism are positively associated with agreement that the war was justified and should not be altered due to rising numbers of casualties or financial costs. These effects are significant in every model, even when considering for political affiliation and other control variables. The success of counterterrorism policies abroad is also positively associated with agreement that the war should continue despite its long duration, though this relationship becomes insignificant when the individual characteristics of the respondents are considered.

LEVEL OF THREAT AND POLICY SUPPORT

Perceptions of a terrorist threat are associated with the level of policy support for the war in Iraq, but the relationship varies depending on the policy question at hand and how the threat is specified. Those who consider terrorism to be a threat to national or personal security are more likely than others to agree that the United States was justified in attacking Iraq after 9/11. The reported probabilities that there would be an attack on U.S. soil or that someone close would be hurt by an attack in the next 2 years are irrelevant.

In contrast, those who assign a higher probability to the likelihood that someone they know will be hurt by a terrorist incident in the next 2 years are more likely than others to support continued fighting in Iraq despite the loss of blood, treasure, and time. This relationship remains significant when controlling for different specifications of threat, political affiliation, and other personal characteristics of the respondents. At the same time, however, the probability of an attack on the U.S. soil is no impact on support for the war.

The perceived existence of a terrorist threat to national or personal security does not have a significant impact on casualty sensitivity or war weariness. Agreement that terrorism is a threat to personal security is initially significant in all three models (column 3), but becomes insignificant when the control variables are considered (column 4). The impact of agreement that terrorism is a threat to national security has a weakly significant impact ($p < .1$) on a willingness to continue fighting despite high financial costs but does not affect casualty tolerance or the willingness to stay in the fight regardless of how long it takes for the United States to accomplish its objectives.

THE IMPACT OF INDIVIDUAL CHARACTERISTICS ON POLICY SUPPORT

Political affiliation, education level, and age have significant effects on policy support for the war in Iraq. Self-identified Democrats, those with higher levels of education, and those who are younger are less likely to agree that the war was justified or should be continued given costs in blood, treasure, and time. In one model, women are more likely than men to agree that the United States was justified in attacking Iraq (Table 2.3, column 8), yet neither gender nor region of the country has an impact on the level of policy support for maintaining U.S. policy in Iraq.

CONCLUSION

Changing levels of trust in the U.S. government during the last 3 years of the George W. Bush Administration affected public perceptions of the threat from terrorism and the level of policy support for the war in Iraq. These effects varied depending on whether trust in the government was defined in terms of the trustworthiness of the information it provided, the integrity of national politicians, or the efficacy of government policy. Unpacking trust that the government is "doing the right thing" into three of its constitutive components reveals that trust in government affects public perceptions of threat and the level of policy support in different ways. Perceptions of the threat of terrorism, in turn, affected policy support differently depending on whether terrorism was considered a threat to national security or personal security. The effect of threat on policy support also varied depending on whether people were asked about the extent to which they agreed that terrorism posed a security threat or the probability that a terrorist attack was imminent.

To this point, I have highlighted several intriguing findings about relationships among trust, threat and policy support that are worthy of additional research. First, the George W. Bush Administration succeeded in mobilizing public opinion. Public perceptions that terrorism was a threat to national security remained high throughout. In addition, while the public remained divided on its support for the war in Iraq, the level of public support for the war and its confidence in the success of the administration's counterterrorism policies actually grew slightly over time.

Second, public trust in the objectivity and truthfulness of the information provided by the government about the war in Iraq was low and declined over time. This decline did not affect perceptions of terrorism as a threat to national security or the anticipation of a future attack, but it did have a significant negative impact in public perceptions of terrorism as a threat to personal security and the level of support for the war in Iraq. Those who distrusted the objectivity of the information provided by the national government about Iraq were less likely to agree that the invasion was justified following 9/11 and less likely to support continuing to fight given its cost in blood, treasure or time.

Third, public trust in the integrity of politicians not to exploit information about Iraq for political or partisan advantage had a significant impact on the perceived threat from terrorism. Those who did not trust the integrity of politicians were more likely to consider terrorism a threat to national and personal security and more likely to anticipate an attack on U.S. soil. This effect is curious as it runs counter to our expectations that people are less likely to accept the administration's signals about the high threat of terrorism when politicians act in more partisan ways. This dynamic is worthy of future research. It may be that opportunism among policymakers is perceived as a lack of seriousness that, in turn, raises uncertainty about the government's responsiveness to terrorism, thus making the threat more dangerous.

While the perceived integrity of politicians affected public assessment of the threat of terrorism, it did not affect the level of policy support for the administration's justification to go to war in Iraq after 9/11 or the public's willingness to continue fighting despite high numbers of casualties and financial costs. A lack of integrity among politicians was, however, associated with a lack of support for continuing the war for long periods of time in order to achieve U.S. objectives. It appears that people were not willing to support continuing a war for the political benefit of their leaders.

Fourth, trust in the success of government policies matters, but the public differentiates successes at home from successes abroad. The perceived success of counterterrorism policies at home is associated with the perception of terrorism as a threat to national security, yet the success of counterterrorism at home had no impact on the level of policy support for the war in Iraq. In contrast, while the perceived success of U.S. counterterrorism policies abroad had no effect on perceptions of threat, that success was consistently and significantly associated with higher levels of policy support for the war in Iraq.

Fifth, perceptions of threat and their impact on the level of policy support varied depending on whether terrorism was framed as a threat national security or personal security, and whether respondents were asked to consider the existence of the threat or the likelihood that an attack was imminent. While some factors affected perceptions of terrorism as a threat to national security and personal security in similar ways, no aspect of trust in government had a significant impact on the perceived likelihood that someone close would be hurt by an attack in the next 2 years.

Yet, the perceived likelihood that someone close would be hurt is positively associated with support for U.S. policy in Iraq.

In sum, trust in the national government is associated with perceptions of threats to national and personal security, and the level of popular support for counter-threat policies. Our surveys and the experiences of the last three years of the Bush Administration suggest that these relationships are more nuanced than is generally acknowledged. To borrow a phrase popularized by Jentleson (1992), the principal lesson for President Obama and other leaders is that the public is "pretty prudent." It values the objectivity of information, the integrity of politicians, and the likely success of government policies, but the impact of each factor varies depending on the issue at hand.

ACKNOWLEDGEMENTS

The author thanks the National Science Foundation and the NSF project team, including co-principal investigators Roxane Silver and Richard Matthew, as well as Scott Blum, Paloma Gonzalez, Bryan McDonald, and Michael Poulin for their work in developing the surveys. He also thanks David Tingle for his contributions to this chapter.

REFERENCES

Abramowitz, A., & Saunders, K. (1998). Ideological realignment in the U.S. electorate. *Journal of Politics, 60*, 634–652.

Ansolabehere, S., Meredith, M., Snowberg, E., & Synder J. (2007). Sociotropic voting and the media: A summary of results from the 2006 ANES Pilot. Working Paper. Ann Arbor, MI: American National Election Studies.

Baker, W., & Oneal, J. (2001). Patriotism or opinion leadership? *Journal of Conflict Resolution, 45*(5), 661–687.

Bennett, S. E., & Flickinger, R. S. (2009). American's knowledge of U.S. military deaths In Iraq, April 2004 to April 2008. *Armed Forces & Society, 35*, 587–604.

Berinsky, A. (2005). *Silent voices: Public opinion and political participation in America.* Princeton, NJ: Princeton University Press.

Berinsky, A. (2007). Assuming the costs of war: Events, elites, and American support for military conflict. *Journal of Politics, 69*(4), 975–997.

Boettcher, W. A., & Cobb, M. D. (2006). Do frames really matter? Causality frames, causality tolerance, and public perceptions of success and failure in the war in Iraq. Paper presented at the 2006 Annual Meeting of the International Studies Association. San Diego, California.

Brady, H., & Sniderman, P. (1985). Attitude attribution: A group basis for political reasoning. *American Political Science Review, 79*, 1061–1078.

Brewer, M., & Brown, R. (1998). Intergroup relations. In D. Fiske & G. Lindzey (Eds.), *Handbook of social psychology* (pp. 554–594). New York, NY: McGraw-Hill.

Brody, R. A. (2002). The American people and President Bush. *The Forum, 1*(1), 1–19.

Brody, R. A., & Shapiro, C. R. (1989). Policy failure and public support: The Iran-Contra affair and public assessment of President Reagan. *Political Behavior, 11*(4), 353–369.

Chanley, V. A. (2002). Trust in government in the aftermath of 9/11: Determinants and consequences. *Political Psychology, 23*(3), 469–483.

Chanley, V. A., Randolph, T. J., & Rahn, W. M. (2000). The origins and consequences of public trust in government: A time series analysis. *Public Opinion Quarterly, 64*, 239–256.

Crawford, V. P., & Sobel, J. (1982) Strategic information transmission. *Econometrica, 50*(6), 1431–1451.

Delii Carpini, M., & Keeter, S. (1996). *What Americans know about politics and why it matters.* New Haven, CT: Yale University Press.

Druckman, J, & Lupia, A. (2000). Preference formation. *Annual Review of Political Science, 3*, 1–24.

Gelpi, C., Feaver, P., & and Reifler, J. (Winter 2005/2006). Success matters: Casualty sensitivity and the war in Iraq. *International Security, 30*(3), 7–46.

Gershkoff, A., & Kushner, S. (2005). Shaping public opinion: the 9/11-Iraq connection in the Bush Administration's rhetoric. *Perspectives on Politics, 3*(3), 525–537.

Groeling, T., & Baum, M. (2008). Crossing the water's edge: Elite rhetoric, media coverage, and the rally-round-the-flag. *Journal of Politics, 70*(4), 1065–1085.

Hetherington, M. J., & Nelson, M. (2003). Anatomy of a rally effect: George W. Bush and the war on terrorism. *PS: Political Science and Politics, 36*(1), 37–42.

Holsti, O. (2004). *Public opinion and American foreign policy, revised edition.* Ann Arbor, MI: University of Michigan Press.

Howell, W., & Kriner, D. (2013). Congressional leadership of war opinion? Backlash effects and the polarization of public support for war. In L. Dodd and B. Oppenheimer (eds.), *Congress Reconsidered*, Volume 10. Thousand Oaks, CA: Congressional Quarterly Press. (Forthcoming).

Huddy, L., Feldman, S., Capelos, T., & Provost, C. (2002). The consequences of terrorism: Disentangling the effects of personal and national threat. *Political Psychology, 23*(3), 485–498.

Huddy, L., Feldman, S., Taber, C., & Lahav, G. (2005). Threat, anxiety, and support for antiterrorism policies. *American Journal of Political Science, 49*(3), 593–608.

ITERATE. (2009). *International terrorism attributes of terrorist events data base.* Created by Mickolus, E. Dunn Loring, VA: Vinyard Software.

Iyengar, S., & Kinder, D. (1985). Psychological accounts of media agenda-setting. In S. Kraus & & R. Perloff (Eds.), *Mass media and political thought* (pp. 117–140). Beverly Hills, CA: Sage Publications.

Jentleson, B. (1992). The pretty public: Post post-Vietnam American opinion on the use of military force. *International Studies Quarterly, 36*, 49–74.

Josiger, W. (2009). How do audiences react to terrorism and why? Ph.D. Dissertation, Georgetown University, in progress.

Joslyn, M. R., & Haider-Markel, D. P. (2007). Sociotropic concerns and support for counterterrorism. *Social Science Quarterly, 88*(2), 306–318.

Kam, C. D., & Ramos, J. M. (2008). Joining and leaving the rally: Understanding the surge and decline in presidential approval following 9/11. *Political Opinion Quarterly, 72*(4), 619–650..

Kinder, D. R., & Kiewiet, D. R. (1979). Economic grievances and political behavior: The role of personal discontents and collective judgments in congressional voting. *American Journal of Political Science, 23*, 495–527.

Kinder, D. R., & Kiewiet, D. R. (1981). Sociotropic politics. *British Journal of Political Science, 11*, 191–161.

Lupia, A. (1994). Shortcuts versus encyclopedias: Information and voting behavior in California insurance reform elections. *The American Political Science Review*, 88(1), 63–76.

Lupia, A., & McCubbins, M. (1998). *The Democratic dilemma: Can citizens learn what they need to know?* New York: Cambridge University Press.

Matthew, R., & Shambaugh, G. (2005). The pendulum effect: Explaining shifts in the Democratic response to terrorism. *Analyses of Social Issues and Public Policies*, 5(1), 223–233.

Mueller, J. (1973). *War, presidents, and public opinion*. New York, NY: Wiley.

Mutz, D. C. (1998). *Impersonal influence: How perceptions of mass collectives affect political attitudes*. Cambridge, UK: Cambridge University Press.

Nacos, B. (2002). *Mass-mediated terrorism*. Lanham, MD: Rowman and Littlefield.

Nacos, B. (2006). *Terrorism and counterterrorism: Understanding threats and responses in the post-9/11 world*. New York, NY: Pearson Longman.

Orren, G. (1997). Fall from grace: The public's loss of faith in government. In J. S. Nye, Jr., P.D. Zelikow, & D. C. King (Eds.), *Why people don't trust government* (pp. 77–107). Cambridge, MA: Harvard University Press.

Page, B., & Shapiro, R. (1992). *The rational public: Fifty years of trends in Americans' policy preferences*. Chicago, IL: Chicago University Press.

Page, B., Shapiro, R., & Dempsey. (1987). What moves public opinion? *American Political Science Review*, 81, 23–44.

Popkin, S. (1994). *The reasoning voter: Communication and persuasion in presidential campaigns*. Chicago, IL: University of Chicago Press.

Powlick, P., & Katz, A. (1998). Defining the American public opinion/foreign policy nexus, *Mershon International Studies Review*, 42, 29–61.

Shambaugh, G., & Josiger, W. (2004). *Public prudence, the policy salience of terrorism and presidential approval following terrorist incidents*. Paper presented at the annual meeting of the American Political Science Association, Washington, D.C.

Shambaugh, G., Matthew R., & McDonald, B. (2008). Post-9/11 America: Conventional wisdom versus popular pragmatism. *Democracy & Society*, 5 (2), 1–23.

Shambaugh, G., Matthew, R., Silver, R. C., McDonald, B., Poulin, M., & Blum, S. (2009). Public perceptions and traumatic events and their effects on policy preferences during the George W. Bush Administration. *Studies in Conflict and Terrorism*, 33(1), 55–91.

Shapiro, R. Y., & Page, B. I. (1988). Foreign policy and the rational public. *Journal of Conflict Resolution*, 32(2), 211–247.

Sniderman, P. M., Brody, R. A., & Tetlock, P. E. (1991). *Reasoning and choice: explorations in political psychology*. Cambridge, UK: Cambridge University Press.

Sobel, J. (1985). A theory of credibility. *Review of Economic Studies*, 52(4), 557–573.

Souva, M., & Rohde, D. (2007). Elite opinion differences and partisanship in congressional foreign policy, 1975–1996. *Political Research Quarterly*, 60(1), 113–123.

Zaller, J. (1991). Information values and opinion. *The American Political Science Review*, 85(2), 1215–1237.

Zaller, J. (1992). *The nature and origins of mass opinion*. New York, NY: Cambridge University Press.

Zaller, J. (1994). Elite leadership of mass opinion: New evidence from the Gulf War. In W. Bennett & D. Patetz (Eds.), *Taken by storm: The media, public opinion, and U.S. foreign policy in the Gulf War* (pp. 186–209). Chicago, IL: University of Chicago Press.

CHAPTER 3
Negative Emotions and Political Engagement
MICHAEL J. STEVENS

"War is politics by other means. Terrorism is the warfare of the weak. Therefore, terrorism is politics" (McCauley, 2006, p. 46). This syllogism has profound meaning in light of how the terrorist attacks of 9/11 and elsewhere altered political landscapes worldwide. That terrorism affects the political responses of ordinary citizens is not surprising. Because terrorism is relatively unusual, yet potentially devastating, the experience and prospect of terrorism elicit cognitive and emotional reactions that influence intended and enacted forms of political engagement. Whether real or simulated, terrorist attacks and the threat of terrorist attacks impact such political responses as support for government retaliation (e.g., DeSouza, Stevens, & Metivier, 2011), trust in government to protect its citizens (e.g., Sinclair & LoCicero, 2010), motivation to seek information about political candidates (e.g., Valentino, Brader, Groenendyk, Gregorowicz, & Hutchings, 2011), intentions to protest government policies (e.g., Iyer, Schmader, & Lickel, 2007), and consumer spending and charitable donations as expressions of patriotism and national unity (e.g., Morgan, Wisneski, & Skitka, 2011).

Although direct and indirect political responses to terrorism have been documented, the psychological mechanisms underlying these responses are less well understood. This chapter reviews a growing literature on the role of negative emotions in political engagement. It examines how anxiety and anger contribute to certain political response tendencies. It also discusses related research on risk perception and how it is tied to distinct emotions that lead to different forms of political engagement. In addition, the chapter shows how demographic and opinion-group membership influence the relationship between negative emotions and political engagement. Theoretical frameworks are described that explain the relationship between certain negative emotions and corresponding forms of political responding.

POLITICAL REACTIONS TO TERRORISM

After the 1993 World Trade Center bombing, opinions about terrorism and terrorists among students and police in New York City ranged from disgust to approval (Takooshian & Verdi, 1993). Reactions in the United States to terrorism became less variable after 9/11, although modest ethnocultural differences emerged (Walker & Chestnut, 2003). Whites reacted more angrily than nonwhites, blaming 9/11 on U.S. geopolitical arrogance and lax immigration laws. By 2005, sentiment among American students that the United States was partly responsible for 9/11 had grown (Sahar, 2008).

Experimental research on government retaliation against terrorism predates 9/11 and typically involved priming respondents with hypothetical terrorist-attack scenarios (Bourne, Healy, & Beer, 2003). When asked to choose the best policy for the United States to adopt in response to terrorism, students responded initially with forgiveness, but became less tolerant as attacks persisted. Field studies confirm that Israelis and Palestinians perceive less international support after being attacked by terrorists and more international condemnation if they favored government retaliation (Shamir & Shikaki, 2002). This hostile-world effect may legitimize support for government retaliation following repeated terrorist attacks. Schema theory has also been advanced as an interpretive framework for this forgiveness–escalation pattern (Herrmann, Voss, Schooler, & Ciarrochi, 1997). Mental representations of countries and groups as either allies or enemies coalesce from past experiences. By accessing country or group images, people can make sense of current circumstances and decide how to respond.

After 9/11, Healy, Aylward, Bourne, and Beer (2009) investigated how aggressively students wanted their government to retaliate after reading various terrorist-attack scenarios. Students favored greater government aggression 1 year after 9/11 than did students who had read similar scenarios before 9/11 (Healy, Hoffman, Beer, & Bourne, 2002), although both groups preferred a gradual escalation of hostilities following repeated attacks. However, a cross-national study by DeSouza et al. (2011) found that American students favored strong government retaliation against a simulated first strike. This study suggests that 9/11, coupled with a heightened sense of vulnerability to terrorism, may have eroded the capacity of Americans for understanding and reconciliation. In comparison, the retaliatory preferences of Peruvian students were more variable and revealed their sensitivity to the economic costs of terrorism. These cross-national differences in support of government retaliation underscore the distinctive ecological contexts in which political opinions form.

American and international groups tend to offer utilitarian moral justifications for aggression when supporting government aggression against another country (e.g., "[it] will prevent more suffering than it will cause") (McAlister, Bandura, & Owen, 2006; Shamir & Shikaki, 2002). For example, the prevailing reaction of Israelis to a simulated terrorist attack was anger and desire for revenge (Desivilya

& Yassour-Borochowitz, 2010). Israelis favored retaliatory action because of the expected benefits for victimized Israelis, and showed less regard for the adverse consequences to out-groups associated with terrorists. Israelis' support for government retaliation also revealed a suspension of generally principled moral reasoning. The policy preference of Israelis for aggressive government protection suggests that protracted conflict may weaken moral perspective taking (Desivilya & Yassour-Borochowitz, 2010).

Some research indicates that gender moderates support for government retaliation against terrorism, with women recommending less severe retaliation (Anthony, Rosselli, & Caparyan, 2003; Bourne et al., 2003; DeSouza et al., 2011; Healy et al., 2002, 2002). Women tend to forgive terrorist attacks in order to preserve international relations (i.e., restorative justice), whereas men prefer retaliatory responses that restore equilibrium in international relations (i.e., retributive justice) (Robinson, 2008). Belief in a government's broad right to use aggression are also stronger in men (Anthony et al., 2003).

This literature indicates that support for government retaliation against terrorism is influenced by the frequency, recency, and target of terrorist attacks, by gender-role socialization, and perhaps by preexisting attitudes toward a government's right to use aggression. Additional evidence suggests that the policy preferences of citizens reflect their enthocultural differences, activation of reference-group schemas, and certain forms of moral reasoning. What remains unclear is the relationship between emotions evoked by terrorism and the political responses that follow.

EMOTIONS AND POLITICAL ACTION

Twenty years ago, scholars emphasized skills and resources as predictors of political engagement (e.g., age, education, income, marital status) (Valentino, Hutchings, Banks, & Davis, 2008). Today, emotions are seen as contributing to the dynamics whereby skills and resources are used to evaluate politicians, government effectiveness, and public policies (Herrmann et al., 1997; Jasper, 2011; Miller, 2011). Studies have debunked the stereotype that politically uninformed and disengaged citizens use emotion versus reasoning to make political choices. Because of their interest in and knowledge of politics, political sophisticates often subject political information to a cost-benefit analysis, report more positive or negative emotions more quickly, and are mobilized to direct resources toward political action (e.g., campaign activism) (Miller, 2011).

Emotions range from transient urges and feelings to enduring affective attachments and aversions as well as moral feelings of approval and disgust. Emotions serve numerous political purposes (Jasper, 2011). Pride can motivate social movements, whereas humiliation can prompt terrorist attacks. Emotion can liberate people from complacency and resignation, and rally action to create a better future. How do emotions increase political involvement and movement toward political goals? In general, emotions focus attention (e.g., reconfiguring foreground and background of a political gestalt), call into question accepted perspectives, recruit others to action, strengthen commitment to a cause, and build solidarity within a political movement (Jasper, 2011). Of particular interest is the contribution of negative emotion to political engagement.

ANXIETY AND FEAR

Anxiety and fear are closely related. Both are normal reactions to the uncertainty and insecurity of threat (Huddy & Feldman, 2011). Anxiety and fear are associated with avoidant behavior because they increase attention to threat as well as responses that minimize threat. In a national survey conducted within 6 months after 9/11 (Huddy, Feldman, Taber, & Lahav, 2005), anxiety appeared to heighten avoidant behavior. Respondents with higher anxiety were less supportive of American military intervention against terrorists, less approving of President George W. Bush, and more inclined toward isolationism. Furthermore, anxiety was not tied to support for efforts to enhance domestic security, such as requiring a national identification card, e-mail and phone surveillance, and legislation that limits civil liberties. Anxiety not only inhibited public support for overseas action that could escalate threat but also weakened support for measures to protect the homeland from threat. Avoidant behavior may reflect the motivation of anxious people to reduce anxiety, even if it undermines protective responses, as these may fuel the already high perceived threat of terrorism. Threat is an outcome of the cognitive appraisal of risk (Lerner, Gonzalez, Small, & Fischhoff, 2003), which is discussed later.

Does threat interact with a sense of personal, as opposed to national, security to influence opinions about security policy? Americans who felt more personally insecure in the 6 months after 9/11, yet perceived the United States as vulnerable to another terrorist attack favored strong security policies at home (e.g., tougher visa checks) and abroad (military involvement in Afghanistan) (Huddy, Feldman, & Weber, 2007). Consistent with Attachment Theory, which holds that personal security is established during infancy and regulates anxiety under conditions of threat, 9/11 minimally affected people's attachment behavioral system. For securely attached Americans, the effect of threat on anxiety and support for counterterrorism measures was moderate (Huddy et al., 2007). Thus, in the wake of a terrorist attack, the impact of threat on anxiety and political engagement may rest on a disposition toward personal security. These findings have implications for how governments garner support for antiterrorism policies and legislation. Contrary to the view that fear-mongering arouses political support, it succeeds only by activating threat in the absence of anxiety, as anxious citizens shy away from military ventures abroad because of worries about vulnerability to future terrorist attacks (Huddy, Feldman, & Cassese, 2009; Huddy et al., 2005).

Endorsement of immigration restrictions, police surveillance, and military action against terrorists have been linked not only to heightened perceptions of threat but also to a purer mental representations of the in-group and sharper in-group–out-group differentiation (Hodson, Esses, & Dovidio, 2006). These findings recall Social Identity Theory, wherein group membership becomes especially salient during intergroup conflict because of intensified awareness of shared grievances and threat (Tajfel & Turner, 1979).

Terror Management Theory also links anxiety and fear to political engagement. This theory holds that anxiety is elicited by awareness of personal mortality and can be regulated by eliminating threats and embracing one's cultural worldview (Pyszczynski, Greenberg, & Solomon, 2003). Existentially speaking, worldview allegiance is triggered by anxiety, which signals mortality threat. Politically speaking, ideology intensifies after a terrorist attack because it buffers the threat of death by reaffirming shared values that provide comforting guidelines for living. Priming mortality has intensified Americans' preexisting political ideologies, support for the USA PATRIOT Act, approval of President Bush and his Iraq policies, and reverence for national symbols, as well as strengthened Israeli support for military force against Palestinians (Morgan et al., 2011; Pyszczynski et al., 2009). In a study by Pyszczynski et al. (2009), Iranian students who had received a mortality prime agreed more with an essay favoring martyrdom attacks against the United States and expressed greater interest in becoming martyrs than did a control group exposed to a distasteful topic unrelated to death. Likewise, mortality-primed American students supported more extreme military intervention, but only among the politically conservative. These findings show that across different cultures, awareness of the inevitability of death hardens cultural narratives of struggle against a mortal enemy, irrespective of the human toll. There are two noteworthy aspects to this study. First, unlike anxiety evoked by 9/11, which is associated with political caution, existential anxiety seemed to motivate risky aggressive action in response to perceived threat. Second, and somewhat contradictory to Terror Management Theory, mortality priming amplified less dominant worldviews that offer a greater sense of security. Returning to a study described earlier (Desivilya & Yassour-Borochowitz, 2010), Israelis' support for government retaliation against terrorists revealed a suspension of otherwise principled moral reasoning. Emergence of an ethnocentric utilitarian orientation under threat suggests the activation of existential anxiety and intensification of a historical narrative of collective survival.

Demographic groups experience anxiety and engage politics differently. Women, African Americans and Latinos/as, younger people, and those with less education generally report greater anxiety, personal threat, and insecurity following 9/11 (Huddy & Feldman, 2011; Huddy et al., 2005, 2007, 2009; Miller, 2011; Skitka, Bauman, Aramovich, & Morgan, 2006; Skitka, Bauman, & Mullen, 2004). Lower social status, which is associated with higher ambient stress, might potentiate anxious reactions to the threat of terrorism in these groups. Women, African Americans and Latinos/as, and more educated citizens are less supportive of military incursions, visa restrictions, surveillance of people with Middle East origins, and deportation of Muslims and immigrants (Huddy et al., 2005, 2007; Miller,

2011; Skitka et al., 2006). Women, however, reported the most consistently elevated level of anxiety in response to terrorism (Huddy et al., 2009) and worry about escalating conflict following government retaliation (Anthony et al., 2003; Bourne et al., 2003; DeSouza et al., 2011; Healy et al., 2002, 2009; Huddy et al., 2009). Women's higher anxiety, personal threat, and insecurity account for their antipathy toward aggressive international and intrusive domestic security policies.

In general, anxiety and fear appear to inhibit political engagement, particularly among women. This inhibitory effect manifests in less support for national security policies that introduce unacceptable personal risk. Insecure attachment may intensify perceptions of threat and anxiety, which reduce support for strong counterterrorism policies. However, the threat of mortality and arousal of existential anxiety may activate aggressive non-dominant worldviews that offer security and assurance of survival.

ANGER

Anger and anger-related emotions (e.g., hostility, outrage) comprise another reaction to terrorism that predicts certain forms of political engagement. In general, anger about 9/11 is related to preferences for aggressive responses to terrorist attacks (Morgan et al., 2011). Unlike anxiety, anger has been tied to support for President Bush and the Iraq War (Huddy & Feldman, 2011). Anger can mobilize other political behavior, including wearing a campaign button, donating money, attending a rally, and volunteering for a campaign (Valentino et al., 2011).

Anger contributes to approach behavior (Huddy & Feldman, 2011) through its effect on cognitive processing. Specifically, anger has been associated with less perceived threat of future terrorist attacks and hence increased willingness to adopt risky political action (Huddy & Feldman, 2011; Huddy et al., 2007; Lerner et al., 2003; Skitka et al., 2006). According to the Cognitive Calculus Model, anger limits information processing by giving greater weight to anger-congruent information, which yields more rapid and punitive policy choices (Sirin, Villalobos, & Geva, 2011; Valentino et al., 2008). For example, anger decreases the amount of policy information reviewed, decreases the time needed to select policies, and increases the chances of picking military responses to scenarios involving ethnic conflict (Sirin et al., 2011). Thus, anger triggers a "cognitive shutdown" (Sirin et al., 2011, p. 44) via optimistic risk assessments about aggressive responses to terrorist attacks and threats. Given the well documented link between public opinion and foreign-policy decisions (Abrams, 2011; Herrmann et al., 1997), politicians may succumb to the demands of angry citizens for swift and decisive, but potentially costly action.

Like the Cognitive Calculus Model, Appraisal Tendency Theory proposes that emotions can cause or be an outcome of cognitive appraisals (i.e., judgments) (Skitka et al., 2004, 2006). This theory posits that emotions are associated with specific cognitive appraisals either of which can facilitate or inhibit behavior (Lerner et al., 2003). Unlike anxiety, which evokes uncertainty and need for personal control, anger elicits certainty and a sense of control (Slovic & Peters, 2006). Appraisal Tendency Theory permits a test of the relationship of distinct emotions on the perceived threat of terrorism. In an analogue study, anger induction reduced estimates of risk to oneself, others, and the nation more so than did fear or sadness (Lerner et al., 2003). Furthermore, anger induction yielded more support for punitive policies (e.g., deportation of suspected terrorist sympathizers) versus conciliatory policies, perhaps due to its modulating effect on perceived risk. These results held for naturally occurring emotions evoked by 9/11, which predicted differential risk estimates 6 to 10 weeks later. Appraisal Tendency Theory also explains the finding that optimistic risk estimates associated with anger may enhance political engagement by activating coping skills and material resources needed to overcome the perceived costs of political action (Valentino et al., 2011).

Intergroup Emotion Theory explains the contradictory behavioral intentions generated by anger versus fear in response to intergroup conflict. Intergroup Emotion Theory gives primacy to the cognitive appraisal of threat vis-à-vis judgments of in-group strength relative to that of an out-group. Appraisal of in-group strength elicits anger and confrontation, whereas appraisal of in-group weakness evokes anxiety and withdrawal. The tenets of the theory have been confirmed (Skitka et al., 2004, 2006), with an additionally informative finding. Anger evoked by 9/11 led to support for expanding the War on Terror beyond Afghanistan and Iraq. Fearful reactions to 9/11 predicted support for deporting Arab-American Muslims and first-generation immigrants. Further confirming Intergroup Emotion Theory, anger partially mediated the effect of political extremism on support for war, whereas anxiety partially mediated the effect of political extremism on support for deportation. Political extremism appears to produce high threat appraisals, strong feelings of anger or fear, and punitive or defensive policy preferences (Skitka et al., 2006). This "overkill response" (Skitka et al., 2006, p. 351) dovetails with value-protection theories, which hold that distress leads people to preserve their threatened moral order (Morgan et al., 2011). It also explains why fear does not always eventuate in avoidant political responses. That fear was influenced by political extremism and led to backing risky polices (e.g., deportation of citizens symbolically connected to 9/11) suggests a specific type of fear more akin to the existential anxiety that drives ethnocentric utilitarian responses (Desivilya & Yassour-Borochowitz, 2010; Pyszczynski et al., 2003).

Moral outrage can also explain how anger contributes to political engagement. Moral outrage is a reaction to the perceived source of threat and restores psychological balance by devaluing that source and instigating action to reduce threat (Huddy & Feldman, 2011; Morgan et al., 2011; Skitka et al., 2006). Moral outrage was included in a test of an integrated model of political intolerance caused by negative emotions to 9/11 (Skitka et al., 2004). Political intolerance was measured by agreement with laws and policies restricting the rights of Arab Americans, Muslims, and first-generation immigrants. Anger and fear both predicted intolerance, but through different routes. Anger weakened tolerance through perceived threat, moral outrage, out-group derogation, and in-group enhancement, whereas fear reduced tolerance via perceived threat, moral outrage, and in-group enhancement. When channeled through value affirmation (i.e., recommitment to positive in-group values), anger and fear strengthened tolerance. This study has two clear implications. First, although post-9/11 anger and fear are associated with approach and avoidant political responses, respectively, both can intensify political intolerance. Second, the effect of anger and fear after 9/11 on political tolerance was partially mediated by moral outrage and value affirmation, which supports value-protection theories that hypothesize worldview defense under conditions of threat. However, unlike Terror Management Theory (Pyszczynski et al., 2009) and the Ethnocentric Utilitarian Perspective (Desivilya & Yassour-Borochowitz, 2010), anger and fear evoked by terrorist threats did not require abandoning prosocial worldviews.

Morally based anger has been linked to protest against national policies that are considered illegitimate (Iyer et al., 2007). Threat to the collective image of a people elicits anger, which can lead citizens to question whether their country's actions have jeopardized that image. Consistent with the view that anger promotes action because of lowered risk estimates, anger predicted support for protest groups advocating withdrawal from Iraq, reparations for those harmed by the Iraq War, and confrontation of governments deemed responsible for the war. Specific political support was based on the target of anger. When image threat elicited anger toward in-group members, anger predicted advocacy for reparations. When image threat elicited anger toward an out-group government, anger predicted support for confronting culpable leaders. Finally, when image threat elicited anger toward an in-group government, anger predicted the backing of military withdrawal, reparations, and holding governments responsible. These findings show that anger stemming from moral judgment can predict political intent, and underscore how targets of morally based anger produce different goals and strategies for political protest against counterterrorism policies and legislation.

To summarize, anger facilitates political engagement by lowering risk appraisals and increasing perceptions of control and in-group strength (Huddy & Feldman, 2011; Lerner et al., 2003; Skitka et al., 2004, 2006), reducing information processing and accelerating decision making (Sirin et al., 2011; Valentino et al., 2008), prompting instrumental strategies and material support to solve political problems (Valentino et al., 2011), and maintaining a core worldview under threat (Iyer et al., 2007; Morgan et al., 2011; Skitka et al., 2004). Anger at terrorist attacks and threats increases approval of politicians, support for and protest against government policies, willingness to expand military operations, and political intolerance. Several studies show that 9/11 evoked different levels of anger depending on demography. Whites, men, older persons, and those less-educated were more likely to report anger after 9/11 (Miller, 2011; Skitka et al., 2004, 2006; Walker & Chestnut, 2003). Men tend to estimate lower costs of another terrorist attack to themselves, other Americans, and the nation generally (Lerner et al., 2003). This gender difference is due in part to men experiencing less anxiety and more anger than women in response to terrorist attacks and threats (Huddy et al., 2009; Lerner et al., 2003).

VOTING BEHAVIOR

Voting is a special form of political engagement that merits special attention. Ideally, voting requires citizens to make choices based on information about candidates, including their character, ideology, policies, and legislative agenda. Anger about the state and direction of the country was positively correlated with participation in the 2008 U.S. presidential election (Valentino et al., 2011). Contrary to the view that anxiety and fear limit political engagement by attenuating the search for political information, recent studies show that these emotions motivate information gathering under conditions of threat (Parker & Isbell, 2010; Valentino et al., 2011). According to Dual Process Theory, anxiety and fear increase attention to threat. Activation of this *surveillance system* prompts citizens to seek information about where candidates stand on issues like terrorism and national security (Marcus, Neuman, & MacKuen, 2000). Because of its association with high threat and risk aversion, anxiety should increase political information gathering and learning prior to voting (Huddy et al., 2007; Valentino et al., 2011). When anxiety was induced by asking Americans to recall anything that made them feel anxious about the 2004 presidential campaign, 40 percent mentioned terrorism or the Iraq War (Valentino et al., 2008). Their anxiety mediated the number of online news articles about political candidates they read and the amount of information they retained (Valentino et al., 2008).

Although anxiety increases consumption of political information, it also can initiate a narrow search for highly relevant information (Huddy & Feldman, 2011; Valentino et al., 2011). After recalling an experience that made them feel either anxious or angry, anxious students spent more time navigating a web site with information about two bogus political candidates (Parker & Isbell, 2010). Anxious students sought more issue-oriented details confirming their political views than general information, which characterized the search of angry participants (Parker & Isbell, 2010). Furthermore, agreement with candidates on issues determined candidate preferences for anxious voters, whereas angry voters chose candidates based on general information (i.e., party affiliation and name recognition). Anxiety, then, may increase the amount and specificity of political information collected along with the depth of information processing (Valentino et al., 2011). These findings suggest that political candidates should package their views on the issues of terrorism and national security to fit the information-processing proclivities of the segment of the electorate for whose vote they are campaigning (e.g., anxious women vs. angry men). As a caveat, anxiety aroused by conditions that heighten personal vulnerability may short-circuit the collection and processing of information about political candidates (Huddy & Feldman, 2011; Morgan et al., 2011; Pyszczynski et al., 2003, 2009; Valentino et al., 2008).

Affective Intelligence Theory explains survey and experimental evidence that, when circumstances produce enough anxiety, politically disengaged citizens make thoughtful decisions about candidates using information related to issues and character (Marcus et al., 2000). Simply put, voters attend more to substantive considerations when anxiety alerts them to threat by triggering a *surveillance system*. Anxiety has been found to lower the impact of partisanship by over half while strengthening the impact of policy preferences, supporting its indirect contribution to voter choice (Ladd & Lenz, 2008). Citizens with acute concerns about terrorism want political candidates to offer thoughtful and informed statements rather than the party line about the threat of terrorism and remedies for it. This theory also holds that anxiety may be of any kind, and its effect on voters' search for meaningful political information and motivation to take political action can either be direct, indirect, or interactive (Brader, 2011).

One salient point emerges from the literature on voting behavior: contrary to evidence that anxiety is associated with avoidant political behavior, Affective Intelligence Theory suggests that anxious citizens may be more discerning than their angry counterparts because they take steps to inform themselves about candidates before voting. Perhaps, anxious citizens are better prepared to engage in politics because of their risk aversion, which is plausible in the uncertain, high-stakes case of anti-terrorism policy. Thus, it may not be that anxious citizens fail to engage politically, but rather that they are inclined toward more informed and less risky forms of political expression. Supporting this argument, Valentino and colleagues (2011) used survey data on presidential elections from 1980 to 2004 to show that anxiety and anger each mobilize participation in "cheap" political acts, such as wearing a campaign button or talking about voting, whereas anger alone boosted costly political participation, including donating money and working for a campaign. The supposition that perceived risk may influence political engagement is examined next.

RISK PERCEPTION

Considerable research on the relationship of negative emotion to political engagement emphasizes threat. Threat can be defined as "any risk of future harm either material or symbolic" (Valentino et al., 2008, p. 157). Fear amplifies risks estimates, whereas anger attenuates them (Lerner et al., 2003). Slovic and Peters (2006) coined the term *affect heuristic* to capture the value of emotional information in making sense of circumstances and guiding adaptive responses to them. When people experience negative feelings about an intended action, they perceive that action as having greater risk than benefit and are less inclined to act; conversely, people are more likely to act when they feel positively and anticipate greater benefit than risk. This *affect heuristic* has predicted attitudinal and behavioral responses to various threats, including terrorism. Because terrorism evokes strong emotions, affect can override reason and substitute possibilistic for probabilistic thinking about risk, termed *probability neglect* (Furedi, 2009). This may be why citizens and government officials often overrespond to the threat of a terrorist attack.

Given the uncertainty of policy outcomes, opinion about policies intended to counter terrorism partly reflect the perceived risk of their implementation. Research has examined how policy preferences vary with the risk conveyed by specific outcome scenarios, or framed choices. A framed choice pits a guaranteed gain or loss against a probabilistic alternative outcome. Decision makers typically choose an assured gain over a more positive probable outcome; conversely, a less negative but probable outcome is selected when the alternative involves certain loss. Prospect Theory (Kahnemann & Tversky, 1979), which captures these findings, assumes that acceptance or avoidance of risk lies in the context of a framed choice. Recently, scholars have extended Prospect Theory to include a trait view of responses to risk, namely risk orientation (Ehrlich & Maestas, 2010; Kam & Simas, 2010). Risk orientation can be defined as a stable emotional response to encounters that have an uncertain likelihood of gain or loss (Ehrlich & Maestas, 2010). Risk avoiders desire security, whereas risk seekers prefer high returns. Evidence for risk orientation lies in enduring individual differences in responding to perceived risk. Risk orientation has been associated with a consistent preference for either assured or risky policies irrespective of expected gain or loss (Kam & Simas, 2010). Risk intolerance predicted preferences for guaranteed outcomes, whereas risk acceptance predicted an inclination toward probabilistic outcomes no matter how policies were framed. Notably few respondents reversed their initial policy preference when given an alternative policy frame later. Risk orientation, then, may lower susceptibility to policy frames, which weakens the claim of Prospect Theory that policy choices are contextually determined.

The relative independence of risk orientation from policy frames has implications for political engagement. The political responses of citizens to anti-terrorism policies espoused by politicians may reflect risk orientation more than the influence of media campaigns (i.e., policy frames) designed to sway the electorate. Although policy frames matter because of the particular issue they tap, such as terrorism, citizens are generally well anchored and not likely to shift toward policies whose risk deviates markedly from their comfort zone. Much like Appraisal Tendency Theory, citizens are sensitive to information about risk that comports with their predispositions. Policy statements may activate risk dispositions that mediate information processing and opinion formation. Clearly, efforts to promote public consensus on policy changes necessitated by the evolving nature of international and domestic terrorism must take stock of risk orientation.

Recent studies confirm the role of risk orientation in determining preferences for actual policies that involve personal risk (Ehrlich & Maestas, 2010). Risk orientation interacted with risk exposure to predict opinions about immigration policy, which has direct implications for employment and financial security. Support for offering citizenship to illegal immigrants declined markedly with a rise in job insecurity, but only among the risk averse; risk-tolerant citizens showed an increase in support for lenient immigration policy notwithstanding a rise in perceived job insecurity. The risk of job loss did not independently predict opinions about immigration. In the real world, risk orientation appears to be a more powerful determinant of policy choices than the personal risk associated with policy outcomes. The application of risk orientation and personal risk in predicting political reactions to terrorism policies awaits investigation.

Little research has examined group differences in risk orientation, perhaps because it is conceived as an individual-difference variable (Kam & Simas, 2010). However, gender yields the most consistent differences on negative emotion and political engagement. Women are generally more anxious and fearful than men, though less likely to have been victimized (Nellis, 2009). Women in New York City and Washington, DC, reported greater risk of another terrorist attack, more worry about becoming victim to terrorism, greater likelihood of seeking information about terrorist threats, and more precautionary behaviors than did men (Nellis, 2009). Perceived risk of terrorism predicted women's fear of being victimized, information seeking, and behavioral avoidance. These results suggest a general vulnerability (i.e., risk orientation) that underlies women's anxiety about terrorism (Nellis, 2009). Conversely, white men perceive less risk to themselves, others, and the nation of future terrorist attacks (Lerner et al., 2003); white men may experience the world as generally safer and risks as worth taking (Finucane, Slovic, Mertz, Flynn, & Satterfield, 2000). Such a risk orientation is presumably well represented among white men who comprise the power elite and who craft policies and laws that minimize risk to themselves.

OPINION-BASED GROUPS

Opinion-based groups are a barometer of the politicization of citizens, and have predicted political responses to 9/11 (Musgrove & McGarty, 2008). Australians who either supported or opposed the War on Terror were sampled to determine whether their emotions following 9/11 mediated the relationship of group membership to political intentions. Prowar advocates were angrier at terrorists, which predicted their support for offensive antiterrorist action. Antiwar proponents directed more anger toward government, which predicted their intention to protest overseas military operations (Musgrove & McGarty, 2008). A shared ideological perspective may facilitate the development of group identity and social movements, particularly if such groups believe they operate from a position of strength, as proposed by Intergroup Emotion Theory. In related research, support for the Afghanistan and Iraq wars and for targeted killing were explained by a model in which anger at 9/11 mediated the personal relevance and intolerance of terrorism, which in turn mediated self-identification as a Christian (Cheung-Blunden & Blunden, 2008). In line with Appraisal Theory, cognitive judgments elicited emotions that determined policy preferences and consequent action. This study also demonstrated that group identity in the form of religious affiliation can be a source of appraisals that bear on political engagement. These findings underscore the significance of identity politics on attitudinal and behavioral responses to terrorism-related issues.

Political conservatism can be construed as an outcome of the need to manage uncertainty when threatened and of "binding" moral values that sustain in-group integrity (De Zavala, Cislak, & Wesolowska, 2010; van Leeuwen & Park, 2009).

Both views dovetail with Terror Management Theory (Pyszczynski et al., 2003) and the Ethnocentric Utilitarian Perspective (Desivilya & Yassour-Borochowitz, 2010). For Dutch students, belief in a dangerous world and in binding moral values predicted political conservatism (van Leeuwen & Park, 2009). Furthermore, binding moral values partially mediated the relationship of perceived social dangers to political conservatism. Like mortality salience, perceptions of threat motivate the preservation of threatened worldviews, which can express itself through political orientation. Moral values, then, may determine political attitudes that are revealed in support for conservative politicians and policies, especially under threat (e.g., support for President Bush and the Iraq War following 9/11) (Abrams, 2011; Huddy & Feldman, 2011).

Need for cognitive closure may explain the tendency of conservatives to aggress against an out-group when threatened (De Zavala et al., 2010). Cognitive closure can be defined as the motivation to establish an unambiguous perspective on an issue (Sirin et al., 2011). The need for cognitive closure in Polish students predicted their willingness to aggress against Germans due to unresolved political issues between the countries, but only for students who self-identified as conservative. Regarding terrorism, an association between the need for closure and hostility toward Arabs held for conservative Polish students, but only for those who perceived a terrorist threat to the nation and public given Poland's involvement in the Afghanistan and Iraq wars. Not unlike Terror Management Theory (Pyszczynski et al., 2009), Intergroup Emotion Theory (Skitka et al., 2004, 2006), and the Ethnocentric Utilitarian Perspective (Desivilya & Yassour-Borochowitz, 2010), cognitive closure plus perceived in-group strength predict hostility toward an out-group when ideological cues are available to justify the use of violence to prevent annihilation.

CONCLUSION

The following observations emerge from this literature review of negative emotions and political engagement. First, political responses to terrorism are partly determined by the frequency, recency, and target of terrorist attacks and by prior attitudes about a government's right to aggression. Second, anxiety and fear are tied to unacceptably high risk, efforts to acquire and evaluate information about salient issues, and cautious political behavior, particularly among women and minorities. This inhibitory effect may not hold when threat is so profound that it precipitates risky aggressive responses aimed at ensuring survival. Third, anger lowers risk perceptions by increasing perceived control and strength, reduces information seeking and processing, and mobilizes adventurous political action to preserve a threatened worldview, particularly among older, less-educated white men. Fourth, risk perception, which is intensified by anxiety and fear and diminished by anger, conveys information that can guide political responses. Risk orientation is a dispositional variable that may account for stable emotional reactions and policy preferences that have varying probabilities of gain or loss. Fifth, women's elevated anxiety and fear, higher risk perception, and greater political caution may reflect their generalized vulnerability to harm, whereas the disregard for risk by white males seems to mirror their privileged and insulated worldview. Political conservatism is linked to a need for closure and for preserving collectively held moral values under threatening conditions, and predicts hostile ethnocentric political preferences. Sixth, several conceptual models have been developed or adapted to explain the association between negative emotions and political engagement: Affect Intelligence Theory, Appraisal Tendency Theory, Attachment Theory, Cognitive Calculus Model, Dual Process Theory, Ethnocentric Utilitarian Perspective, Intergroup Emotion Theory, Prospect Theory, Social Identity Theory, and Terror Management Theory. Each perspective sharpens and deepens the understanding and prediction of political engagement in circumstances that involve terrorism.

What is needed now is a systematic multidisciplinary effort to construct and validate a unifying theory, sensitive to context and culture and unencumbered by methodological confounds, of how demographic and opinion-group membership, personal dispositions, risk perception, and negative emotions together explain the broad spectrum of political opinions, intentions, and actions that follow a terrorist attack and threats of future attacks in the various forms they may take.

REFERENCES

Abrams, M. (2011). Does terrorism really work? Evolution in the conventional wisdom since 9/11. *Defence & Peace Economics, 22*, 583–594.

Anthony, K., Rosselli, F., & Caparyan, L. (2003). Truly evil or simply angry: Individualism, collectivism, and attributions for the events of September 11th. *Individual Differences Research, 1*, 147–157.

Brader, T. (2011). The political relevance of emotions: "Reassessing" revisited. *Political Psychology, 32*, 337–346.

Bourne, L. E., Jr., Healy, A. F., & Beer, F. A. (2003). Military conflict and terrorism: General psychology informs international relations. *Review of General Psychology, 7*, 189–202.

Cheung-Blunden, V., & Blunden, B. (2008). Paving the road to war with group membership, appraisal antecedents, and anger. *Aggressive Behavior, 34*, 175–189.

Desivilya, H. S., & Yassour-Borochowitz, D. (2010). Israelis' moral judgments of government aggression and violations of human rights: Is democracy under siege? *Beliefs & Values, 2*, 38–48.

DeSouza, E. R., Stevens, M. J., & Metivier, R. M. (2011). Government retaliation against terrorism: A cross-national study. *Behavioral Sciences of Terrorism & Political Aggression, 3*(1), 1–19.

De Zavala, A. G., Cislak, A., & Wesolowska, E. (2010). Political conservatism, need for cognitive closure, and intergroup hostility. *Political Psychology, 31*, 521–541.

Ehrlich, S., & Maestas, C. (2010). Risk orientation, risk exposure, and policy opinions: The case of free trade. *Political Psychology, 31*, 657–684.

Finucane, M. L., Slovic, P., Mertz, C. K., Flynn, J., & Satterfield, T. A. (2000). Gender, race, and perceived risk: The "white male" effect. *Health, Risk & Society, 2*, 159–172.

Furedi, F. (2009). Fear and security: A vulnerability-led policy responses. In D. Denney (Ed.), *Living in dangerous times: Fear, insecurity, risk and social policy* (pp. 86–102). Malden, MA: Wiley-Blackwell.

Healy, A. F., Aylward, A. G., Bourne, L. E., Jr., & Beer, F. A. (2009). Terrorism after 9/11: Reactions to simulated news reports. *American Journal of Psychology, 122,* 153–165.

Healy, A. F., Hoffman, J. M., Beer, F. A., & Bourne, L. E., Jr. (2002). Terrorists and democrats: Individual reactions to international attacks. *Political Psychology, 23,* 439–467.

Herrmann, R. K., Voss, J. F., Schooler, T. Y. E., & Ciarrochi, J. (1997). Images in international relations: An experimental test of cognitive schemata. *International Studies Quarterly, 41,* 403–433.

Hodson, G., Esses, V. M., & Dovidio, J. F. (2006). Perceptions of threat, national representation, and support for procedures to protect the national group. In P. R. Kimmel & C. E. Stout (Eds.), *Collateral damage: The psychological consequences of America's war on terrorism* (pp. 109–129). Westport, CT: Praeger.

Huddy, L., & Feldman, S. (2011). Americans respond politically to 9/11: Understanding the impact of terrorist attacks and their aftermath. *American Psychologist, 66,* 455–467.

Huddy, L., Feldman, S., & Cassese, E. (2009). Terrorism, anxiety, and war. In W. G. K. Stritzke, S. Lewandowsky, D. Denemark, J. Clare, & F. Morgan (Eds.), *Terrorism and torture: An interdisciplinary perspective* (pp. 290–312). New York, NY: Cambridge University Press.

Huddy, L., Feldman, S., Taber, C., & Lahav, G. (2005). Threat, anxiety, and support of antiterrorism policies. *American Journal of Political Science, 49,* 593–608.

Huddy, L., Feldman, S., & Weber, C. (2007). The political consequences of perceived threat and felt insecurity. *Annals of the American Academy of Political & Social Science, 614,* 131–153.

Iyer, A., Schmader, T., & Lickel, B. (2007). Why individuals protest the perceived transgressions of their country: The role of anger, shame, and guilt. *Personality & Social Psychology Bulletin, 33,* 572–587.

Jasper, J. M. (2011). Emotions and social movements: Twenty years of theory and research. *Annual Review of Sociology, 37,* 285–303.

Kahnemann, D., & Tversky, A. (1979). Prospect theory: An analysis of decision under risk. *Econometrica, 47,* 263–291.

Kam, C. D., & Simas, E. N. (2010). Risk perceptions and policy frames. *Journal of Politics, 72,* 381–396.

Ladd, J. M., & Lenz, G. S. (2008). Reassessing the role of anxiety in vote choice. *Political Psychology, 29,* 275–296.

Lerner, J. S., Gonzalez, R. M., Small, D. A., & Fischhoff, B. (2003). Effects of fear and anger on perceived risks of terrorism: A national field experiment. *Psychological Science, 14,* 144–150.

Marcus, G. E., Neuman, W. R., & MacKuen, M. B. (2000). *Affective intelligence and political judgment.* Chicago, IL: University of Chicago Press.

McAlister, A. L., Bandura, A., & Owen, S. V. (2006). Mechanisms of moral engagement in support of military force: The impact of Sept. 11. *Journal of Social & Clinical Psychology, 25,* 141–165.

McCauley, C. (2006). Jujitsu politics: Terrorism and responses to terrorism. In P. R. Kimmel & C. E. Stout (Eds.), *Collateral damage: The psychological consequences of America's war on terrorism* (pp. 45–66). Westport, CT: Praeger.

Miller, P. R. (2011). The emotional citizen: Emotion as a function of political sophistication. *Political Psychology, 32,* 575–600.

Morgan, G. S., Wisneski, D. C., & Skitka, L. J. (2011). The expulsion from Disneyland: The social psychological impact of 9/11. *American Psychologist, 66,* 447–454.

Musgrove, L., & McGarty, C. (2008). Opinion-based group membership as a predictor of collective emotional responses and support for pro- and anti-war action. *Social Psychology, 39*, 37–47.

Nellis, A. M. (2009). Gender differences in fear of terrorism. *Journal of Contemporary Criminal Justice, 25*, 322–340.

Parker, M. T., & Isbell, L. M. (2010). How I vote depends on how I feel: The differential impact of anger and fear on political information processing. *Psychological Science, 21*, 548–550.

Pyszczynski, T., Abdollahi, A., Solomon, S., Greenberg, J., Cohen, F., & Weise, D. (2009). Mortality salience, martyrdom, and military might: The Great Satan versus the Axis of Evil. In J. Victoroff & A. W. Kruglanski (Eds.), *Psychology of terrorism: Key readings—classic and contemporary insights* (pp. 281–297). New York, NY: Psychology Press.

Pyszczynski, T., Greenberg, J., & Solomon, S. (2003). *In the wake of 9/11: The psychology of terror.* Washington, DC: American Psychological Association.

Robinson, L. (2008). The moral accounting of terrorism: Competing interpretations of September 11, 2001. *Qualitative Sociology, 31*, 272–285.

Sahar, G. (2008). Patriotism, attributions for the 9/11 attacks, and support for war: Then and now. *Basic & Applied Social Psychology, 30*, 189–197.

Shamir, J., & Shikaki, K. (2002). Self-serving perceptions of terrorism among Israelis and Palestinians. *Political Psychology, 23*, 537–557.

Sinclair, S. J., & LoCicero, A. (2010). Do fears of terrorism predict trust in government? *Journal of Aggression, Conflict & Peace Research, 2*, 57–68.

Sirin, C. B., Villalobos, J. D., & Geva, N. (2011). Political information and emotions in ethnic conflict interventions. *International Journal of Conflict Management, 22*, 35–59.

Skitka, L. J., Bauman, C. W., Aramovich, N. P., & Morgan, G. S. (2006). Confrontational and preventative policy responses to terrorism: Anger wants a fight and fear wants "them" to go away. *Basic & Applied Social Psychology, 28*, 375–384.

Skitka, L. J., Bauman, C. W., & Mullen, E. (2004). Political tolerance and coming to psychological closure following the September 11, 2001, terrorist attacks: An integrative approach. *Personality & Social Psychology Bulletin, 30*, 743–756.

Slovic, P., & Peters, E. (2006). Risk perception and affect. *Psychological Science, 15*, 322–325.

Tajfel, H., & Turner, J. C. (1979). An integrative theory of intergroup conflict. In W. G. Austin & S. Worchel (Eds.), *The social psychology of intergroup relations* (pp. 33–47). Monterey, CA: Brooks/Cole.

Takooshian, H., & Verdi, W. M. (1993). U.S. attitudes toward the terrorism problem. *Journal of Psychology & the Behavioral Sciences, 7*, 83–87.

Valentino, N. A., Brader, T., Groenendyk, E. W., Gregorowicz, K., & Hutchings, V. L. (2011). Election night's alright for fighting: The role of emotions in political participation. *Journal of Politics, 73*, 156–170.

Valentino, N. A., Hutchings, V. L., Banks, A. J., & Davis, A. K. (2008). Is a worried citizen a good citizen? Emotions, political information seeking, and learning via the Internet. *Political Psychology, 29*, 247–273.

van Leeuwen, F., & Park, J. H. (2009). Perceptions of social dangers, moral foundations, and political orientation. *Personality & Individual Differences, 47*, 169–173.

Walker, K. L., & Chestnut, D. (2003). The role of ethnocultural variables in response to terrorism. *Cultural Diversity & Ethnic Minority Psychology, 9*, 251–262.

CHAPTER 4

Beyond the Water's Edge: Threat, Partisanship, and Media

SHANA KUSHNER GADARIAN

Most Americans receive information about terrorism through mass media that emphasize threatening information and de-emphasize reassuring news (Nacos, Bloch-Elkon, & Shapiro, 2007). Scholars and political commentators worry that such evocative terrorism news may scare the public into supporting policies they would not otherwise support by causing them to overestimate the risk of future terrorism (Fischhoff, Gonzalez, Small, & Lerner, 2003). Yet, there are few studies that explore how terrorism news influences perceptions of threat in a politicized context.

By considering how political context affects citizens' evaluations of threatening news, this chapter contributes to the growing literature on the relationship between threat perception and political attitudes. After 9/11, citizens who perceived higher threat from terrorism were more likely to support the wars in Afghanistan and Iraq (Gadarian, 2010; Huddy, Feldman, Taber, & Lahav, 2005), restrictions on civil liberties (Berinsky, 2009; Davis, 2007), and approve of George W. Bush's presidency (Merolla & Zechmeister, 2009; Willer, 2004). Much of the scholarship demonstrating that the news media increased the public's perceptions of threat occurred in the months following the 9/11 attacks (Entman, 2003; Schlenger et al., 2002), during a time of reduced elite opposition to George W. Bush's terrorism policies (Bennett, Lawrence, & Livingston, 2007). However, the bipartisan coalition that formed after 9/11 soon dissipated, and public evaluations of the Bush Administration and foreign policy became the most polarized by party in more than seven decades (Jacobson, 2010).

As elites and the mass public divided on terrorism policy, rejection of terrorism messages from the president became likely among Democrats and liberals because of the tight rhetorical link drawn by the Bush Administration between the threat of terrorism and hawkish counterterrorism policies. Hawkish policy here is defined as foreign policy that is aggressive and punitive in nature. Hawkish public opinion is more supportive of policies such as higher defense spending, armed intervention, and war. Dovish foreign policy is defined as more cooperative than punitive and is expressed by support for policies such as diplomacy, negotiations, and foreign aid. When citizens who disagreed with the hawkish policy solution offered by the president were exposed to subsequent communication about that threat (like a news story), they were motivated to reject the story's message when they recognized the link between the original political rhetoric and the subsequent news message. The likelihood that a backlash would occur increased as the subsequent, nonpersuasive communication became more vivid and evocative (Dillard & Shen, 2005). Conversely, citizens whose policy views conformed to those in the original persuasive communication were likely to accept the subsequent nonpersuasive message (Zaller, 1992).

Terrorism provides an ideal case study to test the conditions under which evocative news messages can affect perceptions about potential threat. On its face, terrorism is inherently dramatic and garners significant media attention. Furthermore, primary exposure to violent news and imagery increases the belief and the fear that future terrorism is likely (Fischhoff et al., 2003). However, because terrorism as a policy area became entangled with one party's policy solutions (i.e., the Republican party) following the 9/11 attacks, citizens' political identities (e.g., partisanship and ideology) could become a basis for interpreting subsequent terrorism information.

To the extent that citizens feel that news stories intentionally create threat and fear in order to affect their policy attitudes, they may be motivated to reject these messages. During the Bush Administration, Democrats and liberals were more likely to perceive the greatest threat to their autonomy from terrorism news stories because these stories were likely to frame the solution to the threat of terrorism as hawkish foreign policy, a solution disliked by many Democrats. As a note, these are not mutually exclusive categories. Democrats, on average, tend to be more liberal than Republicans, yet there is variation within each party on ideological grounds, especially on issues surrounding foreign policy. These groups will be treated as separate empirical categories based on respondents' survey answering self-identifying themselves on ideology and party identification. Republicans and conservatives were unlikely to reject threatening terrorism information since the information pointed them in a policy direction consistent with their prior attitudes. The next section outlines previous literature on threat, the information environment, and reactance to derive hypotheses about how terrorism news affects Americans' emotions and perceptions of threat in a politically polarized environment.

THE INFORMATION ENVIRONMENT: HOW THE NEWS CAN INCREASE THREAT PERCEPTION

Generally speaking, informing the public about possible risks through the mass media increases their perception of risk, even when the potential for harm is very small. For example, MacGregor, Slovic, & Morgan (1994) found that individuals who read a brochure about the risks from electromagnetic fields became more concerned about health risks, even though the communication emphasized that there is no established scientific link between the fields and health problems. As another example, attention to bioterrorism news increases worry about future attacks (Rodriguez & Lee, 2010). However, the belief that government is ready for an attack lessens worry, suggesting that trust in government can help citizens manage risk perception. In the political context explored here, during the Bush Administration, Republicans and conservatives are the most likely to trust in government while Democrats and liberals are likely to be more skeptical. For example, in the 2004 National Election Studies, 62 percent of Republicans trusted the government to do "what is right" most or all of the time compared with 46 percent of Democrats.

Surveys of Americans immediately after the 9/11 terrorist attacks showed a strong connection between media exposure and fear (Schlenger et al., 2002). Even controlling for demographics and direct exposure to the terrorist attacks (i.e., being near the Trade Towers), TV content and hours of exposure were associated with clinically significant distress symptoms. Respondents who saw particularly vivid images of the attacks reported more severe stress (Schlenger et al., 2002). As the amount of television news coverage focusing on terrorism increased from 2001 to 2005, in the aggregate, the public became more threatened (Nacos et al., 2007). In contrast, reassuring terrorism coverage, such as the lowering of the Department of Homeland Security threat advisory, had no significant effect on lowering citizens' risk perceptions (Nacos et al., 2007). These findings lead to the expectation that evocative terrorism news should increase threat perception among all individuals in a nonpoliticized time period like post-9/11. The next section explores the context when threatening news may become less threatening to some individuals.

WHY DEMOCRATS AND LIBERALS MAY REJECT TERRORISM NEWS

Persuasive communications are not always so persuasive. Communication can potentially lead to backlashes, especially when the language is intense, forceful, or dogmatic (Dillard & Shen, 2005), when the message evokes fear (S. Brehm & Brehm, 1981), and when the message runs up against a motivation to remain consistent with prior attitudes (Kunda, 1987). In the case of terrorism during the Bush Administration, Democrats and liberals were the groups most likely to be targeted by persuasive messages to support counterterrorism policies that they normally do not. Democrats and liberals were also more difficult to persuade as the issue of terrorism grew more politicized. Persuasion may break down through several mechanisms whereby individuals choose information that confirms their prior beliefs (even when those beliefs are wrong) (Lord, Ross, & Lepper, 1979; Nyhan & Reifler, 2010), avoid information that disconfirms their beliefs (Arceneaux,

Johnson, & Murphy, 2012; Festinger, 1957), or see biases in stories or news outlets that they disagree with (Baum & Gussin, 2008; Vallone, Ross, & Lepper, 1985).

Persuasion may also break down when individuals consider the persuasive communication itself as manipulative. When an individual perceives that the communication threatens her freedom to act, this may lead to an unpleasant motivational state whereby the individual reestablishes control through engaging in the behavior proscribed by the persuasive message, in a process called reactance (Brehm, 1966). That is, messages may lead to the exact opposite behavior as intended by the communication. Reactance has been identified in reactions to messages against binge drinking, drug use, sun protection, tobacco use, flossing, and fat warning labels (Bushman, 1998; Dillard & Shen, 2005). Two message features increase the probability of reactance, both of which are present in the terrorism case: (1) threat to choice language and (2) vividness. Messages that use forceful and dogmatic language that explicitly pressures listeners to conform to recommendations (Quick & Stephenson, 2008) or vivid and graphic imagery (Bushman, 1998; Quick & Stephenson, 2008) often trigger backlashes. Together, these features suggest that vivid terrorism news stories may invoke a boomerang effect when they are perceived to threaten individuals' freedom to form their own counterterrorism attitudes.

Even communications that are not overtly persuasive may lead to reactance when the images and language in the communication were previously linked to political elites' persuasive rhetoric. In the context of terrorism, images of the World Trade Center (WTC) and terrorism as well as mentions of 9/11 were strongly linked to a set of foreign policy remedies, including military action in Iraq, by the Bush Administration (Gadarian, 2010). This link remained unchallenged by both Democrats and the mass media for some time after 9/11 (Bennett et al., 2007; Entman, 2003). To the extent that citizens whose foreign policy attitudes are inconsistent with the policies advocated in the original rhetoric (in this case, liberals and Democrats), are exposed to terrorism news, they may be motivated to reject that news because of its link to the original communication.

Both the Bush Administration and mass media coverage of terrorism used the "War on Terror" frame in communication about terrorism. The frame defined terrorism as problematic and argued that hawkish foreign policy was the correct policy solution (Entman, 2003). In making the case for war in Iraq, the president juxtaposed references to Iraq with allusions to the 9/11 attacks in his speeches, creating a rhetorical link between threat and military action abroad (Gershkoff & Kushner, 2005). Additionally, several of Bush's campaign ads used images of the WTC and flag-draped coffins of firefighters to promote the president's policies (Farhi, 2004).

Bush's framing of the 9/11 attacks as the commencement of a global war against terrorism that could be won through aggressive military action gained acceptance by Democrats and journalists in the months after 9/11 (Entman, 2003). For example, in *New York Times* front-page coverage of the War on Terrorism from 2001 to 2005, more than 70 percent of stories that used a "terrorism" frame took a promilitary engagement (or hawkish) tone (Boydstun & Glazier, 2012). Politicians have little control over the visuals and language used in news broadcasts, but to the extent that the images and language used by elites appear in news stories, these can be understood to have political meaning by news recipients. Viewers may still associate particular visual cues and language with policies endorsed by politicians, even when political elites do not appear and when the news story itself does not advocate policy positions. These findings lead to the hypothesis that exposure to evocative terrorism news will increase the probability of message rejection and reactance among individuals who perceive the message as manipulating their perceptions and threatening their freedom to form political attitudes. During the post-9/11 Bush Administration, these individuals are more likely to be Democrats or liberals, whose foreign policy views were inconsistent with those of the president.

THE ROLE OF POLITICAL INFORMATION

Political sophistication, that is, paying close attention to and understanding politics, is an important moderator of motivated reasoning, biased information processing, and polarization (Taber & Lodge, 2006). Sophistication allows citizens to recognize when new information clashes with their own opinions and/or the positions of the party with which they affiliate. For example, at the elite level, the Republican and Democratic parties in the United States differ about the causes of climate changes as well as proposed solutions. The Republican party is more skeptical that climate change poses a threat and is less supportive of government efforts to regulate climate change. In the mass public, sophistication allows partisans not to necessarily take the "right" position, but to accept facts that are consistent with those of trusted leaders (Zaller, 1992). As sophistication increases (measured as educational attainment), Democrats become more concerned about climate change, whereas education leads Republicans in the public to become *less* concerned about climate change (Hamilton, 2010). Political sophisticates are also motivated to maintain consistency with their attitudes and more likely to seek out information that conforms to prior beliefs and denigrate information that disagrees with those beliefs. Taber and Lodge (2006) found significant evidence of attitude polarization among politically knowledgeable experimental subjects but not among those with lower levels of knowledge. More knowledgeable partisans are most likely to recognize whether terrorism news conforms to their policy preferences and threat perceptions and thus are more likely to reject terrorism messages that threaten their ability to formulate their own policy views. Therefore, we can expect that during the Bush Administration, more knowledgeable Democrats should be less likely to accept threatening terrorism messages than less knowledgeable Democrats.

RESEARCH HYPOTHESES

To restate the hypotheses, the effect of terrorism news stories on threat perception is conditional on the political identity and political sophistication of news viewers in a politicized policy environment. In the context of this study, which took place during the Bush presidency following 9/11, Democrats and liberals will be the most likely to reject terrorism news when they view the stories as intentionally threatening them in order to advocate hawkish counterterrorism policies that originated with a Republican president. In this context, reactance should be most likely among politically sophisticated Democrats and liberals since they are the most likely to recognize the link between the terrorism news story and calls for hawkish foreign policy from the presidential administration. Since Republicans are more likely to already hold hawkish policy preferences, they would be less likely to view terrorism news stories as problematic and would be more likely to accept the threatening messages. The foreign policy attitudes of Independents (who do not lean toward either party) and moderates fall between those of Democrats and Republicans. Since these groups are less motivated to maintain consistency with their political identity, terrorism news may also increase threat among Independents and moderates.

METHOD

Study 1: Laboratory Experiment

To test the hypothesis that evocative terrorism news may both increase and decrease threat, a lab experiment was run over several months in 2005–2006. Using an experiment avoids the potential confound in survey data that individuals may self-select terrorism information that conforms to their political predispositions. The lab experiment occurred during ongoing political discussion and news coverage of terrorism and a partisan polarization of attitudes toward the Iraq war and the War on Terror more broadly (Jacobson, 2010). This research was approved by the institutional review board at Princeton University in fall 2005.

The sample was composed of 246 undergraduates and graduate students at Princeton University. Fifty-four percent of the respondents identified as Democrats, 20 percent as Independents, and 25 percent as Republicans. Forty-three percent of the sample considered themselves liberal, 20 percent conservative, and 37 percent moderate. Fifty-two percent of the respondents were female and the average age of the sample was 19.5 ($SD = 1.4$) years. Respondents received a small cash payment for participation. The student sample does not allow a test of the hypothesis that political sophistication will moderate reactance because there is little variance on political sophistication, which was measured by the level of education. Rather, the expectation is that reactance will be likely to occur among Democrats and liberals in this sample. College students tend to have stronger cognitive skills and less crystallized attitudes than broader adult samples (Sears, 1986). While the fluidity of students' attitudes may make affecting attitudes easier in this experiment, their stronger cognitive skills may act as a countervailing force against affecting perceptions. Additionally, cognitive ability is correlated with political knowledge and more consistent preferences, meaning that affecting threat perceptions may be more challenging among students.

Lab Experiment Manipulation

The experimental treatments manipulated the presence of threat (threatening vs. nonthreatening) in a real television story about recent terrorist attacks. Participants came to the lab in groups and were assigned to watch one of two story sets on a screen at the front of the lab. Using individual computers, subjects answered questions about their policy attitudes, evaluations of George W. Bush's presidency, and their reactions to the news stories that they watched.

Subjects were randomly assigned to either (1) the control condition where respondents watched one nonterrorism, reassuring foreign policy story (i.e., the North Korea story) or (2) the treatment condition where respondents watched both the nonthreatening foreign policy story (i.e., the North Korea story) and a threatening story about the potential for a new wave of terrorism (i.e., the "Wave of Terror" story). The nonthreatening story recounted a diplomatic breakthrough between the United States and North Korea. The story was positive in valence and provided neither verbal information on threat nor a visual emotional cue to threat.

The threatening terrorism story, the "Wave of Terror," was 2½ minutes in length and was an actual news broadcast from fall 2005. The story outlined recent terrorist attacks and ominously suggested that future terrorism was likely. Not only did the terrorism story provide respondents threatening information, but the story was also edited to enhance the threatening nature of the story by adding frightening imagery. This editing added additional footage of the burning WTC and bloodied victims of the 2005 London transit bombings aimed at increasing the emotional impact. By increasing the emotional intensity of the imagery, the terrorism story is more likely to induce resistance (Dillard & Shen, 2005).

Prior to the lab experiment, all of images added to the "Wave of Terror" story were pretested by a separate sample of 79 students to confirm that the terrorism images provoked emotion. No one dropped out of the study due to distress. Respondents viewed a series of both neutral and evocative photos in random order and answered how afraid, hopeful, and angry each photo made them, on a scale from 1 "not at all" to 10 "very." The neutral images were of a double-decker London bus, a flower, football player, a British flag, sunshine, flames, and a map of the London subway system. The images of terrorism included a picture of the double-decker bus blown apart by terrorists on July 7, 2005 in London, survivors of the London explosions, a picture of a man with his face covered holding an automatic weapon, the Twin Towers on fire on 9/11, survivors from the 9/11 attacks, and a picture of Osama bin Laden. For the seven neutral images, the mean fear score was 1.60 while the average fear score for the terrorism pictures was 4.84 ($p < .01$). Respondents who saw a neutral image of a double-decker London bus ($M_{bus} = 1.70$) were significantly less fearful than those who saw the image of the London bus attacked on July 7, 2005 ($M_{explosion} = 4.91, p < .01$).

Results

The reactance hypothesis suggests that citizens whose policy predispositions are different than the president's (i.e., Democrats and liberals) would be most likely to reject an evocative terrorism story. Figure 4.1 tests this hypothesis by showing the effect of being in the treatment condition (i.e., seeing the Wave of Terror story), compared with the control condition, on respondents' threat level separately by party and ideology. Partisanship was measured with a 7-point scale that ranged from "strong Democrat" to "strong Republican." Independent leaners (i.e., those Independents who say that they are closer to the Republican or Democratic party) are combined with partisans since these Independents behave and vote like party members (Keith et al., 1992). Ideology was measured with a 3-point scale—liberal, moderate, and conservative. Threat perception was operationalized as how likely a respondent believes a terrorist attack is in the next 12 months, on a 4-point scale (scaled from 0 "very unlikely" to 1 "very likely"), measured post-treatment. The figure shows coefficients and 95 percent confidence intervals from an ordinary least

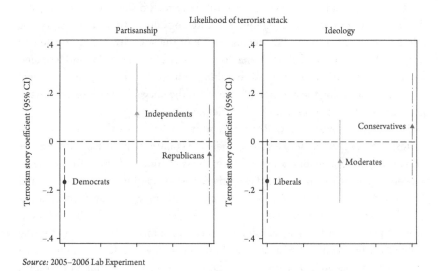

Source: 2005–2006 Lab Experiment

Figure 4.1:
Terrorism news backfires with Democrats and liberals (student sample).

squares (OLS) regression model predicting threat perception as a function of being in the terrorism condition (with no controls). The coefficients can be interpreted as the effect of being in the experimental condition on threat perception compared with the control condition. If exposure to the terrorism story made subjects believe that terrorism was more likely in the near future, the coefficients are positive; if subjects believed that terrorism was less likely, the coefficients are negative.

There are two major findings from Figure 4.1: (1) only Democrats and liberals updated their threat perception based on exposure to the terrorism story, and 2) Democrats and liberals significantly rejected the terrorism story. Contrary to expectations, the treatment condition did not significantly affect threat perception among subjects other than Democrats and liberals.

It is not the case that respondents simply found the treatment story unarousing and that is why the experimental treatments did not significantly affect Republicans' and Independents' threat perception. In a later round of experiments ($N = 48$), respondents answered questions about their emotional reactions to the news stories themselves after answering the threat question and rated the treatment condition as significantly more emotional than the control condition. Respondents evaluated each news story separately for how worried (worried, anxious, unpleasant, nervous, fearful) and angry (angry, enraged, furious, wrathful, and mad) the story made them feel on an 9-point scale from 0 (not at all) to 8 (extremely). These terms were then combined into a worried scale (Cronbach's alpha = .95) and anger scale (Cronbach's alpha = .95). Subjects reported feeling significantly more worried after watching the terrorism story than in the control condition [$M_{control}$ = 1.95 vs. $M_{treatment}$ = 3.51, $t(df = 46) = 2.59$, $p < .01$] and also reported more anger [$M_{control}$ = 1.51 vs. $M_{treatment}$ = 2.29, $t(df = 46) = 1.80$, $p < .05$]. Even Democrats became significantly more worried after watching the evocative terrorism story ($M_{control}$ = 1.20 vs. $M_{treatment}$ = 3.12, $t(df = 23) = 3.18$, $p < .01$).

Consistent with the reactance hypothesis, Democrats and liberals did react after watching the terrorism story by rating terrorism as *significantly less likely* in the treatment condition than in the control condition. Turning back to the OLS models from Figure 4.1, Democrats in the treatment condition lowered their threat perception by .17 (SE = .07) on the 0-to-1 scale, while liberals similarly lowered their threat perception by .16 (SE = .09).

As indirect evidence that Democrats did respond to the terrorism story as linked to previous persuasive messages, an open-ended question that was asked at the end of the second round of experiments ($n = 89$) is used. Respondents in the experimental conditions were asked separately what they thought the goal of the threatening Wave of Terror and the nonthreatening North Korea stories were and whether the stories succeeded in those goals. Each question had a text box for typing a response and subjects had unlimited time to answer. A total of 61 respondents answered about what they thought the goal of the Wave of Terror was, six respondents chose not to answer and 22 saw only the North Korea story. Answers ranged from saying that the story aimed to simply inform the public about the continual threat of terrorism to subjects offering more political goals such as "turning the nation against President Bush" or giving the "government an excuse to take action." Of the 61 respondents, 19 (12 Democrats, 7 Republicans) mentioned that the goal of the terrorism story was to scare/frighten the public about terrorism, which was then coded as a dummy variable indicating that the respondent mentioned "scare" as a goal. In the scary visuals condition, the correlation with threat perception and this "scare" variable is negative for Democrats ($r = -0.31, p < .25$) and positive for Republicans ($r = 0.38, p < .20$). Even though these correlations are not statistically significant at conventional levels given the small sample size, this provides one indirect indication of Democrats' reactance.

As an additional piece of evidence that the message rejection was due to perceived link between threat perception and policy solutions, the effect of exposure to the terrorism condition among respondents who disapproved of Bush's handling of terrorism prior to experimental treatment was explored. Of the 182 respondents who disapproved of Bush's terrorism policies, 19 percent were pure Independents, 7 percent were Republican leaning Independents, and 5 percent were Republicans with the remaining 69 percent made up of Democrats and Democratic leaning Independents. Assuming reactance is due to the link between threat and policy, the respondents who disapprove of the president's counterterrorism policies should also experience less threat from watching the terrorism story. Using an OLS regression to model the effect of the experimental treatment, among the respondents who disapproved of Bush's handling of terrorism prior to exposure to the terrorism story, the results show watching the "Wave of Terror" story significantly lowered their threat perception by 10 percent of the 0-to-1 scale ($b = -.10$, $SE = .06$) compared with the control condition. Together, these two pieces of evidence suggest that Democrats rejected the threatening message because they were more skeptical about the communication whereas Republicans and Independents were not motivated to discount the threatening message.

Study 2: Online Cues Experiment

The lab experiment can only provide indirect evidence of which aspects of the terrorism story Democrats reacted to. The online elite cues experiment relies on an overtly persuasive message from a hypothetical candidate to demonstrate that reactance to the news story was a function of the connection between threat and particular policy solutions. The experiment provides direct evidence that it is the pairing of an emotionally powerful terrorism image and a hawkish foreign policy message that leads Democrats and liberals to reject terrorism news. Democrats and liberals were not motivated to reject a dovish cue paired with an evocative terrorism reminder. The experiment also provides the opportunity to test the hypothesis that political knowledge moderates reactance.

Online Experiment Manipulation

In order to make more generalizable claims about how evocative news may lead to a backlash, this study relies on a nationally representative sample of adults. Study participants were recruited from a Knowledge Networks' (KN) panel of respondents who participated in online research during 2008. During the study, respondents saw a screen that was reported to come from the webpage of a Congressional candidate where subjects read the candidate's stance on foreign policy. Respondents received one foreign policy cue from a single candidate. The experiment varied two dimensions of foreign policy cues: (1) the content of foreign policy cue (hawkish vs. dovish) and (2) the emotion of the cue (negative emotion vs. neutral). After reading the candidate's statement, respondents were asked for their emotional reactions to the cue. The research was approved by the Princeton University institutional review board.

Respondents in the treatment conditions read the candidate's foreign policy statement that claimed that terrorism was a problem and offered either a hawkish or a dovish policy remedy. In the hawkish condition, respondents read a statement that came from George W. Bush's 2002 National Security Strategy that advocated foreign policy based on military strength and a willingness to use force. In the dovish condition, respondents read a statement from the 1956 Democratic national convention statement that advocated foreign policy based on cooperation with allies, diplomacy, and foreign aid.

Half of the respondents in the treatment conditions received only the foreign policy cue while the other half received the cue accompanied by an image of the WTC on fire designed to induce subjects' emotions. Visuals are more powerful tools than nonvisual stimuli in arousing emotion (Brader, 2006; Graber, 1990; Newhagen & Reeves, 1992). By separating the emotional power of the image from the information contained in the foreign policy cue, this experimental design can more precisely illustrate what aspects of television news affect perceptions of future threat.

For the study, 2218 panel respondents were contacted via email and 1400 completed the study over a week in February 2008, for a completion rate of 63.1 percent. KN sampled from a probability-based sample designed to be statistically representative of the United States. All models utilize post-stratification weights to account for nonresponse. Seventy-six percent of the sample identified as white, 9 percent as African American, 8 percent as Latino, and 7 percent as "other" or multiracial, and 18 percent of respondents come from the Northeast. Thirty-one percent of respondents held a college degree or higher, 50 percent were female, and the average age was 48 years old. Including Independent leaners as partisans, 43 percent of respondents identified as Republicans, 53 percent as Democrats, and 4 percent as Independents. In comparison, on the 2008 General Social Survey, 77 percent of respondents identified as white, 14 percent as African American, and 9 percent as "other." Thirty-three percent of respondents identified as Republicans,

49 percent as Democrats, and 8 percent as Independents. Fifty-four percent of GSS respondents were female and 29 percent had a college degree or higher.

To facilitate a comparison between the student sample and the national sample and to test the role of political sophistication in reactance, the national sample was split by whether participants had a bachelor's degree or not. Rather than use the common measure of political sophistication—answers to factual questions about politics—this study uses education as a proxy (Judd, Krosnick, & Milburn, 1981). Because subjects took the survey online, answering factual questions may reflect the ability to find the answer on the Internet as much as stored political knowledge, so the study relies on the education measure as a more reliable proxy of sophistication.

If terrorism images themselves are considered manipulative, then Democrats and liberals who receive the WTC image should be less threatened than those who do not receive the image, regardless of the content of the foreign policy cue. If out-party members react not to the frightening images themselves by to the linkage of those images to (disliked) counterterrorism policies, then exposure to the terrorism image should lead to reactance only among Democrats and liberals who also received the hawkish foreign policy cue. Respondents answered a series of questions about their reactions to the candidate statements that they read during the study. At the end of the study, respondents were asked about their reactions to the candidate's statements and answered how afraid, fearful, angry, furious, depressed, and sad they felt on a scale from 0 (did not feel this emotion at all) to 8 (felt the emotion very strongly). The dependent variable is an index of the two questions "afraid" and "fearful." This measure of emotional reaction is different than the threat perception measure used in the lab experiment. While fear and threat perception are distinct concepts, they are logically related to one another. Citizens unaffected emotionally by terrorism should not perceive a great deal of risk from terrorism. Using the emotion measures also makes for a hard test of the hypothesis since Democrats did react emotionally to the news story in the lab experiment and emotional reactions tend to occur quickly and prior to consciousness.

To further specify the root of reactance, Figure 4.2 shows the effect of exposure to the terrorism image on respondents' self-reported level of fear and worry only among Democrats and liberals, who experienced reactance in the lab study. The figure shows the OLS coefficient (and 95 percent confidence interval) for the effect of exposure to the terrorism image on respondents' level of fear. The two worried terms (afraid, fearful) were combined into a single fear index (Cronbach's alpha = .90) and fear was modeled as a function of seeing the terrorism image (1 = WTC image, 0 = no image), the type of foreign policy cue (1 = hawkish, 0 = dovish), controlling for respondents' anger and sadness. Positive coefficients indicate that seeing the terrorism image increased fear compared with seeing the same foreign policy cue without the terrorism image. Negative coefficients indicate that the terrorism image decreased fear compared with reading the same foreign policy cue without the image.

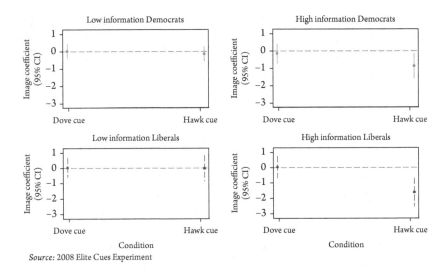

Figure 4.2:
Terrorism images decrease fear among Democrats and liberals (national sample).

Consistent with expectations, Figure 4.2 reveals that sophisticated Democrats and liberals are motivated to reject the tone and content of the persuasive cue when that cue was paired with an evocative terrorism image. The cues experiment augments the lab experiment by demonstrating that Democrats and liberals only display reactance when faced with a hawkish cue paired with the WTC image. Democrats and liberals who were aware of the tight rhetorical connection between threat and Republican counterterrorism policies were most likely to perceive manipulation and a threat to autonomy when exposed to this combination of policy cue and image. Further, the figure provides evidence for the sophistication hypothesis by showing that less knowledge Democrats, who were less aware of the link between the WTC image and hawkish foreign policy made by the Bush Administration, were unmotivated to reject the emotional tone. Low information Democrats and liberals' fear levels were similar regardless of whether they saw the terrorism image or not.

For politically sophisticated Democrats and liberals, the pairing of the iconic terrorism image and a hawkish policy message served to *decrease* their fear level. This finding is consistent with Democrats' reactance in the lab experiment, demonstrating that politically sophisticated Democrats will reject emotionally powerful messages and imagery when those messages are linked to disliked policies. Turning back to the OLS models from Figure 4.2, consider the effect of the terrorism image for sophisticated Democrats who received the hawkish cue, the coefficient farthest to the right in the figure. When the hawkish cue is paired with the terrorism image, politically knowledgeable Democrats report feeling less fearful by .87 (SE = .36) on the 0 to 8 fear scale or a decrease of 10 percent. On the bottom on Figure 4.2, liberals in the hawkish cues condition were similarly motivated to deny its emotion and content when the WTC image appeared. Liberals reported feeling less fearful by 1.62 (SE = .42) on the 0 to 8 scale or, in other words, 19 percent less fearful.

DISCUSSION

The current study utilizes two experiments to evaluate whether there is a relationship between evocative terrorism news, and partisan and ideological ties. The first experiment was conducted in 2005–2006 in a lab with a student sample and tested whether exposure to threatening terrorism news stories affects individuals' beliefs about the likelihood of future terrorism. The second experiment more directly tests whether information about the likelihood of terrorism itself causes some citizens to reject evocative news or whether the link between terrorism images and counterterrorism policies induces reactance. The second experiment suggests that political party affiliation moderated emotional reactions to images of terrorism. Politically sophisticated Democrats reported feeling *less fearful* after hearing a hawkish foreign policy message linked to a terrorism image than when they heard the same message with no image.

Exposure to news stories about terrorism in the lab experiment affected subjects in a variety of ways. Watching a terrorism story did not significantly increase Republicans' (conservatives') or Independents' (moderates') threat perception, but Democrats and liberals actively rejected the threatening tone and message of the terrorism story. If Democrats linked the threat of terrorism to disliked policies, then rejecting the threatening messages allowed them to maintain prior beliefs about the likelihood of terrorism and effective policies to prevent terrorism.

At the time of the lab experiment, threat perception was already relatively high in the American public prior to the survey, which makes affecting these perceptions with a 2½-minute television story difficult. In a January 2006 poll, 53 percent of respondents to a CBS/*New York Times* poll thought that another terrorist attack was likely in the next few months. Additionally, Republicans (conservatives) and Independents (moderates) were less likely to need the perception that terrorism was likely to support the hawkish foreign policy implied by the "Wave of Terror" story. Republican and conservative subjects already overwhelmingly supported the president's handling of the War on Terror prior to watching the terrorism story (84 percent of Republicans, 76 percent of conservatives "approve" or "strongly approved" in a pretest question), and did not need the additional emotional news story to convince them that threat was imminent. Independents and moderates were less supportive of Bush's foreign policy than their Republican counterparts (26 percent of Independents, 28 percent of moderates supported the president), but more supportive than Democrats and liberals, whose support for Bush's War on Terror was in the single digits (5 percent for Democrats, 6 percent for liberals). It may have simply taken a stronger terrorism story in order to significantly change Republicans' and Independents' threat perceptions. Yet, it is not simply that Democrats are cold-hearted or that the news story was not threatening enough to affect threat perception. Rather, Democrats interpreted the Wave of Terror story as manipulating them into supporting counterterrorism policies with which they disagreed, and therefore resisted the major message of the news story that future terrorism was likely. Democrats and liberals fundamentally rejected the major theme of the "Wave of Terror" story—that future terrorism was likely and imminent— because they *understood the terrorism story in persuasive, partisan terms* rather than simply a news story with no persuasive agenda.

The results from the online cues experiment imply that political identities significantly structure the acceptance of threatening information and cues, and that politically sophisticated partisans and ideologues are unlikely to simply accept threatening news without evaluating it. Perceiving more threat from terrorism and worrying about that threat increases support for hawkish foreign policy (Gadarian, 2010). By rejecting the fear-inducing message, high information Democrats and liberals could maintain their more dovish foreign policy views. In the online experiment, respondents answered a question on how the United States should generally pursue foreign policy after exposure to the experimental cue. On average, exposure to the terrorism image decreased Democrats' fear by 10 percent when it was paired with the hawkish cue. Calculating the effect of this 10 percent decrease on 7 point scale where respondents answered whether diplomacy or the military was the best way for the United States to conduct foreign policy, shows that Democrats' fear did not significantly alter Democrats' foreign policy views. By denying their fear of terrorism, Democrats could remain consistent with their prior beliefs about effective counterterrorism policy even despite exposure to persuasive policy arguments counter to these views. When emotional images and news also have political meaning, citizens may refuse to accept the emotional tone when doing so would necessitate updating political attitudes.

CONCLUSION

Through two experiments, this chapter demonstrates that citizens' threat perceptions are structured not only by what they see on television but how their partisan and ideological identities tell them to interpret that information. Across the experiments, the effects of both the terrorism news story as well as the terrorism image were limited to Democrats and liberals. Consistent with the expectations of reactance, Democrats and liberals perceived the terrorism communication as threatening their autonomy to form their political attitudes, and thus, they were motivated to reject the content and emotional tone of both a news story and persuasive campaign appeal. Conversely, Republicans and conservatives were not motivated to reject threatening messages because they were likely to support those policies linked to threatening news messages and images. This also meant that there was simply less room to affect the perceptions of Republicans and Independents, who in this political context, believed terrorism to be likely and supported Republican antiterrorism policies.

By demonstrating that reactance can occur in political communications that are not persuasive on their face in a politicized policy area, this chapter contributes to the reactance literature. There were no quotes from political elites or the president in the threatening terrorism story and only one still image of the president in the nonthreatening North Korea story. Contrary to the concerns that television may manipulate the public into supporting policies they would not otherwise, watching threatening media stories led sophisticated subjects to rely *more* rather than less on their partisan and ideological predispositions. This evidence suggests that subjects interpreted the threatening images as cues and signals of policies to fight terrorism rather than as representations of the threat of terrorism. For those concerned about the power of television news or elites to manipulate the public using emotional rhetoric and imagery, these findings should provide some relief (Fischhoff et al., 2003). Politicians who invoke terrorism in order to promote policies run the risk of appearing manipulative to members of the opposing party.

This chapter also contributes to the literature on threat and political communication by demonstrating that in a polarized political context, news messages intended to identify risks may be met by skepticism and reactance. The experiments demonstrate that messages do not need to originate from political leaders themselves to be seen as advocating policy positions. Using both real news stories and an experiment with a hypothetical candidate, this chapter demonstrates that while news stories may influence citizens' emotions, citizens are not all equally persuaded that threat is imminent. Politically sophisticated Democrats and liberals adjusted their perceptions and emotions in the opposite way intended by both the terrorism news story and the hawkish elite cue because they considered the communication as limiting their freedom and pushing them toward policies with which they disagreed. Democrats who saw the WTC image paired with a dovish policy cue did not become significantly more fearful than those who received the dovish cue with no image, but they were not motivated to reject the message totally.

In the days and months after 9/11, the concern about elite and media coercion of the public might have been justified, but a decade after the terrorist attacks, at least some of the most fear inspiring kinds of media are neutralized by partisan and ideological identification. It is not at all clear, though, that the influence of partisanship and ideology on threat perception is in itself normatively positive. Political elites and the mass media need to communicate about risks to public safety and public health, and these findings suggest that it may be difficult to effectively do so when threats are linked closely with a particular set of partisan policy options. Open questions remain about when the public may be persuaded by elite or media communications about risk. These questions include (1) Would liberals and Democrats be just as skeptical of threatening messages from Barack Obama? (2) If liberals do accept a threatening messages from Democratic leaders but not Republican leaders, are the messages themselves somehow less coercive? (3) Might partisanship fade in the event of another terrorist attack on U.S. soil that provided new frightening imagery? (4) Would sophisticated Republicans react the same way as sophisticated Democrats to images that they associate with polices they do not support? In a polarized political context, when elites and the mass media need to inform the public of legitimate, imminent risks, this chapter implies that the perceptual screen of partisanship will challenge both journalists' and elites' ability to communicate effectively with the mass public and motivate citizens to accept risk information.

REFERENCES

Arceneaux, K., Johnson, M., & Murphy, C. (2012). Polarized political communication, oppositional media hostility, and selective exposure. *Journal of Politics, 74*(1), 174–186.

Baum, M., & Gussin, P. (2008). In the eye of the beholder: How information shortcuts shape individual perceptions of bias in the media. *Quarterly Journal of Political Science, 1*(1–31).

Bennett, W. L., Lawrence, R. G., & Livingston, S. (2007). *When the press fails: Political power and the news media from Iraq to Katrina.* Chicago, IL: University of Chicago Press.

Berinsky, A. (2009). *In time of war: Understanding American public opinion from World War II to Iraq.* Chicago: The University of Chicago Press.

Boydstun, A., & Glazier, R. (2012). The president, the press, and the war: A tale of two framing agendas. *Political Communication, 29*(4), 428–446.

Brader, T. (2006). *Campaigning for hearts and minds: How emotional appeals in political ads work.* Chicago, IL: University of Chicago Press.

Brehm, J. W. (1966). *A theory of psychological reactance.* New York, NY: Academic Press.

Brehm, S., & Brehm, J. W. (1981). *Psychological reactance: A theory of freedom and control.* New York, NY: Academic Press.

Bushman, B. (1998). Effects of warning and information labels on consumption of full-fat, reduced-fat and no-fat products. *Journal of Applied Psychology, 83*, 97–101.

Davis, D. W. (2007). *Negative liberty: Public opinion and the terrorist attacks on America.* New York, NY: Russell Sage Foundation.

Dillard, J. P., & Shen, L. (2005). On the nature of reactance and its role in persuasive health communication. *Communication Monographs, 72*, 144–168.

Entman, R. M. (2003). Cascading activation: Contesting the White House's frame after 9/11. *Political Communication, 20*, 415–432.

Farhi, P. (2004, March 5). Bush ads using 9/11 images stir anger, *The Washington Post*, p. A1.

Festinger, L. (1957). *A theory of cognitive dissonance.* Evanston, IL: Row, Peterson and Co.

Fischhoff, B., Gonzalez, R. M., Small, D. A., & Lerner, J. S. (2003). Judged terror risk and proximity to the World Trade Center. *Journal of Risk and Uncertainty, 26*(2/3), 137–151.

Gadarian, S. K. (2010). The politics of threat: How terrorism news shapes foreign policy attitudes. *Journal of Politics, 72*(2), 1–15.

Gershkoff, A., & Kushner, S. (2005). Shaping public opinion: The 9/11-Iraq connection in the Bush administration's rhetoric. *Perspectives on Politics, 3*(3), 525–538.

Graber, D. (1990). Seeing is remembering: How visuals contribute to learning from television news. *Journal of Communication, 40*(3), 134–155.

Hamilton, L. (2010). Education, politics, opinions about climate change: evidence for interaction effects. *Climatic Change, 104*(2), 4–12.

Huddy, L., Feldman, S., Taber, C., & Lahav, G. (2005). Threat, anxiety, and support of antiterrorism policies. *American Journal of Political Science, 49*(3), 593–608.

Jacobson, G. (2010). Perception, memory, and partisan polarization on the Iraq War. *Political Science Quarterly, 125,* 31–56.

Judd, C., Krosnick, J., & Milburn, M. (1981). Political involvement and attitude structure in the general public. *American Sociological Review, 46*(5), 660–669.

Keith, B., Magleby, D., Nelson, C., Orr, E., Westlye, M., & Wolfinger, R. (1992). *The Myth of the Independent Voter.* Berkeley, CA: University of California Press.

Kunda, Z. (1987). Motivated Inference: Self-serving generation and evaluation of causal theories. *Journal of Personality and Social Psychology, 53*(4), 636–647.

Lord, C., Ross, L., & Lepper, M. (1979). Biased assimilation and attitude polarization: The effects of prior theories on subsequent considered evidence. *Journal of Personality and Social Psychology, 37,* 2098–2109.

MacGregor, D. G., Slovic, P., & Morgan, M. G. (1994). Perception of risks from electromagnetic fields: A psychometric evaluation of a risk-communication approach. *Risk Analysis 14*(5), 815–828.

Merolla, J., & Zechmeister, E. (2009). *Democracy at risk: How terrorist threats affect the public.* Chicago, IL: University of Chicago Press.

Nacos, B. L., Bloch-Elkon, Y., & Shapiro, R. (2007). Post-9/11 terrorism threats, news coverage, and public perceptions in the United States. *International Journal of Conflict and Violence, 1*(2), 105–126.

Newhagen, J. E., & Reeves, R. (1992). The evening's bad news: Effects of compelling negative television images on memory. *Journal of Communication, 42*(2), 25–41.

Nyhan, B., & Reifler, J. (2010). When corrections fail: The persistence of political misperceptions. *Political Behavior, 32,* 303–330.

Quick, B., & Stephenson, M. (2008). Examining the role of trait reactance and sensation seeking on perceived threat, state reactance, and reactance restoration. *Human Communication Research, 34,* 448–476.

Rodriguez, L., & Lee, S. (2010). Factors affecting the amplification or attenuation of dread about bioterrorism attacks. *Homeland Security, 6.* Retrieved from http://www.hsaj.org/?article=6.1.7

Schlenger, W. E., Caddell, J. M., Ebert, L., Jordan, B. K., Rourke, K. M., Wilson, D., ... Kulka, R. A. (2002). Psychological reactions to terrorist attacks: Findings from the national study of Americans' reactions to September 11. *JAMA: The Journal of the American Medical Association, 288*(5), 581–588.

Sears, D. (1986). College sophomores in the laboratory: Influence of a narrow data base on Social Psychology's view of human nature. *Journal of Personality and Social Psychology, 51,* 515–530.

Taber, C., & Lodge, M. (2006). Motivated skepticism in the evaluation of political beliefs. *American Journal of Political Science, 50*(3), 755–769.

The American National Election Studies. (2004). The ANES 2004 Time Series Study.

Vallone, R. P., Ross, L., & Lepper, M. R. (1985). The hostile media phenomenon: Biased perception and perceptions of media bias in coverage of the Beirut massacre. *Journal of Personality and Social Psychology, 49*(3), 577–585.

Willer, R. (2004). The effects of government-issued terror warnings on presidential approval ratings. *Current Research in Social Psychology, 10,* 1–12.

Zaller, J. (1992). *The nature and origin of public opinion.* New York, NY: Cambridge University Press.

CHAPTER 5

The War/Crime Narrative and Fear Content in Leader Rhetoric About Terrorism

KRISTA DE CASTELLA AND CRAIG MCGARTY

The rhetoric used by the leaders of Western democracies about terrorism has attracted considerable attention in political commentary and political science in recent times. A great deal of that attention has been focused on the leaders of the English-speaking Western democracies that have been embroiled in wars in Afghanistan and Iraq for the last decade. The implicit (sometimes explicit) understanding of political rhetoric is that it is designed to advance a leader's political agenda. That is, by framing arguments in particular ways political leaders are seeking to convince audiences to support their political program (e.g., by voting for candidates endorsed by the leader at the next election, endorsing the policies advocated by that leader in opinion polls or other forms of political action).

There has, of course, been a trenchant critique of the approach taken by recent Western leaders in the War on Terror. We will address this in more detail below but the core of this critique is that the rhetorical strategies adopted by Western leaders are duplicitous and even undemocratic (Lawrence, 2006). The leaders are presented as fear mongers (Altheide, 2003; Jackson, 2005; Lawrence, 2006), and, following Hermann and Chomsky (1988), popular consent for their programs is said to be manufactured.

In order to understand the rhetoric of the leaders and the criticism of that rhetoric, we think it is helpful to take a step back to consider the very specific military and political problem that terrorism presents to Western leaders in the 21st century. Terrorist attacks against civilian targets are invariably undertaken by groups with complex motives and agendas for change, but very limited means to bring about a change. Terrorism is a tactic used by groups with minimal military power. The attacks on September 11, 2001, in the United States were appalling, and had massive human and political consequences, but compared with attacks by state actors using military methods and technologies to kill civilians, the most devastating attacks ever carried out by terrorists are relatively small in scale. As Jackson (2005) observed, the loss of life in the Rwandan Genocide of 1994 can be compared with the World Trade Center attacks happening several times a day every day for 100 days. Nevertheless, terrorist attacks take on a broad significance precisely because such attacks are communicative actions that are intended to have consequences far beyond those directly affected.

The motives of the attackers can also be incredibly complex. Thousands of pages have been devoted to analysing the political objectives of Al Qaeda for carrying out the 9/11 attacks. There can be little doubt that the attacks were intended to influence American political opinion, but the intended effect of that influence is less clear. It has been argued that the real political target of the attacks was not America but the governments of Middle Eastern countries that were seen to be its clients (Bergen, 2006). In this view, the purpose of the attacks was not to frighten the American people, but to make them so angry that the United States would attack countries such as Afghanistan and thereby unite Islamic opinion against America (Doran, 2005).

One byproduct of international terrorism is that the targets of the attacks are likely to be poorly informed and very confused. The weak might hate the strong, but we do not expect the weak to attack the strong. Given the surprising, disturbing, and intensely public nature of terrorist acts, terrorism is something that governments need to explain to their populations. This is why leader rhetoric about terrorism is of particular importance. In order to address domestic uncertainty, governments must explain why the attacks took place and how the attacks were possible, as well as what they are doing to make sure they do not happen again.

When facing a threat to civil order that is attributed to the deliberate action of other people, political leaders can draw on two broad narratives identified by Jackson (2005). They can talk about the threat as an act of war or they can talk about it as a crime. The war narrative is epitomized by the rhetoric of British Prime Minister Winston Churchill during World War II (Valiunas, 2002). The war narrative involves stating the justice of the cause, it calls for unity and points to eventual victory so long as we banish fear, calling instead for righteous anger and sacrifice (Valiunas, 2002). Another way to talk about terrorism is as a crime. The hallmarks of the crime narrative are the rights of citizens as a moral community to be safe and the need to bring immoral wrongdoers to justice (Surette, 2010). Citizens are asked to recognise the dangers, to provide information and political support for the campaign against crime, but they are not expected to enlist in the cause of tracking down the wrongdoers or to risk their lives.

At first glance, the war narrative would seem to be the obvious choice for a leader whose country is attacked by terrorists. Surprisingly though, the consistent allegation by critics of Western political leadership has been that they have been engaged in a campaign of fear—mongering (Altheide, 2003; Jackson, 2005; Lawrence, 2006). In other words, critics have claimed that the political aspects of the War on Terror have been prosecuted by frightening the populations who are the victims of attacks. This is an extraordinary claim. Surely it is the role of terrorists to frighten civilians and for governments to protect their citizens? Do not those same governments reduce their chance of winning the conflict by frightening their own side?

Intriguingly, fear campaigns seem better suited to the crime narrative. Yet the War on Terror has been prosecuted by military methods that have led to the deaths of thousands of people. Indeed, the number of U.S. military personnel who have (at the time of writing) died in Afghanistan is very similar to the number of U.S. civilians killed on September 11, 2001. In effect, military methods are being used to conduct operations in response to alleged criminal activities by states or quasi-state actors (i.e., harboring terrorists and their facilities in the case of Afghanistan and concealing weapons of mass destruction that could be used by terrorists in the case of Iraq). We argue that in such cases neither the war nor the crime narrative completely fits the political agenda. Unlike total wars, where sacrifice is demanded from the populace through active participation and support for conscription, in the wars in Afghanistan and Iraq the public was asked to consent to military campaigns conducted largely by professional volunteers. These military personnel performed the social role of police officers and civilian agencies (targeting specific threats and preventing criminal acts against U.S. citizens) but used methods and technologies that are completely inappropriate for conventional police operations.

Thus, we contend that the structural conditions of terrorism (a weak opponent with complex motives, a confused population and the ready availability of seemingly overwhelming military responses) set the scene for the adoption of a blended War/Crime narrative that draws on aspects of both narrative styles. In this way it was possible for leaders to advocate specific military methods without eschewing fear, and it is even possible for fear to become a desirable political commodity. We next consider the elements chosen from each core narrative and the evidence for this content in political rhetoric.

ELEMENTS OF THE WAR NARRATIVE

A common theme drawn from the War narrative is the bipolar representation of "us" and "them," and the portrayal of the "evil other" with language that is simplistic, dichotomous and reductionistic. Discursive bipolarity is apparent in war and crime rhetoric throughout history (Lazar & Lazar, 2004; Phil, Keenan, & Dowd, 2004) and in the rhetoric of leaders on both sides of the conflict (Leudar et al., 2004). Pinter (2005) suggested that this primitive and easily packaged narrative style works to intentionally keep thought at bay. Statements such as "you're either with us or with the terrorists" mute criticism and dissent as "only the evil and the perverted" would seek to justify terrorist acts (Howard, 2002). The logic of binarism further encourages an ethical stance on counterterrorism where the "end justifies the means." It legitimises acts undertaken in the name of good; irrespective of the destruction they may cause and promotes support for draconian, militarist, antiterrorism responses (Kellner, 2004).

A second theme in the *War* on terror narrative is the depiction of terrorists as motivated chiefly by a hatred of the (in this case, Western) values of the target group. This is a powerful technique for enlisting public support, as few would willingly side with people who are portrayed as bent on the destruction of their society. This strategy also makes it extremely difficult to deny the legitimacy of the war, or argue against the necessity or effectiveness of overall counterterrorism measures (Jackson, 2005). Carefully used euphemisms preemptively mute criticism and debate even before such criticisms take place. For example, the term "enemies of freedom," used early in the discourse after 9/11, works to preempt the common observation that "one man's terrorist is another man's freedom fighter" (Jackson, 2005). The "War on Terror" is thus presented as a battle between good and evil; between freedom and tyranny. Kellner (2004) argues that euphemisms in terrorism discourse are so contradictory they contain almost Orwellian features of Doublespeak:

> War against Iraq is for peace, the occupation of Iraq is it's liberation, destroying it's food and water supplies enables humanitarian action, and the murder of countless Iraqis and destruction of the country will produce freedom and democracy (Kellner, 2004, p. 54).

A third common theme relates to information "security," secrecy, and opacity. By drawing on the national security imperative the War on Terror emphasises the need for high levels of secrecy. Where information, strategies, and opinions are publicly presented by leaders, they tend to be sourced to intelligence and other government agencies and thereby imbued with credibility and authority. The secrecy of terrorism "intelligence" is also provided as justification for large omissions in official government discourse and debate. The ability to critically examine claims about terrorism and terrorist threats in the public sphere is therefore limited, restricting thinking around counterterrorism issues while at the same time promoting unity and trust in government (Jackson, 2005). Pallitto and Weaver (2007) argue that, in the name of national security, leaders are increasingly able to claim authority to act unilaterally and secretly, even when their actions may be constitutionally questionable or in violation of criminal law.

In the name of "security," the War narrative invokes widespread acceptance of military spending and other risk-reduction strategies. For example, Braithwaite (2005) pointed out that in 2002, the increase in the United States spending on the war on terrorism was greater than the combined expenditure of all the world's countries on foreign aid. The need for increased security is also used to justify the sacrifice of individual freedoms and human rights (Dinh, 2004). Concessions are called for "at home" with increasing infringements on information privacy and moves toward pervasive surveillance:

> As the criminal justice system turns from a reactive to a proactive approach—from deterrent penalties meted out for past crimes toward preventing attacks before they occur—informational privacy is bound to suffer. Every weapon in the counterterrorism arsenal—searches, detention, interrogations, informants, electronic surveillance, visual surveillance, analysis of bank records and telephone records—increases what is known by the authorities (Dripps, 2003, p. 18).

Even greater sacrifices are demanded from those abroad. Terrorism suspects, for example, may need to be treated in ways that breach international criminal and human rights law. Suspects may be incarcerated indefinitely in detention and subject to harsh interrogation techniques or even torture without the opportunity for judicial oversight or review (Flyghed, 2005). According to Altheide (2003, p. 38), in times of war, "compromises with individual liberty and even perspectives about 'rights', the limits of law, and ethics must be 'qualified' and held in abeyance in view of the threat." All of these strategies mean that the War narrative authorises extreme responses to crimes. The pursuit of criminals is normally directed at their capture, trial and (perhaps) their rehabilitation. In war, the goal of pursuing combatants need only be their elimination (Feldman, 2004). Troublesome intervening steps such as arrests, trials, sentences and appeals are also dispensed.

Finally, the War narrative can be an attractive rhetorical tool for advancing a political or foreign policy agenda. Glassner (1999) argues that fear of terrorism—unlike other fears such as being without health care or employment—is ambiguous, opaque, and immune to policy failure. Any terrorist attack can be constructed as another reason to commit greater resources to manage the "new" and "unpredictable" threat rather than a failure of government policy in the first place. For example:

> "The final thing I want to say is that this country has never been immune from a possible terrorist attack. That remains the situation today and it will be the situation tomorrow. It's important that we continue to mobilise all of the resources of the Commonwealth and the States to fight terrorism" (Australian Prime Minister John Howard, 2005)

In this way, invoking the war narrative encourages citizens to accept unrestricted government powers in exchange for reassurance, and promises of increased (if never complete) protection from terrorist attacks.

ELEMENTS OF THE CRIME NARRATIVE

As noted above, although called a "War" on terror, leader rhetoric about terrorism also draws heavily upon the crime narrative. Terrorism is presented as a symbolic crime (Surette, 2010), focusing on a crisis created by the harmful actions of people who live outside the moral community. Reference to "victims," "acts of murder," the "search for criminals," and the need to "bring to justice" those responsible all invoke the crime narrative (Hodges, 2011, p. 27). Crimes are presented as a challenge to public safety and one's traditional way of life. Yet rather than focusing on sacrifice and participation from the public, the crime narrative calls for citizens to be "on alert." Past crimes and potential threats are also presented as evidence of existing risks and as arguments for changes to criminal justice policy:

> [Symbolic crimes] are taken up by claim makers and forwarded as either "the types of crimes we can expect to happen more often because we have allowed a set of conditions to fester" or as "an example of what a new criminal justice policy will correct if we implement it" (Surette, 2010, p. 42).

In this way, the Crime narrative offers fear as a tool of coercion that promises citizens increased protection only if they consent to the policy changes and measures advocated by their leader.

From the Crime narrative then, comes the depiction of a "dangerous new era"—a narrative strategy allegedly used in the War on Terror to promote and exploit popular fears for narrow political gain (Glassner, 2004). Reference to this new era emerges as a common theme in Western political rhetoric about terrorism:

1. We've entered a new world and a dangerous new war ... For the sake of our security, Congress will need to act and update our laws to meet the threats of this new era (Bush, 2006a).
2. We are in mortal danger of mistaking the nature of the new world in which we live ... The threat we face is not conventional. It is a challenge of a different nature from anything the world has faced before. It is to the world's security, what globalisation is to the world's economy ... (Blair, 2004).
3. I have to say to all of your listeners, to our fellow Australians, that we are living in different world. It's nasty, it's unwelcome, it's more dangerous ... But we have to confront it (Howard, 2002).

Rothe and Muzzatti (2004, p. 327) argue, "While the events of September 11, 2001 were indeed tragic, the construction of a moral panic by the media and politicians to support their interests is a greater social tragedy." They are not the only critics to make such claims. Others argue that fear campaigns have been launched to distract the public from unsavoury public policy (Mueller, 2004; Prewitt et al., 2004); mute criticism and dissent (Furedi, 1997; Krebs & Lobasz, 2007); win elections (Oates, 2006) and promote support for counterterrorism and programmes that increase the coercive powers of the state (Furedi, 1997; Glassner, 2004; Sunstein, 2004).

In addition to benefiting from public fears, Jackson (2005) has argued that the dangerous "new age" theme offers a number of strategic benefits. First, framing 9/11 as the beginning of a "new age" absolves government officials from responsibility in the occurrence of future terrorist attacks as they cannot be held accountable for failing to anticipate threats that are by nature unprecedented and unpredictable. Second, the "new age" narrative entitles governments to even greater political powers as existing laws may be amended and human rights limited to meet "new" and unconventional threats. Third, the "new age" theme also capitalises on a sense of urgency, promoting fear of dissent, disunity and inaction. As Howard (2004) noted:

> All of us, whatever our views may originally have been about Iraq, have to stand together because if we react in a way that encourages more hostages to be taken, and those taken to be murdered, well we can be certain that is exactly what will happen... This is not the time in the history of the world for disunity amongst friends.

This strategy cleverly circumvents any discussion of nonmilitary solutions to the problem of terrorism and warns against openly challenging the government's counter terrorism policies. Interestingly, these appeals often emerge as statements that both relieve and invoke anxiety at the same time. The public is assured that measures are being taken to make them safer, while at the same time warned terrorists could strike at any moment:

> ... we are taking additional precautions. But you can never give an absolute guarantee that all the precautions you take are going to be successful. (Howard, 2001).

Jackson (2005) suggests that these discursive devices create an artificial dependency on the government. The public is grateful to the government for easing their fears, even if they play a role in engendering these fears in the first place.

THE EVIDENCE FOR FEAR APPEALS

Most research on the politics of fear using the War on Terror narrative has involved political commentary and historical analyses of leadership styles and behaviours (see Furedi, 1997; Glassner, 1999; Heldring, 2004; Hooks & Mosher, 2005; Jackson, 2005; Maser, 2004; Padgett & Allen, 2003; Spence, 2005; Stern, 2000). Discourse and content analytic approaches have also been used to examine key political speeches (de Beaugrande, 2004; Graham, Keenan, & Dowd, 2004) involving membership categorisation (Leudar, Marsland, & Nekvapil, 2004), political rhetoric and media coverage (Bligh, Kohles & Meindl, 2004), and the construction of the enemy image (Merskin, 2004). These approaches are rarely used however, to systematically examine *how* fear appeals are constructed or the extent to which such content is actually present in a politician's rhetoric. Furthermore, allegations of political fear mongering have been explicitly disavowed by the leaders accused of these tactics. Krebs and Jackson (2007) argue that proof of fear mongering requires knowledge of a speaker's "real motives" and the ability to distinguish these sincere beliefs from those adopted for strategic purposes. While it therefore is unlikely that researchers will be able to overcome the methodological hurdles necessary to prove emotional manipulation, the explicit content of political communication is accessible and it is possible to explore whether this content is, at least, consistent with such claims.

In our recent work in this area (De Castella & McGarty, 2011; De Castella, McGarty, & Musgrove, 2009), we used an appraisal theory–based content analytic approach to systematically examine emotional appeals in the political rhetoric of three former Western leaders in the War on Terror: former U.S. President, George W. Bush, former British Prime Minister, Tony Blair, and former Australian Prime Minister, John Howard. Speeches were sourced from official government websites and, for all three speakers, we sought to obtain a comprehensive sample of television and radio addresses to the nation on the topic of terrorism within specific date parameters (September 11, 2001, and May 1, 2003, the declared end of major combat operations in Iraq). Press conferences, written statements, press releases, media remarks and conference speeches were excluded, as were speeches that were less than 400 words in length. Where speeches contained sections greater than 500 words that did not relate to the themes of terrorism, these sections were also omitted from coding that the total word count of coded material was reduced accordingly.

According to appraisal theory, fear is elicited by a combination of discrete emotion-eliciting cognitive appraisals (Lazarus, 1991a, 1991b; Smith & Lazarus, 1990, 1993). These include the belief that a situation is (1) personally relevant, (2) potentially harmful, and (3) threatening, as well as the belief that one (4) has uncertain or insufficient ability to cope with the present threat. While appraisal theory has been used previously in research on emotional appeals, causal attributions, and risk assessment (Lerner & Keltner, 2000; Small, Lerner, & Fischhoff, 2006), little work has applied this model to assess emotional content in political rhetoric. Using appraisal theory, we coded key terrorism speeches over time for the presence of statements that contained all four appraisal elements. Examples of statements that met the criteria for fear appraisal include the following:

1. The danger to our country is grave and it is growing... The attacks of September the 11th showed our country that vast oceans no longer protect us from danger (Bush, September 28, 2002).
2. We know that if not stopped, the terrorists will do it again, this time possibly in Britain (Blair, October 8, 2001).
3. We are living in a different world. We're living in a world that is more challenging. We're living in a world where the possibility of a terrorist attack on our own soil is more likely that it would have been a year ago or even six months ago ... (Howard, March 13, 2003).

To establish intercoder reliability, two additional coders independently coded a selection of 20 statements and were required to indicate which if any appraisal elements were present by ticking the appropriate combination of boxes. These included five options: core relational themes, motivational incongruence, motivational relevance, uncertain coping, and no content. A correct answer was recorded when coders ticked the same boxes as the researcher and when they left the same boxes unchecked. In total the 20 statements provided a score out of 20 for each appraisal element with a total set of 120 right or wrong responses. Intercoder reliability for the different speakers ranged from 84 to 92 percent.

The percentage of each speech containing fear content was calculated by dividing the number of statements meeting the criteria for fear appraisal by the total number of sentences in each speech (see De Castella et al., 2009, 2011, for more information on methods and results). Results revealed that fear inducing content was not a constant feature of terrorism rhetoric but was, in fact, highly variable both across speakers and over time (see Figure 5.1). In the rhetoric of all three speakers, fear content was significantly higher in the pre–Iraq war period with a near complete absence of fear-content before this time. Both periods of major combat operations in Afghanistan and Iraq were similarly characterised by comparatively lower levels of fear appraisal content—accounting for less that 10 percent of coded material.

An analysis of U.S. public opinion polls (CNN/*USA Today*/Gallup Polls) found little evidence of a link between fear rhetoric used by President Bush and public fear of terrorism. These results might suggest that if there was a fear campaign it was unsuccessful (at least in generating fear). This is consistent with recent research by Back, K üfner, and Egloff (2010), who found that, while many people experienced heightened anxiety at the time of major attacks, they recovered quickly with anxiety returning to baseline levels. Our analysis of U.S. presidential approval ratings revealed that fear content in Bush's speeches was however, more prevalent during periods of declining support for the administration and their counter terrorism policies. This was most clearly seen in the lead-up to the War on Iraq and lends some support to claims that fear may be employed with the aim of bolstering support for political leaders and their policy agenda at times of heightened political uncertainty, conflict, and declining support for the government and their campaigns (Altheide, 2003; Jackson, 2005; Pyszczynski, 2004; Robin, 2004; Rothe & Muzzatti, 2004; Sunstein, 2004).

The correlated pattern of fear appeals across speakers is also indicative of a general trend in the "War on Terror" rhetoric. Political leaders are deliberate actors and select their words strategically to make the most convincing case for their policy agenda at certain times. It is also important to recognise that the content of Bush, Blair, and Howard's speeches is not independent of each other. This is partly because they were talking about the same events and were working in concert. Because the speeches were public they were also readily available to other speakers and their speechwriters. The content and styling of a speech by one leader may thus

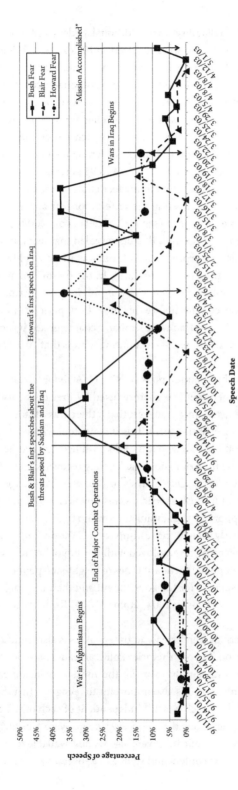

Figure 5.1:
Proportion of fear appraisal content in Howard, Bush, and Blair's political speeches about terrorism

be echoed in the speech of another. Pfiffner (2007) argues that there is also evidence to indicate that, by April 2002, George Bush and Tony Blair had agreed that there needed "to be a political plan in place to convince public and world opinion that war [against Iraq] was necessary" (p. 215). Rhetorical appeals to fear in this rhetoric would, therefore, be consistent with such a plan but are not proof of its existence.

SPEECHES BY BUSH, BLAIR, AND BIN LADEN

To explore the different rhetorical styles of leaders on both sides of the War on Terror, and how their communication may have changed over time, we conducted a textual analysis of six speeches by George Bush, Tony Blair, and Osama bin Laden (for a textual analysis of speeches by Australian Prime Minister John Howard, see De Castella et al., 2009). We were particularly interested in contrasting early public addresses on terrorism in 2001 with later speeches in 2006, well after the official end of the War on Iraq.

GEORGE W. BUSH: SPEECH NO. 1

Bush's address to the nation on September 11 was his first public address on the topic of terrorism. In this speech, he publicly condemns the attacks on the United States, and expresses his resolve to "bring to justice" those responsible. The speech is very short (594 words) and is characterised by the use of metaphors as well as motivational and patriotic appeals to unity and strength. There is little effort to describe the "terrorists" who are simply referred to as "those behind" these attacks and only one statement was consistent with fear appraisal: "Our first priority is to . . . take every precaution to protect our citizens at home and around the world from further attacks." Thus, in this early speech the typical characteristics of fear appeals were not present in Bush's rhetoric.

GEORGE W. BUSH: SPEECH NO. 2

The first speech by Bush to display a marked increase in fear-appraisal content was his address to the nation on October 7, 2002. Bush explains in his opening address that he hopes "to take a few minutes to discuss a grave threat to peace" namely, the threat posed by weapons of mass destruction, and "America's determination to lead the world in confronting that threat." In this speech Bush argues for the invasion of Iraq. The speech is a total of 3352 words and it contains a total of 44 statements (22 percent) that meet the criteria for fear appraisal. Fear content emerges in statements that caution listeners about the dangers posed by "massive stockpiles" of biological, chemical and nuclear weapons "capable of killing millions." For example, quotes from Bush's October 7 speech include:

1. The attacks of September the 11th showed our country that vast oceans no longer protect us from danger ... Today in Iraq, we see a threat whose outlines are far more clearly defined, and whose consequences could be far more deadly ...
2. Iraq could decide on any given day to provide a biological or chemical weapon to a terrorist group or individual terrorists. Alliance with terrorists could allow the Iraqi regime to attack America without leaving any fingerprints.

Fear appeals also arise as warnings against dissent, indecision, and inaction:

3. Facing clear evidence of peril, we cannot wait for the final proof—the smoking gun—that could come in the form of a mushroom cloud ... we have every reason to assume the worst, and we have an urgent duty to prevent the worst from occurring.
4. Failure to act would embolden other tyrants, allow terrorists access to new weapons and new resources, and make blackmail a permanent feature of world events.

GEORGE W. BUSH: SPEECH NO. 3

In Bush's commemoration speech on September 11, 2006 (Bush, 2006b), he reiterates his condemnation of the attacks 5 years earlier. He goes on to summarise all that has been accomplished in this time and encourages renewed effort and determination in the War on Terror. The speech is 2623 words in length and 13.9 percent of the content in this speech meets the criteria for fear appraisal. These statements emerge as overt or implied warnings of the risks still facing America and the "nature of the threat before us." Bush reminds his audience that "today, we are safer, but we are not yet safe":

1. We saw what a handful of our enemies can do with box-cutters and plane tickets. We hear their threats to launch even more terrible attacks on our people. And we know that if they were able to get their hands on weapons of mass destruction, they would use them against us. We face an enemy determined to bring death and suffering into our homes.

Fear content also emerges in statements cautioning against inaction, disunity and dissent:

2. On September the 11th we learned that America must confront threats before they reach our shores ..

3. The worst mistake would be to think that if we pulled out, the terrorists would leave us alone. They will not leave us alone. They will follow us. The safety of America depends on the outcome of the battle in the streets of Baghdad ... If we yield to men like bin Laden, our enemies will be emboldened; they will gain a new safe haven; they will use Iraq's resources to fuel their extremist movement ...

In contrast to Bush's 2001 speeches, in these later speeches fear content is more prevalent and the "evil enemy" is more clearly defined. Bush makes direct attributions about terrorists and their motives and the presence of statements promoting uncertain coping emerge in arguments warning against dissent, inaction, or withdrawal from Iraq. Hart and Childers (2005) argue that while he had been tentative during the 2000 election campaign, by 2004 Bush had found an important narrative to tell about terrorism and a forceful way of telling it.

OSAMA BIN LADEN'S SPEECHES

We next sought to contrast Bush's later speeches on terrorism with a speech delivered by Osama bin Laden (2006). Sections of this audio address were aired on Al-Jazeera and the entire speech was published on the Al-Jazeera web site. The *Associated Press* translated the text into English from Arabic. Unlike other speeches by Bin Laden this speech was addressed to a Western audience and was titled "Message to the Americans." The speech is 1509 words in length and bin Laden begins by stating, "My message to you is about the wars in Iraq and Afghanistan and the ways to end them." He continues:

1. I plan to speak about the repeated errors your President Bush has committed in comments on the results of your polls that show an overwhelming majority of you want the withdrawal of American troops from Iraq ...

Fear appeals are more clearly present occupying approximately 10 percent of coded content. Appraisal elements emerge in statements intended to threaten and discourage American support for the Bush Administration:

2. The war in Iraq is raging with no let-up, and operations in Afghanistan are escalating in our favour, thank God, and Pentagon figures show the number of your dead and wounded is increasing not to mention the massive material losses, the destruction of the soldiers' morale there and the rise in cases of suicide among them.
3. We are people who do not stand for injustice and we will seek revenge all our lives. The nights and days will not pass without us taking vengeance like on Sept. 11, God permitting. Your minds will be troubled and your lives embittered. As for us, we have nothing to lose. A swimmer in the ocean does not fear the rain.

You have occupied our lands, offended our honour and dignity and let out our blood and stolen our money and destroyed our houses and played with our security and we will give you the same treatment.

4. Don't let your strength and modern arms fool you. They win a few battles but lose the war...

Interestingly, bin Laden also makes appeals to sympathy for American soldiers with vivid descriptions that conjure images of their physical and emotional suffering:

5. You can imagine the state of psychological breakdown that afflicts a soldier as he gathers the remains of his colleagues after they stepped on land mines that tore them apart... [your soldiers are] under psychological pressure, fear and humiliation while [their] nation is ignorant of that (what is going on). The soldier has no solution except to commit suicide. That is a strong message to you, written by his soul, blood and pain... The solution is in your hands if you care about them.

Osama bin Laden also attributes blame and accountability to American and coalition soldiers for their actions in Iraq, Afghanistan, Abu Ghraib, and Guantanamo:

6. There is no difference between this criminality [committed by the U.S. army] and Saddam's criminality, as it has reached the degree of raping women and taking them as hostages instead of their husbands. As for torturing men, they have used burning chemical acids and drills on their joints. And when they give up on (interrogating) them, they sometimes use the drills on their heads until they die. Read, if you will, the reports of the horrors in Abu Ghraib and Guantanamo prisons.

As it might be expected, fear content is present in bin Laden's speech and occupies approximately 10 percent of coded content. However, there are also some unexpected variations on emotional appeals such as appeals to anger, remorse, and sympathy for U.S. soldiers. It is also somewhat surprising that fear appeals are not more prevalent in this speech, given that it is delivered by a *terrorist* who is threatening further attacks on the United States. Instead, we see similar and even higher levels of fear content in the majority of speeches delivered by Western leaders (President Bush and Australian Prime Minister Howard, see figure).

TONY BLAIR: SPEECH NO. 1

Tony Blair's statement to Parliament on September 14, 2001, was his first political speech about the 9/11 terror attacks. In this speech, Blair publicly expresses his condemnation of the attacks and his commitment to support the United States in "bringing to justice those responsible." The speech is 1722 words in length but only one statement met the criteria for fear appraisal (<1 percent). Similar to Bush's first speech on September 11, 2001, Blair established in his speech the importance and personal relevance of the attacks by describing them as "murder of British citizens," as "hideous and foul events," "an act of wickedness" and a "tragedy of epoch making proportions." Elements of the traditional War narrative are also present in statements describing the attacks as an assault on shared human values:

1. These attacks were not just attacks upon people and buildings; nor even merely upon the USA; these were attacks on the basic democratic values in which we all believe so passionately and on the civilised world

As in Bush's first speech, statements of blame and accountability are attributed to terrorists. However, they are defined in relatively broad terms as "our enemies," a "form of terror" and a "menace." Blair even acknowledged, "we do not yet know the exact origin of this evil." And so, while accountability is clearly attributed to an "evil out-group," ambiguity makes it difficult to classify these statements as traditional emotional appeals as there is not a clear object to which blame can be attributed. Fear content is even more infrequent with only one statement meeting the criteria for fear appraisal:

2. We know, that they would, if they could, go further and use chemical or biological or even nuclear weapons of mass destruction. We know, also, that there are groups or people, occasionally states, who trade the technology and capability for such weapons . . .

These results indicate that while there is some content consistent with key appraisal elements, traditional fear appeals are largely absent in this initial speech made by Tony Blair.

TONY BLAIR: SPEECH NO. 2

Blair's speech on March 21st 2006 was the first in a series of three speeches on foreign policy and defense with the second and third speeches delivered to American and Australian audiences. Blair explains that in this speech he hopes to "set out the thinking behind the foreign policy we have pursued [in Iraq] . . . " and to "describe how I believe we can defeat global terrorism and why I believe victory for democracy in Iraq and Afghanistan is a vital element of doing that." In its entirety, this speech is 4830 words long. The introductory section (850 words) on defense and foreign policy made no reference to terrorism and was removed from the analysis.

In contrast to later speeches presented by Bush, Bin Laden and Howard (see De Castella et al., 2009; De Castella & McGarty, 2011), Blair's speech contains a marked absence of content that meets appraisal criteria for fear (less than 0.01 percent). While there are many statements discussing the personal relevance and importance of the War on Terror, Blair refers primarily to a "fundamentalist ideology" rather than an explicit or evil "other" to which blame and accountability can be attributed. Rather than seeking to assign blame, Blair also acknowledges the intrinsic societal and ideological problems that give rise to fundamentalism: "The roots of global terrorism and extremism are indeed deep. They reach right down through decades of alienation, victimhood and political oppression in the Arab and Muslim world." Statements promoting uncertain coping are also virtually nonexistent. Instead, Blair's speech is largely motivational, optimistic and progressive in tone advocating a better understanding of Islam and culture in the Middle East:

1. The most remarkable thing about reading the Koran—in so far as it can be truly translated from the original Arabic—is to understand how progressive it is. I speak with great diffidence and humility as a member of another faith ... But as an outsider, the Koran strikes me as a reforming book ... It is inclusive. It extols science and knowledge and abhors superstition. It is practical and way ahead of its time in attitudes to marriage, women and governance ...
2. Extremism is not the true voice of Islam ... It is, as ever, to be found in the calm, but too often unheard beliefs of the many Muslims, millions of them the world over ... who want what we all want: to be ourselves free and for others to be free also; who regard tolerance as a virtue and respect for the faith of others as part of our own faith.

Rather than relying on emotional appeals and elements from the traditional War/Crime narrative, Blair's speech is characterised by the presence of well-developed, two-sided arguments and attention to the complexities associated with the "war in Iraq." Blair reiterates in detail the views expressed by his opponents and then proceeds to deconstruct and critique them in advocating his own:

3. The majority view of a large part of western opinion... [believes] that the policy of American since 9/11 has been a gross overreaction; George Bush is as much if not more of a threat to world peace as Osama bin Laden; and what is happening in Iraq, Afghanistan or anywhere else in the Middle East, is an entirely understandable consequence of U.S./UK imperialism or worse, of just plain stupidity. Leave it all alone or at least treat it with sensitivity and it would all resolve itself in time ...

Blair continues ...

4. This world view—which I would characterise as a doctrine of benign inactivity sits in the commentator's seat, almost as a matter of principle ... it is a posture of weakness, defeatism and most of all, deeply insulting to every Muslim who

believes in freedom for the majority... we can no more opt out of this struggle than we can opt out of the climate changing around us. Inaction, pushing the responsibility on to America, deluding ourselves that this terrorism is an isolated series of individual incidents rather than a global movement and would go away if only we were more sensitive to its pretensions; this too is a policy. It is just that; it is a policy that is profoundly, fundamentally wrong.

Two-sided arguments have traditionally been considered to be most effective when an audience is intelligent, aware that there are two contradictory sides to an issue and when the audience is not already in agreement (Johnston, 1994). Such appeals have also been found to enhance a speaker's credibility, promote more enduring attitude change and prepare an audience to resist future persuasion by opponents (Johnston, 1994). Blair's (2006) speech demonstrates that a different rhetoric about terrorism is possible and may even be more persuasive among critical and unsympathetic audiences.

DIFFERENCES BETWEEN SPEAKERS AND OVER TIME

A review of key political speeches made between 2001 and 2006 revealed that fear arousing content is present to varying degrees in the rhetoric of leaders on both sides of the War on Terror. The quantity and form of these appeals however, varied substantially over time and between speakers. In Bush's rhetoric, the strongest fear appeals emerged in late 2002 when advancing arguments for the U.S.-led invasion of Iraq. Closer examination of Bush's speeches revealed that by 2002, the terrorist "other" had been more clearly defined using the language of demagoguery to position "the enemy" in binary opposition to America and its citizens (Jackson, 2005b). Volkan points out that this language of demonisation and dehumanisation mirrors the union of religion and politics in the rhetoric of Islamic extremists and that "when 'Gods' are involved in human group conflict, tragedies follow because 'Gods' do not negotiate, 'they' give permission to destroy the 'evil'" (2004, p. 167). Fear appeals, while largely absent in Bush's 2001 speech, also became a prominent part of his later speeches about terrorism. These speeches were also more characteristic of traditional fear appeals, containing a sharp increase in statements promoting uncertainty around coping with the terrorist threat. Such statements warn of future terrorist attacks and weapons of mass destruction, as well as the risk of inaction and dissent. At the same time, these arguments serve to legitimise counterterrorism policies and military intervention in Iraq.

An analysis of Osama bin Laden's message to the Americans (January 13, 2006) revealed that fear content arose primarily in warnings to Americans that they were losing and would lose the war in Iraq. Despite this threatening tone, only 10 percent of this speech meets the criteria for fear-appraisal. Instead, bin Laden also appeals to anger, remorse, and even sympathy with statements attributing blame to the

Bush Administration and the American military for atrocities committed in Iraq, Afghanistan, Abu Ghraib, and Guantanamo.

In stark contrast with speeches presented by George Bush and Osama bin Laden, fear appeals are often absent in Tony Blair's political rhetoric. Blair frequently refers to terrorist groups in abstract terms describing the problems that give rise to a "fundamentalist ideology" rather than attributing blame to a clearly defined out-group. In Blair's later speech (March, 2006) there is also little content that meets the criteria for fear appraisal. Instead, his language is motivational, progressive and optimistic in tone and characterised by the use of well-developed two-sided arguments.

THE ALTERNATIVE TO FEAR

An analysis of emotional appeals in the rhetoric of different speakers and over time revealed several unexpected findings. First, the terrorism speeches delivered by different political leaders vary markedly in fear content and fluctuate a great deal over time, likely as a function of context. Second, even an extremely threatening speech delivered by a terrorist leader (Osama Bin Laden) to a Western audience, contains comparatively fewer fear-arousing statements than observed in many national addresses by Western leaders. Third, despite the frightening nature of the 9/11 attacks, explicit fear content only emerged much later in speeches by Bush, Blair and Howard (De Castella et al., 2009; De Castella & McGarty, 2011) and was also nearly completely absent in later (2006) speeches by former British Prime Minister Tony Blair.

The findings that fear appeals emerged much later in political rhetoric are particularly noteworthy for two main reasons. First, the absence of fear content at other times demonstrates that fear arousing communication is not a permanent or inevitable aspect of political communication—even when discussing provocative and frightening topics. Second, the fact that fear content varies across speakers demonstrates that even at politically turbulent times, appeals to fear are not always necessary or consistently used by speakers to generate support for the government or its foreign policy agenda (Flyghed, 2005; Furedi, 1997; Jackson, 2005; Sunstein, 2004).

Are there alternatives to the War/Crime narrative? We believe there are. Blair's later speech on terrorism presents a series of persuasive arguments to support his political agenda with an almost complete absence of fear arousing content (0.01 percent). Instead of a simplistic, emotive depiction of the evil terrorist "other" Blair's later rhetoric focuses on understanding the motives and environmental context that gives rise to "fundamentalist ideologies" and terrorist events.

Research into the motives of suicide terrorists also paints a more complex picture. Robert Pape (2005) conducted one of the largest research projects ever seen on suicide terrorism around the world, analysing 315 attacks that took place between 1980 and 2003. He discovered that, suicide terrorists are not inherently evil, deviant, or destitute individuals; they are not driven by hatred of Western values; they are not emotionally or psychologically unstable; and they do not stem primarily from regions promoting religious fundamentalism. What all suicide terrorists do have in common, however, is a key strategic objective—to coerce modern democracies to withdraw military forces from regions that they perceive as their homeland. Far from the prevailing stereotypical murderer, cult member, or fundamentalists, most suicide terrorists are young, intelligent, socially integrated, capable people acting on their own rational judgment. Pape (2005) argues that the profile fits more closely to that of a well-educated and politically conscious individual that would join a grass-roots movement or political party. Pape (2005) also discovered that most suicide terrorists do not engage in such activities from a position of intense hatred, manipulation or depression, but rather that they have altruistic motives, and a sense of duty and responsibility, similar to the reasoning of a soldier who chooses to engage in a suicide mission for their country.

As with constructions of the "terrorist other," the "new age" narrative could also be framed very differently. In an historical analysis of conflict and terrorism trends, Mueller (2004) argued that September 11, 2001, was not the beginning of a new era, but rather part of an ongoing conflict of violence and counter violence between America and Al Qaeda since 1991. Jackson (2005) also pointed out that the attacks on the World Trade Center were tragic, yet highly atypical events—unusual both in terms of terrorist ability and an uncommon failure of American intelligence. Talking about terrorism squarely as a crime rather than, as a war would also promote the application of police methods and the criminal justice system suggesting that appropriate action entails capture and trial rather than obliteration. It would also create opportunities for new and creative counterterrorism approaches, reducing the focus on military intervention.

Placing risks and dangers in proportion with other threats might further reduce unnecessary fear of terrorism. Barker (2002) explains that the actual risk of being killed in a terrorist attack is statistically lower than deaths resulting from home improvement accidents, bee stings and lightning strikes. Even in the worst years on record in the United States the annual death toll from terrorism does not even begin to compare with the number of deaths from gun-related homicides or alcohol-related motor vehicle accidents (Glassner, 2004).

The language of threat and danger that pervades political rhetoric makes it appear perfectly normal to be afraid. However, there are many alternatives to the War/Crime discourse of terror. By calling on the public to put their fears in proportion, the official discourse could aim to reduce public anxiety around terrorism. A reflective discourse of proportional concerns and rational two-sided arguments for foreign policy would provide the greatest protection for true democracy and freedoms as the greatest dangers are posed not by terrorists, but the consequences of overreaction, rash counterterrorism measures, and a discourse that promotes destruction and dehumanisation.

REFERENCES

Altheide, D. L. (2003). Notes towards a politics of fear. *Journal for Crime, Conflict and the Media, 1*, 37–54.
Back, M. D., K üfner, A. C. P., & Egloff, B. (2010). The emotional timeline of September 11, 2001. *Psychological Science, 21*, 1417–1419.
Barker, J. (2002). *The no-nonsense guide to terrorism*. Oxford, UK: W.W. Norton & Company
Bergen, P. (2006). *The Osama bin Laden i know: An oral history of al Qaeda's leader* (p. 229). New York, NY: Free Press.
bin Laden, O. (2006, January 19). Message to the Americans. Speech aired on Al-Jazeera. Retrieved from http://www.nytimes.com/2006/01/19/international/20tapefulltext.html?pagewanted=all
Blair, T. (2001, September 14). Response to September 11. Speech delivered to the House of Commons. Retrieved from http://www.guardian.co.uk/politics/2001/sep/14/houseofcommons.uk1
Blair, T. (2004, March 5). The Continued Threat of Global Terrorism. Speech delivered in Sedgefield, County Durham, UK. Retrieved from http://www.guardian.co.uk/politics/2004/mar/05/iraq.iraq
Blair, T. (2006, March 21). Foreign policy in Iraq and Afghanistan speech delivered at Reuters Newsmaker event, London, UK. Retrieved from http://www.guardian.co.uk/politics/2006/mar/21/iraq.iraq1
Bligh, M. C., Kohles, J. C., & Meindl, J. R. (2004). Charting the language of leadership: A methodological investigation of President Bush and the crisis of 9/11. *Journal of Applied Psychology, 89*, 562–574.
Braithwaite, J. (2005). Pre-empting terrorism. *Current Issues in Criminal Justice, 17*, 96–114.
Bush, G. W. (2001, September 11). A great people has been moved to defend a great nation. Address to the nation: Oval Office, Washington, D.C. Retrieved from http://www.americanrhetoric.com/speeches/gwbush911addresstothenation.htm
Bush, G. W. (2002, October 7). President Bush Outlines Iraqi Threat. Remarks by the President on Iraq, Cincinnati Museum Center,, Cincinnati, Ohio. Retrieved from http://georgewbush-whitehouse.archives.gov/news/releases/2002/10/20021007-8.html
Bush, G. W. (2006a, September 6). President Bush's speech on terrorism Address from the White House, Washington, D. C. Retrieved from http://www.nytimes.com/2006/09/06/washington/06bush_transcript.html?pagewanted=all
Bush, G. W. (2006b, September 11). The fifth anniversary of September 11, 2001. Address to the nation: Oval Office, Washington, D.C. Retrieved from http://georgewbush-whitehouse.archives.gov/news/releases/2006/09/20060911-3.html
de Beaugrande, R. (2004). Critical discourse analysis from the perspective of ecologism. *Critical Discourse Studies, 1*, 113–145.
De Castella, K., & McGarty, C. (2011). Two leaders, two wars: A psychological analysis of fear and anger content in political rhetoric about terrorism. *Analyses of Social Issues and Public Policy, 11*, 180–200.
De Castella, K., McGarty, C., & Musgrove, L. (2009). Fear arousing content in political rhetoric about terrorism: An analysis of speeches by Australian Prime Minister Howard. *Political Psychology, 30*, 1–26.
Dinh, V. D. (2004). Forward: freedom and security after September 11. In G. Martin (Ed.), *The new era of terrorism: Selected readings* (pp. 23–26). Thousand Oaks, CA: SAGE Publications.
Doran, M. S. (2005). *Understanding the war on terror*. New York, NY: Norton.

Dripps, D. A. (2003) Terror and tolerance: Criminal justice for the new age of anxiety. *Ohio State Journal of Criminal Law, 1*, 9–43.

Feldman, N. (2004). Choices of law, choices of war. In G. Martin (Ed.), *The new era of terrorism: Selected readings* (pp. 72–87). Thousand Oaks, CA: SAGE Publications.

Flyghed, J. (2005). Crime-control in the post-wall era: the menace of security. *Journal of Scandinavian Studies in Criminology and Crime Prevention, 6*, 165–182.

Furedi, F. (1997). *Culture of fear: Risk-taking and the morality of low expectation*. London, UK: Cassell.

Glassner, B. (1999). *The culture of fear: Why Americans are afraid of the wrong things*. New York, NY: Basic Books.

Glassner, B. (2004). Narrative techniques of fear mongering. *Social Research, 71*, 819–826.

Graham, P., Keenan, T., & Dowd, A. (2004). A call to arms at the end of history: A discourse-historical analysis of George W. Bush's declaration of war on terror. *Discourse & Society, 15*, 199–221.

Hart, R. P., & Childers, J. P. (2005). The evolution of candidate Bush: A rhetorical analysis. *American Behavioral Scientist, 49*, 180–197.

Heldring, M. (2004). Talking to the public about terrorism: Promoting health and resilience. *Systems & Health, 22*, 67–71.

Hermann, E. S., & Chomsky, N. (1988). *Manufacturing consent: The political economy of the mass media*. New York, NY: Pantheon Books.

Hodges, A. (2011). *The war on terror narrative*. Oxford, UK: Oxford University Press.

Hooks, G., & Mosher, C. (2005). Outrages against personal dignity: Rationalizing abuse and torture in the war on terror. *Social Forces, 83*, 1627–1646.

Howard, J. (2001, October 8). U.S. retaliation against Afghanistan. Retrieved from http://www.australianpolitics.com/news/2001/01-10-08.shtml

Howard, J. (2002, October 14). Attacks on mainland a possibility. Retrieved from http://www.australianpolitics.com/news/2002/10/02-10-14.shtml

Howard, J. (2004, April 6). Gutsy Australians want to see things through. Retrieved from http://www.australianpolitics.com/news/2004/04/04-04-16.shtml

Howard, J. (2005, November 8). Howard pays tribute to ASIO and federal police for terror arrests. Press conference at Parliament House, Canberra. Retrieved from http://australianpolitics.com/2005/11/08/howard-pays-tribute-to-asio-for-terror-arrests.html

Jackson, R. (2005). *Writing the war on terrorism: Language, politics and counter-terrorism*. Manchester, UK: Manchester University Press.

Johnston, D. D. (1994). *The art and science of persuasion*. Madison, WI: Brown and Benchmark.

Kellner, D. (2004). 9/11, spectacles of terror, and media manipulation: A critique of Jihadist and Bush media politics. *Critical Discourse Analysis, 1*, 41–64.

Krebs, R. R., & Jackson, P. T. (2007). Twisting tongues and twisting arms: The power of political rhetoric. *European Journal of International Relations, 13*, 35–66.

Krebs, R., & Lobasz, J. (2007). Fixing the meaning of 9/11: Hegemony, coercion, and the road to war in Iraq. *Security Studies, 16*, 409–451.

Lawrence, C. (2006). *Fear and politics*. Melbourne, Australia: Scribe Short Books.

Lazarus, R. S. (1991a). Cognition and motivation in emotion. *American Psychologist, 46*, 352–367.

Lazarus, R. S. (1991b). Progress on a cognitive-motivational-relational theory of emotion. *American Psychologist, 46*, 819–834.

Lazar, A., & Lazar, M. M. (2004). The discourse of the new world order: Out-casting the double face of threat. *Discourse & Society, 15*(2–3), 223–242.

Lerner, L. S., & Keltner, D. (2000). Beyond valence: Toward a model of emotion-specific influences on judgment and choice. *Cognition & Emotion, 14(4),* 473–493.

Leudar, I., Marsland, V., & Nekvapil, J. (2004) On membership categorization: Us, them and doing violence in political discourse. *Discourse & Society, 15(2–3),* 243–266.

Maser, C. (2004). *The perpetual consequences of fear and violence: Rethinking the future.* Washington, DC: Maisonneuve Press.

Merskin, D. (2004). The construction of Arabs and enemies: Post-September 11 discourse of George W. Bush. *Mass Communication & Society, 7,* 157–177.

Mueller, J. (2004). Harbinger or aberration? A 9/11 provocation. In G. Martin (Ed.), *The new era of terrorism: Selected readings* (pp. 42–46). Thousand Oaks, CA: SAGE Publications.

Oates, S. (2006). Comparing the politics of fear: The role of terrorism news in election campaigns in Russia, the United States and Britian. *International Relations, 20(4),* 425–437.

Padgett, A. & Allen, B. (2003). Fear's slave: The mass media and Islam after September 11. *Media International Australia Incorporating Culture & Policy, 109,* 32–40.

Pallitto, R. M., & Weaver, W. G. (2007). *Presidential secrecy and the law.* Baltimore, MD: John Hopkins University Press.

Pape, R. (2005). *Dying to win: The strategic logic of suicide terrorism.* Melbourne, Australia: Scribe.

Pfiffner, J. P. (2007). Intelligence and decision making before the war with Iraq. In G. C. Edwards & D. King (Eds.), *The polarized presidency of George W. Bush* (pp. 213–244). Oxford, UK: Oxford University Press.

Phil, G., Keenan, T., & Dowd, A. (2004). A call to arms at the end of history: A discourse-historical analysis of George W. Bush's declaration of war on terror. *Discourse & Society, 15(2–3),* 199–221.

Pinter, H. (2005). *Nobel Lecture: Art, truth & politics.* Retrieved from http://nobelprize.org/literature/laureates/2005/pinter-lecture-e.html

Prewitt, K., Alterman, E., Arato, A., Pyszcycnski, T., Robin, C., & Stern, J. (2004). The politics of fear after 9/11. *Social Research, 71,* 1129–1146.

Pyszczynski, T. (2004). What are we so afraid of? A terror management theory perspective on the politics of fear. *Social Research, 71,* 827–848.

Robin, C. (2004). *Fear: The history of a political idea.* Oxford, UK: Oxford University Press.

Rothe, D., & Muzzatti, S. L. (2004). Enemies everywhere: Terrorism, moral panic, and U.S. civil society. *Critical Criminology, 12,* 327–350.

Small, D. A., Lerner, J. S., & Fischhoff, B. (2006). Emotion priming and attributions for terrorism: Americans' reactions in a national field experiment. *Political Psychology, 27(2),* 289–298.

Smith, C. A., & Lazarus, R. S. (1990). Emotion and adaptation. In L. A. Pervin (Ed.), *Handbook of personality: Theory and research* (pp. 609–637). New York, NY: Guilford.

Smith, C. A., & Lazarus, R. S. (1993). Appraisal components, core relational themes and emotions. *Cognition and Emotion, 7,* 233–269.

Spence, K. (2005). World risk society and war against terror. *Political Studies, 53,* 284–304.

Stern, S. (2000). Why politicians want to scare us. *New Statesman, 129,* 29–31.

Sunstein, C. R. (2004). Fear and liberty. *Social Research, 71,* 967–996.

Surette, R. (2010). *Media, crime and criminal justice: Images, realities and policies.* Lansing, MI: Thomson/Wadsworth.

Valiunas, A. (2002). *Churchill's military histories: A rhetorical study.* MD: Rowman & Littlefield Publishers.

CHAPTER 6

Fear of Suicide Terrorism: Consequences for Individuals and Politics

C. DOMINIK GÜSS, ALEXANDRA FOUST, AND
DIETRICH DÖRNER

Suicide terrorism can be defined as a premeditated attack by someone who is willing to kill himself or herself and others to achieve a political goal (Bloom, 2005; Güss, 2011; Merari, 2005). Suicide terrorism (see also "Islamic martyrdom," Güss, Tuason, & Teixeira, 2007) has been a form of terrorism applied in many countries in the past (Pape, 2005; Silke, 2006), most widely in Palestine and Israel, and in recent years in Afghanistan and Iraq. According to Atran (2006, p. 127), "During 2000–2004, there were 472 suicide attacks in 22 countries, killing more than 7000 and wounding tens of thousands. Most have been carried out by Islamist groups claiming religious motivation, also known as jihadis." For example, an average of more than one suicide attack per day occurred in 2005 in Iraq (MacDonald, 2005). One reason for the prevalence of suicide terrorism is its "success"—being relatively cheap and killing on average four times more people than other terrorist acts (Hoffman, 2006).

A suicide attack involves several groups of people. We distinguish at least five groups of people in order to discuss their distinct emotional reactions, their coping, and consequences for their actions. These groups are (1) the directly targeted victims and their families; (2) the attacker, and the organization that organizes and sponsors the attack; (3) the wider local and national population that learns about the suicide attack through the media or through other formal or informal channels; (4) local and national political leaders; and, since suicide attacks are often carried out in countries with foreign occupiers, (5) foreign military forces.

Although suicide terrorism triggers many emotions (e.g., anger and sadness), this chapter focuses on fear as the primary emotional reaction. We will discuss fear in the context of PSI-Theory. PSI-Theory (Dörner, 1999) is named after the Greek letter "Ψ," which often symbolizes *psychology*. The theory describes the interaction of motivational, emotional, and cognitive psychological processes. PSI-Theory allows psychologists in a range of subfields to analyze human behavior as a result of specific arrangements of activated needs.

In this chapter, we use PSI-Theory to highlight the consequences of fear for human information processing. We explore how fear of suicide terrorism impacts political attitudes. Due to space limitations, the discussions of the consequences of fear focus on groups 1, 3, and 4 mentioned earlier (i.e., the victims of suicide attacks and their families, the wider population affected by suicide terrorism including their attitudes towards government and political leaders, and political leaders). We focus on Iraq and Afghanistan to discuss reactions to suicide attacks.

HUMAN EMOTION REGULATION: FEAR

Most psychological research regards fear as a basic emotion that every human being experiences across cultures (e.g., Ekman, 2007). From an evolutionary psychology perspective, fear ultimately helps humans survive by triggering fight or flight tendencies, and desire to avoid dangerous situations.

A computational model of emotions, the PSI-Theory (Dörner, 1999, 2003; Dörner & Güss, 2013) describes fear from a slightly different perspective. The theory focuses not only on emotions but also on their interaction with motivation and cognition. Following this theory, emotions are not separate constructs, but emerge from the specific constellation of motivations, modulation parameters, and behavior tendencies that are elicited in certain contexts.

Motivations result from needs. The theory postulates five basic groups of needs similar to the ones of Maslow (1954; physiological needs, safety and security, love and belongingness, self-esteem, self-actualization): *existential needs* such as pain avoidance, hunger, and thirst; *sexuality*; *affiliation* such as belonging to a group or social network; *certainty* related to the predictability of events and one's own actions; and *competence* related to the capability to solve problems and change the environment (see Figure 6.1).

Needs exist within the architecture as homeostatic systems, each with an ideal set-point unique to each human. A set-point deviation activates a need. Homeostasis means the desire to maintain a balance in each of the five groups of needs in light of environmental influences on a person. Together with a goal, the need becomes a motivation. For example, during a horrific suicide attack, the existential need for survival and protection of one's health becomes a highly activated motivation, precipitating the goal to protect oneself and leave the situation. Later, the need for certainty becomes active when the affected persons realize that they can hardly predict future suicide attacks. Existential needs, certainty needs, and competence needs activate in different timeframes when someone experiences fear related to suicide terrorism.

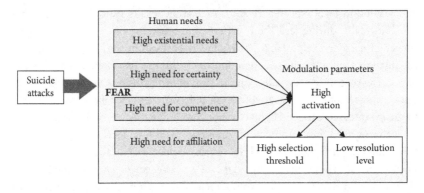

Figure 6.1:
The effects of fear of suicide bombings for individuals

Although some researchers try to identify common traits of suicide bombers (Lester, Yang, & Lindsay, 2004), there is no dominant profile of a suicide bomber (Crenshaw, 2007; Hirsh et al., 2005; Hoffman, 2003). Volunteers vary greatly in their demographic characteristics (Pape, 2005; Reuter, 2004; Soibelman, 2004). Most are men, but the numbers of women and children are rising (Cook, 2005). It can be someone motivated by religious convictions or by political convictions, or both (Atran, 2006); someone who is rich or poor, well educated or not (Krueger & Maleckova, 2003); someone who experienced cruelties by the occupiers or by a corrupt regime (Pape, 2005). As Reuter (2004, p. 204) noted, "Most Islamic martyrs are normal, fearless people with strong convictions." People commit suicide attacks for any number of complex combinations of personal convictions and shared ideology.

Only if one analyzes the motivations in terms of the specific macro-socio-historical-political context, mechanisms of the human psyche, and group processes can one attempt to understand a person's decision to become a suicide bomber (Güss, Tuason, & Teixeira, 2007). But fear follows any suicide attack, and instigating this fear in the population motivates terrorist groups to use suicide terrorism as a strategy to ultimately achieve their political goals.

Feelings of low control also characterize fear. Despite the hard truth that we cannot prevent attacks, we see many measures to increase perceived control and safety. For example, many restaurants in Israel employ guards who examine every client for explosives. On a national scale, the United States introduced a color code to indicate the likelihood of terrorist attacks. In 2011, the National Terrorism Advisory System replaced the color code. It provides warnings and information specific to the threat. However, there is no certainty that suicide attacks will not happen, especially in countries such as Iraq and Afghanistan, where they increased in the last decade.

The activated existential needs and needs for certainty and competence affect internal cognitive processes and external human behavior. Three modulation parameters influence the internal processes: activation, selection threshold, and resolution level (see Figure 6.1). Activation results from low competence. Physiologically, during fear, the heart rate and breathing rate increase. The body prepares for action (Selye, 1956). The higher the activation, the higher is the second modulation parameter, the selection threshold. This means no other needs become active. The person focuses solely on the current active need. A person truly in the grips of physiologically activated fear can only scan his environment and attempt to escape or avoid danger. High activation also influences internal cognitive processes through the third modulation parameter, resolution level of thinking. When activation is high, the resolution level of thinking decreases. One does not process details; one does not think of potential causes or consequences. Thinking becomes short term in orientation and narrow in focus. One is prone to using shortcuts such as heuristics and stereotypes (e.g., Hall, 2002).

Low resolution of thinking on a pervasive scale and for an extended period of time explains the widespread stereotyping of suicide bombers. People who constantly fear suicide terrorism attempt to safeguard themselves with the mental shortcut of lumping suicide terrorists into one cohesive group. Inhabitants of Gardez, Afghanistan, who experienced a suicide attack characterized the attackers as "bad Muslims who pervert Islam" (Williams, 2001). A spokesperson of the U.S. Department of Defense characterized attackers from the Taliban as "the enemies of Afghanistan" (Canadian Broadcasting Corporation, 2006).

Using stereotypes leads to an increase in certainty. The stereotype allows a person to identify suicide attackers with greater probability, easily placing people into discrete in-group/out-group categories. Making the enemy predictable by labeling them using stereotypes decreases uncertainty. Often times, these stereotypes put down or dehumanize the enemy (Baumeister, 1996). That way, one feels superior, which ultimately leads to an increase in competence, perceived control, and a sense of safety.

In short, PSI-Theory describes emotions as specific constellations of parameters. Humans experience fear as parameters set to high existential needs, low certainty, low competence, high activation, high selection threshold, and low resolution level of cognitive processes. The constellation of low certainty and low competency in fear leads to five dominant behavior tendencies: flight, aggression (fight), safeguarding behavior, affiliative tendencies, and confirmatory perception (see Figure 6.2). Both on the individual and group level, we exhibit specific behaviors in response to the fear of suicide terrorism, which illustrates the uniqueness of this particular fear.

BEHAVIORAL CONSEQUENCES OF FEAR FOR THE AFFECTED INDIVIDUALS AND POPULATION

The strongest reactions to fear are *flight* and *aggression*. If people experience fear and have their backs to the wall, they might become aggressive, especially when they feel capable of action. (Due to space limitations we will not discuss aggression in detail.) As mentioned previously and referring to evolutionary psychology,

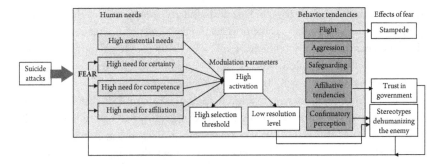

Figure 6.2:
The effects of fear of suicide bombings for individuals and society. (Connections between human needs and behavior tendencies are not shown to increase visibility of the figure.)

fear elicits survival by evoking urges to fight, avoid, or flee in dangerous situations (Cannon, 1915). The human brain evolved to process these urges subconsciously as to not waste time to analyze the situation in detail. Plus, given humans' extreme social nature, the flight response happens whether danger is real or perceived, as illustrated in the example below.

The flight response developed in the human psyche so that we could protect ourselves from outside threats, but in modern society, sometimes flight results in the opposite effect. This happened on August 31, 2005 (Cable News Network World, 2005). About 1 million Shiite pilgrims were on their way to the Al Kadhimiya Mosque in Baghdad. When a rumor spread that a suicide attacker was among the Shiite procession, the crowd panicked. It was not unreasonable for the Shiite pilgrims to panic, because Sunnis carried out several suicide and mortar attacks on big Shiite gatherings in the past. Some people in the crowd ran toward a bridge and opened the closed gate to escape. However, they could not open the locked gate on the other side of the bridge. Hundreds of pilgrims shoved each other off the bridge into the Tigris River below and died. The stampede resulted in almost 1000 deaths (Worth, 2005).

Fear also triggers *safeguarding*—constantly checking the environment for relevant stimuli. One focuses his/her cognitive capacity on monitoring the situation for potentially threatening stimuli; thus, the internal cognitive processes are shallower (low resolution level of thinking). Many studies empirically demonstrate this increase in cognitive vigilance, anxiety, and fear (e.g., Valentino, Hutchings, Banks, & Davis, 2008).

Affiliative tendencies are a third group of behavior tendencies. The literature has well established the intense human need for social connection and affiliation (e.g., Ainsworth, 1991; Bowlby, 1969). Since the targets of suicide terrorism have almost no influence on the situation, individuals try to gain some kind of control or consolation through contact with other individuals, groups, or local or national political leaders, given the way we organize ourselves in societies. This is a cry for help, an appeal to the basic animal instinct of safety in numbers. Pervasive fear of potential violent death causes low competence and affiliative tendencies, which may lead people to trust any leader capable of reducing the threat of suicide terrorism. On the other hand, affiliative tendencies can also drive people to support terrorist groups, a concept we explore later.

A recent study with U.S. university students investigated the trust and reliance on government leaders in relation to fears of terrorism (Sinclair & LoCicero, 2010). Controlling for demographic and psychosocial variables, regression analyses demonstrated that fear of terrorism significantly predicted trust in government. The more fear participants experienced, the higher their trust in government. Researchers added indicators of the impact of the color code threat level alert system in a last step of the regression and found that the system was also a significant predictor—the higher the threat level, the higher is the trust in government. The authors explained their findings using attachment theory and evolutionary theory. Similar to a child who seeks protection of a parent in a dangerous situation, individuals seek protection from government leaders. From an evolutionary viewpoint, humans have adapted to trust a stronger leader when their own resources cannot effectively deal with the situation. PSI-Theory, combining attachment and evolutionary theory, also explains the phenomenon that fear of terrorism predicts trust in government. An increase in affiliative tendencies (similar to attachment theory) plus lowered competence (similar to evolutionary theory) prompt fear of terrorism and trust in government.

The fourth possible fear reaction is *confirmatory perception*, where a person only perceives information in the environment that confirms prior assumptions and world knowledge. We perceive suicide attackers according to the hypotheses and stereotypes we have about them. For example, Güss (2011) conducted a study investigating associations to five terms used in the suicide terrorism literature: *suicide bomber, suicide terrorist, Islamic martyr, martyr, volunteer*. Every participant (U.S. students) received a list of six words. One word was from that list of suicide terrorism terms, and the other five words were neutral words such as box, breeze, hair, day, pants. Participants were asked to list as many associations for each word as possible. The negative associations mentioned most frequently (in order of frequency) for *suicide bomber* were death, killing, pain, terrorist, and crazy; for *suicide terrorist*, 9/11, death, angry, mean, and religion; for *Islamic martyr*, religion, belief, foreign, terrorist, and death; for *martyr*, death, sacrifice, blood, brave, and religion; and for *volunteer*, helpful, nice, free, kind, and caring. The number of negative associations decreased and the number of positive associations increased from *suicide bomber* to *suicide terrorist* to *Islamic martyr* to *martyr* to *volunteer*. These findings show that people have specific connotations with the words used to describe suicide terrorists.

In extreme fear, the resolution level of thinking is low and one does not consider causes and ramifications of suicide attacks. Instead, one only considers information that confirms one's worldview and cognitive structures—hence labels for suicide bombers like "evil" or "crazy fanatics" or "psychologically sick" or "bad

Muslims who pervert Islam." Perceived threat is considered the single best group-level predictor of exclusionism and intolerance (Quillian 1995; Sullivan, Pierson, & Marcus 1982).

Fear generally triggers these four behavior tendencies. An individual's cultural norms, stored in long-term memory, as well as the unique situational context, inform the nature, order, and extent of behavior tendencies an individual displays in his/her reaction to motivations and needs activated by fear of suicide terrorism.

FEAR OF SUICIDE TERRORISM: CONSEQUENCES FOR POLITICIANS AND GOVERNMENTS

Williams (2001, p. 1) describes the fear of Afghans after a suicide attack:

> When I interviewed locals who were still traumatized by the [suicide] attack, I began to understand the impact that a single bombing has on a community. As I talked to bewildered villagers who cursed the bombers as "bad Muslims who pervert Islam" or "enemies of Afghanistan," their shock and fear were palpable. It reminded me of the fear that struck America when the so-called Beltway Sniper roamed the Washington, D.C., area in 2002 killing innocent victims at random.

Some researchers have distinguished between personal fear and national fear (e.g., Lavanco, Romano, & Milio, 2008; Pedhazur & Canetti-Nisim, 2010) or personal fear and sociotropic fear (Beckenridge & Zimbardo, 2007). Previous discussions focused on personal fear of suicide terrorism, how individuals fear for their lives and their loved ones, and the implications for individual behavior and health. This fear can extend to national fear or sociotropic fear, which relate to political attitudes and expectations for public policy decisions. Many interpret terrorism as a threat to the existing political system or the stability of society. At the same time, people employ terrorism to express discontent with existing political and societal structures.

The fear that outside oppressors or a "puppet" government jeopardize a nation's Muslim identity can outweigh that of suicide attacks. This fear can even lead to support for suicide terrorism, especially if the oppressors are primarily targets. Data from the Pew Research Center (2010) shed some light on how other countries view the United States and its politics. Unfortunately no data were available from Iraq and Afghanistan, but we can compare several predominantly Muslim countries such as Egypt, Jordan, Turkey, and Pakistan. In those nations, favorability ratings of the United States increased slightly with Obama's election, but by 2010 they fell back to the ratings under Bush in 2008 of less than 20 percent. Less than one third of participants said they were confident that the United States "will do the right thing in world affairs," with Pakistan only showing 8 percent in 2010. It follows that about two-thirds of respondents residing in the aforementioned countries want coalition troops out of Afghanistan.

Another question asked about support for suicide bombing. The percentage of Muslim participants who indicated in 2010 that suicide bombing is "often or sometimes justified" was 39 percent for Lebanon, 20 percent in Jordan, 8 percent in Pakistan, and 20 percent in Egypt. Although these percentages are lower than the ones 5 to 8 years before, they are still considerably high. One also has to consider that these numbers could be low estimates. Terrorist groups could use suicide terrorism to play on ensuing increases in affiliative tendencies if a significant portion of the population views it as an effective tool against an occupying force or ineffectual government. More often, terrorist organizations employ suicide terrorism for the chaos it creates.

Before discussing the consequences of fear of suicide terrorism for politicians and governments, we should mention the scarcity of research and reliable data. Our arguments rely heavily on news media or state organizations and have to be seen in light of these potential biases and incomplete historical backgrounds. This caveat generates tentative future discussions.

Due to space limitations, discussion of implications of suicide terrorism for politics focuses on Iraq and Afghanistan, as these countries saw the most deaths due to global terrorism. Furthermore, the United States invaded Iraq and Afghanistan with the primary goal—at least officially—to eradicate terrorism. According to the U.S. National Counterterrorism Center (2010), in 2009, 3654 people died in Iraq and 2778 people died in Afghanistan due to terrorist attacks, which include but are not limited to suicide terrorism. In 2009, Afghanistan had the highest number of suicide attacks (99), followed by Pakistan (84), and then Iraq (82). Suicide attacks in Iraq, Afghanistan, and Pakistan in 2008 accounted for about 60 percent of all terrorist attacks worldwide (National Counterterrorism Center, 2010, p. 11).

AFGHANISTAN: FEAR OF SUICIDE TERRORISM AND POLICY IMPLICATIONS

Suicide terrorism started very slowly in Afghanistan. The first suicide attack in Afghanistan happened in September of 2001 (United Nations Assistance Mission to Afghanistan [UNAMA], 2007). Two attacks occurred in 2003, and six occurred in 2004 (Karzai, 2006). The number of suicide attacks increased steadily from 22 in 2005 to 160 in 2007 before falling to 99 in 2009 (Williams, 2001), probably because terrorist organizations saw the success of this method against the overwhelming military superiority of coalition forces in Iraq and recognized the profound effect the first suicide attacks had in Afghanistan. As the UNAMA (2007, p. 34) reported, "Notably in Palestine and Afghanistan, survey data show that even publics which once completely eschewed suicide attacks condemn it less over time." Most of the attacks over the years occurred in the two biggest cities, Kabul and Kandahar.

In Afghanistan, suicide terrorist attacks target U.S. military and other occupying forces, the Afghan population, and the various Afghan institutions and government officials. However, "while groups using the tactic appear almost exclusively to target national and international security forces, their victims are overwhelmingly civilians" (UNAMA, 2007, p. 5). Despite this disheartening reality, hope for a peaceful Afghanistan lies in its people's very low support of the Taliban, the primary terrorist organization in the nation. Islamist extremism drives a significant portion of suicide terrorism in Afghanistan. But perhaps the majority of suicide bombers aim to attack occupying military forces and those Afghan forces seen as Western proxies (UNAMA, 2007). Furthermore, the UNAMA (2007) summarizes data that indicates that the Taliban coerces a large portion of volunteers for suicide missions. The small section of the Afghan public that supports the Taliban and its missions do so not from a religious or ideological base, but from a perspective of very limited options and out of pervasive fear from the longtime violence prompted by the U.S. and coalition forces (especially in the form of air strikes).

Afghanistan is among the poorest 15 countries worldwide according to the International Monetary Fund (2012). Only 6 percent of the population has access to electricity, and only 23 percent has access to drinking water (Europäische Kommission, 2007–2013). Fewer than a third of Afghans older than 15 can read and write (Europäische Kommission, 2007–2013). In many areas of Afghanistan and Pakistan, the Taliban provides the only option for education to desperate parents. The Taliban often recruits children and adolescents in Afghanistan or Pakistan to train and educate them for suicide missions (News 24, 2012; UNAMA, 2001–2007). The combination of poverty, political instability, unemployment, and illiteracy leads to an experience of deprivation and dissatisfaction in the population, and potentially leads to support of terrorism, especially among those Afghans who do not perceive an improvement in living conditions since the fall of the Taliban.

Politically speaking, it seems that outside nations with a religious/political/economic agenda can easily operate within such a vulnerable, chaotic nation as Afghanistan to achieve their respective objectives. The sociopolitical situation in Afghanistan contributes to this dynamic, where on the one hand government officials want to promote a young democracy, and on the other hand there are ingrained economic, social, and political factors working against this process. PSI-Theory provides insight into how emotion (fear)-activated motivations provoke behavior aimed at improving feelings of competence, security, and affiliation, which ultimately drive individual leaders' as well as citizens' decision-making (see Figure 6.3).

Interestingly, although Afghan discontent with the United States remains highly publicized, Afghans seem to feel very dissatisfied with their own national forces and politicians. Many Afghans actually see the Karzai Administration as a "puppet" of the U.S. government. For example, an ABC poll found that almost half of over 1000 Afghans interviewed in 2006 suspected fraud in the parliamentary elections. In an interview, 23-year-old Tahir, arrested in Kabul, admitted to planning suicide terrorism and criticized his government (UNAMA, 2007, p. 71).

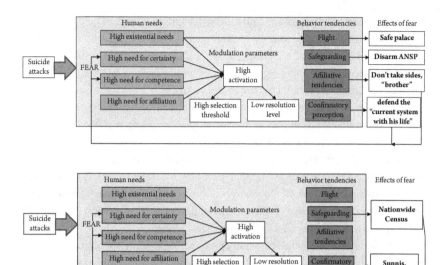

Figure 6.3:
Consequences of suicide terrorism fear for decisions of Karzai (above) and al-Maliki (below).

> Regarding the government, it is not an elected Afghan government. The voters who were brought there were not real Afghans. There is a difference between Karzai and Babrak Karmal. One came with U.S. plans the other with the U.S.SR. Both are puppet regimes and they will be toppled.

When terrorist bombs were detonated in Kabul and other provinces in April 2012, the opposition criticized Karzai's government. The former Vice President Ahmad Zia Massoud of the National Front party said: "A government that can neither implement the laws nor maintain its security, and which cannot provide social and economical facilities for the people of Afghanistan: the Afghan people don't need such a government" (ToloNews, 2012).

Ahmad Zia Massoud openly said that he had no power as vice president. Daiyar (January 24, 2012) writes in a blog about accumulation of power in Karzai's hands. Karzai condemns calls for reforms, saying "Afghanistan is not the political laboratory of foreigners to test new systems" and that he will defend the "current system with his life" (see Figure 6.3). Daiyar interprets the political situation in Afghanistan as far from a real democracy due to the prevalence of authoritarian attitudes. Furthermore, Karzai's confusing messages supporting the Taliban (often calling them "brothers," Rubin & Bowley, 2012), rejecting the United States, and struggling to consolidate his own power indicate that he responds to the fear of suicide terrorism much as any other Afghan (Rubin & Bowley, 2012). He struggles to maintain perceived control and a sense of affiliation in the face of ongoing violence.

Meanwhile, the United States and coalition forces have distinct motivations from Karzai, although they all officially fight the same war together. Like Afghans,

North Americans and Europeans suffer from national fear of suicide terrorism. If measurable, we would expect to see lower individual levels of fear in typical North Americans and Europeans than for Afghans (and many other Middle Eastern people) due to different attack frequencies. Nevertheless, the fear held by people in North America and Europe sparked their entry into costly wars in search of an obscured enemy.

As the greatest danger to the country, Afghan participants in the ABC poll identified the Taliban (41 percent), drug traffickers (28 percent), warlords (22 percent), the United States (4 percent), and the Afghan government (2 percent). Nevertheless, when the Taliban approach Afghans and asks for food and money, many Afghans help the Taliban because of religious duty, agreement with their goals, and coercion (UNAMA, 2007). The reason most often given is that the Taliban can provide security and stability (UNAMA, 2007). Roughly 10 percent of Afghans expressed that suicide attacks can be justified (UNAMA, 2007). One has to be cautious with these numbers, because social desirability might affect answers to the question if suicide attacks are justified. Answers might also depend on the format of the question (e.g., written, oral, on the phone). Such data reveal that a population faced with a strong, enduring fear of physical danger might support whichever organization provides the greatest sense of security, regardless of the more abstract political picture.

Such nuanced political dynamics underscore the relevance of social and behavioral psychological constructs in the war on terror. Karzai, as the leader of the Islamic republic elected by his people, should—according to both the basic nature of human interaction predicated on our need for affiliation, as well as the basic nature of a democratic republic—act on behalf of his constituents and protect them from all acts of terrorism. Even though Karzai attempts to distinguish his position of power following suicide attacks, his people, made vulnerable by fear, might support the Taliban if they see the latter as more powerful.

IRAQ: FEAR OF SUICIDE TERRORISM AND POLICY IMPLICATIONS

Suicide attacks in Iraq have been very frequent. There were more attacks in 2005 and 2006 in Iraq than in the whole Middle East in the last 25 years (Hassan, 2008). In 2005, more than one suicide attack per day occurred on average in Iraq (MacDonald, 2005). The overall number of suicide attacks even increased in 2006 and 2007 before it declined (National Counterterrorism Center, 2010). In 2010, there were still more than 50 suicide attacks in Iraq. Researchers estimate that more than 13,000 people have been killed and more than 16,000 people have been wounded in Iraq due to suicide bombings by 2008 (Fisk, 2008).

Suicide bombings increased in response to two kinds of events: (1) military events, as terrorists seek to demonstrate their willingness to strike back, persevere, and defend their lives (Hafez, 2007), and (2) political changes that suggest democratization, such as the drafting of an Iraqi constitution by an Assembly elected in January 2005.

Hassan (2008, p. 279) lists 4 primary goals of Iraqi insurgents: "1. Drive the U.S. and coalition forces out of Iraq, 2. Overthrow the new Iraqi government and deprive it of popular legitimacy, 3. Keep Iraqi forces from becoming effective, and 4. Create a climate of general insecurity in the country" (see also Cordesman, 2005; Tosini, 2010). We should also consider two pieces of demographic information pertinent to suicide terrorism in Iraq. In terms of per capita gross domestic product (GDP), Iraq ranks 162 of 226 nations globally (CIA World Factbook, 2011 estimate). To gloss over an immensely complicated issue, religion also plays a big role in the context of suicide terrorism in Iraq. The vast majority (80 to 90 percent) of Muslims in the world are Sunni, and the Shia account for the minority. But in Iraq, 60 to 65 percent of Muslims are Shia (CIA World Factbook), creating a centuries-old breeding ground for intra-Muslim violent conflict.

Like in Afghanistan, suicide bombings receive public support in Iraq. In 2005, 82 percent of Iraqis wanted a near-term U.S. withdrawal (Hassan, 2008), and 61 percent of Iraqis supported attacks against U.S.-led forces (Program on International Policy Attitudes, 2006). As suicide terrorism is often a reaction to foreign oppression (Pape, 2005), perhaps one reason for the eventual decline in suicide terrorist activity stems from the agreement between the U.S. and Iraqi governments in 2008 (U.S.-Iraq Status of Forces Agreement), which outlined a withdrawal of U.S. troops from Iraqi cities by June 30, 2009, and from Iraq altogether by December 31, 2011. This satisfies the first goal of the insurgents.

But suicide terrorism in Iraq differs from that in Afghanistan, and the targets and the organizations that claim responsibility have changed over the years. While in 2003 about two thirds of the targeted victims were coalition forces, in 2005 and 2006, less than 10 percent of the targets were coalition forces (Hafez, 2007). In the same timeframe, the percentage of targeted Iraqi Security Forces increased to about 50 percent, and the percentage of civilians targeted increased to 20 to 40 percent, depending on the month data were collected (Hafez, 2007). One reason for this change in targeted groups relates to the fact that coalition forces withdrew and Iraqi Security Forces took over the responsibility to maintain order.

A change in terrorist groups claiming responsibility for the attacks coincided with the change in targets. In 2003 and 2004, pro-Baathists (mainly Sunnis) claimed responsibility for roughly one third of the attacks, Al-Qaeda in Iraq (AQI) claimed responsibility for roughly another third of the attacks, Ansar al-Islam and Ansar al-Sunna claimed responsibility for roughly another third of the attacks, and for roughly 10 percent no one claimed responsibility (Hafez, 2007).

In 2005 and 2006, however, Al-Qaeda in Iraq (AQI) claimed responsibility for roughly a third of the attacks, and no one claimed responsibility for the remaining two thirds. One reason for that change could be that some groups melded together with other groups. Second, as Shias account for most of the targeted victims, perhaps Baathist and Sunni attackers avoid claiming responsibility for fear of retaliation by Shia militia. Additionally, it seems that corrupt factions of government and, more recently, prisons are new breeding grounds for jihadists. Iraqi officials reported bribes to get AQI suicide bombers through security checkpoints or to get cell phones for AQI-related prisoners (Benraad, 2009). Thus, fighting corruption is one necessary step in the fight of suicide terrorism. Increasing transparency in republic and democratic-style governments should enhance citizens' sense of affiliation, certainty, and competence related to the ability to meet existential and higher-order needs.

Based on the high rates of suicide attacks on civilians, Iraqis must live with extreme fear. Humans, as social animals, place an upmost importance on belonging to a group. If the sociological or political structure prevents certain religious minorities from realizing this need for affiliation, as is the case in Iraq, the resulting insecurity can rival the intensity of fear for physical danger. The extreme nature of this fear could drive some to sympathize with terrorist cells. Of course, the fear of physical harm from ongoing violence only exacerbates the fear of psychological and political oppression.

How does the Nouri al-Maliki Administration in Iraq deal with the fear of suicide terrorism? The coalition forces and the Iraqi regime could not defeat the insurgency. It seems that the opportunistic strategy of suicide terrorism paid off and was at least partially successful in Iraq. Iraqi people supported the withdrawal of the United States and coalition forces because that remains the primary goal of the majority of suicide terrorists. But we saw that suicide terrorism continued even after the withdrawal of coalition troops began. Probably terrorist organizations realized the enormous psychological effect of these operations and are now applying the technique to reach other goals, such as destabilization of the government.

In Iraq, the tribal structure dominated for centuries and remains the most respected and knowledgeable organization of power in the nation. There are about 150 tribes in Iraq (Khan, 2007). As Khan (2007) puts it, "Only by acknowledging and demonstrating sensitivity towards tribal society will the Iraqi government, as well as the United States, be able to work alongside the tribal network to curb, and ultimately rein in, terrorist elements within Iraq." Prime Minister Nouri al-Maliki urged every province in Iraq to establish its own "salvation council" similar to the one in al-Anbar (Khan, 2007). A salvation council is an organization of tribal leaders including armed militias to fight terrorist groups. Such salvation councils might work in some regions but might not work in heterogeneous communities or where tribal loyalty is weak. Highly nuanced dynamics and alliances among tribes present further problems for the al-Maliki government. For best results, the Iraqi government must tactfully consider tribes on an individual basis and use caution when rewarding them.

Bin Hassan (2006) argues that we can only defeat Al Qaeda by defeating the radical ideology and propaganda. Military operations only represent one—relatively unsustainable—tactic to reach the ultimate goal. To achieve this goal, says bin Hassan, moderate Muslims must gain predominance over radical Muslims, and alternatives to the terrorist ideology must be presented.

These tasks seem incredibly daunting given the great risk tribal leaders who stand up and criticize Al Qaeda face. Many have been kidnapped and killed. The follower of Zarqawi, Abu Hamza al-Muhajir, the leader of Al Qaeda in Iraq (AQI), threatened to attack tribal leaders who cooperate with the Iraqi government (Hafez, 2007).

The Iraqi regime realized that popular support for suicide terrorism has to be reduced. As Crenshaw (2007, p. 158) discussed, "Changing popular attitudes to reduce support for suicide attacks is another solution that is often proposed." In terms of PSI-Theory, addressing the cultural constructs that determine the Iraqi view of affiliation, specifically easing tensions between Sunni and Shia sects of Islam, would significantly reduce the shared fear of one another within those groups which leads them continually attack one another. How to ease these tensions is, of course, a difficult problem.

Coalition forces implemented other measures since the war in Iraq with mixed results include tighter border controls to avoid smuggling of weapons, and administration of a nationwide census in Iraq as a first step and basis to implement law and order (knowing, for example, residents' addresses and vehicles) (Kuan, 2004).

A recent crackdown against Sunni politicians and the detention of hundreds of them by al-Maliki's security forces (*USA Today*, 2012) will certainly be perceived by the Sunni population as a widening of Shia influence and will probably result in more violence. Such a crackdown was probably only made possible by a series of severe suicide attacks and the subsequent fear of the primarily Shia population. McDermott and Zimbardo (2007) demonstrate how politicians can strategically use fear and anger to manipulate the public and justify tough political decisions. The crackdown might, however, increase sympathy towards terrorists in the Sunni population, because "fear for one's country and for one's identity as Muslim believers were the second major sources of legitimization for suicide bombing" (Chiozza, 2009, p. 4; the main reason was "disaffection towards the American people," Chiozza, p. 4).

"Politics and public opinion form the major confluence of events that can force terrorist groups to review their modalities. Public disapproval also plays a huge role in a review of terrorists' policies" (Zaidi, 2009, p. 416). Suicide terrorism is a complex problem related to historic, political, societal, cultural, and individual psychological factors (Güss, Tuason, & Teixeira, 2007). Only if those factors are targeted together, can the problem be addressed adequately.

CONCLUSION

We began this chapter with an overview of PSI-Theory through the emotion of fear. We treated fear of suicide terrorism as a specific version of fear, which activates motivations, cognitive processes, and behaviors in a specific constellation relative to the cultural and situational context. We attempted to demonstrate the complexity of the individual's response to personal fears of suicide terrorism, be it in the immediate aftermath of an attack or as a member of a community exposed to regular attacks. The politician's fear of suicide terrorism builds on that of the average citizen's in complexity: as an individual, he/she shares in much of the average person's experience, but as a national leader, his/her primary responsibility remains consideration of the sociotropic fear. Furthermore, a government must ultimately consider the causality of fear and suicide attacks among the contentious factions of its society. If they wish to make headway in the war on terror, national and regional governments must engage all relevant parties inside and outside their territories in a way that addresses the role that fear and the subsequent need for affiliation plays into their war tactics.

In Afghanistan, fear affects Karzai's behavior as a national leader primarily as a result of the uncertain and changing affiliations among the various parties in the conflict: the United States, coalition forces, intelligence agencies, the Taliban, al-Qaeda, Pakistan and other neighbors, the Karzai Administration, politicians from other parties, and the Afghan people. Decreasing uncertainty and increasing security and competence among Afghan people certainly represent primary ways to ameliorate terrorism, but we still do not know how to go about achieving that complex goal. While the behavioral responses to fear are very obvious, the motivations remain veiled.

Westerners often make the mistake of discussing the wars in Iraq and Afghanistan as extensions of one another—we hope that, if anything, we have at least demonstrated the error of this thinking. Al-Maliki in Iraq faces a different set of complexities. Although the shifting relationship with U.S. and coalition forces equally complicates his responses to terrorism in the long-term sense, al-Maliki does not face quite the desperation of impoverished masses as does Karzai. Using PSI-Theory and countless examples from political history, we contend that when basic existential needs go unsatisfied, violence becomes more and more justified as an attempt to reconcile unmet needs, and the resolution level of thinking decreases. Furthermore, in an ancient, shifting, multifaceted conflict as the war on terror, the lines between in-group and out-group are so blurry that those involved can hardly ascertain the appropriate group with which to affiliate and thereby decrease fear.

Certainly these conclusions only lead to more questions, and perhaps history as it unfolds will provide some answers. Our attempt to connect individual psychological constructs to political problems is an attempt to provide explanations. This novel approach, which considers the extent fear plays into political behavior, cannot provide the solutions to the conflict per se, but hopefully a better understanding and ultimately an approach to dealing with the complex problem of suicide terrorism.

REFERENCES

Ainsworth, M. D. S. (1991). Attachments and other affectional bonds across the life cycle. In C. M. Parkes, J. Stevenson-Hinde, & P. Marris (Eds.), *Attachment across the life cycle* (pp. 33–51). London, UK: Routledge.

Atran, S. (2006). The moral logic and growth of suicide terrorism. *The Washington Quarterly, 29,* 127–147.

Baumeister, R. F. (1996). *Evil: Inside human violence and cruelty.* New York, NY: Freeman.

Beckenridge, J. N., & Zimbardo, P. G. (2007). The strategy of terrorism and the psychology of mass-mediated fear. In B. Bongar, L. M. Brown, L. E. Beutler, J. N. Breckenridge, & P. G. Zimbardo (Eds.), *Psychology of terrorism* (pp. 116–134). New York, NY: Oxford University Press.

Benraad, M. (2009, December). Prisons in Iraq: A new generation of jihadists? *CTC Sentinel, 2*(12), 16–18.

Bin Hassan, M. H. (2006). Key considerations in counterideological work against terrorist ideology. *Studies in Conflict & Terrorism, 29,* 531–558.

Bloom, M. (2005). *Dying to kill: The allure of suicide terror.* New York, NY: Columbia University Press.

Bowlby, J. (1969). *Attachment and loss. Vol. 1: Attachment.* New York, NY: Basic Books.

Canadian Broadcasting Corporation *CBC News.* (January 16, 2006). Taliban attacks kill at least 24 in Afghanistan. Retrieved from http://www.cbc.ca/news/world/story/2006/01/16/taliban-attacks060116.html#ixzz0lfUBQfiX

Cannon, W. B. (1915). *Bodily changes in pain, hunger, fear and rage.* New York, NY: Appleton.

Chiozza, G. (November 11, 2009). *How to win hearts and minds? The political sociology of the support for suicide bombing.* Retrieved from http://www.elecdem.eu/media/universityofexeter/elecdem/pdfs/giacomochiozzatraining/How_to_Win_Hearts_and_Minds.pdf

CNN World. (September 1, 2005). Iraq mourns stampede victims. Retrieved from http://articles.cnn.com/2005-09-01/world/iraq.main_1_mortar-attack-annual-hajj-pilgrimage-stampede?_s=PM:WORLD

Cook, D. (2005). Women fighting in Jihad? *Studies in Conflict and Terrorism. Special Issue: Women and Terrorism, 28,* 375–384.

Cordesman, A. H. (2005). *Iraq's evolving insurgency.* Washington, DC: Library of Congress.

Crenshaw, M. (2007). Explaining suicide terrorism: A review essay. *Security Studies, 16,* 133–162.

Daiyar, A. (April 25, 2012). *Our brothers. Kabul perspective.* Retrieved from http://kabulperspective.wordpress.com/

Daiyar, A. (January 24, 2012). *The kingdom of Kabul.* Kabul perspective. Retrieved from http://kabulperspective.wordpress.com/2012/01/24/the-kingdom-of-kabul/

Dörner, D. (1999). *Bauplan für eine Seele* [Blueprint for a soul]. Reinbeck, Germany: Rowolt.

Dörner, D. (2003). The mathematics of emotion. In F. Detje, D. Dörner, & H. Schaub (Eds.), *Proceedings of the Fifth International Conference on Cognitive Modeling. The logic of cognitive systems* (pp. 75–80). Bamberg, Germany: Universitäts-Verlag.

Dörner, D., & Güss, C. D. (2013). PSI: A computational architecture of cognition, motivation, and emotion. *Review of General Psychology.*

Ekman, P. (2007). *Emotions revealed: Recognizing faces and feelings to improve communication and emotional life* (2nd ed.). New York, NY: Owl Books.

Euopäische Kommission. (2007–2013). *Länderstrategiepapier Islamische Republik Afghanistan 2007–2013.* Retrieved from http://eeas.europa.eu/afghanistan/csp/07_13_de.pdf

Fisk, R. (2008). The cult of the suicide bomber. *The Independent*, March 14, 2008. Retrieved from http://www.independent.co.uk/opinion/commentators/fisk/robert-fisk-the-cult-of-the-suicide-bomber-795649.html

Güss, C. D. (2011). Suicide terrorism: Exploring Western perceptions of terms, context, and causes. *Behavioral Research in Terrorism and Political Aggression, 3*, 97–115.

Güss, C. D., Tuason, M. T., & Teixeira, V. (2007). A cultural-psychological theory of contemporary Islamic martyrdom. *Journal of the Theory of Social Behaviour, 37*(4), 415–445.

Hafez, M. M. (2007). *Suicide bombers in Iraq: The strategy and ideology of martyrdom*. Washington, DC: United States Institute of Peace.

Hall, K. (2002). Reviewing intuitive decision-making and uncertainty: The implications for medical education. *Medical Education, 36*, 216–224.

Hassan, R. (2008). Global rise of suicide terrorism: An overview. *Asian Journal of Social Science, 36*, 271–291.

Hirsh, M., Hosenball, M., Peraino, K., McGuire, S., Flynn, E., Underhill, W., ... Klaidman, D. (2005). It can happen anywhere. *Newsweek*, 8/1/2005, Vol. *146*(5), 36–39.

Hoffman, B. (2003). The logic of suicide terrorism. Retrieved from http://www.theatlantic.com/magazine/archive/2003/06/the-logic-of-suicide-terrorism/2739/

Hoffman, B. (2006). *Inside terrorism* (rev. and expanded ed.). New York, NY: Columbia Press.

International Monetary Fund. (2012). *World Economic Outlook Database-April 2012*. Retrieved from http://www.imf.org/external/pubs/ft/weo/2012/01/index.htm

Karzai, H. (2006). *Afghanistan and the logic of suicide terrorism*. Retrieved from http://www.rsis.edu.sg/publications/Perspective/IDSS0202006.pdf

Khan, J. (2007). The Iraqi tribal structure. Background and influence on counter-terrorism. Retrieved from http://www.terrorismanalysts.com/pt/index.php/pot/article/view/2/html

Krueger, A., & Maleckova, J. (2003). Education, poverty, political violence and terrorism: Is there a causal connection. *Journal of Economic Perspectives, 17*, 119–144.

Kuan, E. K. P. (2004). How to combat car suicide bombings in Iraq? Retrieved from http://www.ipcs.org/article/suicide-terrorism/how-to-combat-car-suicide-bombings-in-iraq-1532.html

Lavanco, G., Romano, F., & Milio, A. (2008). Terrorism's fear: Perceived personal and national threats. *International Journal of Humanities & Social Sciences, 2*, 186–189.

Lester, D., Yang, B., & Lindsay, M. (2004). Suicide bombers: Are psychological profiles possible? *Studies in Conflict & Terrorism, 27*, 283–295.

MacDonald, N. (2005). Suicide Attack Every Day in the New Iraq. *Financial Times*, July 14, 2005. Retrieved from http://news.ft.com/cms/s/7c74abf8-f495-11d9-9dd1-00000e2511c8.html;

Maslow, A. (1954). *Motivation and personality*. New York, NY: Harper & Row.

McDermott, R., & Zimbardo, P. G. (2007).The psychological consequences of terrorist alerts. In B. Bongar, L. M. Brown, L. E. Beutler, J. N. Breckenridge, & P. G. Zimbardo (Eds.), *Psychology of terrorism* (pp. 357–371). New York, NY: Oxford University Press.

Merari, A. (2005). Social, organizational and psychological factors in suicide terrorism. In T. Bjørgo (Ed.), *Root causes of terrorism* (pp. 70–86). London, UK: Routledge.

News 24 (February 20, 2012). *Afghans rescue 41 child suicide bombers*. Retrieved from http://www.news24.com/World/News/Afghans-rescue-41-child-suicide-bombers-20120220

Pape, R. (2005). *Dying to win*. New York, NY: Random House.

Pedhazur, A., & Canetti-Nisim, D. (2010). *The impact of terrorism on political attitudes: A two-edged sword*. PowerPoint presentation. Retrieved from http://www.docstoc.com/docs/657226/The-Impact-of-Terrorism-on-Political-Attitudes

Pew Research Center (2010). *Obama more popular abroad than at home, global image of U.S. continues to benefit. 22-Nation Pew Global Attitudes Survey*. June 17, 2010. Retrieved from http://pewresearch.org/pubs/1630/obama-more-popular-abroad-global-american-image-benefit-22-nation-global-survey

Program on International Policy Attitudes. (September 27, 2006). *The Iraqi public on the U.S. presence and the future of Iraq—A World Public Opinion.org Poll*. Washington, DC: Program on International Policy Attitudes (PIPA).

Quillian, L. (1995). Prejudice as a response to perceived group threat: Population composition and anti-immigrant and racial prejudice in Europe. *American Sociological Review, 60*, 586–611.

Reuter, C. (2004). *My life is a weapon: A modern history of suicide bombing*. Princeton, NJ: Princeton University Press.

Rubin, A. J., & Bowley, G. (2012). With eye on past, Karzai lays out vision for an independent Afghanistan, *New York Times*, April 17, 2012. Retrieved from http://www.nytimes.com/2012/04/18/world/asia/with-eye-on-past-karzai-lays-out-vision-for-independent-afghanistan.html

Selye, H. (1956). *The stress of life*. New York, NY: McGraw-Hill.

Silke, A. (2006). The role of suicide in politics, conflict, and terrorism. *Terrorism and Political Violence, 18*, 35–46.

Sinclair, S. J., & LoCicero, A. (2010). Do fears of terrorism predict trust in government. *Journal of Aggression, Conflict and Peace Research, 2*, 57–68.

Soibelman, M. (2004). Palestinian suicide bombers. *Journal of Investigative Psychology and Offender Profiling, 1*, 175–190.

Sullivan, J., Pierson, J., & Markus, G. (1982). *Political tolerance and American democracy*. Chicago, IL: Chicago University Press.

The National Counterterrorism Center (2010). *2009 NCTC Report on Terrorism*. Retrieved from http://www.nctc.gov/witsbanner/docs/2009_report_on_terrorism.pdf http://www.fbi.gov/stats-services/publications/terror_08.pdf

ToloNews (April 16, 2012). Reactions and reassurances in wake of Kabul attacks. Retrieved from http://tolonews.com/en/afghanistan/5935-reactions-and-reassurances-in-wake-of-kabul-attacks

Tosini, D. (2010). Al-Qaeda's strategic gamble: The sociology of suicide bombings in Iraq. *Canadian Journal of Sociology/Cahiers canadiens de sociologie, 35*(2), 271–308.

United Nations Assistance Mission to Afghanistan (UNAMA). (2007). *Suicide attacks in Afghanistan (2001–2007)*. Retrieved from http://www.unhcr.org/refworld/pdfid/49997b00d.pdf

U.S.A Today. (2012). Suicide bomber kills 33 at Shiite funeral in Iraq. Retrieved from http://www.usatoday.com/news/world/story/2012-01-28/iraq-suicide-bombing/52835372/1

Valentino, N. A., Hutchings, V. L., Banks, A. J., & Davis, A. K. (2008). Is a worried citizen a good citizen? Emotions, political information seeking, and learning via the Internet. *Political Psychology, 29*, 247–273.

Williams, B. G. (2001). Mullah Omar's missiles. A field report on suicide bombers in Afghanistan. Retrieved from http://www.mepc.org/journal/middle-east-policy-archives/mullah-omars-missiles-field-report-suicide-bombers-afghanistan

Worth, R. F. (September 1, 2005). 950 Die in Stampede on Baghdad Bridge. Retrieved from http://www.nytimes.com/2005/09/01/international/middleeast/01iraq.html?pagewanted=all

Zaidi, S. M. A. (2009). Organizational profiling of suicide terrorism: A Pakistani case study. *Defence Studies, 9*, 409–453.

CHAPTER 7
Policy Preference in Response to Terrorism: The Role of Emotions, Attributions, and Appraisals

GEOFFREY WETHERELL, BRADLEY M. WEISZ, RYAN M. STOLIER, ADAM J. BEAVERS, AND MELODY S. SADLER

In the wake of terrorist attacks, such as those of September 11, 2001, people experience diverse reactions that influence subsequent behaviors and preferences for policies intended to thwart future terrorism. Perhaps not surprisingly, much literature is devoted to understanding the detrimental consequences terrorism has on mental health, particularly among people directly impacted by the attacks. Increased rates of depression and posttraumatic stress disorder have been well documented following acts of terrorism in the United States, including those of 9/11 (e.g., Galea et al., 2002; Schlenger et al., 2002) and the Oklahoma City bombing (North, 2010). Many U.S. citizens reported feeling strong emotions following acts of terrorism (Saad, 2001 as cited in Fredrickson, Tugade, Waugh, & Larkin, 2003). People expressed anger toward those who were responsible for the attacks, fear that more attacks could occur, uncertainty concerning America's ability to manage this new terrorist threat, and sadness for the enormous loss of life to family members, friends, and fellow Americans.

The personal impact felt by the U.S. populace translated into attitudinal and behavioral changes in the aftermath of 9/11. Americans became more unified, and experienced increased national pride (Smith, Rasinski, & Toce, 2001). Time spent volunteering (Traugott et al., 2002), blood donations (Linden, Davey, & Burch, 2002), and American flag displays (Skitka, 2005) all increased. There is evidence that political attitudes became more conservative (Bonanno & Jost, 2006; Nail & McGregor, 2009). For example, soon after 9/11, terrorism-related distress—defined as being upset by reminders of the attacks, having disturbing memories, and feelings of ongoing threat—was associated with a desire for revenge towards terrorists (i.e., aggressive antiterrorism policy preferences; Kaiser, Vick, & Major, 2004).

The purpose of the current chapter is to provide a social-psychological examination of the cognitive and emotional processes affecting political decision-making in response to terrorism, particularly endorsements of disparate antiterrorism policies. This chapter focuses on how attributions elicit specific emotions (i.e., what/whom one believes caused an event to occur) and appraisals (i.e., the perceived ability to cope with an event) following terrorist actions. Subsequently, the consequences of experiencing these specific negative emotions on policy preferences is discussed, specifically, the link between anger, fear, and sadness on support for either aggressive (e.g., war) or preventative (e.g., increasing airport security) antiterrorism policies is detailed.

AFFECT AS UNDIFFERENTIATED EMOTION

Early conceptualizations of emotion focused on global feelings, or affect, stratified by valence (i.e., positive vs. negative feelings; Schwarz & Clore, 1983). The valence of an affective state can influence how people interpret a situation (e.g., as risky or threatening) and how they decide to handle it, a process known as an "affective heuristic" (Schwarz & Clore, 1983; Wyer & Carlston, 1979). For example, participants in a bad mood report lower life satisfaction than those in a good mood (Schwarz & Clore, 1983). More germane to the current purposes, negative affect increases the tendency to perceive risk perceptions in the environment, while positive affective decreases it (Finucane, Alhakami, Slovic, & Johnson, 2000; Johnson & Tversky, 1983).

Accordingly, negative affect arising from terrorist threats leads people to overestimate the risk of future attacks, and increases overly cautious reactions to terrorism, such as recommending people regularly check their mail for anthrax (Sunstein, 2003). Negative affect also appears to be associated with support for hawkish foreign policy. For example, negative affect in response to terrorist attacks relates to increased support for military retaliation to terrorism, sending troops but not aid to the Sudan, and increased military spending in Iraq (Gadarian, 2010).

Although this research demonstrates a relationship between affect and preference for specific antiterror policies, it does not account for cognitive evaluations of the threat associated with terrorism, nor does it examine the effects of specific emotions on policy preferences in response to terrorist acts. Specific emotions, as opposed to general affect, are associated with specific responses (called "action tendencies;" discussed below) that influence how people react to emotion provoking situations (Smith & Ellsworth, 1985). Thus, in order to predict support for aggressive versus preventative antiterrorism policies, it is important to differentiate the specific negative emotions people experience.

ATTRIBUTIONS AND APPRAISALS PROMPT EMOTIONS

Emotions are elicited from a combination of external stimuli, internal understanding, and evaluation of the environment. Emotions enhance survival by regulating assessments of risk or gain, preparing physically for fight or flight, and conveying internal states to friends or foes. Emotions are composed of bodily sensations, arousal, affect, and outward expression (Schwarz & Clore, 1996, as cited in Higgins & Kruglanski, 1996). Emotions also accompany judgments about the cause of events, called "attributions" (Weiner, 1985), and perceived implications of environmental circumstances for the individual, called "appraisals" (Ellsworth & Smith, 1988; Lerner & Keltner, 2000). Two prominent theories, attribution theory (e.g., Weiner, 1985; Weiner, Perry, & Magnusson, 1988) and appraisal theory (e.g., Ellsworth & Smith, 1988; Lerner & Keltner, 2000;), describe the manner in which attributions and appraisals relate to particular emotions, and beget specific "action tendencies," or tendencies to either approach and aggress, or to avoid and flee (Frijda, 1986).

Attributions

People desire a sense of control over their environment, which leads them to search for the causes of circumstances (White, 1959). This is more likely to occur when a situation seems threatening or uncertain (Brader, 2006; Marcus, Neuman, & Mackuen, 2000; Schwarz, 1990). Attribution theorists explore three dimensions of judgment of the cause of behavior: internal vs. external attributions, controllable vs. uncontrollable attributions, and stable vs. unstable attributions. *Internal* attributions are beliefs that an action is self-motivated by the actor, while external attributions are beliefs that the cause of behavior is driven by the environment or situation in which the actor finds himself/herself. *Controllable* attributions refer to attributions concerning whether or not a person (be it the self or another) is in control of their actions. Attributions of *stability* suggest that a person's actions are based on unchangeable traits, while attributions of instability suggest that a person's behavior may change, or be changed over time. When people make internal attributions for the harmful behavior of others, they tend to experience anger and punish transgressors, whereas situational attributions for other's behavior are related to sympathy and a desire to help victims of circumstance (Carroll, Perkowitz, Lurigio, & Weaver, 1987; Weiner, 1993).

Attribution theory has implications for terrorism policy preference. People harbor "hedonic biases," the tendency to make situational attributions for harmful in-group behavior (i.e., external, uncontrollable attributions), and dispositional attributions for harmful out-group behavior (i.e. internal, controllable attributions; Harvey & Weary, 1981; Kunda, 1990; Ross, 1977; Weiner, 1985). For example, political conservatism was associated with fewer attributions that the policies and actions of the United States provoked the attacks of September 11 (Sahar, 2008), and more forgiving attributions for United States Marines accused of killing Iraqi civilians (Morgan, Mullen, & Skitka, 2010). Overall, attribution theory demonstrates that people attempt to assess the underlying causes of behavior and process information in ways that fit their expectations or motives.

Appraisals

While attributions concern a person's beliefs about the cause of an event, appraisals are a person's beliefs about their ability to cope with the event. Appraisals are important predictors of emotional reactions, and may mediate the relationship between attributions and emotional reactions (Smith, Haynes, Lazarus, & Pope, 1993). The appraisal-tendency theory of emotion suggests emotions are composed of six dimensions (e.g., Smith & Ellsworth, 1985; Smith & Lazarus, 1990): *certainty* refers to how sure one is about a particular situation, *pleasantness* refers simply to whether the emotion is positive or negative (a dimension akin to affective states), *attentional activity* refers to the level of attention associated with an emotional state, *anticipated effort* refers to the amount of effort a person needs to devote to a situation, *control* refers to the extent to which a person feels they have control over a situation, and *responsibility* refers to the extent to which a person feels responsible for a situation. These dimensions can apply to the self or to others, although appraisal-tendency theorists tend to focus on the perceived ability of the self to cope with circumstances (e.g., Smith et al., 1993). Of note is the fact that two of the six appraisal dimensions, control and responsibility, are complementary to the causal ascriptions that predominate attribution theory.

In addition to functioning at the individual level, it is important to note that appraisals can function at the group level. People desire social group membership (Grieve & Hogg, 1999; Hogg, 2000), especially with cohesive groups (Hogg, Sherman, Dierselhuis, Maitner, & Moffitt, 2007). Social identity theorists argue that cohesiveness leads people to feel like "prototypical group members" who integrate group membership into their sense of self, quelling uncertainty in response to threat (Hogg et al., 2007; Hogg, Adelman, & Blagg, 2010; Hogg & Turner, 1987). Group identification has implications for the study of emotions because people may base appraisals on how well their group can deal with a dangerous or stressful situation (Smith, Seger, & Mackie, 2007). Given that indicators of group identification such as feelings of national pride (Smith et al., 2001) increased in response to the 9/11 attacks, it may be that the appraisals of the U.S. citizenry outside of the areas directly impacted by the attacks (e.g., New York, Washington D.C.) were made with respect to the group's ability to cope rather than with respect to the individual's ability to cope. In sum, when circumstances are unexpected and/or important, people search for their cause, attach attributional significance to the actions of others (Gans, 1979; Weiner, 1985; Wong & Weiner, 1981), and experience a resulting emotional reaction which may then influence support for particular antiterrorism policies.

EMOTIONAL PRECURSORS TO ANTITERRORISM POLICY SUPPORT

Research on emotional reactions to terrorism often distinguishes the emotions of anger, fear, and sadness (e.g., Sadler, Lineberger, Correll, & Park, 2005). These emotions arise from different attributions and appraisals of terrorism, and have disparate implications for antiterrorism policy preferences. Broadly, attributions and appraisals associated with anger vary from those of fear and sadness. The following sections present evidence that anger is associated with support for aggressive strategies to combat terrorism while fear and sadness are related to support for more defensive strategies.

Anger

Anger was a common emotional response to the attacks on 9/11. Anger is elicited when a person or group's negative or harmful actions are seen as controllable, unstable, and emanating from internal traits (Weiner, 1985). Similarly, work based on appraisal tendency theory suggests that anger is related to perceptions that negative events are predictable, under human control, and caused by others (Scherer, 1999). Moreover, appraisal theorists have found that anger is associated with low risk perception and increased certainty for the perceiver (Lerner & Keltner, 2000; 2001). Emotions related to certainty, such as anger, are related to decreased information processing and search (Tiedens & Linton, 2001).

Both attribution and appraisal theorists find that anger relates to increased support for retaliatory policies in response to terrorism. For example, when Israeli Palestinians and Jews attributed responsibility for negative acts to one another, each side showed less support for peace and more support for violence, suggesting a responsibility–anger link (Kimhi, Canetti-Nisim, & Hirschberger, 2009; for an alternative perspective, see Tagar, Federico, & Halperin, 2011). Sadler et al. (2005) found that participants who felt anger in response to images of the September 11 attacks were more likely to support aggressive foreign policy (e.g., assassination of terrorist leaders in foreign countries, war against countries who harbor terrorists), and less likely to support humanitarian aid in countries known to harbor terrorist organizations (e.g., Afghanistan). Similarly, anger in response to the September 11 attacks was related to increased support for confrontational as opposed to preventative policies (Skitka, Bauman, Amarovich, & Morgan, 2006), increased moral outrage, and outgroup derogation toward Arab Americans, Palestinians, and people living in the Middle East (Skitka, Bauman, & Mullen, 2004).

Work based in Intergroup Emotion theory (see Smith, 1993) demonstrates collective emotional orientations may exacerbate conflict and terrorism when they are based in anger. For example, feelings of anger on the part of Israelis towards Palestinians before the Gaza War became worse over time, and were increased by perceptions of unfairness (Halperin & Gross 2011). Feelings of efficacy, the belief that the United States was capable of winning in wartime, were positively and directly related to anger, support for war and killing in both Afghanistan and Iraq in response to the September 11 attacks (Cheung-Blunden & Blunden, 2008). These results lend further support to the idea that anger is related to beliefs that one (or one's group) can handle present circumstances, as well as increased support for retaliatory measures.

Fear

As opposed to anger, fear is related to the perception that negative events are unpredictable and influenced by situational circumstances (Lerner & Keltner, 2000). The belief that one is unable to effectively navigate potentially harmful circumstances undergirds fear, and leads people to seek out information about the environment in an attempt to find a way to reduce the danger (Litz & Keane, 1989).

In general, people who respond to terrorist acts with fear tend to avoid policies that promote direct aggression, instead favoring policies that propose internal solutions. Experiencing anxiety is predictive of decreased support for the war in Afghanistan, involvement in world affairs, and presidential candidates who favor aggressive policies (Huddy, Feldman, Lahav, & Taber, 2005). Amongst participants high on Right-Wing Authoritarianism (RWA), fear predicts support for deporting Middle Eastern immigrants, whereas anger predicts support for expanding the war on terror beyond Afghanistan (Skitka et al., 2006). Research also suggests that fear after September 11 was related to decreased support for civil liberties in the name of security (Davis & Silver, 2004)—a defensive, rather than aggressive policy. Over the year following September 11, the perceived threat of terrorism predicted increased support for government surveillance and restriction of civil liberties (Cohrs, Moschner, Maes, & Kielmann, 2005), in support of the idea fear leads to preference for internal solutions. Thus, fear in response to terrorism is generally associated with opposition to aggressive anti-terrorism policy and support for defensive policy (Lerner, Gonzalez, Small, & Fischhoff, 2003).

Fear can also be influenced by the perception that one's group is at risk, independent of risk to oneself. For example, leading Dutch people to see themselves as Westerners, as opposed to simply Europeans (vs. Americans), led them to feel greater fear in response to 9/11, to search for information about the attacks, and to favor extending help and support to victims (Strelan & Lawani, 2010). These results demonstrate that inclusion in a group under terrorist threat increases fear, as well as a desire to support those in need. In its totality, research suggests that fear in response to terrorism relates to decreased confidence in one's ability to handle terrorist threat, decreased retaliatory aggression, and increased support for policies designed to prevent terrorism indirectly.

Sadness

Sadness and fear lead to similar, but not identical, outcomes concerning terrorism policy. Sadness relates to the perception that no one in particular is responsible for negative circumstances, and that outcomes are not understandable or predictable (Ellsworth & Scherer, 2003). Sadness is also associated with increased perceptions of risk, decreased support for hawkish foreign policy, and increased support for protective, nonaggressive measures. For example, sadness in response to terrorism reduces support for strong military responses and a desire to engage in the 'War on Terror', but increases situational attributions for terrorist attacks and feelings of inability to cope (Sadler et al., 2005).

THE INTERPLAY OF COGNITION AND EMOTION IN RESPONSES TO TERRORISM

In an attempt to integrate research on attributions, emotions, and policy preferences, Sadler et al. (2005) examined how anger, fear, and sadness relate to support for hawkish versus dovish policy in response to the September 11 attacks. To encourage reconstruction of initial emotional responses to the attacks, participants viewed videos with coverage of the events as they unfolded that day. The first video included clips that depicted planes striking the World Trade Center's North Tower, South Tower, and the Pentagon and crashing into a field in Pennsylvania, followed by a montage of images of the human impact of the attacks. Participants next wrote about their emotional reactions and completed measures of anger, fear, and sadness. Based on the assumption people would endorse a combination of negative emotions, the authors developed measures of the extent that each participant felt an emotion relatively more than the others. Thus, the emotion measures represented how much people's emotional reaction was predominated by anger, for example, relative to fear or sadness.

In addition to emotional responses, participants were asked how much they endorsed various causal attributions for the attacks. Possibilities included internal attributions such as blaming the terrorists themselves, and external attributions to security lapses at U.S. airports and the impoverished situation of the terrorists' home countries. Finally, participants were asked how much they endorsed whether or not the U.S. government should respond to the attacks with war (e.g., moderate and/or strong military responses), increased security at airports and border crossings, or humanitarian aid to foreign countries.

Results showed that the more participants blamed the terrorists for the September 11 attacks (as opposed to their situation, such as the life circumstances of the attackers), the more anger they reported, and the more support they showed for hawkish foreign policy, such as a strong military response. The more external attributions participants made (e.g., the attacks were the result of impoverished circumstances in other countries), the more sadness they reported concerning 9/11, and the less likely they were to support hawkish foreign policy. Interestingly, participants who were fearful did not evidence a strong pattern of attributions, yet they too were not likely to support hawkish policy. The lack of association among attributions and fear in these samples is not altogether surprising when one takes into account the fact that people who are fearful are least certain about what has transpired in a situation, or will transpire in the future, compared with people who are angry or sad (Roseman, 1984; Scherer, 1984; Tiedens & Linton, 2001).

The researchers also tested the causal relationships among attributions, emotions, and policy endorsement. Results supported a causal chain in which attributions lead to emotional reactions that lead to policy endorsement, in the case of anger and sadness. Specifically, assigning blame to the terrorists for causing the attacks led people to be angry, which in turn led them to support military responses but deny humanitarian aid. In contrast, making external attributions for the attacks (i.e., impoverished life circumstances in foreign countries were to blame) led people to feel more sadness, which in turn led to endorsement of providing humanitarian aid to foreign countries. It is noteworthy that demonstrated causal relationships held for people with both conservative and liberal political ideologies. Moreover, the reverse causal path—attributions mediating the relationship between emotions and policy preference—was tested but not supported. Overall, the results of this work suggest that anger, rather than fear, may be the emotional state most indicative of postterrorism aggression (c.f., Gadarian, 2010).

CONCLUSIONS

The emotions preceding terrorism policy preferences are founded on people's causal ascriptions for terrorism and how they appraise their ability to cope. If one believes others are responsible for terrorism and that one can handle the attacks, anger and support for offensive reactions to terrorism are likely to result. On the other hand, if one believes that situational factors are responsible for terrorism and that one is not capable of coping with terrorism, fear and/or sadness are most likely to emerge, as well as support for defensive/nonaggressive policy responses. These processes are suggested to occur both among people directly (e.g., people in New York City during 9/11) and indirectly (e.g., the U.S. populace at large) affected by terrorism. That is, emotions may emerge from attributions and appraisals made with regard to the safety of the self or on behalf of the safety of the country's citizenry, a group with which one shares a social identity.

The research summarized here shows that subtle differences in assessments of the causes of terrorism, and the ability to cope, lead to different emotional reactions and conclusions about what types of policies should be used to combat terrorism. This point becomes relevant when one considers the media coverage that followed 9/11 and preceded the U.S. invasion of Iraq. Looking back, critics have blamed the media for dictating public discourse, and creating an atmosphere that made war with Iraq seem inevitable without considering more diplomatic alternatives. This media-created atmosphere has often been labeled as "fear-mongering" (Brzezinski, 2007); however, the research presented in this chapter suggests that this label may not be accurate. In general, because fear and sadness are associated with decreased support for aggressive foreign policy, and greater support for protective measures, while anger is associated with endorsement of aggressive foreign policy, we suggest that a new label, "anger-mongering," may more accurately capture the media firestorm that followed the 9/11 terrorist attacks.

Understanding the interplay between attributions, appraisals, emotions and policy support has direct implications for institutions capable of influencing public discourse concerning terrorism, and thus, influencing people's beliefs about how to properly respond to terrorist acts. Framing terrorism as a function of the disturbed actions of a few deranged individuals, or as a function of the environment in which those individuals live, may sway public opinion towards war or peace, depending on the attributions and appraisals the public makes based on this information. Perhaps if policymakers and the media have a more complete understanding of how terrorism policy preferences are shaped by cognitive and emotional reactions, they will be more cognizant of the way they portray acts of terrorism. Future research should address if comprehensive media coverage of internal and external attributions for the cause of an attack, as well as multipronged strategies that include both offensive and defensive tactics to cope with an attack, reduce the tendency for a people's policy preference to default to war, and to reduce civil liberties in trade for a sense of increased security in response to terrorism.

REFERENCES

Bonanno, G. A., & Jost, J. T. (2006). Conservative shift among high-exposure survivors of the September 11 terrorist attacks. *Basic and Applied Social Psychology*, 28(4), 311–323.
Brader, T. (2006). *Campaigning for hearts and minds*. Chicago, IL: University of Chicago Press.
Brzezinski, Z. (2007). Terrorized by war on terror. *Washington Post*, 25, 2007.
Carroll, J. S., Perkowitz, W. T., Lurigio, A. J., & Weaver, F. M. (1987). Sentencing goals, causal attributions, ideology, and personality. *Journal of Personality and Social Psychology*, 52(1), 107–118.
Cheung-Blunden, V., & Blunden, B. (2008). Paving the road to war with group membership, appraisal antecedents, and anger. *Aggressive Behavior*, 34(2), 175–189.
Cohrs, J. C., Moschner, B., Maes, J., & Kielmann, S. (2005). The motivational bases of right-wing authoritarianism and social dominance orientation: Relations to values and attitudes in the aftermath of September 11, 2001. *Personality and Social Psychology Bulletin*, 31(10), 1425–1434.
Davis, D. W., & Silver, B. D. (2004). Civil liberties vs. security: Public opinion in the context of the terrorist attacks on America. *American Journal of Political Science*, 48(1), 28–46.

Ellsworth, P. C., & Scherer, K. R. (2003). Appraisal processes in emotion. In R. J. Davidson, K. R. Scherer, & H. Goldsmith (Eds.), *Handbook of affective sciences* (pp. 572–595). New York, NY: Oxford University Press.

Ellsworth, P. C. & Smith, C. A. (1988). From appraisal to emotion: Differences among unpleasant feelings. *Motivation and Emotion, 12*, 271–302.

Finucane, M. L., Alhakami, A., Slovic, P., & Johnson, S. M. (2000). The affect heuristic in judgments of risks and benefits. *Journal of Behavioral Decision Making, 13*, 1–17.

Fredrickson, B. L., Tugade, M. M., Waugh, C. E., & Larkin, G. R. (2003). What good are positive emotions in crises? A prospective study of resilience and emotions following the terrorist attacks on the United States on September 11, 2001. *Journal of Personality and Social Psychology, 84*, 365–376.

Frijda, N. H. (1986). *The emotions*. London, England: Cambridge University Press.

Gadarian, S. K. (2010). The politics of threat: How terrorism news shapes foreign policy attitudes. *Journal of Politics, 72*(2), 469–483.

Galea, S., Ahern, M., Resnick, H., Kilpatrick, D., Bucuvalas, M., Gold, J., & Vlahov, D. (2002). Psychological sequelae of the September 11 terrorist attacks in New York City. *The New England Journal of Medicine, 13*, 982–987.

Gans, H. (1979). *Deciding what's news*. New York, NY: Pantheon.

Grieve, P., & Hogg, M. A. (1999). Subjective uncertainty and intergroup discrimination in the minimal group situation. *Personality and Social Psychology Bulletin, 25*, 926–940.

Halperin, E., & Gross, J. J. (2011). Intergroup anger in intractable conflict: Long-term sentiments predict anger responses during the Gaza War. *Group Processes & Intergroup Relations, 14*(4), 477–488.

Harvey, J. H., & Weary, G. W. (1981). *Perspectives on Attributional Processes*. Dubuque, IA: Wm. C. Brown.

Hogg, M. A. (2000). Subjective uncertainty reduction through self-categorization: A motivational theory of social identity processes. *European Review of Social Psychology, 11*, 223–255.

Hogg, M. A., Adelman, J. R., & Blagg, R. D. (2010). Religion in the face of uncertainty: An uncertainty-identity theory account of religiousness. *Personality and Social Psychology Review, 14*(1), 72–83.

Hogg, M. A., Sherman, D. K., Dierselhuis, J., Maitner, A. T., & Moffitt, G. (2007). Uncertainty, entitativity, and group identification. *Journal of Experimental Social Psychology, 43*(1), 135–142.

Hogg, M. A., & Turner, J. C. (1987). Intergroup behavior, self-stereotyping and the salience of social categories. *British Journal of Social Psychology, 26*, 325–340.

Huddy, L., Feldman, S., Taber, C., & Lahav, G. (2005). Threat, anxiety, and support of antiterrorism policies. *American Journal of Political Science, 49*(3), 593–608.

Johnson, E., & Tversky, A. (1983). Affect, generalization, and the perception of risk. *Journal of Personality and Social Psychology, 45*, 20–31.

Kaiser, C. R., Vick, S. B., & Major, B. (2004). A prospective investigation of the relationship between just-world beliefs and the desire for revenge after September 11, 2001. *Psychological Science, 15*(7), 503–506.

Kimhi, S., Canetti-Nisim, D., Hirschberger, G. (2009) Terrorism in the eyes of the beholder: The impact of causal attributions on perceptions of violence. *Peace and Conflict: Journal of Peace Psychology, 15*(1), 75–95.

Kunda, Z. (1990). The case for motivated reasoning. *Psychological Bulletin, 108*, 480–498.

Lerner, J. S., Gonzalez, R. M., Small, D. A., & Fischhoff, B. (2003). Effects of fear and anger on perceived risks of terrorism: A national field experiment. *Psychological Science, 14*(2), 144–150.

Lerner, J. S., & Keltner, D. (2000). Beyond valence: Toward a model of emotion-specific influences on judgement and choice. *Cognition & Emotion, 14*(4), 473–493.

Lerner, J. S., & Keltner, D. (2001). Fear, anger, and risk. *Journal of Personality and Social Psychology, 81*(1), 146–159.

Linden, J. V., Davey, R. J., & Burch, J. W. (2002). The September 11, 2001 disaster and the New York blood supply. *Transfusion, 42,* 1385–1387.

Litz, B. T., & Keane, T. M. (1989). Information-processing in anxiety disorders: Application to the understanding of post-traumatic stress disorder. *Clinical Psychology Review, 9*(2), 243–257.

Marcus, G. E., Neuman, W. R., & MacKuen, M. B. (2000). *Affective intelligence and political judgment.* Chicago, IL: University of Chicago Press.

Morgan, G. S., Mullen, E., & Skitka, L. J. (2010). When values and attributions collide: Liberals' and conservatives' values motivate attributions for alleged misdeeds. *Personality and Social Psychology Bulletin, 36*(9), 1241–1254.

Nail, P. R., & McGregor, I. (2009). Conservative shift among liberals and conservatives following 9/11/01. *Social Justice Research, 22*(2-3), 231–240.

North, C. S. (2010). A tale of two studies of two disasters: Comparing psychosocial responses to disaster among Oklahoma City bombing survivors and Hurricane Katrina evacuees. *Rehabilitation Psychology, 55*(3), 241–246.

Roseman, I. J. (1984). Cognitive determinants of emotion: A structural theory. *Review of Personality & Social Psychology, 5,* 11–36.

Ross, L. (1977). The intuitive psychologist and his shortcomings. In L. Berkowitz (Ed.), *Advances in experimental social psychology,* Vol 10 (pp. 173–220). New York, NY: Academic Press.

Saad, L. (2001). Personal impact of Americans' lives. *Gallup News Service.* Retrieved from http://www.gallup.com/poll/4900/Personal-Impact-Americans-Lives.aspx

Sadler, M. S., Lineberger, M., Correll, J., & Park, B. (2005). Emotions, attributions, and policy endorsement in response to the September 11 terrorist attacks. *Basic and Applied Social Psychology, 27*(3), 249–258.

Sahar, G. (2008). Patriotism, attributions for the 9/11 attacks, and support for war: Then and now. *Basic and Applied Social Psychology, 30*(3), 189–197.

Scherer, K. R. (1984). Emotion as a multicomponent process: A model and some cross-cultural data. *Review of Personality & Social Psychology, 5,* 537–563.

Scherer, K. R. (1999). Appraisal theory. In T. Dalgleish & M.J. Power (Eds.), *Handbook of cognition and emotion* (pp. 637–663). Chichester, England: Wiley.

Schlenger, W. E., Caddell, J. M., Ebert, L., Jordan, B. K., Rourke, K. M., Wilson, D., . . . Kulka, R. A. (2002). Psychological reactions to terrorist attacks—Findings from the national study of Americans' reactions to September 11. *JAMA-Journal of the American Medical Association, 288*(5), 581–588.

Schwarz, N. (1990). Feelings as information: Informational and motivational functions of affective states. In E. T. Higgins & R. M. Sorrentino (Eds.), *Handbook of motivation and cognition: foundations of social behavior* (Vol. 2, pp. 527–561). New York, NY: Guilford.

Schwarz, N., & Clore, G. L. (1983). Mood, misattribution and judgments of well-being: Informative and directive functions of affective states. *Journal of Personality and Social Psychology, 45,* 513–523.

Schwarz, N., & Clore, G. L. (1996). Feelings and phenomenal experiences. In E. T. Higgins & A. W. Kruglanski (Eds.), *Social psychology: Handbook of basic principles* (pp. 433–465). New York, NY: Guilford.

Skitka, L. J. (2005). Patriotism or nationalism? Understanding post-September 11, 2001, flag-display behavior. *Journal of Applied Social Psychology, 35*(10), 1995–2011.

Skitka, L. J., Bauman, C. W., Aramovich, N. P., & Morgan, G. S. (2006). Confrontational and preventative policy responses to terrorism: Anger wants a fight and fear wants "them" to go away. *Basic and Applied Social Psychology, 28*(4), 375–384.

Skitka, L. J., Bauman, C. W., & Mullen, E. (2004). Political tolerance and coming to psychological closure following the September 11, 2001, terrorist attacks: An integrative approach. *Personality and Social Psychology Bulletin, 30*(6), 743–756. doi:10.1177/0146167204263968

Smith, C. A., & Ellsworth, P. C. (1985). Patterns of cognitive appraisal in emotion. *Journal of Personality and Social Psychology, 48*, 813–838.

Smith, C. A., Haynes, K. N., Lazarus, R. S., & Pope, L. K. (1993). In search of the "hot" cognitions: Attributions, appraisals, and their relation to emotion. *Journal of Personality and Social Psychology, 65*, 916–929.

Smith, C. A., & Lazarus, R. S. (1990). Emotion and adaptation. In L. A. Pervin (Ed.), *Handbook of personality: theory and research* (pp. 609–637). New York, NY: Guilford.

Smith, E. R. (1993). Social identity and social emotions: Toward new conceptualizations of prejudice. In D. M. Mackie & D. L. Hamilton (Eds.), *Affect, cognition, and stereotyping: interactive processes in group perception* (pp. 297–315). San Diego, CA: Academic Press.

Smith, E. R., Seger, C. R., & Mackie, D. A. (2007). Can emotions be truly group level? evidence regarding four conceptual criteria. *Journal of Personality and Social Psychology, 93*(3), 431–446.

Smith, T. W., Rasinski, K. A., & Toce, M. (2001). *American rebounds: A national study of public response to the September 11 terrorist attacks.* Chicago: NORC.

Strelan, P., & Lawani, A. (2010). Muslim and Westerner responses to terrorism: The influence of group identity on attitudes towards forgiveness and reconciliation. *Peace and Conflict: Journal of Peace Psychology, 16*, 59–79.

Sunstein, C.R. (2003). Terrorism and probability neglect. *The Journal of Risk and Uncertainty, 26*, 121–136

Tagar, M. R., Federico, C. M., & Halperin, E. (2011). The positive effect of negative emotions in protracted conflict: The case of anger. *Journal of Experimental Social Psychology, 47*(1), 157–164.

Tiedens, L. Z., & Linton, S. (2001). Judgment under emotional certainty and uncertainty: The effects of specific emotions on information processing. *Journal of Personality and Social Psychology, 81*(6), 973–988.

Traugott, M., Brader, T., Coral, D., Curtin, R., Featherman, R. G., Hill, M., . . . & Willis, R. (2002). How Americans responded: A study of public reactions to 9/11/01. *Political Science and Politics, 35*, 511–516.

Weiner, B. (1985). An attributional theory of achievement motivation and emotion. *Psychological Review, 92*, 548–573.

Weiner, B. (1993). On sin versus sickness—a theory of perceived responsibility and social motivation. *American Psychologist, 48*(9), 957–965.

Weiner, B., Perry, R., & Magnusson, J. (1988). An attributional analysis of reactions to stigmas. *Journal of Personality and Social Psychology, 55*, 738–748.

White, R. W. (1959). Motivation reconsidered: The concept of competence. *Psychological Review, 66*, 297–333.

Wong, P. T. P., & Weiner, B, (1981). When people ask "why" questions, and the heuristics of attributional search. *Journal of Personality and Social Psychology, 40*, 650–663.

Wyer, R. S., & Carlston, D. E. (1979). *Social cognition, inference and attribution.* Hillsdale, NJ: Erlbaum.

PART TWO

CHAPTER 8
The Legacy of Fear in Northern Ireland
RACHEL MONAGHAN

The "Troubles" in Northern Ireland began in the late 1960s and ushered in nearly 30 years of political violence between the state and republican and loyalist paramilitaries. More than 3600 people lost their lives (McKittrick, Kelters, Feeney, & Thornton, 2001) with another 50,000 to 100,000 injured (Breen-Smyth, 2012; French, 2009). The signing of the Belfast/Good Friday Agreement in April 1998 and its subsequent endorsement in referenda by its electorate (71.2 percent) and voters in the Republic of Ireland (94 percent) appears on the surface at least to signal a political solution to Northern Ireland's Troubles. Pivotal to the success of this transition from political conflict to peace was the introduction of a new power-sharing executive, with an inclusive system of decision-making. Furthermore, those parties involved in the peace process had to eschew the use of violence by signing up to the Mitchell principles of democracy and non-violence, and affirm their commitment to "democratic and exclusive peaceful means of resolving political issues" (Belfast Agreement, 1998: section 4:1). Both the British and Irish governments formally resolved their historical differences through the general and mutual acceptance of the principle of consent; thus, Northern Ireland would remain a part of the United Kingdom so long as the majority of its population wished it to remain so. The Republic of Ireland's constitution (articles 2 and 3) was amended to reflect this and power was devolved to a locally elected Northern Ireland Assembly (Darby, 2003).

In addition, the Agreement contained measures designed to create a "normal and peaceful society in Northern Ireland" including the early release of paramilitary prisoners, parallel reviews of the policing and criminal justice systems, the establishment of a new independent Human Rights and Equality Commissions, and a commitment by all parties involved to total disarmament of all paramilitary organizations by working with the independent International Body on Decommissioning. The devolved Assembly has been suspended on a number of occasions as a result of Unionist demands in relation to the decommissioning of

Provisional Irish Republican Army (PIRA) weaponry, prosaically described as "no guns, no government" (Knox & Monaghan, 2002).

As Shirlow and McEvoy (2008) observed, since 1998 there has been a significant growth in support for both Sinn Féin (the political wing identified with the PIRA) and for the Democratic Unionist Party (DUP), who were initially anti-Agreement in outlook. Furthermore, they note in the period following the suspension of the Assembly in 2002 to its reinstatement in 2007 that the main focus in political negotiations had been on persuading these two main parties to share power (Shirlow & McEvoy, 2008). Thus, acceptance of the St. Andrew's Agreement together with the complete decommissioning of PIRA weaponry and Sinn Féin's endorsement of the reformed Police Service of Northern Ireland (PSNI) led to the restoration of devolution (Owen, 2006). As Shirlow and McEvoy (2008, p. 5) explain this resulted in the,

> Improbable scenario of a DUP/Sinn Féin power-sharing executive. The subsequent image of Martin McGuinness (Sinn Féin) and Ian Paisley (DUP), men who had been at the forefront of political contestation in Northern Ireland since the 1960s, sharing power at Stormont has been widely lauded locally and internationally as confirmation *par excellance* of political conflict transformation in action.

However, as Mac Ginty, Muldoon, and Ferguson (2007, p. 1) aptly note, "reaching a peace deal is not the same as reaching peace," and Northern Ireland continues to experience low levels of political violence (Police Service of Northern Ireland, 2012a, 2012b, 2012c) and remains a deeply divided society (Hughes, Campbell, Hewstone, & Cairns, 2008). This divide can be seen as "essentially ethnic notwithstanding the fact that it is denoted by the religious labels 'Catholic' and 'Protestant'" (Doherty & Poole, 2002, p. 75). Census data reveals that 40 percent of the population identified themselves as Catholic and 46 percent as Protestant (Northern Ireland Statistics and Research Agency, 2008). The following chapter considers, first, the continuing threat posed by terrorism in Northern Ireland before addressing the legacy of fear some 14 years after the signing of the Good Friday Agreement. To this end, it will examine some of the policies pursued by the state to reduce terrorism and political violence; it will explore the continued divided nature of Northern Irish society before looking at violent republican groups and their activities.

THE CONTINUING THREAT POSED BY TERRORISM

The Independent Monitoring Commission (IMC), an independent watchdog set up by the British and Irish governments, began reporting in 2004 on the continuing activities of the various paramilitary groups in existence in Northern Ireland. In its last and final report, the IMC provided this overview of paramilitary activities between 2004 and 2011:

> Twenty-one murders; over eight hundred reported casualties of paramilitary violence; the robbery at the Northern Bank in December 2004; the feud between the Ulster Volunteer Force (UVF) and the Loyalist Volunteer Force (LVF) in 2004–05 in which the UVF murdered five people; the resurgence of serious violence by dissident republicans in 2009 and 2010 in which four [two soldiers and two police officers] have been murdered (IMC, 2011, p. 12).

According to the British domestic security services, MI5, the current terrorist threat level of Northern Ireland-related terrorism is rated as severe; this means that a terrorist attack is highly likely in Northern Ireland, and in Great Britain (England, Scotland, and Wales), the threat is deemed substantial with a strong possibility of an attack (MI5, 2011). Indeed, the activities of violent dissident republican groups, namely the Real IRA and the Continuity IRA, have been placed alongside those of international terrorism as a "tier one" security risk to the national security of the United Kingdom based on an assessment of the probability of the risk arising and its likely impact (HM Government, 2010).

Counterterrorism Measures

Throughout the course of the Troubles, the government introduced measures that it hoped would reduce the levels of political violence in Northern Ireland. A number of these measures will be explored and their unintended consequences explored. In 1971, internment without trial was reintroduced in Northern Ireland and people suspected of being members of paramilitary groups were arrested and detained. The Home Secretary stated in the House of Commons that the aim of "the internment policy is to hold in safety, where they can do no further harm, active members of the I.R.A. and secondly, to obtain more information about their activities, their conspiracy and organisation, to help the security forces in their job of protecting the public as a whole..." (cited in Spjut, 1986, p. 715). The information supplied by the Royal Ulster Constabulary (RUC) to the military for the purposes of Operation Demetrius was found to be inaccurate in that many innocent or inactive mainly nationalist or republican suspects were interned (Bruce, 1992). As Coogan (1995, p. 126) noted "the army quite often simply picked up the wrong people, a son for a father, the wrong 'man with a beard living at no. 47' and so on." Internment was extended to include loyalists and lasted until December 1975, and in this time a total of 1981 people were detained. The vast majority (1874) were Catholic/republican, with only 107 being from the Protestant/loyalist community (CAIN, 2012b). This policy designed to reduce the levels of violence in Northern Ireland is widely credited as a catalyst for increased community support and an influx of new recruits for both republican and loyalist paramilitary groups (Bruce, 1992; Hillyard, 2005).

As Walker (1992) observed, the PIRA had launched a sustained bombing campaign in 1973 "when there were no fewer than eighty-six explosions resulting in one death and over 380 injured. In the first ten months of 1974, there were ninety-nine further incidents, producing seventeen deaths and 145 other casualties" (Walker, 1992, p. 32). With the worsening security situation both in Northern Ireland and in England, the government introduced the first Prevention of Terrorism (Temporary Provisions) Act in 1974. This legislation was introduced following the PIRA's bombing of two Birmingham pubs in November 1974, which resulted in the deaths of 21 people and injured a further 180 persons (Pantazis & Pemberton, 2009). The Prevention of Terrorism Act "provided the police with extended powers of arrest and detention and gave them new powers to control the movement of persons entering Great Britain and Northern Ireland" (Hillyard, 1993, p. 4). The Act also made the IRA a proscribed organization and displays of support for the group became illegal. Additionally, the Secretary of State was given the power to exclude individuals from parts of the United Kingdom through the use of exclusion orders. Although as Doody (2012, p. 83) noted, "The reality of the measure was that someone who was suspected of terrorist connections was not acceptable in GB, but it was quite acceptable for them to be in NI." This view is confirmed by the numbers of persons subject to exclusion orders up to 1982, which showed 37 persons from the Republic of Ireland had been excluded from Great Britain and 230 persons from Northern Ireland had been excluded from Great Britain (Lord Jellicoe, 1983).

Research conducted by Hillyard (1993) explored the experiences of Irish people in Britain in relation to the Prevention of Terrorism Act between 1978 and 1991. He found that some 6097 (85 percent) of the 7052 persons detained as a result of the legislation were subsequently released without charge (Hillyard, 1993, p. 257). This led him to conclude that the legislation had created a "suspect community":

> The wide powers of examination, arrest and detention, the executive powers to proscribe selected organisations, the range of specific offences under the Acts, the power to issue exclusion orders and a whole new range of provisions covering seizure and investigation, have all played their part in making the Irish living in Britain, or Irish people travelling between Ireland and Britain, a suspect community ... (Hillyard, 1993, pp. 257–258).

Thus, the Irish in Britain and Catholics in Northern Ireland were feared by the general population and subject to intensive surveillance by the state. Hillyard's view is supported by Doody's (2012) research on the use of exclusion orders, which noted that the legislation reinforced the "othering" of the republican/nationalist community. "Othering" like the creation of a suspect community involves the designation of a segment of society as an "other," a group opposed to the rest of society (Boréus, 2009; Eyben & Lovett, 2004). Subsequently as Young (2003, p. 455) explains, "a series of binaries are set up: us-them, majority-minority, pure-impure, and with a seeming inevitability law-abiding-criminal, normal deviant" (Young, 2003, p. 455). In Northern Ireland, an additional binary or "us" and "them" pairing was created, in the form of terrorist-non-terrorist. Indeed, a popular stereotype at least within the Protestant community was that Catholics were terrorist supporters in that they "supported Sinn Fein, and since Sinn Fein was inextricably connected with the IRA and hence a terrorist organization . . . Catholics supported terrorists" (Herbert, 2007, p. 352). This stereotype was reinforced by Unionist politicians referring to Sinn Féin/IRA.

A Deeply Divided Society

Social psychologists have found that fear and anxiety are dominant emotions that inhibit contact between groups (Bar-Tal, 2001; Blair, Park, & Bachelor, 2003). As Bar-Tal (2001, p. 603) explains, "Fear constitutes combined physiological and psychological reactions programmed to maximize the probability of surviving in dangerous situations in the most beneficial way." Likewise, anxiety and more specifically intergroup anxiety, which are experienced as a result of actual interactions with individuals belonging to another group or the thought of potential interactions, can also result in negative effects on intergroup relations. Therefore in the context of Northern Ireland, if the source of fear is the "other" community then avoiding members of that community represents a protective behavior. Additionally, "anxiety, like fear, increases the desire to distance oneself form the out-group and avoid intergroup contact" (Hughes, Campbell, Hewstone, & Cairns, 2008, p. 529); thus, segregation can be seen as expressions of both fear and intergroup anxiety of the "other" community.

As previously noted, Northern Ireland remains a deeply divided society despite continuing results from the Northern Ireland Life and Times Survey (NILTS) that suggest that relations between Catholic and Protestants are improving; for example, when asked whether relations between the two main communities were better than they were 5 years ago, more than 60 percent of respondents have agreed with the statement over the past 7 years (NILTS, 2012). Societal divisions can be observed in a number of key areas, namely within education and residential segregation.

According to NILTS (2012), 70 percent of respondents in 2010 expressed the view that they would like to send their children to a mixed-religion school; however, more than 90 percent of children attend either a Catholic or Protestant school, with only 5 percent of children attending an integrated school, in which Catholics and Protestants are taught together in an environment that recognizes and promotes the expression of both traditions (Lloyd & Robinson, 2011). Previous research on education in Northern Ireland has identified a number of problems associated with separate schools and their long-term effects on social attitudes. Brocklehurst (2006, p. 92) argues that the separate "school is essentially a closed environment where potent sentiments expressed between children can ramify their notions of religious difference, and physical bullying and peer pressure can reinforce concepts of identity." Hughes (2011, p. 829) in her qualitative study of a Protestant school found evidence of "a relationship between ethnic isolation experienced by children and negative intergroup social attitudes."

In terms of NILTS, 83 percent of respondents in the 2010 survey expressed a wish to live in a mixed-religion area (NILTS, 2012). Despite this wish, somewhere between 30 to 40 percent of the Northern Ireland population live in segregated neighborhoods (Hughes, Campbell, Hewstone, & Cairns, 2008). Moreover, segregation is most evident in disadvantaged working-class neighborhoods and, in particular, in social housing. The strategic housing authority for Northern Ireland, the Northern Ireland Housing Executive suggested that some 98 percent of social housing in Belfast was segregated, that is to say more than 90 percent of residents on a particular housing estate were from a particular religious background. The figure for Northern Ireland as a whole was 71 percent (Byrne, Hansson, & Bell, 2006).

Residential segregation is not a new phenomenon in Northern Ireland, and in the case of Belfast, it can be traced back to the city's founding in the early seventeenth century (Boal, 2002). Early residual clustering according to Boal (2002, p. 690) served to provide to newcomers to the city both "a supportive community environment . . . and a response to hostile surroundings where the Irish immigrants were not welcomed with open arms by members of the respective 'host' populations." Throughout the course of the twentieth century, particularly in working-class areas, residential segregation increased (Boal, 2002; Shirlow & Murtagh, 2006). The outbreak of the Troubles saw some 1500 Catholic families left homeless between July and September 1969 as a result of being burnt out by loyalist mobs in Belfast alone (Whelan, 2009). The early years of the Troubles saw the "'largest forced population movements in Western Europe since the aftermath of World War II' up to that point, and in Belfast nearly one quarter of all households moved house between 1969 and 1974" (French, 2009, p. 888). Such segregation can serve a number of functions for individuals living in such areas including feelings of safety and security, community solidarity, the provision of a setting for intergenerational transmission of cultural tradition including collective remembering and an understanding of the "other" community (Boal, 2002). Subsequently, fear of being a victim of either a sectarian attack or terrorist incident meant many people developed comprehensive knowledge of "safe" and "unsafe" places (Burton, 1978).

Research has found that individuals living in segregated areas, while feeling safe in their own areas, maintained considerable fears in relation to areas dominated by the "other" community. The presence of such fears has often been identified as a tool used by both political and paramilitary groups to create and sustain territoriality. Territoriality is concerned with bordering, that is to say the marking out of boundaries and their maintenance and the creation of politicized spaces (Eyben & Lovett, 2004). Thus, segregated areas in Northern Ireland are often demarcated by flags, painted curbstones, and/or wall murals or even subliminal messages that you are in the "other" community's territory, such as a place name or local area/estate with a legacy of violence. As Shirlow and Murtagh (2006, p. 28) explain:

> Ethno-sectarian conflict has reproduced spatial enclosure and behavioural practices that are partly-dictated by widespread fears and prejudices. Presenting the 'other' community as fearsome and pathological was employed as a tactic that aimed to communities and reinforce spatial enclosure.

In segregated areas of Belfast levels of avoidance strategies remain high with large numbers refusing to use public facilities situated in locations within the confines of the "other" community. Shirlow and Murtagh's (2006) survey of over 9000 individuals found that in some areas three quarters of respondents would not use their nearest health center if it was situated in the "other" community's area. Moreover, 80 percent would travel to an area dominated by their own community if the closest social security benefits office was located in the "other" community, while less than a fifth of those surveyed would on a weekly basis undertake consumption-based activities such as shopping and socializing in areas dominated by the "other" community. They also found that just one in eight people worked in an area in which the "other" community was dominant. Survey respondents explained their decisions not unsurprisingly in terms of a fear of being verbally or physically attacked by members of the "other" community but also in terms of a fear of being disloyal to their own community by spending their money in areas dominated by the "other" community. As Shirlow and Murtagh (2006, p. 174) note,

> segregation is reproduced not by the boundaries between places but through the deeds and actions that maintain the need and desire to remain separate. Somewhat depressingly, and despite the decline in violence, identity formation remains influenced by real and imagined presence of an ontological 'other' that is 'threatening.'

Another dimension of residential segregation is the existence of interface communities; these are areas in which members of the two main communities in Northern Ireland exist with a common boundary. This boundary can be physical, for example, a road, park or the form of a "peace wall," or mental barriers. Physical interfaces were initially introduced to control violence and unrest between the two opposing communities. As Byrne (2011, p. 62) observes,

> From the outset peace walls were incorporated into the military's strategy of reducing and restricting levels of violence between communities ... There is no doubting that there was an immediate decrease in incidents of communal rioting, and damage to properties as soon as the peace walls were constructed within those areas.

However, over the long term, interfaces became the frontlines in the conflict, with a third of politically motivated deaths occurring within 820 feet (250 meters) of an interface and nearly 85 percent of such deaths took place within 3280 feet (1000 meters) of all segregated boundaries in Belfast (Shirlow & Murtagh, 2006). The Community Relations Council, an independent company with charitable status, which was set up to promote better community relations between Protestants and Catholics, describes interface barriers as more than physical barriers:

> They are the structures which remind us that hostility, fear and anger of the past remain alive and continue to threaten the peace of people and communities on either side of the barrier. The barriers separate communities in which fear remains that, without the barrier, lives will be put at risk. They freeze the geography and demography of single-identity communities and prevent all sorts of normal freedom of movement (Community Relations Council, 2009, p. 3).

Thus, the boundaries between segregated communities have become symbols of division, suspicion and mistrust. They have further reinforced community identity and territory, and more recently have inadvertently served as magnets for the exploitation and/or the expression of community tensions whereby youths engage in what has frequently referred to as recreational rioting (Byrne, 2005). As Feldman (1991, p.37) contends, "The wall itself becomes the malevolent face of the people who live on the other side."

The actual number of "peace walls" in Belfast is disputed with Byrne (2011) identifying 42 peace walls constructed by the Northern Ireland Office throughout the city, whereas a recent report by the Belfast Interface Project (2012) identifies 99 separate security barriers and defensive architecture including metal fencing, solid walls, roads with gates that are occasionally closed, roads that have been closed to vehicles but permit pedestrian access, fences with vegetation that acts as a buffer, and walls with metal fencing above. What is clear that despite reductions in the levels of political violence in Northern Ireland, additional peace walls have been built and none thus far have been dismantled.

Indeed in 2007, the Northern Ireland Office agreed following consultation with the PSNI, local communities, and statutory sympathizers to construct a new 25-foot-high "peace wall" in the grounds of the Hazelwood Integrated Primary School in north Belfast. Justifying this decision, the Security Minister for Northern Ireland said:

> My first obligation is to protect people's lives and to protect people's homes. Therefore it would be irresponsible for me to take down those barricades if it exposed people to risk and to threat, and I cannot run that risk. And as much as I want to see the end of these barricades I can't risk a family having their home firebombed, losing their lives in the process and that has to be my first and foremost responsibility (Goggins, 2008).

Also in 2007, the US-Ireland Alliance commissioned a study that sought to find out the views of interface residents in relation to "peace walls." The study asked over

1037 people living in three specific Belfast interface areas: the Falls/Shankill, East Belfast (Short Strand and Templemore Avenue), and North Belfast (Antrim Road and Tigers Bay). Of those surveyed, 81 percent wanted the walls to come down, of which 60 percent qualified their response by arguing that they did not want this to happen at present but only when it was safe to do so (Vargo, 2008).

THE IMPACT OF THE TROUBLES ON HEALTH AND THE CONTINUANCE OF FEAR

Some scholars believe that "inter-community tensions are damaging to the physical and mental health of the people of NI" (French, 2009, p. 889). The Cost of the Troubles Study undertook a survey of 1356 persons across Northern Ireland with the aim of capturing the experience and impact of the Troubles (Fay, Morrissey, Smyth, & Wong, 2001). They found that of respondents living in areas with a high Troubles-related death rate (defined as more than seven deaths per thousand), more than 25 percent experienced dreams and nightmares, a third reported involuntary recall, nearly 25 percent had taken some form of medication to counter such efforts while just over a fifth acknowledged an increase in their alcohol consumption. Additionally, in terms of their entire sample, approximately 30 percent were considered to be exhibiting post-traumatic stress (Fay, Morrissey, Smyth, & Wong, 2001). Subsequent research has found that patients affected by the Troubles present with both a range of physical problems such as injuries from "punishment" beatings and shootings, arthritis and diabetes, and psychological problems including stress, depression, and anxiety (Hamilton, Byrne, & Jarman, 2003). The recent WAVE report into the needs of individuals and their families injured as a result of the Troubles found "significant numbers of injured people reported on-going concerns about their own personal security. These fears have an isolating effect and many injured people chose to stay within their own local communities because of such fears" (Breen-Smyth, 2012, p. 11).

VIOLENT DISSIDENT REPUBLICANISM

While the Provisional Irish Republican Army (PIRA), the Ulster Volunteer Force (UVF), the Red Hand Commando (RHC), the Ulster Defence Association (UDA), and its affiliated group, the Ulster Freedom Fighters (UFF), namely those paramilitary groups committed to the peace process, have decommissioned their weapons, a small number of dissident republican groups opposed to the peace process continue to engage in acts of political violence. The Real IRA was established in 1997 by former members of the PIRA who were opposed to the peace process. The group was responsible for the Omagh bombing in 1998, which saw the largest loss of life in a single terrorist incident in Northern Ireland (29 people plus two unborn children). While the group apologized for those civilians killed, the attack was condemned by leading mainstream republicanism. Sinn Féin, the political wing of the PIRA, had consistently refused over the years to condemn acts of republican political violence, but in the wake of the bombing, its president Gerry Adams publicly stated, "I am totally horrified by this action. I condemn it without any equivocation whatsoever" (McKittrick, Kelters, Feeney, & Thornton, 2001, p. 1442).

The group suspended its military operations following the Omagh bombing but relaunched its campaign of violence in 2000 with a bomb attack on army barracks in Ballykelly, Co. Londonderry (Frampton, 2010). The group continued to target army bases and the Police Service of Northern Ireland (PSNI). In its attacks on the PSNI, the group attempted to murder two off-duty Catholic officers in 2007, and the following year a car bomb seriously injured another Catholic officer. In 2009, the group claimed responsibility for the murder of two soldiers at Massereene Barracks in Antrim (Horgan & Morrison, 2011).

A faction within the Real IRA utilizes the name of Oglaigh nahEireann (ONH) when claiming responsibility for terror attacks (Frampton, 2010). For example, a number of car bomb attacks aimed at PSNI officers including that of Paedar Heffron, an Irish language specialist, who lost a leg and had his bowel removed as a result of the attack have been claimed by ONH (BBC News, 2010a). The IMC, in its penultimate report, said of the Real IRA and its ONH faction "in terms of weapons, money, personnel and support the present dissident campaign in no way matches the range and tempo of the PIRA campaign of the Troubles" (IMC, 2010a, p. 6).

The other main violent dissident republican group is the Continuity IRA, which, although established in 1986, did not engage in a campaign of violence until the mid-1990s. The group was responsible for a number of attacks including the bombing of the Killyhelvin Hotel, Enniskillen, which injured 17 people in 1996, and the detonation of a large car bomb outside the police station in Moria, Co. Down in 1998. The group also claimed responsibility for the murder of Stephen Carroll in 2009, the first police officer to be killed since the formation of the PSNI (BBC News, 2012a; CAIN, 2012a). Speaking in relation to the Continuity IRA's murder of the PSNI officer, Martin McGuinness, the Deputy First Minister of the Northern Ireland Assembly and former PIRA commander, said, "These people are traitors to the island of Ireland, they have betrayed the political desires, hopes and aspirations of all the people who live on this island and they don't deserve to be supported by anyone" (BBC News, 2012b).

In the year following Carroll's murder, the IMC found that the Continuity IRA was not as active or as violent as their counterpart, the Real IRA. Moreover, their activities were concerned with training members in weapon handling and bomb construction, recruiting new members, attempting to obtain weapons, and the surveillance of potential targets (IMC, 2010b). The IMC concluded that the Continuity IRA "remained a major threat" (IMC, 2010b, p. 9).

Additionally, paramilitary groups retain a threat of political violence toward members of their own communities in working-class areas. Throughout the course of the Troubles, paramilitary groups both republican and loyalist alike operated an informal system of justice incorporating the use of "punishment" shootings, beatings, and the exiling/banishment of unwanted individuals from their areas (Monaghan, 2004; Monaghan & McLaughlin, 2006). This informal justice was developed in working-class areas albeit for different reasons. Initially, in Protestant working-class areas, patrols by paramilitaries were designed to assist the police in a period of increasing intercommunal tensions, rioting, and political violence. In Catholic working-class areas, paramilitary justice was in part a response to community pressure for organizations like the PIRA "to do something" about crime in their areas following the creation of a policing vacuum due to the conflict occurring within Northern Ireland. In addition, both republican and loyalist paramilitaries have used "punishments" to deal with transgressions by their own members or members of rival groups. Thus, in both communities, a graduated scale of "punishments" developed. "Punishment" beatings and shootings continued to exist for three main reasons during the course of the Troubles: the absence of a legitimate policing in republican areas and an adequate policing service in loyalist areas; the rising levels of petty crime and "antisocial behavior" occurring in working-class areas; and, the perceived failure of the formal criminal justice system to deal with those criminals apprehended by the police and prosecuted (Knox & Monaghan, 2002).

Within mainstream republicanism, there is an acceptance of the peace process; this is evidenced by the PIRA declaring its war was over, its subsequent decommissioning of weapons in September 2005 and the fact that the group has not undertaken any "punishment" attacks since February 2006 (IMC, 2010b). Additionally, Sinn Féin has given its formal backing to the PSNI in January 2007. Despite these developments, republican paramilitary "punishments" still occur; moreover, they are now undertaken by dissident republicans. In recent times, the levels of loyalist paramilitary "punishments" have decreased considerably and there have been no "punishment" shootings attributed to loyalist groups since 2009; in the same period, there have been 111 shootings by republican groups (PSNI, 2012d). The two main dissident groups, the Real IRA and the Continuity IRA, have both moved into the administration of informal justice in the areas in which they operate with acts of violence and intimidation being directed at community members for alleged drug dealings and other antisocial behavior. The Real IRA is believed to be responsible for the majority of "punishment" shootings attributed to dissident republicans, while the Continuity IRA has also been accused of "punishment" beatings and exiling (IMC, 2009).

The continued existence of paramilitary "punishments" is not surprising for a number of reasons. First, within republican working-class areas, the historic alienation of such communities from "any normal conception of interaction with the police" is not going to disappear overnight (Topping & Byrne, 2012, p. 44). Thus, even the most basic of cooperation between republican working-class areas and the police remains tense (Topping, 2008). Second, there is a perception (among residents) that such areas are plagued by "crime," and antisocial behavior and groups such as the Real and Continuity IRA are willing to deliver "punishment" shootings and beatings and exile undesirables given that the PIRA is no longer involved in such activities (Monaghan, 2004; Topping & Byrne, 2012).

Within republican areas of Northern Ireland's second largest city and Britain's City of Culture for 2013, Derry, the establishment of a group calling itself Republican Action Against Drugs (RAAD) has resulted in a recent upsurge in "punishments." Since its formation in 2008, RAAD, which is believed to be composed of former PIRA members, has embarked on a campaign to "clean up" nationalist areas and has targeted those involved in the drugs trade in Derry (*Derry Journal*, 2009a). In its first 18 months of operation, the group exiled more than a dozen individuals, shot and wounded 15 men, and undertook a number of pipe-bombings targeting those it believed were involved in the drugs trade (BBC Spotlight, 2010; *Derry Journal*, 2009b). In addition, to targeting those selling illegal drugs, the group have also attacked local businesses selling "legal highs." In February 2010, a lone gunman walked into Raymond Coyle's shop in the city center and shot him several times in the leg; his "crime" was to sell such products (McDermott, 2010). In the past year, RAAD has expelled more than 200 people from the city and continued to shoot those it alleges are involved with drugs (McDonald, 2012). In March 2012, a mother accompanied her 18-year-old son to an "appointment" to be shot once in each leg. She explained her reason to accompany her son was based on a fear for the safety of her other children: "I couldn't have them [RAAD] coming to the house to attack him as I have other young children to protect" (*Derry Journal*, 2012a).

In another incident, in the same month, a former republican prisoner had to take his son to an alleyway and watch as both his son and nephew were shot a number of times following a drunken row with a member of RAAD. Speaking after the attack, Ciaran McFadden stated "These people are really scary. They are very dangerous people and they listen to no-one . . . They are flexing their muscles since killing of Andrew Allen. They are scaring the community now, they have crossed a line" (*Derry Journal*, 2012b). Allen had left Derry following a RAAD death threat and had set up home across the border in Buncrana in the Republic of Ireland; he was shot dead by the group in February 2012. His mother has said that the "peace process no longer meant anything to her or her family" and that she, like many others, was "existing 'in a city of fear'" (McDonald, 2012, p. 1).

A further development in the activities of RAAD occurred on June 2, 2012, when for the first time they targeted the PSNI, who were involved in a house search in the Creggan area of Derry. They launched a bomb attack on a police vehicle; the vehicle suffered extensive damage and the police are treating the incident as attempted murder (*Derry Journal*, 2012c). This incident marks not only a shift in targeting away from alleged drug dealers and antisocial elements within their community to the police but also an escalation in the levels of violence to which they resort.

THE CONTINUANCE OF "OTHERING"

Despite the existence of a political settlement to the conflict, the process of "othering" still continues within Northern Ireland. A recent survey of the Orange Order, the largest Protestant organization in Northern Ireland found that 60 percent of its members agreed with the statement "most Catholics are IRA sympathizers" (BBC News, 2011). Indeed, figures released in terms of the number of stops and searches made by the police under Section 44 of the Terrorism Act (which allows police to act without reasonable suspicion) show that in 2008–2009, the antiterror legislation was used on nearly 10,000 occasions, but in terms of the northwest of Northern Ireland, the figure was over 2500. This is an area characterized by dissident republican activity and support (Frampton, 2010; IMC, 2010b). A Sinn Féin spokesperson noted that "these statistics . . . show that Derry and Strabane, which are predominantly republican areas, had the highest volume of stop-and-search incidents anywhere in the North" (BBC News, 2010b) and suggest that young republican males were being treated as a "suspect community" within the larger Catholic community in the area.

CONCLUSION

What is clear from the discussion above is that government policies adopted in the Troubles have lasting legacies in the Northern Ireland of today. The creation of a "suspect community" through the use of internment, the implementation of the Prevention of Terrorism Act and its corresponding use of exclusion orders together with self-imposed residential segregation and the construction of "peace walls" and defensive architecture has resulted in increased fear, tension and violence in interface areas (Hamilton, Hansson, Bell, & Toucas, 2008; Shirlow, 2003). Although Northern Ireland in general has moved into what could be considered a postconflict phase with the vast majority of people accepting the Belfast/Good Friday Agreement, with politicians divided by decades of animosity working together in the Northern Ireland Assembly (evidenced by the First Minister, Peter Robinson, coming from the Democratic Unionist Party and the Deputy First Minister, Martin McGuinness coming from Sinn Féin), Northern Ireland still remains a deeply divided society. Pockets remain within society in which the continuing fear of the "other" community is played out either through the segregated nature of people's lives or through the persistence of low levels of political violence. While recognizing that some of these fears may well be imagined, we must remember that "all fears matter because they are real to the people who hold them" (Gold & Revill, 2003, p. 34).

REFERENCES

Bar-Tal, D. (2001). Why does fear override hope in societies engulfed by intractable conflict, as it does in the Israeli society? *Political Psychology*, 22, 601–627.
BBC News. (2010a). Car bomb officer Paedar Heffron's leg amputated. January 13. Available at: http://news.bbc.co.uk/1/hi/northern_ireland/8457169.stm, accessed May 14, 2012.

BBC News. (2010b). Police stop-and-search powers used most in North West. January 21. Available at: http://news.bbc.co.uk/1/hi/northern_ireland/foyle_and_west/8471871.stm, accessed May 10, 2012.

BBC News. (2011). 60 percent of Order view Catholics as "IRA sympathisers." November 22. Available at: http://www.bbc.co.uk/news/uk-northern-ireland-15832376, accessed May 4, 2012.

BBC News. (2012a). The story of the Stephen Carroll murder trial. March 30. Available at: http://www.bbc.co.uk/news/uk-northern-ireland-17220730, accessed May 14, 2012.

BBC News. (2012b). Constable Carroll murder united Northern Ireland in revulsion. Available at: http://www.bbc.co.uk/news/uk-northern-ireland-17562192, accessed May 14, 2012.

BBC Spotlight (2010, March 9) Blood Summons. Broadcast BBC Northern Ireland.

Belfast Agreement (1998) *The agreement reached in the multi-party negotiations*. Belfast: Northern Ireland Office.

Belfast Interface Project (2012). *Belfast Interfaces: Security barriers and defensive use of space.* Belfast: BIP.

Blair, I.V., Park, B., & Bachelor, J. (2003). Understanding intergroup anxiety: Are some people more anxious than others? *Group Processes & Intergroup Relations*, 6, 151–169.

Boal, F.W. (2002). Belfast: Walls within. *Political Geography*, 21, 687–694.

Boréus, K. (2009). Discursive discrimination: A typology. *European Journal of Social Theory*, 9, 405–424.

Breen-Smyth, M. (2012). *The Needs of Individuals and their Families Injured as a Result of the Troubles in Northern Ireland*. Belfast: WAVE.

Brocklehurst, H. (2006). *Who's Afraid of Children? Children, Conflict and International Relations*. Aldershot: Ashgate.

Bruce, S. (1992). *The Red Hand: Protestant Paramilitaries in Northern Ireland*. Oxford: Oxford University Press.

Burton, F. (1978). *The Politics of Legitimacy: Struggles in a Belfast Community*. London: Routledge.

Byrne, J. (2005). *Interface Violence in East Belfast During 2002*. Belfast: Institute for Conflict Research.

Byrne, J. (2011). *Belfast's Peace Walls: Agenda Dynamics and Actors in the Emerging Policy Process* (unpublished doctoral thesis). University of Ulster, Northern Ireland.

Byrne, J., Hansson, U., & Bell, J. (2006). *Shared Living: Mixed Residential Communities in Northern Ireland*. Belfast: Institute for Conflict Research.

CAIN. (2012a). Abstracts of organisations. Available at: http://cain.ulst.ac.uk/othelem/organ/corgan.htm, accessed May 14, 2012.

CAIN. (2012b). Internment—Summary of events. Available at: http://cain.ulst.ac.uk/events/intern/sum.htm, accessed May 15, 2012.

Community Relations Council. (2009). *Towards Sustainable Security: Interface Barriers and the Legacy of Segregation in Belfast*. Belfast: CRC.

Coogan, T.P. (1995). *The Troubles: Ireland's Ordeal 1966–1996 and the Search for Peace*. London: Hutchinson.

Darby, J. (2003). Northern Ireland: The background to the peace process. Available at: http://cain.ulst.ac.uk/events/peace/darby03.htm, accessed May 10, 2012.

Derry Journal. (2009a, August 18). Ex-Provos swell RAAD ranks. Available at: http://www.derryjournal.com/news/local/ex-provos-swell-raad-ranks-1-2139816, accessed May 2, 2012.

Derry Journal. (2009b, December 14). RAAD Bomb Blitz. Available at: http://www.derryjournal.com/news/local/raad-bomb-blitz-1-2142681, accessed May 1, 2012.

Derry Journal (2012a, April 30). "I hope he listens now"—Mum ordered to bring so to be shot. Available at: http://www.derryjournal.com/news/local/i-hope-he-listens-now-mum-ordered-to-bring-son-to-be-shot-1-3789831, accessed May 5, 2012.

Derry Journal. (2012b, March 9). "I had to watch my son get shot." Available at: http://www.derryjournal.com/news/local/i-had-to-watch-my-son-get-shot-1-3606580, accessed March 9, 2012.

Derry Journal. (2012c, June 4). RAAD admit attack on police. Available at: http://www.derryjournal.com/news/local/raad-admit-attack-on-police-1-3916693, accessed June 4, 2012.

Doody, J. (2012). Creating suspect communities: Exploring the use of exclusion orders in Northern Ireland. *Behavioral Sciences of Terrorism and Political Aggression, 4*, 77–98.

Doherty, P., & Poole, M.A. (2002). Religion as an indicator of ethnicity in Northern Ireland—an alternative perspective. *Irish Geography, 35*, 75–89.

Eyben R., & Lovett J. (2004). *Political and Social Inequality: A Review*. IDS Development Bibliography 20. Brighton: Institute of Development Studies.

Fay, M.T., Morrissey, M., Smyth, M., & Wong, T. (2001). *The Cost of the Troubles Study* (2nd Edn). Derry: INCORE.

Feldman, A. (1991). *Formations of Violence: The Narrative of the Body and Political Terror in Northern Ireland*. Chicago: University of Chicago Press.

Frampton, M. (2010). *The Return of the Militants: Violent Dissident Republicanism*. London: International Centre for the Study of radicalisation and Political Violence.

French, D. (2009). Residential segregation and health in Northern Ireland. *Health & Place, 15*, 888–896.

Gold, J.R., & Revill, G. (2003). Exploring landscapes of fear. *Capital & Class, 80*, 27–50.

Goggins, P. (2008, September 5). *The Wall*. Belfast: Radio Ulster.

Hamilton, J., Byrne, J., & Jarman, N. (2003). *A Review of Health and Social Care Needs of Victims and Survivors of the Northern Ireland Conflict*. Eastern Health and Social Services Board (unpublished).

Hamilton, J., Hansson, U., Bell, J., & Toucas, S. (2008). *Segregated Lives: Social Division, Sectarianism and Everyday Life in Northern Ireland*. Belfast: Institute for Conflict Research.

Herbert, D. (2007). Shifting securities in Northern Ireland: "Terror" and "the Troubles" in global media and local memory. *European Journal of Cultural Studies, 10*, 343–359.

Hillyard, P. (1993). *Suspect Community: People's Experience of the Prevention of Terrorism Acts in Britain*. London: Pluto Press.

Hillyard, P. (2005). *ECLN essays: The "War on Terror"—Lessons from Ireland*. Available at: www.ecln.org, accessed May 10, 2012.

HM Government. (2010). *A Strong Britain in an Age of Uncertainty: The National Security Strategy*. London: HM Government.

Horgan, J., & Morrison, J.F. (2011). Here to stay? The rising threat of violent dissident republicanism in Northern Ireland. *Terrorism and Political Violence, 23*, 642–669.

Hughes, J. (2011). Are separate schools divisive? A case study from Northern Ireland. *British Educational Research Journal, 37*, 829–850.

Hughes, J., Campbell, A., Hewstone, M., & Cairns, E. (2008). "What's there to fear?"—A comparative study of responses to the out-group in mixed and segregated areas of Belfast. *Peace & Change, 33*, 522–548.

Independent Monitoring Commission (2009). *Twenty-second report*. London: The Stationery Office.

Independent Monitoring Commission. (2010a). *Twenty-Fifth report*. London: The Stationery Office.

Independent Monitoring Commission (2010b). *Twenty-Third report*. London: The Stationery Office.

Independent Monitoring Commission. (2011). *Twenty-Sixth and final report*. London: The Stationery Office.

Jellicoe, Lord (1983) *Review of the operation of the Prevention of Terrorism (Temporary Provisions) Acts 1976*. Cmnd. 8803. London: The Stationery Office.

Knox, C., & Monaghan, R (2002). *Informal Justice in Divided Societies*. Basingstoke: Palgrave Macmillan.

Lloyd, K., & Robinson, G. (2011). Intimate mixing—bridging the gap? Catholic-Protestant relationships in Northern Ireland. *Ethnic and Racial Studies, 34*, 2134–2152.

Mac Ginty, R., Muldoon, O.T., & Ferguson, N. (2007). No war, no peace: Northern Ireland after the Agreement. *Political Psychology, 28*, 1–11.

McDermott, E. (2010, January 10). Shot man not warned over selling "legal highs." *Belfast Telegraph*, p. 16.

McDonald, H. (2012, May 14). Fear and republican vigilantes stalk new city of culture. *The Guardian*, p. 1.

McKittrick, D., Kelters, S., Feeney, B. & Thornton, C. (2001). *Lost Lives*. Edinburgh: Mainstream Publishing.

MI5 (2011). Terrorist threat levels. Available at: https://www.mi5.gov.uk/output/threat-levels.html, accessed May 12, 2012.

Monaghan, R. (2004). An imperfect peace: Paramilitary "punishments" in Northern Ireland. *Terrorism and Political Violence, 16*, 439–461.

Monaghan, R., & McLaughlin, S. (2006). Informal justice in the City. *Space and Polity, 10*, 171–186.

Northern Ireland Life and Times Survey (2012). Module: Community Relations. Available at: http://www.ark.ac.uk/nilt/results/comrel.html, accessed May 30, 2012.

Northern Ireland Statistics and Research Agency (2008). 2001 Census: Key statistics to output area level. Available at: http://www.nisra.gov.uk/Census/2001%20Census%20Results/Key%20Statistics/KeyStatisticstoOutputAreaLevel.html, accessed May 10, 2012.

Owen, P. (2006, October 17). What is the St. Andrews Agreement? *The Guardian*. Available at: http://www.guardian.co.uk/politics/2006/oct/17/northernireland.devolution1, accessed May 6, 2012.

Pantazis, C., & Pemberton, S. (2009). From the "old" to the "new" suspect community. *British Journal of Criminology, 49*, 646–666.

Police Service of Northern Ireland (2012a). Deaths due to the Security Situation in Northern Ireland 1969–29 February 2012. Available at: http://www.psni.police.uk/deaths_cy.pdf, accessed May 14, 2012.

Police Service of Northern Ireland (2012b). Persons Injured as a Result of the Security Situation in Northern Ireland 1968–29 February 2012. Available at: http://www.psni.police.uk/persons_injured_cy.pdf, accessed May 14, 2012.

Police Service of Northern Ireland (2012c). Security-Related Incidents 1969–29 February 2012 Available at: http://www.psni.police.uk/security_related_incidents_cy.pdf, accessed May 14, 2012.

Police Service of Northern Ireland (2012d). Casualties as a Result of Paramilitary-Style Attacks 1973–29 February 2012. Available at http://www.psni.police.uk/ps_attacks_cy.pdf, accessed May 15, 2012.

Shirlow, P. (2003). Ethnosectarianism and the reproduction of fear in Belfast. *Capital & Class, 80*, 77–93.

Shirlow, P., & McEvoy, K. (2008). *Beyond the Wire: Former Prisoners and Conflict Transformation in Northern Ireland*. London: Pluto Press.

Shirlow, P., & Murtagh, B. (2006). *Belfast: Segregation, Violence and the City*. London: Pluto Press.

Spjut, R.J. (1986). Internment and detention without trial in Northern Ireland 1971–1975: Ministerial policy and practice. *Modern Law Review, 49*, 712–739.

Topping, J. (2008). Diversifying form within: Community policing and the governance of security in Northern Ireland. *British Journal of Criminology, 18*, 377–398.

Topping, J., & Byrne, J. (2012). Paramilitary punishments in Belfast: Policing beneath the peace. *Behavioral Sciences of Terrorism and Political Aggression, 4*, 41–59.

Vargo, T. (2008). Belfast residents asked if peace lines should come down. US-Ireland Alliance. Available at: http://www.us-irelandalliance.org/wmspage.cfm?parm1=779, accessed January 15, 2009.

Walker, C. (1992). *The Prevention of Terrorism in British Law* (2nd edn.). Manchester: Manchester University Press.

Whelan, P. (2009). Remembering the Past: Bombay Street, 1969. August 13. *An Phoblacht*. Available at: http://www.anphoblacht.com/news/detail/38678, accessed May 5, 2012.

Young, J. (2003). To these wet and windy shores: Recent immigration policy in the UK. *Punishment & Society, 5*, 449–462.

CHAPTER 9
A New Normal? Australian Responses to Terrorism and Their Impacts
ANNE ALY

In March 2002, with much pomp, the Bush administration's new Department of Homeland Security introduced its color-coded terror alert system: green, "low"; blue, "guarded"; yellow, "elevated"; orange, "high"; red, "severe." The nation has danced ever since between yellow and orange. Life has restlessly settled, to all appearances permanently, on the redward end of the spectrum, the blue-greens of tranquility a thing of the past. "Safe" doesn't even merit a hue. Safe, it would seem, has fallen off the spectrum of perception. Insecurity, the spectrum says, is the new normal.

Massumi, 2005, p. 31

The terrorist attacks on the United States in September 2001, we were told, changed the world forever: a tragic harbinger of a new era of insecurity. An era in which warfare extended beyond the traditional boundaries of combat and the battlefields of "ideological struggle" (Bush, 2006) are our homes, our backyards, and our living rooms.

Australia's cultural kinship with the United States drew Australia, along with the rest of the Western world, into a global battle of "good versus evil." Australia was positioned as a possible target for terrorists whose only motivation was an intense desire to annihilate the "free" world. In October 2002, the Bali bombings consolidated terrorism as a problematic issue in the Australian public's consciousness. Eighty-six Australians were among the 202 fatalities when dual bombs exploded at popular nightspots in Kuta. The attacks were constructed in the political and popular media as a direct attack on Australia by an irreconcilable, incomprehensible, and unappeasable enemy motivated only by hatred:

> Just as we love Australia, the evil men who murdered our people and others in Bali, they surely hate Australia. And why do they hate us . . . . They hate us for our oddly persistent goodness (Sheridan, 2002, p. 13).

In the "new normal" (Massumi 2005, p. 31), we are urged to "be alert but not alarmed," and insecurity is transformed from a situational emotional response (Cameron & McCormick, 1954) to a persistent state of alarm and terrorism is imagined as an unknown, but impending, doom. Everyday situations (traveling to and from work; visiting crowded shopping centers) and objects (a back-pack, a credit card, a mobile phone) become subliminally associated with the threat of terrorism. The terrorist threat, articulated through images of the mundane and banal, is situated in the ordinary: normalizing threat and reconstructing what would otherwise be considered exceptional measures as rational, prudent, even necessary (Huysmans, 2004). The heightened security measures at airports, the perpetual salience of the *National Security Public Information Campaign* urging Australians to look out for Australia by reporting anything suspicious, and the progressive introduction of over 30 legislative amendments in the interests of national security invoke the specter of security and amplify threat in the public imagination.

In public use, the term "terrorism" takes on an expanded meaning and refers as much to an act of terrorism as a state of terror. Perhaps the most telling example of how the boundaries of meaning of terrorism and terror have become collapsed in public use is the widely used term "war on terror" in reference to what is essentially a "war on terrorism." What is particularly interesting here is that terror describes a state of intense or extreme fear. The very use of terror over terrorism implies that fear, or terror, has become the most pervasive element of terrorism. Terrorism (what we fear) is reinscribed as terror (the state of intense fear) and the "war on terror" is a referent for the "war on terrorism." As Aly and Balnaves (2005, para.7) note, "Terrorism has become the new metonym for our time where the 'war on terror' refers to a perpetual state of alertness as well as a range of strategic operations, border control policies, internal security measures and public awareness campaigns such as 'be alert, not alarmed.'"

THE TERRORIST THREAT AND PUBLIC PERCEPTION

According to the Global Terrorism Database (GTD), in the decade between 2001 and 2011, Australia experienced six terrorist incidences. Of these incidences, only one resulted in five fatalities. This incident, though categorized as a terrorist incident by the GTD, occurred when an explosion on board the SUSPECTED ILLEGAL ENTRY VESSEL (SIEV) 36 resulted in the deaths of five asylum seekers in April 2009. Of the remaining listed terrorist attacks, two were attacks on Mosques (Perth 2010 and Brisbane 2001), one was an unknown chemical agent in a letter to the United States Consulate in Melbourne, one was an explosion on a private business (Broadbeach 2006), and one was an armed assault on a synagogue in Sydney in 2006.

Since September 12, 2001, Australia's National Terrorism Public Alert System has been set at medium (terrorist attack could occur), the second level of four tiers. More than 10 years after the terrorist attacks on the United States and the Bali bombings, the threat of terrorism continues to be at the forefront of government policy-making despite what appears to be waning public interest. In a 2006 study on the fear of terrorism, Balnaves and Aly (2007) polled a representative sample of Australian households. The Aly-Balnaves metric of fear surveyed comparative feelings of safety before and after the terrorist attacks of September 11 and applied a 23-question fear scale designed to test behavioral modifications in response to perceived terrorist threat. The study by Balnaves and Aly (2007) found that a range of restrictive and protective behaviors had been adopted in response to elevated levels of fear after the 9/11 terrorist attacks. The Australian Election Study found that, at the time of the 2004 election, 67.7 percent of voters thought Australia's involvement in the war in Iraq had increased the threat of terrorism on home soil. The same study found that this figure had slipped to 56.5 percent at the 2007 election, although 65.7 percent of Australians polled did express concern about a major terrorist attack on Australian soil (Megalogenis, 2008). A poll by Roy Morgan in 2005 reported that 46 percent of Australians ranked the terrorist threat as the most significant problem facing the world. Four years later, only 2 percent ranked terrorism as a significant world problem and only 1 percent considered terrorism to be the most significant issue for Australia (Flitton, 2010). A similar pattern was recorded by the ACNielsen Global Consumer Opinion Survey, which found that terrorism was a major concern for 64 percent of Australians polled in 2004 but only 12 percent in June 2005 and 14 percent in June 2006 (Nielsen, 2006).

Such results have prompted politicians and media commentators to ask whether the sense of complacency reflected in opinion polls and surveys is in the national interest. In May 2012, then Defence Minister Stephen Smith warned that Australia needed to "stay alert" to the threat of terrorism. The minister described the publication of Osama bin Laden's personal correspondence in which the former Al Qaeda leader reinforced his focus on the United States as a target for terrorism as a "regrettable feature of post-September 2001 life—the ever-present international terrorist threat and a continued need to be vigilant" (Australian Associated Press, 2012).

The failed attempt by Umar Abdulmutallab to detonate the explosive Pentaerythritol tetranitrate (PETN) on a U.S. bound flight on Christmas Day 2009 raised inevitable questions about public vigilance and the effectiveness of security. In an article entitled "How We Lost the Fear of Terror," *Sydney Morning Herald* journalist, Daniel Flitton (2010) asked, "Has Western society, now more than eight years after the shock of the September 11 attacks, become too complacent about the terrorist threat?" Flitton acknowledged that years of persistent warnings and heightened security measures are more likely to contribute to the sense of public complacency around the threat of terrorism.

While public opinion polls suggest public fatigue with the protracted campaign against terrorism, other studies demonstrate that the fear of terrorism is a latent fear that flows in and out of the public consciousness. Just a few weeks after a 2009 Roy Morgan poll showed that only 2 percent of Australians considered terrorism a significant problem, a survey by the Lowy Institute reported that 68 percent of Australians agreed that combating international terrorism was a critical problem. The apparent contradiction in the results of the two surveys is explained by the fact that in July of that year, mid-way through the polling period, a coordinated attack on the JW Marriott and the Ritz Carlton Hotels in Jakarta killed nine people, including three Australians. The two polls had, quite by accident, recorded the public reaction to the news of the bombings (Flitton, 2010).

Similar patterns of response were reported by the ACNielsen Global Consumer Opinion Survey (Nielsen, 2006), which found that concerns about the threat of terrorism were higher during, and in the lead up to major events. In November 2005, immediately preceding the Commonwealth Games in Melbourne, 36 percent of consumers rated terrorism as their number one concern. Six months later, a follow-up survey revealed that these fears had plummeted to 17 percent. These findings support those of a study conducted by Aly (2010), which found that public fears of terrorism were higher in the presence of images, objects or situations subliminally associated with terrorism. Aly concluded that the salience of terrorism in the media and the existence of resonant images of terrorism in the individual's immediate proximity heighten perceptions of the terrorist threat and produce fear responses associated with mortality risk. The fear of terrorism may therefore remain dormant in the subconscious mind of individuals until aroused by the presence and combination of resonant images in the individual's immediate proximity. Situations that are constructed as threat situations draw on the individual's schematic knowledge of previous terrorist attacks developed through their interaction with media images of the attacks.

Behavioral and psychological responses to the fear of terrorism are generally undetectable until the individual finds him/herself confronted by the specter of terrorism. For example, a female participant in Aly's (2010) study who had lost a close family member in the Bali bombings of 2002 did not believe that this experience had made her more fearful of a terrorist attack. However, she did recall a recent incident in Perth (Western Australia's capital city) in which police sealed the city centre in response to a bomb threat. Trapped in a bus for 2 hours, she began to feel more and more anxious about a terrorist attack: "and so it just went through my head . . . is this real? Can this happen again?" It is not unusual for people who would normally describe themselves as rational to assess their fear of terrorism as irrational particularly when that fear is only salient in the presence of images largely perpetuated by the media discourse on terrorism.

Another of Aly's (2010) participants (also female) recalled an incident in which she encountered an unattended bag on an inner city tram. She began to feel anxious and eventually reported the bag to the tram driver before disembarking and seeking another form of transport. Her response, which manifested in the preventative behavior of removing herself from the place of threat, is based on her construction of the situation as a threat situation. The situational factors: an unattended bag; public transport; a major city centre, all resonate with the media images of the London bombings in 2005. As these stories suggest, messages of fear may be latently subsumed into cultural practices and brought into play in certain situations of fear salience where individuals are suddenly aware of ubiquitous threat of terrorism embodied in their surroundings.

Although public opinion polls and surveys offer a broad brush indication of public concerns, they do not extend an understanding of what exactly is the nature of those concerns. Is the public fear of terrorism strictly a mortality fear aroused in the presence of images or events that have come to be associated with the threat of terrorism? Or, is the fear of terrorism more broadly associated with a perceived *state of terror*: a kind of new world order in which insecurity, suspicion and the manipulation of fear for political purposes are the norm?

THE FEAR OF TERRORISM

The literature on the fear of terrorism distinguishes between two kinds of fear, often in tension with each other: fear that is historically specific and serves a political purpose and fear that is inherent to our psychological makeup and serves a deep psychological need. When viewed from the perspective of political fear, fear of terrorism is typically characterized as the fear of an external threat and presumes a community with a shared identity and common political values and interests (Robin, 2004). From a psychoanalytic perspective, the human response to terrorism is a metaphor for the innate fear of death in humans (Pyszcynski, Solomon, & Greenberg, 2003). In both approaches, the fear of terrorism is a powerful driver of collective identity. From a political perspective, terrorism is presented as politically void and the objects of fear are constructed as ideological enemies that cannot be appeased or confronted through conventional means of warfare. From a psychological perspective, the human response to the fear of terrorism results in a search for ontological security and manifests in reaffirmation of collective identity and aggression toward anything perceived to be a threat to that identity.

In a survey conducted in the months after the September 11 attacks, 90 percent of Australians felt sadder as a result of the attacks, while a majority rated their levels of distress at very high (Bradley, 2003). The same survey also revealed a high level of support among Australians for the use of violence in retaliation for the terrorist attacks. These results reinforce the hypothesis that terrorist attacks threaten people's ontological security and engender fear that motivates a range of actions or reactions designed to diminish the threat. Often these reactions are expressed in terms of violent retaliation toward an imagined enemy or "other." Actions that would otherwise be considered atypical are moralized as a justified response to suffering. The state of insecurity belies community anxiety and fear that finds expression in increased aggression toward the perceived source of threat, greater in-group solidarity and support for extraordinary measures directed at members of the threatening group (Huddy et al., 2005). Through fear, society can reaffirm its commitment to a set of common political values that are threatened by an identified enemy. At an individual or group level, this reaffirmation may be expressed through a renewal of nationalist ideologies and patriotic behaviors. As Falk (2002) states, "When a society is threatened by an external enemy there is a strong tendency to express patriotic feelings through tribal and ultra-nationalist displays of unconditional support" (p. 331).

Terror Management Theory (TMT; Pyszcynski et al., 2003), despite its name, has little to do with the managing the threat of terrorism. TMT does however offer an understanding of human behavior in the face of terror and, as such, a way of understanding the popular response to September 11. At its core, TMT posits that humans have an innate awareness of their own mortality that gives rise to potentially overpowering feelings of terror and the need to maintain "psychological equanimity" in their lives (p. 16). This potential for terror is managed through the construction and maintenance of cultural worldviews that serve to reduce anxiety about the inevitability of death by providing a sense of meaning, stability, permanence and order. The very existence of culturally constructed beliefs that serve to maintain a sense of equanimity and immortality gives rise to feelings of anxiety and apprehension toward those who oppose these beliefs:

> Encountering people with different beliefs and accepting the possible validity of their conceptions of reality necessarily undermines (implicitly or explicitly) the confidence with which people subscribe to their own death-denying conceptions and, in so doing, threatens to unleash the overwhelming terror normally mitigated by the secure possession of one's existing beliefs (Pyszcynski et al., 2003, p. 29).

A core element of TMT is the mortality salience and worldview defense paradigm (Pyszcynski et al., 2003). TMT posits that national identity is central to people's worldviews and to explaining hostilities among different societies and nations. Thus, when confronted with their own mortality (mortality salience), people are motivated to protect their own world views and react positively to anything that upholds their cultural world views and negatively to anything perceived to threaten these world views. Through empirical research, the authors of TMT claim to have proved that mortality salience does indeed provoke positive reactions towards things that reinforce cultural world views and negative reactions to those that threaten or violate these views. The range of behavioral responses to mortality salience includes prejudice, aggression and the marginalization of those considered to have different world views that do not conform to a particular cultural stereotype.

The use of the fear of terrorism to generate social unity and consensus in the "war on terror" is well documented (Aly, 2010; Chermak, 2003; Chomsky, 2002; Gale, 2004; Hollander, 2004; Jamrozik, 2002; Young, 2003; Prewitt, 2004). Altheide (1997) defines fear in terms of a "vocabulary of motive" which identifies objects of fear through particular attributes and characteristics, and motivates responses to "fearing acts" (p. 663). The politics of fear concerns the manipulation of widespread community anxieties about danger, risk, or threat by decision makers to achieve particular goals. Jamrozik (2002) maintains that the use of fear as a political tool has been used historically to gain approval for policies that would not normally meet with resistance and disapproval. Aly and Balnaves (2005) propose that the fear of terrorism is essentially political fear that finds expression in affecting collective identity against a perceived threat.

Hobbes is accredited as the first theorist to recognize how fear could proliferate beyond the objective fact of a distant danger and transformed, in the minds of the public into a pending, inevitable threat (Robin, 2004). Similarly, Massumi (2005) contends that unknowability is a precondition of fear, "A threat is only a threat if it retains an indeterminacy. If it has a form, it is not a substantial form, but a time form: a futurity" (p. 35). In this sense, fear in response to a threat is not an existing precondition but rather may be constructed through acts which magnify risk and "calibrate the public's anxiety" (Massumi, 2005, p. 32). According to Hobbes, the promotion of fear allowed the state to consolidate and maintain control by instilling the population with a sense of dread of an unknown and inexperienced collective harm (Robin, 2004).

From a Hobbesian perspective, the fear of terrorism in Australia is political in that it is not a proportionate reaction to a clear and present danger in the real world (Michaelsen, 2005). Instead it is a reaction to an unknown danger transmitted through the preventative principle. When compared with Australia's actual risk profile, the fear of terrorism hinges on chimera: on the ability of the state to induce and influence collective opinion by magnifying the actual threat of terrorism (Robin, 2004). Howie's (2005) study of the behavioral responses to the fear of terrorism among Melbourne office workers concludes that the fear of terrorism is akin to dread in that it is devoid of rationality and is based on a sensationalized, mediated threat. The threat of terrorism is communicated via the range of official and institutional responses to global terrorist acts, which Michaelsen (2005) maintains are disproportionate to the actual threat of a terrorist attack.

Since the September 11 attacks, the Australian government has progressively introduced a range of counter terrorism measures including over 30 legislative amendments to the Criminal Code, Crimes Legislation (2006), Australian Security Intelligence Organisation Legislation, Telecommunications Act (2004, 2005, 2006, and 2007), Customs Legislation (2006) and the introduction of the Anti-terrorism Bill 2004, the Surveillance Devices Bill 2004, National Security Information (Criminal Proceedings) Bill 2005, and the Aviation Transport Security Bill 2003. More recent amendments to the Aviation Transport Security Bill in 2007 made regulations to cover liquids, aerosols, and gels and to allow for appropriate frisk searches. The Anti-Terrorism Bill 2005 amended existing offences in the Criminal Code to clarify that it is not necessary to identify a particular terrorist act upon proving an offence (Parliament of Australia, 2007).

In response to the London terrorist bombings in 2005, the government also announced amendments to terrorism legislation that increased powers for the police to detain persons of interest suspected of sedition. Such measures exemplify what Massumi (2005) terms "affective modulation" whereby the human response to the fear of terrorism, that of a reinforcement and renewal of collective identity, has been modulated and transformed from an affective *response* to an affective *state* of anxiety. Affect for Massumi can be inscribed in the flesh as "traces of experience"—an accumulation of affects. It is in this way that Massumi views affect as "autonomous." Aly and Balnaves (2005, para.12), in applying Massumi's notion of affective modulation to the "war on terror," note that: "In the Australian context, after more than four years of collected traces of experiences of images of threat, responses to terrorism have become almost reflexive-even automated."

Affective modulation relies on the regenerative capacity of fear, in Massumi's (2005) terms its "ontogenetic powers" (p. 45) to create an ever present threat and maintain fear as a way of life. In this way, affective modulation presents as a mechanism for politicizing the fear of terrorism and sustaining a persistent state of anxiety and tension. Thus, engaging a range of counter terrorism strategies that are disproportionate to the actual risk of a terrorist attack defines terrorism as an object of fear that would direct public concern and positions the public as potential victims of an ever present threat.

FEARING TERROR

Whether the fear of terrorism is politically motivated and historically specific or hardwired into our psyche, the fear response has implications beyond immediate reactions of retaliation, aggression or vilification. The fear of terrorism is not exclusively a fear of being physically harmed in a terrorist attack. Alongside the fear of an actual terrorist attack in Australia, is the fear of the government's response to terrorism and its implications. In this sense the fear of terrorism is a response to both a perceived threat of physical harm (however unreal that threat may be) and the actual, lived experiences of how terrorism has impacted on the everyday lives of people. Anxiety, worry, distress, concern, and fear about the social and political responses to terrorism such as an increased security presence, heightened discrimination and vilification of Muslims, social disharmony, and the manipulation of community fear for political ends have long-term consequences for the everyday lives of individuals. To conceptualize the fear of terrorism wholly in terms of the fear of physical harm ignores the myriad of ways in which people experience the fear of terrorism and views terrorism simply in terms of acts perpetrated by terrorists while denying the ripples that emanate from such acts.

In her study on the fear of terrorism among Australians, Aly (2010) highlighted four distinct but related categories of the fear of terrorism among Australians. Aly's study found that, apart from the fear of being physically harmed in a terrorist attack, Australians also expressed fear of the government response to terrorism; fear of losing civil liberties in the security rich environment of the "new normal"; and the fear of feeling insecure.

POLITICAL FEAR

In today's media savvy culture, there are arguably few people who would not have some awareness of how images and news items are manipulated to serve a broader agenda. Popular films such as *The Truman Show, The Matrix,* and *Wag the Dog* have developed public consciousness about the role of the media in the construction of images and discourses that serve political or institutional purposes. In the "war on terror," the political rhetoric serves to create a sense of perpetual threat and elevates terrorism in the public conscious as a subject of concern. The question of whether public awareness of the political manipulation of fears for political purposes impacts on the perceived threat of terrorism and levels of fear was asked by Aly (2010) in her research. She found that the political fear of terrorism actually generated a different kind of fear: one that was associated with the impending advent of utilitarianism and heightened political conservatism. Political fear was a cause of anxiety and concern because it represented a threat to liberal democratic values: "The terror actually lies in and it comes back down to that one thing: that our ability to discover the truth is actually outstripped by our ability to manifest deceit and it's just getting worse and worse" (Male, age 40–54).

The manipulation of fear for political purposes also raises anxieties about the social consequences of fear that targets and demonizes a particular section of the community. The social impact of politically motivated fear and the fracturing of Australian society along lines of religious and/or cultural difference is, in and of itself, a cause for fear. Those from ethnic backgrounds may be particularly concerned about the impact of political fear on their personal safety. Unlike the fear of a terrorist attack, which in Australia is based on a perceived threat of terrorism as opposed to actual experiences of terrorism, this kind of fear is grounded in personal experiences of being vilified or discriminated against in the aftermath to terrorist attacks. In the wake of terrorist attacks in New York, Bali, Madrid and London, Muslim Australians and those of Arab or Middle Eastern background suffered vilification and even physical attacks as they became the objects of fear.

While the theoretical conceptualization of political fear is premised on a common understanding of terrorism as nonpolitical, the findings of Aly's (2010) study suggest that the conceptualization of terrorism as a political phenomenon is also a source of fear. Participants in Aly's study who understood terrorism in a political context expressed fearfulness, anxiety, and concern about the political dimensions of terrorism. In these cases, the political response to terrorism, the "war on terror" and the invasion of Iraq, is what strikes fear:

> It's interesting to see how often the government tries to enforce the message that Australia is at threat, when I think that generally people don't actually think we are in a particularly dangerous position at the moment. It just seems to be suspicious that the people who are supposed to be protecting us are the ones that are promoting this fear the most (Male, aged 30–45).
>
> Probably the best way to stop the terrorism is not to be involved in it. That seems the best way to avoid it. If you don't want people to bomb you, you don't piss them off, don't bomb them. But that's not really an option to us so we'll just tie everything up and have everyone on guard, have everyone watching each other's backs and have cameras everywhere (Female, aged 30–45).

FEAR OF LOSING CIVIL LIBERTIES

In 2005, shortly after the London terrorist bombings, much attention focused on how proposed new legislative measures to counterterrorism in Australia and other parts of the world constituted a departure from the key principles of liberal democracy and could severely curtail civil liberties. Australia's counterterrorism legislation introduced in response to subsequent global terror attacks are, arguably, the most drastic antilibertarian measures Australia has witnessed and constitute a disproportionate response to Australia's overall risk profile (Michaelsen, 2005). In March 2005, the Club de Madrid released the Club de Madrid Series on Democracy and Terrorism, the outcome of the largest summit to date on terrorism. In the final of three volumes of this series, *Towards a Democratic Response*, members of the working group expressed a unanimous concern that democracies could be attracted to responding to terrorist attacks by enacting strategies that curtail civil liberties, warning that "If this was to happen, the terrorists' . . . aim of undermining democracy would, in part, be fulfilled" (p. 21). The working group stressed the importance of considering measures designed to preserve democratic institutions alongside counterterrorism strategies that focus on security. In a joint report on the (then) proposed counterterrorism measures of the federal government, a conglomerate of community groups including the Civil Rights Network reiterated the sentiments of the Club de Madrid and expressed concern that the proposed measures constitute an attack on political freedoms and that they would negatively impact on Muslim communities. In such circumstances, "Not only will there be a serious breach of the principle of equality before the law but also an erosion of this country's commitment to multiculturalism, by excluding or placing under suspicion a class of people in the community" (Chong et al., 2005, pp. 5–6).

Huysmans (2004) refers to the curtailment of civil liberties bound in the security responses to the September 11 attacks in terms of political exceptionalism. Security responses such as those undertaken by the Australian government have the capacity to establish political exceptionalism as the most prudent response based on fear. Security policy thus becomes paradoxical as it risks undermining the very ethos of the liberal democratic values it seeks to protect. Similarly, Stern (2004) argues that "perhaps the most troubling side-effect of the war on terrorism has been the temptation to imagine that the threats we face are so extreme that ordinary moral norms and laws do not apply" (p. 1115). The kinds of measures introduced by the Australian government in response to the London bombings (such as those regarding detaining and interrogating suspected terrorists) would once have seemed an unthinkable assault on civil liberties and unreasonably authoritarian. Yet in the "war on terror," framed as a global battle between good and evil, policies and strategies that once seemed impossible suddenly become constructed as rational, if not prudent (Stern, 2004).

In times of crisis, the reasoned negotiation of risk is marginalized. In the case of the "war on terror," the use of discourses of national security and sovereignty were central to intensifying the fear of terrorism and hence marginalizing the reasoned negotiation of the risk and potential impact of a terrorist attack (Spence, 2005). Such extreme responses result in the implementation of risk reduction strategies such as the "shoot to kill" policy adopted by London police, which resulted in the death of an innocent bystander mistaken for a terrorist. This dynamic reflects perceived rather than actual danger. Often these strategies and policies do not give full consideration to the longer-term impacts on community relations and the possibility of actually heightening real risk. Hence, the instigation of the "war on terror" in reaction to September 11 may actually have increased the risk of further terrorist attacks in retaliation (Stern, 2004).

Anxiousness, fear, and concern about a potential loss of civil liberties and personal freedoms associated with an increased security environment are another kind of fear of terrorism. The range of strategies introduced in the wake of the New York, Bali, and London bombings, including public debates around the introduction of a national identity card, sedition laws, increased powers to federal and state police, and closed circuit television in public places, aroused concerns among Australian's about the loss of certain freedoms and the erosion of democratic values, as demonstrated in the following excerpt from Aly's (2010) study:

> Every new law that we pass in regards to terrorism is an infringement on the civil liberties of Australians anyway. There's a fine line to walk between how much power the government should have over individuals and how much freedom we should have as well. I think that the government views the terrorist attacks as a way to become a bit more Big Brotherish in this country. There's been laws passed in the name of terrorism that really when looked at properly will affect all Australians and I don't think Australians are actually seeing that. They're giving up some of their rights (Female, aged 18–35).

FEELING INSECURE

For Australians, the Bali bombings of October 2002, constructed in the media and political discourse as a direct attack on Australia, impacted significantly on feelings of security. The Bali bombings signaled that Australia was no longer viewed as a passive partner in the "war on terror," which had been a source of comfort and security. Australia was now a real player, a terrorist target and a potential victim of further terrorist attacks. Bali, the backyard playground of generations of Australia, was no longer viewed as an idyllic holiday spot. Instead, it became associated in the minds of Australians with death, destruction, and the inevitable threat of terrorism. While terrorist attacks in New York, London, and Bali heralded a "new world order" in which the ongoing war on terrorism was constructed as an ongoing battle between good and evil, the fear of terrorism was also roused by its responses.

Australia, like much of the world, has witnessed the introduction of successive security measures, often in response to successful or attempted terrorist attacks. One of the most predominant responses to international terrorism is the heightened security environment, most observable at domestic and international airports. X-ray machines, explosive trace detection equipment, surveillance and closed circuit television, armed police or paramilitary, passenger screening, identity checks, passenger interrogation including racial profiling of Arab passengers at some airports, and sniffer dogs are just some of the security measures introduced since September 2001 designed to prevent potential hijackings, bombings, or other forms of terrorist attacks.

Where security has failed to detect or prevent potential terrorists, airport security measures have attracted criticism as being ineffective prompting even more layers of security and debates about whether more invasive security processes such as full body screening using millimeter waves, which can see through clothing, are warranted. Progressive security measures introduced in response to terrorist attacks and new threats have continually raised fears about the impact on civil liberties and privacy. Civil liberty advocates around the world raised concerns that the millimeter wave scanners could breach people's privacy, while surveillance measures such as closed circuit television, which use face recognition software, have also sparked concerns about the impact of a security culture on civil liberties.

Security measures are introduced in response to the possibility of terrorist acts which are imagined to be limitless in their voracity and capacity for destruction. In this sense, security responses to the risk of terrorism are influenced not by real risk but by speculative risk about the vulnerability of potential targets. Such responses promote, rather than contain, the sense of dread and fear toward terrorism. Furedi (2002) warns that the focus on speculative risk draws attention away from actual risks making it more difficult to manage real threats. Apart from the fear of losing civil liberties, an increased security culture raises anxiety and fears about the loss of security. The specter of security stimulates the public's imagination in relation to the terrorist threat and rouses latent fears of terrorism. Like the examples referred to earlier in this chapter, individuals are prompted to recall the threat of terrorism in the presence of images or situations subliminally associated with terrorism.

Beyond being a fleeting fear that shoots in and out of the public consciousness in times of perceived crisis or threat, the loss of insecurity is related to feelings of safety in the everyday lives of individuals. The fear of terrorism, as it relates to the feeling insecure, is expressed (here by one of Aly's study participants) as a profound and incessant influence on the everyday lives of individuals:

> With the London bombings... once again and it was... terror... being terrorised... and I sort of started to think about what it would be like to live there and I think that really impacted me. When I go to Perth station and I get off at the station and there are signs up everywhere 'please keep all parcels and baggage with you at all times'. Talking with people who are having to deal with this in the workforce... I think that's really a practical way that I view life and my expectation of what may happen here in our own shores and I guess their concentration on trying to tighten security and prepare for disaster... has affected the way I think about my own life and my own family (Female, aged 30–44).

Alternatively, or even concurrently, the specter of security also raises fears about the loss of innocence and an intensified security culture. The salience of security at airports, in streets, shopping centers, and at public events signals the need for vigilance and foreshadows the possibility of disaster. The specter of security stands as an ominous reminder that we are not safe and the security culture makes us all suspicious, encouraging us to "spy on your neighbors... Just make sure that strange smell coming from next door is actually curry and not something else":

> I just recently went overseas and when I get to the airport the thing that sent chills down my spine, that our society has progressed to the stage where there was such high level security, and I was travelling at the time where you couldn't have any cosmetics or anything like that. That sent chills down my spine, and when I got onto the plane where typically you might start to feel those types of threats of terrorism, I wasn't concerned in any way, shape or form. It was the shock and sadness that I felt about how far our society has progressed in terms of giving up all this freedom and living our lives in fear that scared me more than any threat of terrorism. (Female, aged 25–39)

CONCLUSION

Public fears of terrorism, so the surveys tell us, are abating amid a global financial crisis, out of control military budgets and public disillusionment with the prolonged war in Afghanistan. Surveys however, only present part of the picture. What exactly is the fear of terrorism? It is simply the fear or dread associated with being physically harmed in a terrorist attack? Or is the fear of terrorism a more complex phenomenon than that captured by opinion polls? Terrorism, though often applied subjectively to a violent act carried out for a social, political, or ideological cause, is rarely a single act or event and its effects extend far beyond a tangible incident or the immediate victim. Through the magic of television, audiences around the globe witness terrorist events such as those in New York, Madrid, London, and Bali—the images of these events transcend space and time and position us all as bystanders to tragedy. We are invited to participate in the immediate and distal responses to these attacks. Those responses include fear and anxiety about a possible recurrence.

After the September 11 attacks, Australians, who live almost 12,000 miles from New York City, reported feeling anxious, fearful, or unsafe in public places. Those responses also include an intensified quest for meaning and value; heightened patriotism and nationalistic sentiment; the suppression of dissent; and the acceptance of measures that would otherwise be considered excessive in the name of protecting us from terror. Responses to terrorism can, and do, elicit as much fear as terrorism itself. The policy response to terrorism creates a security culture that communicates the pervasive threat of terrorism—from billboards urging us to "say something" to the ubiquitous cameras capturing our every movement, we are constantly reminded that the threat is ever present. More security, however, does not necessarily mean less fear. As governments continue to counter terrorism with security responses that become inscribed into a security culture, publics continue to question the political motives for measures that curtail civil liberties, perpetuate fear and insecurity.

REFERENCES

Altheide, D. L. (1997). The news media, the problem frame, and the production of fear. *The Sociological Quarterly*, 38(4), 647–668.

Aly, A. (2010). *A study of audience responses to the media discourse about the "other": The Fear of terrorism between Australian Muslims and the broader community*. New York, NY: The Edwin Mellen Press.

Aly, A., & Balnaves, M. (December 2005). The atmosfear of terror: Affective modulation and the war on terror," *M/C Journal*, 8(6). Retrieved from http://journal.media-culture.org.au/0512/04-alybalnaves.php

Australian Associated Press. (2012). Australia must stay alert to terror-Smith. Retrieved from http://www.news.com.au/breaking-news/australia-must-stay-alert-to-terror-smith/story-e6frfku0-1226346632197

Balnaves, M., & Aly, A. (2007). Media, 9/11, and fear: a national survey of Australian community responses to images of terror. *Australian Journal of Communication* 343, 101–112.

Bradley, P. (2003). A war on violence? How Western societies are reacting to terrorism. *Inpsych*, (February 2003), 11–13.

Bush, G. W. (2006). President's address to the nation. Retrieved from http://www.whitehouse.gov/news/releases/2001/09/20010920-8.html.

Cameron, W. B., & McCormick, T. C. (1954). Concepts of security and insecurity. *The American Journal of Sociology*, 59(6), 556–564.

Chermak, S. (2003). Marketing fear: Representing terrorism after September 11. *Journal for Crime, Conflict and the Media*, 1(1), 5–22.

Chomsky, N. (2002). *September 11*. Crows Nest: NSW, Allen & Unwin.

Chong, A., Emberton, P., Kadous, W., Pettitt, A., Sempill, S., Sentas, V., ... Tham, J. (2005). *Laws for insecurity? A report on the federal government's proposed counter-terrorism measures*. Retrieved from http://www.amcran.org/images/stories/Laws%20for%20 Insecurity%20Report.pdf.

Club de Madrid. (2001). *Towards a democratic response. The Club de Madrid series on democracy and terrorism volume III*. Madrid, Spain: Club de Madrid

Falk, R. (2002). Testing patriotism and citizenship in the global terror war. In K. Booth & T. Dunne (Eds.), *Words in collision: Terror and the future of global order* (pp. 325–335). New York, NY: Palgrave Macmillan.

Flitton, D. (2010). How we lost the fear of terror. *The Sydney Morning Herald*. Retrieved from http://www.smh.com.au/world/how-we-lost-the-fear-of-terror-20100101-lls8. html#ixzz24AnShwge.

Furedi, F. (2002). *Refusing to be terrorised: Managing risk after September 11th*. Kent, UK: Global Futures.

Gale, P. (2004). The refugee crisis and fear: Populist politics and media discourse. *Journal of Sociology*, 40(4), 321.

Hollander, J. (2004). Fear itself. *Social Research*, 71(4), 865.

Howie, L. (2005). There is nothing to fear but fear itself (and terrorists): Public perception, terrorism and the workplace. *Proceedings Social Change in the 21st Century Conference*. Carseldine, Australia: Queensland University of Technology.

Huddy, L., Feldman S., et al. (2005). Threat, anxiety and support of antiterrorism policies. *American Journal of Political Science*, 49(3), 593–608.

Huysmans, J. (2004). Minding exceptions: The politics of insecurity and liberal democracy. *Contemporary Political Theory*, 3(3), 321–322.

Jamrozik, A. (2002). From lucky country to penal colony: How the politics of fear have changed Australia. *Refugees and the Lucky Country Forum*. Melbourne, Australia: RMIT.

Massumi, B. (2005). Fear (the spectrum said). *Positions*, 13(1), 31.

Megalogenis, G. (2008) Voters cool on war but fear terrorism. *The Australian*. Retrieved from http://www.theaustralian.com.au/national-affairs/defence/voters-cool-on-war-but-fear-terrorism/story-e6frg8yx-1111117233332.

Michaelsen, C. (2005). Antiterrorism legislation in Australia: A proportionate response to the terrorist threat? *Studies in Conflict and Terrorism*, 28(4), 321–340.

Nielsen, A.C. (2006) *ACNielsen Global Consumer Opinion Survey*. Retrieved from http:// au.nielsen.com/news/20060811.shtml.

Parliament of Australia. (2007). Internet resource guide: Australian terrorism law. Retrieved from http:www.aph/gov/au/library/intguide/law/terrorism.htm.

Prewitt, K., Alterman, E., Arato, A., Pyszcynski, T., et al. (2004). The politics of fear after 9/11. *Social Research*, 71(4), 1129.

Pyszcynski, T, Solomon, S, & Greenberg, J. (2003) *In the wake of 9–11: The psychology of terror*. Washington, DC: American Psychological Association.

Robin, C. (2004). *Fear: The history of a political idea*. New York, NY: Oxford University Press.

Sheridan, G. (2002, October 17). This nation we love must face the threat and fight. *The Australian*, 13.

Spence, K. (2005). World risk society and war against terror. *Political Studies*, 53(2), 284–304.

Stern, J. (2004). Fearing evil. *Social Research*, 71(4), 1111–1117.

Young, J. R. (2003). The role of fear in agenda setting by television news. *The American Behavioral Scientist*, 46(12), 1673.

CHAPTER 10

Psychological Determinants of the Threat of Terrorism and Preferred Approaches to Counterterrorism: The Case of Poland

KATARZYNA JAŚKO, MAŁGORZATA KOSSOWSKA, AND MACIEJ SEKERDEJ

Terrorist attacks have contributed to a growing fear of terrorism in many Western societies (e.g., Goodwin, Willson, & Gaines, 2005; Huddy, Khatib, & Capelos, 2002; McCauley, 2004; Paez Rovira, Martinez-Sanchez, & Rime, 2004). Many studies have documented that such prolonged anticipatory fear is likely to have significant negative consequences for an individual's well-being (Ronen, Rahav, & Appel, 2003; Schuster et al., 2001; Somer, Ruvio, Soref, & Sever, 2005; Somer, Tamir, Maguen, & Litz, 2005; Zimbardo, 2003) as well as intergroup dynamics (Lauterbach & Vrana, 2001; Norris, Friedman, & Watson, 2002). Threats of terrorism are also related to specific policy choices and support for counterterrorism actions (Davis & Silver, 2004; Huddy et al., 2005).

Although past research has focused mostly on reactions to terrorism in societies that have suffered directly from terrorist attacks (i.e., Bonanno & Jost, 2006; Echebarria-Echabe & Fernández-Guede, 2006), responses to terrorism in social contexts that have been unaffected by such acts have also been the subject of recent investigation (e.g., Golec de Zavala & Kossowska, 2011; Kossowska et al., 2011; Lemyre et al., 2006). This research suggests that terrorism as a global threat can induce fear, among other negative consequences, in people and societies that have had no direct contact with it.

Moreover, data on the level of terrorist threats in various European Union countries has shown that fear of a terrorist act in a respondent's own country is positively correlated with having experienced terrorism in the past. The perception of terrorist threats in Europe however varies across different countries and is related to experience with terrorism to a lesser extent than fear of a terrorist act in one's own country. More precisely, data from The European Social Survey conducted in 2006 showed that fear of terrorist acts in one's own country was highest in the United Kingdom (84 percent of respondents agreed that terrorist act was probable), Russia (65 percent) and Spain (58 percent); while it was lowest in Finland (5 percent) (Domański, 2009). In Poland, fear was moderate (37 percent). However, when the perceived risk of possible terrorist attacks in Europe was taken into account, the highest level of fear was again found in the United Kingdom (90 percent), but the level of fear was comparable to that found in Norway (84 percent) and Finland (83 percent). Seventy percent of Polish people agreed that there is a risk of terrorist attacks in Europe. Using another set of data, the correlation between the objective risk of terrorism, which was defined as a rate of deaths and injuries caused by terrorism per 1 million inhabitants, and the level of fear of terrorism among European countries surveyed in 2002 was rather low (Treisman, 2011).

What these data show is that there is great variability in the perceived risk of terrorism across different countries, and that experience with terrorism or direct involvement in a "war on terror" are only a couple of the factors that can account for the level of fear associated with attacks and attitudes toward counterterrorist actions. The purpose of this chapter is to review several universal psychological variables moderating the relationships between feeling the threat of terrorism and preferred approaches to counterterrorism. A closer examination of these variables in societies such as Poland may offer insight into cultural and social factors, beyond direct experiences that shape individual and societal reactions to terrorism. This examination seems important because terrorism often evokes actions that demand either passive support or active participation from yet uninvolved political actors. Therefore, the underpinnings of risk assessment, and the emotions and attitudes of such actors are of high importance from the perspective of both domestic and international politics. Moreover, such an analysis is an important part of risk management and planning because it can help to prepare for specific actions in case of a future terrorist attack.

TERRORIST THREATS IN POLAND

When we consider the current level of terrorist threats in Poland, we observe a low to moderate intensity of fear. Data gathered in 2010 from a representative sample of Polish adults (CBOS, 2010) show that one third (32 percent) of Polish adults agreed with the statement that there was a real threat of terrorism. However, 30 percent of respondents claimed that the threat of terrorism was exaggerated, and 26 percent saw no real threat of terrorism. Those numbers were more pronounced when the question was related to a personal threat. The great majority, 72 percent of respondents, was not afraid of being a victim of a terrorist attack, and only 25 percent of Polish people admitted to being afraid of this possibility.

Looking at the changes in the threat of terrorism in Polish society over time, it is clear that the level of threat depends significantly on the salience of terrorist attacks. After the attacks in Madrid in March 2004 and in London in July 2005 there was a sharp increase in terrorist threats (CBOS, 2004, 2005). Similarly, after Osama bin Laden was killed by the U.S. Central Intelligence Agency, the fear of terrorism increased as well: the percentage of Polish people who indicated that they were personally afraid of terrorist acts rose immediately from 25 percent to 35 percent (CBOS, 2011).

When it comes to threats of terrorism, not only does the general level of fear matter, but attitudes toward specific counterterrorist policies also matter. Most Poles (85 percent) agree with controlling borders, airports, and railway stations to prevent threats of terrorism. However, they are much less willing to spend additional money on security (49 percent agree), and they are definitely against allowing state institutions to control their communications (73 percent disagree) or to engage in telephone monitoring (72 percent) (CBOS, 2010). It is of note that just after the attacks in the United States (2001), Spain (2004) and London (2005), public approval of such actions was much higher. For example, in 2005 (CBOS, 2005), support for control over communications was given by 46 percent of Poles. This finding suggests that under conditions of salient terrorist threats, public approval of counterterrorism politics that limit individual liberties is more probable.

Similarly, when asked about their support for the protection of individual freedom or security and the fight against terrorism, Polish people declared that they are more attached to individual freedom. However, this preference for freedom is also correlated with the subjectively experienced level of terrorist threats. Among those who believed there was a real threat of terrorism and those who were personally afraid of attacks, support for severe counterterrorism policies was higher (37 percent) and the preference of personal freedoms and individual rights was lower (47 percent) than it was among those who did not see any threat of terrorism at the moment (18 and 68 percent, respectively) (CBOS, 2008).

To create a more precise view of the Polish context with regard to the threat of terrorism, it should be added that although Poland has not been affected directly by large-scale terrorist attacks, the Polish army participated in the antiterrorism coalition and cooperated closely with the United States during both wars in Afghanistan and Iraq. As a result, the public's perception of terrorist threats has changed. After the 9/11 attacks, 77 percent of Polish people agreed that Poland, as a member of the North Atlantic Treaty Organization (NATO), was obliged to demonstrate solidarity with the United States and join the Allied operation (CBOS, 2001). Due to the involvement of Poland in these counterterrorism actions, we would expect a temporary increase in people's awareness of terrorist threats and more pronounced changes in the fear experienced by Polish society in comparison to countries that have had no such involvement.

Variability in attitudes toward the war on terror is also observed among countries directly involved in the war. For example, when comparing opinions of public security after the death of Osama bin Laden, research has shown that 54 percent of Americans believed that bin Laden's death would make the United States safer from terrorism and that only 28 percent feared that it would make it less safe (Gallup Organization, 2011). These findings can be contrasted with the results of a survey conducted in Poland after the death of bin Laden. According to those data, 47 percent of Polish people claimed that bin Laden's death would increase the general threat of Islamic terrorism, while only 17 percent predicted a decrease in the threat of Islamic terrorism (CBOS, 2011). In the following section of this chapter, we will review research and analyses that offer some insight into the mechanisms accounting for the emotional responses and the level of support in Polish society for specific counterterrorism actions.

PERCEPTIONS OF TERRORISM AND TERRORISTS

People react to a threat primarily according to their interpretations of the threatening stimuli and the particular characteristics that they attribute to them. Therefore, the specific perceptions of and attributions made about terrorism that are shared in a given society can affect reactions to terrorist threats, sometimes irrespective of actual threatening events occurring. According to Slovic and Weber (2002), there are two important dimensions that predict the perceived risk associated with every threatening phenomenon (e.g., nuclear power, smoking, x-rays, terrorism). The "dread risk" dimension refers to the lack of control over the threat, the catastrophic potential and the fatal consequences of the hazardous phenomena. The second dimension—the "unknown risk" dimension—refers to the unobservable, unknown, new, or delayed qualities of the threat. Given that terrorism is likely to be perceived as both a dreaded and an uncertain risk, it evokes more fear than do other, more controllable hazards. Indeed, in a study by Kawalec (2010), Polish students pointed to terrorism as the second highest "dreaded" and uncertain risk, ranking it after a nuclear explosion but before fatal diseases, whirlwind, fires, floods, and car accidents.

However, people hold different views of terrorism, and those specific perceptions can mediate the relationship between the objective presence of a threat and the emotional responses and preferred reactions to it. Data obtained from a representative sample of Polish adults (CBOS, 2005) show that a slight majority of Polish people (51 percent) believed that terrorism was an attempt to instill feelings of danger and fear in society, and 19 percent perceived acts of terror as a means to achieve wealth and power. However, there were also more justifying interpretations of terrorism. Thirteen percent of Poles believed that terrorism was a contemporary way of fighting with an enemy, and 11 percent saw it as an act of despair and a way to attract attention. Similarly, there were differences in perceptions of the specific causes of terrorism. Although the majority (65 percent) of Polish people attributed terrorism to religious (52 percent) and political (13 percent) fanaticism, a smaller group of people (31 percent) pointed toward external causes for terrorism, such as poverty, lack of other opportunities, lack of freedom, helplessness, and cultural differences.

Similar differences were found in our studies of lay perceptions of al-Qaeda terrorists, which were conducted in four European countries (Poland, Belgium, United Kingdom, and Spain). Specifically, the following four images of terrorists emerged: psychopathic criminals, ideologues, strategists, and desperate combatants (Kossowska et al., 2011; Kossowska, Golec de Zavala, & Kubik, 2010). These perceptions differed from each other with regard to underlying motivations, causes for terrorist acts, and specific characteristics attributed to terrorists and were also related to different preferred reactions to terrorism.

For example, psychopathic criminals were perceived as motivated by selfish goals and as being evil and immoral. This image presented terrorists as cynical, mad, barbaric, vicious, ruthless, and savage. In contrast, ideologues were perceived as fanatical, cowardly, and acting in their God's name. They are driven by a cause and they stand for what they believe is justified. They serve a higher goal according to their subjective logic, which is beyond the understanding of external observers. What those two images have in common is that they depict terrorists' motivations and actions as unpredictable and uncontrollable. Because the prevention of terrorist acts seems to be impossible when terrorists are perceived in this way, terrorism under this view is catastrophized and people experience more fear. Such images bring terrorism closer to hazards like natural disasters that cannot be prevented (Kossowska et al., 2010).

According to the third type of perception of terrorists as strategists, terrorists act rationally and in a predictable manner. They are associated with traits such as being power hungry, being focused on a political goal, and seeking publicity. This image is not associated with heightened fear, which is in line with past results showing that when people perceive terrorists as rational warriors fighting for a specific cause, they experience less anger and fear in response to terrorism and are more willing to use diplomatic approaches to counterterrorism (Pronin et al., 2006; Slovic, 2000). We found these three images of terrorists in all four of the social contexts that were examined.

Interestingly, the fourth image of terrorists, which portrayed them as desperate combatants, was specific to the Polish context (see Kossowska et al., 2010). People who shared this image of terrorists perceived them to be victims of the system who are uncompromising and desperate. The presence of this image exclusively in the Polish context raises a question about the possible underpinnings of such a perception. We believe that Poland's historical experiences with fighting for independence, during which various methods were used, can make Polish people more understanding toward using violent means in a political fight. Perceptions of terrorists as people who are frustrated, alienated, and oppressed by an overwhelming power can resonate with Polish historical memories and evoke more empathy and understanding than in countries without such historical experiences. This perception is also consistent with the finding from the Polish sample described earlier that there is a group of people who choose external attributions for terrorism. Importantly, this image is not related to fear of future terrorism (Kossowska et al., 2010).

It is noteworthy that the images of al-Qaeda terrorists as criminals and soldiers roughly correspond to the typical frames used by the media (described by McCauley, 2007) and to two of the popular metaphors inspired by the first-hand experiences of the terrorist threat in the United States (Kruglanski et al., 2007). The frames corresponding to the image of al-Qaeda terrorists as ideologues and desperate combatants were not identified by McCauley (2007), but they can be derived from metaphors described by Kruglanski et al. (2007). Thus, the four images of al-Qaeda terrorists differentiated in empirical studies correspond to those proposed in theoretical analyses.

What our studies show (Kossowska et al., 2010) is that those images of terrorists can predict not only the general level of fear evoked by terrorism but also specific reactions to it. For example, in one study, we tested whether people's images of terrorists could predict attitudes toward the placement of the American National Missile Defense system (NMD) in Poland (Kossowska et al., 2010; study 3). The NMD system is a military installation that protects the U.S. territory (and that of its allies) against intercontinental ballistic missiles (Górka-Winter, 2005; Gray, 2002). From opinion polls, we know that the installation of the NMD in Poland has been perceived as risky, making Poland vulnerable to terrorist threats. The results of this study indicate that people who viewed terrorists as criminals and ideologues were more likely to fear terrorist attacks and to oppose the installation of the missile shield system as a risky move, reducing the country's security and exposing it to future terrorist attacks. Interestingly, the image of terrorists as desperate combatants predicted neither feelings of being threatened nor negative attitudes toward the NMD system. We think that this interpretation of terrorism puts more stress on the social underpinnings of terrorism and sees terrorism as an outcome of external forces instead of internal motivations, which takes part of the responsibility away from terrorists and locates it in the environment. Therefore, military actions and the NMD installation do not seem like adequate responses because they do not address the real cause of terrorism.

Analogous distinctions among the images of terrorists found in different countries demonstrate that even in countries unaffected by terrorist acts, a popular view of terrorists is formed in a similar way to countries experienced with direct attacks, suggesting that global awareness and communication about terrorist threats have an overwhelming impact on public opinions, independent of actual experience. An interesting question that was not investigated in our studies is whether the same representations of terrorists and terrorist acts evoke similar reactions across various social settings.

Results such as those described above can have direct implications regarding strategies for communicating about threats of terrorism. Because different images of terrorists result in different preferred courses of counterterrorism action, the way that the media and public authorities present threats of terrorism can have consequences for public support of specific actions. For example, although it might be expected that those who feel particularly threatened by terrorism would support actions that reduce the effectiveness of terrorist acts, our results systematically indicate that the perception of terrorists as irrational and the fear of terrorism are related to opposition of those solutions (Kossowska et al., 2010, 2011). Presumably, people who feel the most threatened by terrorism prefer counterterrorism actions that appear immediate and definitive.

BELIEF SYSTEMS AND THREATS OF TERRORISM

Ideology

An individual's ideological beliefs about the social world shape his or her opinion about a number of politically relevant issues (Altemeyer, 1988, 1998). Thus, ideological variables are likely to shape individual and collective experiences of terrorist threats as well as emotional responses to terrorism (see Van Hiel & Kossowska, 2007). Important ideological orientations that underlie people's social attitudes are right wing authoritarianism (RWA; Altemeyer, 1996) and social dominance orientation (SDO; Sidanius, Pratto, & Rabinowitz, 1994). RWA is defined by submissiveness (to the power holder), aggression (aimed at individuals or groups that violate the accepted and legitimized standards of society), and conventionalism (i.e., support of conventional social regulations). People high in RWA tend to have pro-war sentiments more than those low in RWA across a number of different international contexts (e.g., Cohrs & Moschner, 2002; Crowson, 2009; Doty, Winter, Peterson, & Kemmelmeier, 1997; Izzett, 1971).

Authoritarians strongly supported military responses to the 9/11 attacks (e.g., Henderson-King, Henderson-King, Bolea, Koches, & Kauffman, 2004) and belligerent and coercive strategies to reduce the threat of terrorism. They also support actions typical for police prosecution of criminals to protect the social system (e.g., Cohrs, Moschner, Maes, & Kielmann, 2005). Authoritarians may also be more likely to support the restriction of human rights and civil liberties, such as freedom of speech, freedom of the press, and the right of assembly (Altemeyer, 1996; Cohrs et al., 2005; Crowson & DeBacker, 2008; McFarland & Mathews, 2005). High authoritarians are prepared to accept any ideas that provide support and protection, even if they violate democratic values. Therefore, restrictions of civil liberties presented by governments as a way of strengthening national security and protecting societies from the threat of future terrorist activities are policies that should attract high RWA support, independently of the cultural context.

A social dominance orientation is a desire for a hierarchical social order. People high in this orientation strive to belong to dominant groups, suffer if they do not, and support beliefs that legitimize and maintain existing social inequalities (Jost & Thompson, 2000; Pratto, Sidanius, Stallworth, & Malle, 1994). People high in SDO are motivated by the goals of dominance, superiority and power. They view the social world as a competitive jungle and intergroup relations as a struggle for dominance. Their hostility is directed toward groups that arouse their competitiveness over status or power (e.g., Duckitt, 2006; Duckitt et al., 2002). People high in social dominance fight to win, because otherwise, they will lose. They attempt to dominate because they fear being dominated themselves.

In other words, people who endorse high levels of RWA and people high in SDO are hostile for different reasons and often toward different groups. Importantly, RWA and SDO develop from different motivational goals and are associated with different worldviews (Duckitt, 2006; Duckitt & Fisher, 2003;Duckitt et al., 2002). RWA and SDO are related to different emotions (e.g., Kossowska, Bukowski, & van Hiel, 2008; Van Hiel & Kossowska, 2006), personality traits (e.g., Ekehammar et al., 2004), and values (Cohrs, Kielmann, Maes, & Moschner, 2005; Duriez & van Hiel, 2002).

In a series of studies, we investigated the consequences of ideological beliefs with respect to preferred counterterrorism actions in Poland. In one study, which was conducted in the United Kingdom and Poland (Golec de Zavala & Kossowska, 2011), we measured levels of RWA and SDO, images of terrorists as criminals and soldiers and preferences for different types of counterterrorism actions, namely, criminal prosecution and/or military counterstrikes. What these studies show is that ideological orientations, particularly SDO, strengthen the link between terrorist images and counterterrorist actions and make this link more consistent. We found that that participants high in SDO not only preferred military actions when they perceived terrorists as soldiers, but when they did not perceive terrorists as soldiers, they were actually opposed to military actions. Framing terrorists as soldiers may appeal especially to people high in SDO who are concerned with intergroup power struggles. Their social world is based on characteristics such as force, influence, power, and competition. We think that individuals high in SDO tend to see terrorists as a collective enemy rather than individual deviants. In response, they are likely to prefer coercive, group-based actions against terrorists. They tend to invest group resources only when such a collective enemy is dangerous and threatening. If those conditions are not met, they prefer to stay clear.

In turn, participants high in RWA tend to see terrorists as individual deviants, but they are not significantly opposed to seeing them as enemy soldiers. Perhaps this reaction is due to the very structure of RWA. Because RWA encompasses conventionalism, authoritarian submission and authoritarian aggression (Altemeyer, 1996), it is particularly focused on the in-group. Previous research has shown that RWA correlates with trust in political leaders (Altemeyer, 1981), preferences for severe punishment of lawbreakers, unless they were considered a part of authority and their deeds were aimed at unconventional, norm-violating individuals or groups (Altemeyer, 1981, 1988), and positive attitudes toward conventional groups and negative attitudes toward unconventional groups (Lambert & Chasteen, 1997). Therefore, people high in RWA are more interested in catching wrongdoers after they have already insinuated themselves into the in-group than they are in open intergroup conflict.

Although both ideologies—RWA and SDO—encompass beliefs that support a social hierarchy, they have distinct consequences for attitudes toward terrorism and counterterrorism actions. In another study, we focused specifically on the impact of RWA on attitudes toward restrictions of civil rights in response to terrorist threats. We showed that RWA positively predicts the presence of those attitudes, independently of the cultural context and experience with terrorist attacks (Kossowska et al., 2011). Therefore, we believe that culture-based variables, such as the dominant ideology and the political climate, constitute important contextual factors that shape the relationship between feelings about terrorist threats and support for specific counterterrorism strategies.

Nationalism

Past research has shown that external threats enhance group identity because uncertainty motivates people to look for a secure and stable environment provided by social groups (Hogg, 2000). Additionally, a number of findings from research on terror management theory (TMT; see, e.g., Mikulincer, Florian, & Hirschberger, 2003; Vaes, Heflick, & Goldenberg, 2010) clearly show that establishing and maintaining positive relations with others, particularly with the members of one's own group, is one of the important adaptive mechanisms as far as primordial anxiety is concerned. Therefore, this anxiety leads to a greater acceptance of group norms, respect for the group's leaders and pressure on those who violate the rules (e.g., Duckitt, 2006; Sidanius & Petrocik, 2001). Given that terrorism is usually aimed at a national group, an interesting question is raised about the impact of national attachment on reactions to terrorism. In one line of research, we focused on the role of nationalism in restrictions of civil liberties in response to a terrorist threat and its dependency on perceptions of terrorism (Sekerdej & Kossowska, 2011).

First, our research revealed that nationalism correlated positively with feelings of being threatened such that individuals high in nationalism were more afraid of terrorist attacks. In other words, these individuals were more concerned that terrorism posed a serious threat to their country, its cherished social order, and its citizens. Moreover, participants high on the nationalism scale were generally in favor of limiting civil liberties. We also found, to a large degree, that nationalism mediated the direct effect of the perception of terrorism as war on the level of support for restrictions of civil liberties, whereas there was no such mediation when terrorism was perceived as a crime. In light of these studies, we have hypothesized that there can be a certain "social feedback" between the perception of terrorist threats and the strength of national attitudes. People high on the nationalism scale tend to feel more threatened than people low on the nationalism scale, and in the face of the actual increased threat following a terrorist attack, this perception of threat further increases. Additionally, a stronger perception of terrorism as a war produces stronger national attitudes. However, when people perceive terrorism as a crime, there is no effect on national attitudes. We think that the war metaphor activates and threatens group identity more strongly, which subsequently evokes stronger national attachment.

In follow-up studies conducted in Poland, we expanded on the analysis of the influence of national attitudes on preferences for counterterrorism actions (Sekerdej, Kossowska, & Trejtowicz, 2012). This time, according to social-psychological tradition, we split national attitude into identification with one's own nation and the feeling of superiority and dominance over other national groups. We called the latter attitude chauvinism. In these studies, we additionally assessed the perceived entitativity of the threatening group (al-Qaeda). The perceived entitativity of an out-group facilitates attributing to it the common out-group intentions (Castano, 2004) and collective responsibility (Denson, Lickel, Curtis, Stenstrom, & Ames, 2006) and enhances the taking of nonspecific retaliating actions toward that group (Lickel, Miller, Stenstrom, Denson, & Schmader, 2006).

The data revealed that both national chauvinism and the perceived entitativity of Al-Qaeda increased support for social control as a state's counterterrorism strategy. Moreover, similar positive correlations were found between those variables and support for taking preventive actions against international terrorism. All in all, these findings show that individual perceptions of the in-group as well as the out-group can play an important moderating role in the relationship between feeling threatened by terrorism and the preferred approaches to counterterrorism.

Religion

Another, closely related sociocultural factor that can influence perceptions and reactions to threats of terrorism is religion, both the level of religiosity and the specific religion that dominates a given society. It can shape reactions on both individual and national levels. Why is religion important? First, Islamic terrorism itself is, in a large part, rooted within religion. Therefore, religious identity can easily be activated during a threat of terrorism. In Polish society, believers are a clear and strong majority. Ninety-eight percent of individuals are believers, and specifically 95 percent are Catholics. Therefore, the possible influence of religious identification on the perception and experience of a terrorist threat is important in this social context. There are several paths through which religiosity might activate concerns about terrorism.

On the one hand, religiosity might increase the level of experienced fear. Among religious people, terrorism can pose not only a greater realistic but also a greater symbolic threat than it does among nonreligious individuals. The perception of fundamental conflicts between religions is more threatening to highly religious individuals than to nonreligious people. Moreover, religiosity is highly correlated with conservative views, and some researchers perceive both worldviews as means to reduce feelings of uncertainty and threat.

Therefore, people with such underlying predispositions may experience more fear when faced with external threats such as terrorism. This view is supported by data showing positive relationships between religiosity and fear of terrorism, and between Catholicism specifically and fear (Domański, 2009). In addition, an analysis of the relationship between various social attitudes and generalized fear demonstrated that fearfulness correlated strongly with the dominant religious tradition and with the proportions of citizens who believed in Heaven (negatively) and in Hell (positively) (Treisman, 2011). These data, although rather scarce, suggest that religiosity—high in Polish society—should be correlated positively with experienced fear.

On the other hand, religiosity might serve as a tool for coping with terrorist threats. For example, drawing from terror management theory (Solomon, Greenberg, & Pyszczynski, 2004), religion offers a cultural worldview that successfully buffers existential threats raised by terrorism. However, although there is some evidence that religion is positively related to emotional responses to stress (Mickley, Carson, & Soeken,1995; Myers & Diener, 1995), there are many studies without conclusive results. An important factor that can moderate the impact of religiosity on emotional responses to threats is whether it is intrinsic or extrinsic religiosity. While intrinsically religious individuals are concentrated on meaning and values, extrinsically religious people use religion to gain social status (Allport & Ross, 1967).

Intrinsic religiosity has been found to be related positively to coping with terrorist threats (Fischer, Greitemeyer, Kastenmüller, Jonas, & Frey, 2006). Specifically, intrinsically religious people experienced more positive emotions and fewer negative emotions under conditions of high terror salience than did nonreligious participants. The mechanism that mediated this relation was self-efficacy, which was influenced negatively by threats of terrorism among non-religious participants but not among intrinsically religious participants. This distinction also mattered when it came to preferred counterterrorism policies. Under existential threats, people who were intrinsically religious supported diplomatic counterterrorism strategies more often than aggressive ones (Golec de Zavala, Cichocka, Orehek, & Abdollahi, 2012). Similar results were obtained in U.S., Iranian, and Polish samples, which suggest that the effect of intrinsic religiosity is also independent of direct experience with terrorism.

TRUST IN GOVERNMENT AND THREAT OF TERRORISM

Another social factor that plays an important role in reactions to the threat of terrorism is the level of social trust and, specifically, trust in public institutions. Numerous studies have demonstrated how trust in public institutions and regulatory authorities can influence perceptions of risk, intensity of experienced emotions and support for specific actions taken by those institutions to deal with risk (Bronfman, López

Vázquez, & Dorantes, 2009; Siegrist & Cvetkovich, 2000). The basic relationship is that belief in the efficacy and trustworthiness of public institutions is related to lower levels of feeling threatened by terrorism and at the same time increases public acceptance of risk (Trumbo, McComas, & Besley, 2008). Social trust is especially important in judgments about risks that people lack knowledge about (Siegrist & Cvetkovich, 2000) and when they experience less personal control over the risk (Lion, Meertens, & Bot, 2002). Under such conditions, belief that external authorities can make trustworthy decisions can decrease fear. This compensatory control over risk is especially important in the context of terrorist threats. Given that this risk is perceived as highly uncontrollable (Slovic & Weber, 2002), people are more likely to rely on information and actions taken by institutions and experts than they are in the context of more controllable hazards. Therefore, when a given society lacks social trust, people might react to the terrorist threats with more intensive anxiety and fear than under conditions of higher trust. At the same time, they might be less accepting of the actions and less persuaded by precautions (i.e., imprisonment and torturing of terrorists, participation in the war on terror) taken by unreliable authorities than by legitimate institutions. Therefore, actions aimed at building the level of social trust can have important consequences for dealing with terrorist threats (ter Huurne & Gutteling, 2009).

Because Poland is a country with one of the lowest levels of social trust and trust in political institutions in Europe (Domański, 2009), the role of this factor is of great importance in Poland. With regard to the threat of terrorism, national survey data show that many people are convinced that public institutions cannot communicate efficiently about terrorist threats. Sixty-nine percent of Polish people feel they are not informed about possible terrorist threats, and only 23 percent of people agree that they are informed about them (CBOS, 2010). Because these figures resemble the level of general political trust in Poland, we suppose that there might be a close relationship between general trust and belief in the efficacy of Polish political institutions in dealing with terrorist threats. This supposition is supported by data on acceptance of the war in Iraq gathered from a representative sample of Polish people. The level of approval of this war was dependent on the level of trust in international institutions such as NATO, the European Union, and the United Nations, but it was also predicted by the general level of trust in other people (Skarżyńska & Chmielewski, 2007).

The inverse relationship between threats of terrorism and trust in institutions is also worth examining. Past research has offered compelling evidence that terrorism salience is related to elevated trust in public institutions (Chanley, 2002; Gaines, 2002; Ladd, 2007). This relationship was indicated by increases in George W. Bush's approval ratings following the 9/11 attacks and after each subsequent terrorism warning issued between 2001 and 2004 (Willer, 2004). This rallying effect of terrorism salience was demonstrated in other studies as well, including when an experimental design was adopted (Lambert et al., 2010, Landau et al., 2004). Importantly, the salience of terrorist threats increased political system legitimacy not only in the United States but also in other social contexts untouched by direct experience with terrorism (Ullrich & Cohrs, 2007). To our knowledge, there have been no studies on the threat of terrorism and political trust in Poland. However, after the plane crash on April 10, 2010, in which many Polish political authorities died including the Polish president Lech Kaczyński, and his wife, and many other Polish politicians, trust in political authorities increased (CBOS, 2010). We think it demonstrated the same psychological effect of increased support for the political system and public authorities after the experience of a threat (Jost et al., 2010) as can be noted after terrorist attacks. Although the type of threat was different, this result is worth noting because, as we mentioned, general trust in public institutions in Poland is very low (Domański, 2009). This result suggests that the absolute level of trust does not moderate the impact of a threat on subsequent support for political authorities, which is critical when future reactions to external dangers are considered. However, it is possible that under circumstances of extremely low levels of social trust and low levels of confidence in the legitimacy of public institutions, threats will not strengthen the system but will instead affect it negatively.

NEGATIVE EMOTIONALITY

Finally, we look at the psychological factors that are very specific to Polish society, namely the level of pessimism and a general propensity to experience negative emotions. Although they have not been directly investigated in the context of terrorist threats, we believe that they offer an interesting empirical question. One relevant study showed that various kinds of fears correlate strongly with each other across different domains (i.e., health, politics, economy) (Treisman, 2011). For example, in a sample of Western European countries, fear of terrorism was significantly correlated with fear of new viruses and fear of medical errors. This result suggests that there is a common underlying predisposition to react with fear in response to different kinds of threatening stimuli. In that analysis, Poland was placed in the group of highly fearful nations. Although data on the Polish sample did not include information about fear of terrorism specifically, high correlations between this type of fear and others found in a sample of other countries allow for the assumption that the picture would be similar if fear of terrorism had been included.

It has been demonstrated that this generalized propensity to experience fear can be partly predicted by a nation's level of pessimism; 25 percent of cross-national variance in fear can be explained by variation in the pessimism index (Treisman, 2011). According to those results, higher levels of fear expressed by Polish respondents could be predicted on the basis of their overestimation of the likelihood of unpleasant outcomes. Those results can be supported by other data. For example, Czapiński & Panek (2003) showed that, on average, Polish people believe that they are less likely to experience positive outcomes in life than other people. This pessimistic bias is in opposition to the results that are usually reported with regard to life expectations.

This lack of optimism among Polish people is also evident when we look at the data regarding risk taking. According to the prospect theory, people play it safe when it comes to gains and prefer smaller but certain positive outcomes. Yet, they choose risky options more often when it comes to losses (Kahneman & Tversky, 1979). Interestingly, Polish people are risk aversive both when it comes to gains and losses. While in the original study by Tversky and Kahneman (1979) 91 percent participants chose a risky option in the loss condition, 79 percent of Polish people chose a certain loss and did not decide to take a risk (Czapiński, 2005). We think that this lack of belief in good fortune in life can also have consequences for the evaluation of terrorist threats. The tendency to have more negative expectations for the future, especially with regard to macro-social events, can prevent people from engaging in actions that they perceive as risky (i.e., participation in the war on terror), even when such actions could eliminate the threat completely.

In addition to being pessimistic and risk averse, Polish people have a general propensity to experience negative emotions and a tendency to negatively evaluate the social world (Wojciszke, 2005). This effect is more pronounced during emotional reactions to distant events and phenomena and those that are more abstract and less concrete examples (Czapiński & Panek, 2003). While Polish people are rather satisfied with their children and spouses, when it comes to the country's future or predicted economic situation, they declare high levels of dissatisfaction. This dissatisfaction is not correlated with the actual economic and political situation because, despite changes that have occurred in those areas across time, the low level of satisfaction has remained stable (Wojciszke, 2005), although it seems to have increased slightly in recent years (Czapiński, 2009).

Wojciszke, Pieńkowski, and Krzykowski (1995) have even suggested that there is a social norm of negativity that prescribes complaining as a desirable behavior. Corroborating this suggestion, data show that only 23 percent of Polish people agree that it is acceptable to talk about one's own happiness, and most of them agreed that past times were better than present and future ones. This norm of negativity is also visible on the level of experienced emotions. For example, while most of the time American students declared that their mood was better than average (Johnson, 1937), Polish students on average felt worse (Doliński, 1996). This effect has been replicated in other studies as well, and it was found to be even stronger among older adults (Wojciszke, 2005), which was interpreted as a sign of a stronger and more developed social norm of complaining. Although complaining during social contacts does not in fact improve mood (Wojciszke et al., 2009), among Polish people, it is perceived as a means to achieve a better connection between people. Conversations based on complaining were judged to be deeper and more honest than conversations during which people engaged in affirmations (Szymków, Wojciszke, & Baryła, 2003).

Is it possible that this general level of negativity plays a role in shaping reactions to the threat of terrorism in Polish society? We hypothesize that it can affect perceptions of and reactions to this risk for several reasons. First, it is known that affect influences risk estimation. Negative emotions increase the perceived probability of a risk (Sjöberg, 2007; Slovic & Weber, 2002). Although research shows that there is a need for studying specific emotions because fear and anger can exert an opposite influence on risk estimation (i.e., Lerner, Gonzalez, Small, & Fischhoff, 2003; Skitka, Bauman, Aramovich, & Morgan, 2006), it is also possible that generalized mood affects the way people process information regarding risk. Second, past research also points to the role of emotionality in coping with terrorist threats such that positive emotions were related to better coping with threats (Fredrickson et al., 2003). Therefore, it is likely that negative emotions indicate fewer resources for coping with any threat, including the threat of terrorism. Moreover, because positive emotions are related to the experience of control, domination of negative affect may decrease self-efficacy when a person is faced with threatening stimuli, which can subsequently increase the perception of a threat.

These suggestions with regard to the Polish society are only hypothetical and need further empirical investigation. Psychological resources such as optimism and positive emotions are usually studied on an individual level. Those results suggest that the relationships between those variables and risk perception on a macro-social level are worthy of investigation because societies can differ with regard to the chronic level of those resources. Such a multilevel analysis could offer some insight into the roles of those coping mechanisms on both individual and social levels, which is important because in the context of terrorism, actions are taken on both levels.

SUMMARY

The harrowing events of September 11, 2001, revealed how quickly and unpredictably acts of terror can strike innocent lives. Given the enhanced global focus on terrorism since these events and the continued high frequency of planned or attempted terrorist attacks, understanding how the awareness of terrorism affects people's beliefs and attitudes may have important real-world implications. Many studies have revealed that terrorism has the potential to evoke strong psychological reactions. The importance of considering the broader context in research on perceptions of terrorism is further underscored by recent findings. Thus, the current analysis has focused on the social and psychological effects of terrorism by identifying critical social and psychological factors that predict how individuals will respond to the threat of terrorism.

In this chapter, we have argued that the effects of terrorism are not limited to those directly associated with the occurrence of an attack. Awareness of a threat itself can lead to adverse effects on psychological well-being, the economy, or intergroup relationships, as well as to indirect effects of concern (Lemyre et al., 2006; Slovic, 2002). We reviewed the effects of the perception of terrorism, ideological factors, social trust, and emotionality on the experience of fear and preferred courses of counterterrorism actions. Together, these findings highlight the universal, context-independent psychological mechanisms evoked by threats of terrorism and their potential social and political consequences. We aimed to demonstrate how those universal mechanisms translate into specific reactions in Polish society. At the same time, we wanted to reveal some specificity of this social context, which suggests future directions for terrorism research and has practical implications. For example, it has been argued that management of such complex risks as terrorism should include efforts to enhance transparency and dialogue, as well as engagement of the public as an active partner in terrorism risk management (Fischhoff et al., 2003). Knowledge about the specific context in which the terrorist threat occurs makes such recommendations more concrete by referring to the specific demands of that society.

ACKNOWLEDGMENTS

The research was supported by grant MNiSW 0624/K03/2007/32 awarded to Małgorzata Kossowska.

REFERENCES

Allport, G., & Ross, M. (1967). Personal religious orientation and prejudice. *Journal of Personality and Social Psychology, 5,* 432–443.

Altemeyer, B. (1981), *Right-wing authoritarianism.* Winnipeg, Manitoba, Canada: University of Manitoba Press.

Altemeyer, B. (1988). *Enemies of freedom: Understanding right-wing authoritarianism.* San Francisco, CA: Jossey-Bass.

Altemeyer, B. (1996). *The authoritarian specter.* Cambridge, MA: Harvard University Press.

Altemeyer, B. (1998). The other "authoritarian personality." In M. Zanna (Ed.), *Advances in experimental social psychology* (Vol. 30, pp. 47–92). San Diego, CA: Academic Press

Bonanno, G. A., & Jost, J. T. (2006). Conservative shift among high-exposure survivors of the September 11th terrorist attacks. *Basic and Applied Social Psychology, 28,* 311–323.

Bronfman, N. C., López Vázquez, E., & Dorantes, G. (2009). An empirical study for the direct and indirect links between trust in regulatory institutions and acceptability of hazards. *Safety Science, 47,* 686–692.

Castano, E. (2004). In case of death, cling to the ingroup. *European Journal of Social Psychology, 34,* 1–10.

CBOS. (2001). Czy Polsce zagraża terroryzm? [Does terrorism threaten Poland]. Retrieved from http://www.cbos.pl/SPISKOM.POL/2001/K_123_01.PDF

CBOS. (2004). Wzrost poczucia zagrożenia terroryzmem [Threat of terrorism]. Retrieved from http://www.cbos.pl/SPISKOM.POL/2004/K_059_04.PDF

CBOS. (2005). Poczucie zagrożenia terroryzmem oraz akceptowane działania zwiększające bezpieczeństwo obywateli [Threat of terrorism and support for actions increasing public safety]. Retrieved from http://www.cbos.pl/SPISKOM.POL/2005/K_144_05.PDF

CBOS. (2010). Rola instytucji rządowych i samorządowych w zakresie informowania obywateli o zagrożeniach terrorystycznych [The role of government and non-government institutions in communications of threat of terrorism]. Retrieved from https://www.google.pl/url?sa=t&rct=j&q=&esrc=s&source=web&cd=1&cad=rja&ved=0CC8QFjAA&url=http%3A%2F%2Fwww.antyterroryzm.gov.pl%2Fdownload%2F5%2F896%2FRola_instytucjI_rzadowych_w_zakresie_informowania_obywatelI_o_zagrozeniach_terro.pdf&ei=y4tiUcvYIYmEO7KRgKgI&usg=AFQjCNGP34rHDFP4SpXw0-Xwf9IR9FQraQ&sig2=ofVZ67ggcFjXaQv7KYeYUQ&bvm=bv.44770516,d.ZWU

CBOS. (2011). Poczucie zagrożenia terroryzmem po śmierci Osamy ben Ladena [Threat of terrorism after Osama ben Laden death]. Retrieved from http://www.cbos.pl/SPISKOM.POL/2011/K_057_11.PDF

Chanley, V. A. (2002). Trust in government in the aftermath of 9/11: Determinants and consequences. *Political Psychology, 23*, 469–483.

Cohrs, J. C., & Moschner, B. (2002). Antiwar knowledge and generalized political attitudes as determinants of attitude toward the Kosovo War. *Peace and Conflict: Journal of Peace Psychology, 8*, 141–157.

Cohrs, J. C., Moschner, B., Maes, J., & Kielmann, S. (2005). The motivational bases of right-wing authoritarianism and social dominance orientation: Relations to values and attitudes in the aftermath of September 11, 2001. *Personality and Social Psychology Bulletin, 31*, 1425–1434.

Crowson, H. M. (2009). Are all conservatives alike? A study of psychological correlates of cultural and economic conservatism within a U.S. population sample. *Journal of Psychology: Interdisciplinary and Applied, 5*, 449–463.

Crowson, H. M., & DeBacker, T. K. (2008). Belief, motivational, and ideological correlates of human rights attitudes. *Journal of Social Psychology, 148*, 293–310.

Czapiński, J. (2005). Optymiści i ryzykanci. Polskie paradoksy [Optimists and adventurers]. In M. Drogosz (Ed.), *Jak Polacy przegrywają—jak Polacy wygrywają?[How do Poles lose—how do Poles win?]* (pp. 127–149). Gdańsk, Poland: Gdańskie Wydawnictwo Psychologiczne.

Czapiński, J. (2009). Zadowolenie z poszczególnych dziedzin i aspektów życia [Satisfaction from certain domains and aspects of life]. In J. Czapiński & T. Panek (Eds.), *Diagnoza społeczna 2009. Warunki i jakość życia Polaków [[Social Diagnosis 2009. Conditions and life quality of Poles]* (pp. 151–228). Retrieved from http://www.diagnoza.com/pliki/raporty/Diagnoza_raport_2009.pdf.

Czapiński J., & Panek, T. (Eds.) (2003). *Diagnoza społeczna 2003. Warunki i jakość życia Polaków [Social Diagnosis 2003. Conditions and life quality of Poles]*. Retrieved from http://www.diagnoza.com/files/raport2003.pdf

Czapiński J., & Panek T. (Eds.) (2005). *Diagnoza społeczna 2005. Warunki i jakość życia Polaków [Social Diagnosis 2003. Conditions and life quality of Poles]*. Retrieved from http://www.diagnoza.com/pliki/raporty/Diagnoza_raport_2005.pdf

Davis, D., & Silver, B. (2004). Civil liberties vs. security in the context of the terrorist attacks on America. *American Journal of Political Science, 48*, 28–46.

Denson, T., Lickel, Brian, Curtis, M., Stenstrom, D., & Ames, D. (2006). The roles of entitativity and essentiality in judgments of collective responsibility. *Group Processes & Intergroup Relations, 9*, 43–61.

Domański, H. (2009). *Społeczeństwa europejskie, stratyfikacja i systemy wartości [European societies, stratification and value systems]*. Warszawa, Poland: Wydawnictwo Naukowe Scholar.

Doliński, D. (1996). The mystery of the Polish soul. *European Journal of Social Psychology, 26*, 1001–1005.

Doty, R., Winter, D., Peterson, B., & Kemmelmeier, M. (1997). Authoritarianism and American students' attitudes about the Gulf War, 1990–1996. *Personality and Social Psychology Bulletin, 23,* 1133–1143.

Duckitt, J. (2006). Differential effects of right wing authoritarianism and social dominance orientation on outgroup attitudes and their mediation by threat from and competitiveness to outgroups. *Personality and Social Psychology Bulletin, 32,* 684–696.

Duckitt, J., & Fisher, K. (2003). The impact of social threat on worldview and ideological attitudes. *Political Psychology, 24,* 199–222.

Duckitt, J., Wagner, C., du Plessis, I., & Birum, I. (2002). The psychological bases of ideology and prejudice: Testing a dual process model. *Journal of Personality and Social Psychology, 83,* 75–93.

Duriez, B., & Van Hiel, A. (2002). The march of modern fascism. A comparison of social dominance orientation and authoritarianism. *Personality and Individual Differences, 32,* 1199–1213.

Echebarria-Echabe, A., & Fernandez-Guede, E. (2006). Effects of terrorism on attitudes and ideological orientation. *European Journal of Social Psychology, 36,* 259–265.

Ekehammar, B., Akrami, N., Gylje, M., & Zakrisson, I. (2004). What matters most to prejudice: Big Five personality, social dominance orientation, or right-wing authoritarianism. *European Journal of Personality, 18,* 463–482.

Fischer, P., Greitemeyer, T., Kastenmüller, A., Jonas, E., & Frey, D. (2006). Coping with terrorism: The impact of increased salience of terrorism on mood and self efficacy of intrinsically religious and non-religious people. *Personality and Social Psychology Bulletin, 32,* 365–377.

Fischhoff, B., Gonzalez, R., Small, D., & Lerner, J. (2003). Evaluating the success of terror risk communication. *Biosecurity and Bioterrorism: Biodefense Strategy, Practice, and Science, 1*(4), 255–258.

Fredrickson, B. L., Tugade, M., Waugh, C., & Larkin, G. (2003).What good are positive emotions in crises? A prospective study of resilience and emotions following the terrorist attacks on the United States on September 11th, 2001. *Journal of Personality and Social Psychology, 84,* 365–376.

Gaines, B. J. (2002). Where's the rally? Approval and trust of the president, cabinet, congress, and government since September 11. *Political Science and Politics, 35,* 530–536.

Gallup Organization. (May 4, 2011). *Majority in U.S. Say Bin Laden's Death Makes America Safer.* Retrieved from http://www.gallup.com/poll/147413/majority-say-bin-laden-death-makes-america-safer.aspx.

Golec de Zavala, A., Cichocka, A., Orehek, E., & Abdollahi, A. (2012). Intrinsic religiosity reduces intergroup hostility under mortality salience. *European Journal of Social Psychology, 42,* 451–461.

Golec de Zavala, A., & Kossowska, M. (2011). The role of ideological orientations in terrorist perception. *European Journal of Social Psychology, 41,* 538–549.

Goodwin, R., Willson, M., & Gaines, S. (2005). Terror threat perception and its consequences in contemporary Britain. *British Journal of Psychology, 96,* 389–406.

Górka-Winter, B. (2005). System obrony przeciwrakietowej Stanów Zjednoczonych. Implikacje dla Polski [US National Missile Defense System: Implications for Poland]. Warszawa, Poland: Ekspertyzy, Biuro Bada [nacut e] i Analiz, Polski Instytut Spraw Międzynarodowych.

Gray, C. S. (2002). *European perspective on U.S. Ballistic Missile Defense.* Fairfax, VA: National Institute for Public Policy.

Henderson-King, D., Henderson-King, E., Bolea, B., Koches, K., & Kauffman, A. (2004). Seeking understanding or sending bombs: Beliefs as predictors of responses to terrorism. *Peace and Conflict: Journal of Peace Psychology, 10,* 67–84.

Hogg, M. A. (2000). Subjective uncertainty reduction through self-categorization: A motivational theory of social identity processes. *European Review of Social Psychology*, 11, 223–255.

Huddy, L., Feldman, S., Taber, C., & Jahav, G. (2005). Threat, anxiety, and support of antiterrorism policies. *American Journal of Political Science*, 49, 593–608.

Huddy, L., Khatib, N., & Capelos, T. (2002). The polls-trends: Reactions to the terrorist attacks of September 11, 2001. *Public Opinion Quarterly*, 66, 418–450.

Izzett, R. (1971). Authoritarianism and attitudes toward the Vietnam war as reflected in behavioral and self-report measures. *Journal of Personality and Social Psychology*, 17, 145–148.

Johnson, W. B. (1937). Euphoric and depressed mood in normal subjects. *Journal of Character and Personality*, 6, 79–98.

Jost, J. T., Liviatan, I., van der Toorn, J., Ledgerwood, A., Mandisodza, A., & Nosek, B. A. (2010). System justification: How do we know it's motivated? In: R. Bobocel et al. (Eds.), *The psychology of justice and legitimacy: The Ontario symposium* (Vol. 11, pp. 173–203). Hillsdale, NJ: Erlbaum.

Jost, J. T., & Thompson, E. P. (2000). Group-based dominance and opposition to equality as independent predictors of self-esteem, ethnocentrism, and social policy attitudes among African Americans and European Americans. *Journal of Experimental Social Psychology*, 36, 209–232.

Kahneman, D., & Tversky, A. (1979). Prospect theory: An analysis of decision under risk. *Econometrica*, 47, 263–291

Kawalec, K. (2010). Wpływ środków masowego przekazu na poczucie zagrożenia terroryzmem oraz na poparcie dla ograniczania swobód obywatelskich jako jednej z metod walki z terroryzmem [Media, threat of terrorism and support for civil right limitations as counterterrorism strategy]. Unpublished master's thesis. Jagiellonian University.

Kossowska, M., Bukowski, M., & Van Hiel, A. (2008), The impact of submissive and dominant authoritarianism and negative emotions on prejudice. *Personality & Individual Differences*. 45, 744–749.

Kossowska, M., Golec de Zavala, A., & Kubik, T. (2010). Images and threat: Impact of the way people perceived terrorists on the fear of future terrorist attacks. *Behavioral Sciences of Terrorism and Political Aggression*. 3, 1–19.

Kossowska, M., Trejtowicz, M., de Lemus, S., Bukowski, M., Van Hiel, A., & Goodwin, R. (2011). Relationships between right-wing authoritarianism, terrorism threat and attitudes toward restrictions of civil rights: A comparison among four European countries. *British Journal of Psychology*, 102, 245–259.

Kruglanski, A. W., Crenshaw, M., Post, J., & Victoroff, J. (2007). What should this fight be called? Metaphors of counterterrorism and their implications. *Psychological Science in the Public Interest*, 8, 97–133.

Ladd, J. M. (2007). Predispositions and public support for the president during the war on terrorism. *Public Opinion Quarterly*, 71, 511–538.

Lambert, A. J., & Chasteen, A. L. (1997). Perceptions of disadvantage vs. conventionality: Political values and attitudes toward the elderly vs. blacks. *Personality and Social Psychology Bulletin*, 23, 469–481.

Lambert, A. J., Scherer, L. D., Schott, J. P., Olsen, K. R., Andrews, R., O'Brien, T., & Zisser, (2010). Rally effects, threat, and attitude change: An integrative approach to understanding the role of emotion. *Journal of Personality and Social Psychology*, 98, 886–903.

Landau, M. J., Solomon, S., Greenberg, J., Cohen, F., Pyszczynski, T., Arndt, J., ... Cook, A. (2004). Deliver us from evil: The effects of mortality salience and reminders of 9/11 on support for President George W. Bush. *Personality and Social Psychology Bulletin*, 30(9), 1136–1150.

Lauterbach, D., & Vrana, S. (2001). The relationship among personality variables, exposure to traumatic events, and severity of posttraumatic stress symptoms. *Journal of Traumatic Stress, 14*, 29–46.

Lemyre, L., Turner, M. C., Lee, J. E. C., & Krewski, D. (2006). Public perception of terrorism threats and related information sources in Canada: Implications for the management of terrorism risks. *Journal of Risk Research, 9*, 755–774.

Lerner, J. S., Gonzalez, R. M., Small, D. A., & Fischhoff, B. (2003). Effects of fear and anger on perceived risks of terrorism: A national field experiment. *Psychological Science, 14*, 144–150.

Lickel, B., Miller, N., Stenstrom, D. M., Denson, T. F., & Schmader, T. (2006). Vicarious retribution: The role of collective blame in intergroup aggression. *Personality and Social Psychology Review, 10*, 372–390.

Lion, R., Meertens, R. M., & Bot, I. (2002). Priorities in information desire about unknown risks. *Risk Analysis, 22*, 765–776.

McCauley, C. (2004). Psychological Issues in understanding terrorism and the response to terrorism. In: C. Stout (Ed.), *Psychology of terrorism: Coping with the continuing threat, condensed edition* (pp. 33–65). Westport, CT: Praeger Publishers/Greenwood Publishing Group.

McCauley, C. (2007). War versus justice in response to terrorist attacks: Competing frames and their implications. In B. Bongar, et al. (Eds.), *Psychology of terrorism* (pp. 13–31). New York, NY: Oxford University Press.

McFarland, S., & Mathews, M. (2005). Who cares about human rights? *Political Psychology, 26*, 365–385.

Mickley, J. R., Carson, V., & Soeken, K. L. (1995). Religion and adult mental health: State of the science in nursing. *Issues in Mental Health Nursing, 16*, 345–360.

Mikulincer, M., Florian, V., & Hirschberger, G. (2003). The existential function of close relationships: Introducing death into the science of love. *Personality & Social Psychology Review, 7*, 20–40.

Myers, D. G., & Diener, E. (1995). Who is happy? *Psychological Science, 6*, 10–19.

Norris, F., Friedman, M., & Watson, P. (2002). 60,000 disaster victims speak: Part II. Summary and implications of the disaster mental health research. *Psychiatry: Interpersonal and Biological Processes, 65*, 240–260.

Paez Rovira, D., Martinez-Sanchez, F., & Rime, B. (2004). Los effectos del compartimento social de las emociones sobre la trauma del 11 de Marzo en personas no afectadas directamente. [Effects of social sharing of emotion about March Eleven trauma on vicarious victims] *Ansiedad y Estres, 10*, 219–232.

Pratto, F., Sidanius, J., Stallworth, L. M., & Malle, B. F. (1994). Social dominance orientation: A personality variable predicting social and political attitudes. *Journal of Personality and Social Psychology, 67*, 741–763.

Pronin, E., Kennedy, K., & Butsch, S. (2006). Bombing versus negotiating: How preferences for combating terrorism are affected by perceived terrorist rationality. *Basic And Applied Social Psychology, 28*, 385–392.

Ronen, T., Rahav, G., & Appel, N. (2003). Adolescent stress responses to a single acute stress and to continuous external stress: Terrorist attacks. *Journal of Loss and Trauma, 8*, 261–282.

Schuster, M., Stein, B., Jaycox, L., Collins, R., Marshall, G., Elliott, M., … Berr y, S. (2001). A national survey of stress reactions after the September 11, terrorist attacks. *New England Journal of Medicine, 345*, 1507–1512.

Sekerdej, M., & Kossowska, M. (2011). Motherland under attack! Nationalism, terrorist threat, and support for the restriction of civil liberties. *Polish Psychological Bulletin, 42*, 11–19.

Sekerdej, M., Kossowska, M., & Trejtowicz, M. (2012). Bytowość, postawy narodowe i reakcje wobec obcych [Entitivity, national attitudes and reactions to outgroup members]. In M. Drogosz & M. Kofta (Eds.), *Poza stereotypy [Beyond stereotypes]* (pp. 15–44). Warszawa, Poland: PWN.

Sidanius, J., & Petrocik, J. R. (2001). Communal and national identity in a multiethnic state: A comparison of three perspectives. In R. D. Ashmore, L. Jussim, & D. Wilder (Eds.), *Social identity, intergroup conflict, and conflict reduction* (Rutgers Series on Self and Social Identity, Volume 3, pp. 101–129). New York, NY: Oxford University Press.

Sidanius, J., Pratto, F., & Rabinowitz, J. (1994). Gender, ethnic status, ingroup attachment and social dominance orientation. *Journal of Cross-Cultural Psychology, 25,* 194–216.

Siegrist, M., & Cvetkovich, G. T. (2000). Perception of hazards: The role of social trust and knowledge. *Risk Analysis, 20*(5), 713–719.

Sjöberg, L. (2007). Emotions and risk perception. Paper prepared for the Preference Elicitation Group workshop on Risk perception, attitudes, and behavior. Retrieved from http://www.dynamit.com/lennart/pdf/Emotions%20and%20risk%20perceptio1%0noc.pdf

Skarżyńska, K., & Chmielewski, K. (2007). Percepcja sytuacji międzynarodowej: rola zaufania i schematu międzynarodowego aktora. *Psychologia Społeczna, 2,* 28–45.

Skitka, L. J., Bauman, C. W., Aramovich, N. P., & Morgan, G. S. (2006). Confrontational and preventative policy responses to terrorism: Anger wants a fight and "fear" wants them to go away. *Basic and Applied Social Psychology, 28,* 375–384.

Slovic, P. (2000). *The perception of risk.* London, UK: Earthscan.

Slovic, P., & Weber, E. (2002). *Perception of risk posed by extreme events.* Paper presented at Risk Management Strategies in an Uncertain World, Palisades, NY, April 12–13, 2002.

Solomon, S., Greenberg, J., & Pyszczynski, T. (2004). The cultural animal: Twenty years of terror management theory and research. In J. Greenberg, S. L., Koole, & T. Pyszczynski (Eds.), *Handbook of experimental existential psychology* (pp. 13–34). New York, NY: Guilford.

Somer, E., Ruvio, A., Soref, E., & Sever, I. (2005). Terrorism, distress and coping: High versus low impact regions and direct versus indirect civilian exposure. *Anxiety, Stress & Coping, 18,* 165–182.

Somer, E., Tamir, E., Maguen, S., & Litz, B. (2005). Brief cognitive-behavioral phone based intervention targeting anxiety about the threat of attack: A pilot study. *Behaviour Research & Therapy, 43,* 669–679.

Szymkow, A., Wojciszke, B., & Baryla, W. (2003). Psychologiczne funkcje narzekania [Psychological functions of complaining]. *Czasopismo Psychologiczne, 9,* 47–64.

ter Huurne, E., & Gutteling, J. M. (2009). How to trust? The importance of self-efficacy and social trust in public responses to industrial risks. *Journal of Risk Research, 12,* 809–824.

Treisman, D. (2011). The geography of fear. *NBER Working Paper Series,* Vol. w16838. Retrieved from http://ssrn.com/abstract=1770390

Trumbo, C., McComas, K., & Besley, J. (2008)., Individual- and community-level effects on risk perception in cancer cluster investigations. *Risk Analysis, 28,* 161–178.

Ullrich, J., & Cohrs, J. C. (2007). Terrorism salience increases system justification: Experimental evidence. *Social Justice Research, 20,* 117–139.

Vaes, J., Heflick, N. A., & Goldenberg, J. L. (2010). "We are people": In-group humanization as an existential defense. *Journal of Personality and Social Psychology. 98,* 750–760.

Van Hiel, A., & Kossowska, M. (2006). Having few positive emotions, or too many negative feelings? Emotions as moderating variables of authoritarianism effects on racism. *Personality and Individual Differences, 40,* 913–930.

Van Hiel, A., & Kossowska, M. (2007). Contemporary attitudes and their ideological representation in Flanders (Belgium), Poland and the Ukraine. *International Journal of Psychology: Behavioral, 42*, 16–26.

Willer, R. (2004). The effects of government-issued terror warnings on presidential approval ratings. *Current Research in Social Psychology, 10*, 1–12.

Wojciszke, B. (2005). Morality and competence in person and self perception. *European Review of Social Psychology, 16*, 155–188.

Wojciszke, B., Baryła, W., Szymków-Sudziarska, A., Parzuchowski, M., & Kowalczyk, K. (2009). Saying is experiencing: Affective consequences of complaining and affirmation. *Polish Psychological Bulletin, 40*, 74–84.

Wojciszke, B., Pienkowski, R., & Krzykowski, G., (1995). Polska norma negatywnego myślenia o świecie społecznym: niezadowolenie z życia, kraju i prezydenta [Polish negativity norm in perception of the social world: Dissatisfaction with life, country and its president]. *Kolokwia Psychologiczne, 4*, 23–411.

Zimbardo, P. (2003). Overcoming terror. Retrieved from http://www.psychologytoday.com/htdocs/prod/ptoarticle/pto-20030724-000000.asp.

CHAPTER 11

An Exposure Effect? Evidence From a Rigorous Study on the Psychopolitical Outcomes of Terrorism

DAPHNA CANETTI, CARMIT RAPAPORT, CARLY WAYNE,
BRIAN J. HALL, STEVAN E. HOBFOLL

This chapter examines a number of questions posed by a reality in which millions of people live under the clouds of war, terror, and violence. How are these people affected and why do some suffer from lifelong trauma while others seem to maintain psychological balance? Why do some endorse aggressive behavior whereas others seek conciliatory repertoires? Answering these questions may give us not only the keys to preserve the well-being of entire societies but also insights into the origins of resilience and other conditions that can serve as protective factors for those exposed to repeated war-related trauma. Understanding how psychological distress, threats, and fears facilitate the inhibition of a distorted outlook about the other may offer policymakers pathways to break this self-perpetuating cycle of violence and retribution.

The Israeli-Palestinian conflict is one of the world's most fundamentally intractable, violent, and prolonged conflicts. For most Israelis and Palestinians, hostility, psychological distress, perceived threats, hatred, fear, violence, and terrorism truly represent *the exhausting daily routine*. This protracted climate of violence naturally leads to key questions regarding how citizens are affected by this prolonged environment of stress, threat, fear, and violence that characterizes intractable conflicts such as the Israeli-Palestinian conflict. Israeli and Palestinian citizens have both been the victims of tremendous acts of violence and war that continue to have a profound effect on citizens' physical and emotional well-being, as well as their political viewpoints and actions with regard to the conflict. Since 2000 alone, 6,489 Palestinian citizens have been killed by Israeli security forces; likewise, 1096 Israeli citizens have been killed by Palestinians (B'Tselem).[1] Many other statistics are just

---

1. B'Tselem Statistics (Data, September 29, 2000, to June 30, 2012) Retrieved from http://old.btselem.org/statistics/english/Casualties.asp

as staggering. As of 2006, almost 4.5 million Palestinians were officially registered as refugees in Jordan, Lebanon, Syria, the West Bank, and the Gaza Strip (*BBC News*).[2] Meanwhile, in just the past 2 years, Israeli civilians have had to contend with 731 rockets and 314 mortar shells launched by Palestinian militants from the Gaza Strip into southern Israel (B'Tselem).[3]

Life under such conditions of continuous threat and uncertainty often induces high levels of trauma and stress in civilian populations. The sustained, long-term nature of the threats facing individual Israeli and Palestinian citizens exacerbates this high level of stress and trauma caused by exposure to conflict-related events. Terrorism in particular can be extremely stressful for civilian populations, causing lasting psychological trauma due to its purposefully random nature, striking at places with heavy civilian traffic such as buses, restaurants, and nightclubs. This type of political violence led to the deaths of about 1000 Jews and Arabs from September 2000 until 2006, as well as thousands of casualties—physically and mentally, mostly as a result of suicide bombings from the Al Aqsa intifada (Israel Ministry of Foreign Affairs, 2007). Likewise, the Palestinian population is consistently exposed to violent, war-related events that deeply affect civilian populations. For example, in Operation Cast Lead alone—a 3-week armed conflict that took place in the Gaza Strip during the winter of 2008–2009, at least 1259 Palestinians were killed and over 4000 wounded (*CBS News*, 2009). According to the Israeli human rights organization B'Tselem, 773 of the Palestinians killed did not take part in the hostilities, including 320 minors and 109 women over the age of 18.[4]

The psychological impact of exposure to conflict events in Israel and in the Palestinian Territories is clear. In a large survey study (Chipman, Palmieri, Canetti, Johnson, & Hobfoll, 2011), almost a third of the sample reported some form of impairment caused by post-traumatic stress, and a fifth of these respondents met the full criteria for diagnosis with post-traumatic stress disorder (PTSD). A second study (Canetti et al., 2010), discovered that the prevalence of PTSD and depression for Palestinians in the West Bank, Gaza, and East Jerusalem was extremely high. The daily violent reality of the Israeli-Palestinian conflict clearly takes its toll.

This psychological distress can play a critical role in determining how individuals perceive potential threats and, in turn, impacts their political decisions—namely, their support for compromise versus militancy or out-group tolerance versus exclusion, which may have important consequences on peacemaking and reconciliation processes. In this chapter, we examine the linkages between the psychological consequences of exposure to political violence, threat perceptions, feeling of fear, and political attitudes as outcomes, in the context of protracted conflicts. As this chapter will demonstrate, the psychological distress associated with this prolonged

---

2. *BBC News*. (May 2008). Facts and figures: Israel at 60. Retrieved from http://news.bbc.co.uk/2/hi/middle_East/7375994.stm

3. B'Tselem. (January 2011). Attacks on Israeli civilians by Palestinians. Retrieved from http://www.btselem.org/israelI_civilians/qassam_missiles#data

4. http://www.btselem.org/press_releases/20090909

exposure to violence can have a major impact on political behavior, fueling and prolonging the destructive cycle of violence between the two sides.

Analyzing this process of how exposure to terrorism and war can affect political behavior, along with resilience versus vulnerability following this exposure, is critical to our understanding of human behavior in conflict zones. This chapter applies in-depth theoretically driven rigorous-empirical research methods based on representative samples of terror-exposed populations in Israel and also in Northern Ireland, developing a stress-based model of political action that may provide answers to these pressing issues. The results of these studies provide clear implications for Israeli and Palestinian citizens and other citizens in various countries around the globe living under situations of conflict and violence.

Toward a Psychological Distress-Based Model of Political Extremism

The aim of this chapter is to propose a new stress-based theory on the psychopolitical consequences of terrorism based on evidence derived from a decade of large-scale studies of the psychopolitical responses of Israelis and Palestinians to terrorism, war, and the threat of future conflict. This theory could be applied not only to the consequences of terrorism but also to the consequences of other types of massive political violence. So far, political models of conflict resolution, ethnic conflicts, and other forms of political violence have mainly emphasized the *individual level* of terrorism exposure. This model, however, follows the psychological tradition and allows for a more refined understanding of intergroup conflict by exploring support for the denial of social and political rights for minority group members within society as a whole, as well as attitudes toward reconciliation and willingness to compromise for peace within and between societies affected by terrorism. The model therefore provides a multidimensional mechanism for explaining the exposure–political behavior linkage. Our studies show that psychological distress and perceived threat are key to understanding whether exposure to conflict will lead to greater support for violence or increased willingness to compromise for peace.

Exposure to Terrorism and Psychological Distress

In societies in conflict, citizens are often exposed to daily acts of violence, bloodshed, and terror. This prolonged exposure to violence has important implications on citizens' psychological distress, physiological health, threat perceptions, emotional orientation, and, importantly, their political beliefs and actions. Although exposure to terrorism might be direct (e.g., injury or death of oneself or a close person) or indirect (injury of an acquaintance, or consumption of media reporting on terrorism attacks) (Hobfoll et al., 2008), either way it has been found to be an important predictor of stress and, in turn, lead to concrete political outcomes

(Hobfoll, Canetti-Nisim, & Johnson, 2006). The widespread stress caused by terrorism is most likely due to the concept of terrorism itself. Terrorism, as a form of psychological warfare, is specifically designed to elicit maximum psychological distress amongst civilian populations by creating the impression that any citizen is vulnerable to physical harm; thus, even those who are not directly exposed to a terrorist attack can experience extreme psychological distress. Consequently, personal exposure may include actual physical proximity to a terror incident (Besser, Neria, & Haynes, 2009), emotional proximity (Huddy et al., 2002), or both (Galea et al., 2002; Lerner, Gonzalez, Small, & Fischhoff, 2003). As a result, two major immediate consequences emerge, psychological distress and increased perceptions of threat, which both have an important impact on political behavior.

A potentially traumatic event is generally defined as a threatening or harmful event that elicits fear, helplessness, horror, or distress. Psychological distress in this context is typified by PTSD, one of the most prominent expressions of psychological distress following severe attacks. And, in fact, PTSD is a common psychological reaction to exposure to terrorism (Bleich, Gelkopf, & Solomon, 2003; Galea et al., 2002; Miguel-Tobal et al., 2006; Rubin et al., 2007; Schuster et al., 2001; Shalev & Freedman, 2005; Silver et al., 2002). Symptoms of PTSD include reexperiencing of the traumatic event (e.g., intrusive memories and nightmares), active avoidance of reminders of the trauma, and hyperarousal (e.g., anger, sleep disturbance) (American Psychiatric Association). Studies of the psychological implications of terrorist attacks in the United States (Galea et al., 2002; Schuster et al., 2001; Silver et al, 2002), Spain (Miguel-Tobal et al., 2006), and Israel (Bleich et al., 2003; Canetti-Nisim et al., 2009; Shalev & Freedman, 2005) have pointed to PTSD as one of the most prominent and prevalent expressions of psychological reactions following exposure to terrorism (Canetti-Nisim et al., 2009; Canetti et al., 2010; Hobfoll et al., 2006, 2011).

This stress response is characterized by both emotional and physical manifestations, often leading to activation of various physiological systems (Lewitus, Cohen, & Schwartz, 2008). Canetti, Russ, Luborsky, and Hobfoll (2012) took a biopolitics approach and found that Israelis who suffered high levels of exposure to rocket and terrorist attacks possessed greater levels of C-reactive protein and anti-cytomegalovirus—chemicals associated with increased inflammation and immune system compromise, demonstrating the physiological impact of stress and fear of terrorism. This linkage among stress, immune system compromise, and inflammation is not new (Segerstrom & Miller, 2004); yet the exploration of this relationship in the context of war and terror is completely novel. By conducting rigorous empirical field research in a real conflict zone, this research for the first time provides definitive support for the hypothesis that there is an effect of cumulative stress and trauma on inflammation among citizens exposed to chronic stress due to the long-term threat of attack and the frequent actual attacks prevalent in conflict zones.

Clearly, long-term exposure to war and terrorism can have an important impact on psychological and physical well-being and their subsequent political attitudes toward the conflict (Laor et al., 2010; Bonanno & Jost, 2006). It is therefore critical that more research be done in conflict zones to examine the impact of this type of chronic exposure to conflict, which differs considerably in its effects from singular conflict events. For example, studies on the aftermath of 9/11 suggest marked impact at the time of the attack for those nearby (Galea et al., 2002; Schlenger et al., 2002) but found that initial severe symptoms in response to the 9/11 attacks subsided within several months (Galea et al., 2003). In contrast, in a study conducted in Israel that examined responses to ongoing terrorism in a national sample, marked effects on depression and moderate effects of PTSD were noted, demonstrating the difference between acute and chronic exposure to violence (Bleich et al., 2003). Thus, chronic exposure to war and terrorism clearly has important long-lasting effects on civilians in conflict zones, not only damaging their own well-being but also potentially contributing to an ongoing cycle of violence as affected citizens harden their political viewpoints in an attempt to cope with stress and reduce the threat of additional resource loss. Therefore, untangling the psychopolitical, biopolitical, and neuropolitical mechanisms expressed among those exposed to ongoing violence by means of empirical and systematic research is invaluable for studies on the consequences of terrorism and conflict resolution research, with applications for practitioners and policymakers alike.

Buffers and Resilience to Psychological Distress

Psychological and emotional distress is a common outcome of exposure to terrorism (Bleich et al., 2003). However, despite the saliency of PTSD symptoms, there are still individuals who demonstrate resiliency and succeed in returning to their normal routines after exposure to a traumatic event (Hobfoll et al., 2009). Such resiliency can be explained by Conservation of Resources (COR) theory (Hobfoll, 1989), which stipulates that higher levels of stress are the result of a threat and fear of the loss of valuable resources, such as relationships, standard of living, objects and physical assets, or personal characteristics. During and after exposure to a traumatic event, those who hold fewer resources, or are less capable of conserving or gaining new resources, suffer more stress. COR theory thus emphasizes resources as the single unit necessary for understanding stress.

For example, with regard to the political behavior of citizens in conflict zones, several elements have already been found to have a significant effect on the psychological and political outcomes of exposure to terrorism. Such elements include the loss of economic resources (Hobfoll et al., 2006), locus of control (Hallis & Slone, 1999), religion (Solomon & Berger, 2005), and commitment to ideology (Bonanno & Jost, 2006; Kaplan et al., 2005; Punamaki, 1996; Shechner, Slone, & Bialik, 2007). Our argument is that the subjective experience of psychological distress caused by protracted exposure to terrorism can be a major mediating factor in determining both citizens' perception of threat and their subsequent political attitudes toward peace and conflict. Specifically, we suggest two key political-psychological mechanisms, political efficacy and ethos of the conflict, which may limit the effect of exposure to terrorism on psychological distress among citizens in conflict zones

Political Efficacy

Political efficacy is a "feeling that individual political action does have, or can have, an impact upon the political process, i.e., that it is worthwhile to perform one's civic duties" (Campbell, Gurin, & Miller, 1954, p. 187). Canetti et al. (2011) suggest that political efficacy can serve as a resource for citizens in coping with exposure to terrorism. They used two dimensions of political efficacy: a *subjective* dimension that refers to perceived attentiveness of the central government to the needs of communities amid war and terrorism and an *objective* dimension referring to the development of collective political efficacy as a function of spatial-political relations (Gidengil, 1990; Gottmann, 1980; Sampson, Morenoff, & Earls, 1999; Wolin, 2004); hence, one representation of objective efficacy is the type of locality and is related to geography (Campbell et al., 1954; Lane, 1959). Dekel and Nuttman-Schwartz (2009) have shown that those residing in different locality types (as an expression of political efficacy) exhibit different levels of emotional well-being.

Canetti et al. (2011) found that above and beyond other factors, there is a moderating effect of political efficacy on the degree to which psychological well-being will be guided by levels of exposure to war and terrorism. Those residing in peripheral towns suffered the most from higher levels of distress following exposure to terrorism. Furthermore, subjective political efficacy (as a perception of government care) was found to moderate the relationship between exposure and well-being. Those who indicated the government did not care at all about their town exhibited a stronger relationship between exposure and distress (less well-being), particularly those residing in conflict areas near the Gaza Strip border (a socioeconomically challenged, periphery area subject to intense rounds of rocket fire from the Palestinian militant group Hamas). These findings suggest that political efficacy can serve as a protective resource for resilience and better coping with exposure to terrorism, as it buffers the psychological distress of citizens.

Ethos of Conflict

Ethos of conflict is an ideology that is defined as "a configuration of central shared societal beliefs that provide a particular dominant orientation to a society and give meaning to societal life under conditions of intractable conflict" (Bar-Tal, 2000, p. 139). According to Bar-Tal (2007, 2009b), ethos of the conflict serves as a mechanism for individuals living under concrete and continuous threat, which allows construing new experiences and information and provides meaning and sense to the interpretation of the situation. In the Israeli-Palestinian case, basic ethos components include societal beliefs regarding the justness of the conflict's goals, beliefs regarding victimization, and beliefs that refer to security and ways to achieve it (Bar-Tal et al., 2009a). Ethos of conflict is yet another factor that can buffer the link between exposure to terrorism and physical expressions of PTSD. Lavi et al. (2012) examined the role played by ethos of the conflict, as an ideological belief system, in buffering the relationship between exposure to terrorism and exhibition of distress symptoms. Ideology is strongly rooted in one's culture and frames and gives meaning to political events, particularly when facing a threat, be it a threat to the nation or to an individual. Unlike political efficacy, the ethos of conflict has no direct bolstering role between exposure to terrorism and psychological distress; however, it has a dual function in mediating this link. Israelis and Palestinians who indicated low levels of adherence to the ethos of conflict reported higher levels of depression and psychological distress following exposure to terrorism. This was not the case for those with higher levels of ethos, most of whom indicated much lower levels of psychological distress following exposure to terrorist attacks. These results indicate that ethos of conflict is a double-edged sword, which both protects from and protracts the conflict. Stated differently, although the ethos serves as an engine in fueling the conflict by arousing and nurturing negative emotions in the direction of the opponent, it also plays a meaningful role as an empowering force for those suffering the psychological burden of an ongoing conflict. In fact, due to its protective properties in the face of conflict exposure, the ethos might actually gain more extreme expressions amid war and terrorism, broadly increasing support for militant actions toward the adversary.

Terrorism Fears and Political Outcomes

Emotional distress both causes and is caused by perceived threat and fear, thereby serving as a key explanatory mechanism for the variation in levels of fear, threat, and anxiety among individuals in conflict zones. Perceived threat can be generally described as an individual's *cognitive evaluation* regarding the manner in which outgroup members interfere or threaten with the achievement of individual or group goals. Perceived threat in turn influences and is influenced by experiences of psychological distress. For example, although actual exposure to terrorism will, of course, worsen the psychological and political effects of an attack (Huddy & Feldman, 2011, p. 461), the *threat* of imminent terrorism can also be extremely detrimental to citizens' psychological well-being. It is important to note here that perception is critical to evaluations of threat; thus, it is not the objective risk of attack of threat that matters as much as the subjective interpretation of vulnerability to threat and attack that is critical to triggering experiences of fear and psychological distress and informing citizens' political behavior.

But what specifically causes groups and individuals to feel threatened? Integrated threat theory (Stephan & Stephan, 2000) breaks down this general conception of perceived threat into two main types of threat: (1) intergroup anxiety and negative stereotypes as an expression of threat on the *individual* level and (2) realistic and symbolic threats, which reflect threats stemming from the *collective/group* level. Within this second group, the distinction between realistic versus symbolic threat is important (Legge, 1996; Berinsky, Crenshaw, & Mendelberg 2004). While realistic threat refers mainly to a potential harm to tangible or concrete objects (e.g., money, land, human life) and has a basis in realistic group conflict theory (LeVine & Campbell, 1972; Sherif, 1966), symbolic threat (which has a basis instead in social identity theory, e.g., Tajfel & Turner, 1979) contains various potential threats to relatively abstract aspects of the state, such as threats to the in-group's identity, value system, belief system, or worldview (e.g., language, religion, morality) (Duckitt, 2003).

Several studies have demonstrated the link between both symbolic threat and realistic economic threat on exclusionary political attitudes (Espenshade & Hampstead, 1996; Esses, Dovidio, Jackson, & Armstrong, 2001; Halperin, Pedahzur, & Canetti-Nisim, 2007; Stephan et al., 1998; Stephan & Stephan, 2000). Following 9/11, however, there was a renewed interest in the impact of realistic *security* threat on political attitudes (e.g., Huddy et al., 2002; Sniderman, Hagendoorn, & Prior, 2004). The September 11 attacks increased public support for conservative views compared with shortly before. Among survivors, three times as many become more conservative compared with becoming more liberal during the 18 months after the attacks (Jost & Amodio, 2012). Canetti, Ariely, and Halperin (2008), examined the impact of security threat on exclusionist political attitudes to minority out-group society members in the Israeli context, finding that perceived security threat was indeed a significant predictor of exclusionist political attitudes toward minority out-group members. In another study analyzing the relationship between exposure and negative out-group attitudes, Hall and colleagues (Hall, Hobfoll, Canetti, Johnson, & Galea, 2009) found that reports of psychological growth are a potential mediating pathway. When Israeli Jews reported greater growth following terror exposure (e.g., feeling closer with in-group members), they also evidenced greater ethnic exclusion and threat perception of Palestinians. This provided evidence that, following terrorism, people may report feeling greater connection to others in their in-group and personal strength, but at the price of exclusionary attitudes toward the out-group that undermine peace.

Other distinctions between types of threat perception are also important, for example, the impact of personal versus collective threat on political attitudes. Studies have found that *personal* threat is a much more powerful predictor of exclusionist attitudes than collective threat, thereby reaffirming the importance of *personal* exposure to conflict events in forming subsequent political attitudes toward the conflict and conflict out-group. For instance, Huddy, et al., (2002) conducted a study that explored the degree to which personal and national threat perceptions of terrorism risk affected political attitudes. They found that "individuals who felt personally threatened by terrorism were expected to take or support actions that decreased their exposure to terrorism ... such actions are motivated by a desire to reduce the negative emotions, such as fear, associated with threat" (Huddy et al., 2002, p. 506). Though not explicitly tested in this particular study, the authors postulate that these results may indicate that personal threat of terrorism may motivate "support for national policies designed to minimize the risk of terrorism, such as tightened homeland security policies and the curtailment of civil liberties" (Huddy et al., 2002, p. 506).

THREAT PERCEPTION AND FEAR

Fear and threat are closely related, and fear is often claimed to be an integral aspect of threat perceptions. Fear can be categorized as a discrete subjective aversive emotion that arises in situations of perceived threat or danger to a person or his or her society that enables the person to respond adaptively (Gray, 1987; Ohman, 1993). It is often accompanied by both the perception of relative weakness and low coping potential with the threatening event (Roseman, 1984). In the context of terrorism and war, as the parties perceive each other to be a threat, both experience high levels of fear. In other words, fear is an emotional response that typically follows the subjective appraisal of threat. This relationship between fear and threat is particularly problematic in situations of conflict, as fear leads to risk-aversion, a refusal to interact with the threatening object and, in extreme cases, reflexive violent reactions designed to reduce the perceived threat posed by the opposing side. Fear stemming from threat has been found to reduce Israelis' willingness to compromise for peace with the Palestinians and end the long-lasting conflict (Bar-Tal, 2001; Gordon & Arian, 2001; Maoz & McCauley, 2005).

Intergroup threat occurs when "one group's actions, beliefs, or characteristics challenge the goal attainment or well being of another group" (Riek, Mania, & Gaertner, 2006). These threats can be both realistic, a threat to tangible resources and physical well-being, and symbolic, a threat to a group's values and norms. In the case of terrorism, a violent strategy specifically designed to invoke both types of threat, exposed individuals will feel intense threat and fear and, in turn, adopt more conservative stances and be less supportive of conciliatory policies. People judged by both themselves and others as being more fearful, are more likely to possess more conservative political views. Research has found that political orientation is influenced by short-term events related to fear. Reminding people of the existence of threats such as terrorism caused political views to become more conservative (Jost & Amodio, 2012).

Stress-Based Model of Political Consequences of Exposure

Thus far we have discussed two main consequences following personal exposure to terror: post-traumatic stress symptoms and increased levels of perception of threat.

We argue, however, that these two psychological responses to exposure also lead to important *political* outcomes. In 2009, Canetti, Halperin, Sharvit, and Hobfoll analyzed this hypothesis—whether personal exposure to terrorism, and the resulting psychological distress, would substantially impact political attitudes. Personal exposure in this context includes both direct losses and indirect experiences of exposure through loved ones and acquaintances. The concept of personal exposure does, however, preclude exposure to "mere knowledge" of terrorism, as in media coverage, which constitutes an important source of indirect exposure to terrorism. Through this study, the authors outlined a new *Stress-Based Model of Political Extremism* in which psychological distress—which had until then largely been overlooked in political scholarship—and threat perceptions mediate the relationship between exposure to terrorism and attitudes toward minorities (Canetti, Halperin, Sharvit, & Hobfoll, 2009). In this study, conducted in the Jewish-Israeli context, the authors found that personal exposure to terrorism predicted psychological distress, which predicted perceived threat from Palestinian citizens of Israel, which, in turn, predicted exclusionist attitudes toward Palestinian citizens of Israel. These findings provide solid evidence and a mechanism for the hypothesis that personal exposure to terrorism introduces nondemocratic attitudes threatening minority rights, presumably to reduce the psychological distress and fear caused by the enhanced threat perceptions that exposed individuals feel.

Canetti et al. (2012) then tested this conclusion at the inter-state level (rather than the in-group/out-group level). Specifically, the main question was, does exposure to terrorism and political violence lead to an increased willingness to compromise for peace? The authors hypothesized that threat perceptions in the face of long-lasting conflict would undercut support for willingness to make compromises for peace or reconcile differences. In turn, exposure to terror and political violence would induce elevated threat perceptions, which would buffer or reduce support for reconciliation policies and promote animosity toward a threatening enemy. Findings from nationally representative two-wave samples of Israeli Jews, West Bank and Gaza Palestinians, Northern Irish Catholics, and Irish Protestants confirm the political effects of threat. Citizens in all four areas demonstrated similar response patterns in the face of exposure to conflict events, whereby this exposure triggered psychological distress and enhanced levels of threat perception that in turn led to important changes in political attitudes and behavior. However, in the Israeli and Palestinian groups, psychological distress played an important role as a mediator between exposure and threat perception, while it did not for the Northern Irish groups (perhaps due to the distance of the psychological distress in the Northern Irish case since the violence of the conflict has long since subsided). These results indicate a cross-border process of political responses to politicized violence, with distinct psychological effects among those exposed to political violence amid enduring conflicts.

These findings therefore suggest that psychological distress plays an important role in political decision making and should be incorporated into models drawing upon political psychology. Exposure to terrorism, by definition, causes fear, disrupts life routine and leads to subjective experience of "psychological insecurity." Such perception of insecurity, or threat, was found to induce intolerance and exclusionist attitudes (Hobfoll, Canetti, & Johnson, 2006). At the international level, threat derives from an outside group, which will lead to citizens' being less willing to compromise for peace (Canetti et al., 2012).

The complementary theory of COR (Hobfoll, 1988) suggests that stress experiences are a function of resource loss and gain resulting from a given event. Accordingly, the level of stress experienced in response to an event may vary depending on the reserves of sustainable resources that are available to different individuals (Hobfoll, 2001). Further, in their Appraisal Theory of Stress, Lazarus & Folkman, (1984) suggest that different individuals may experience different levels of stress in response to similar events due to individual differences in their cognitive appraisals of the situation. These theories are consistent with the proposition that mere exposure is insufficient to explain the political implications of terrorism, and subjective psychological experiences must be taken into account as well. This idea concurs with the generally accepted approach in social psychology, according to which behaviors are a function of both situational and individual dispositional factors (Ross & Nisbett, 1991). Emotions are essentially a response to an individual's subjective interpretation of an event. Thus, feelings of fear and threat perception (and their resulting political consequences) depend in large part on the individual's appraisal of the conflict-related event.

These myriad studies have all demonstrated the clear link between personal exposure, stress, psychological buffers, threat perception, and political responses (Figure 11.1). But what explanations are there for explaining this strong connection? One potential explanation in addition to COR theory is the Shattered Assumptions Approach (Janoff-Bulman, 1992) which explains that, following traumatic events, people often face major challenges to their basic assumptions about the world/themselves. This can trigger enhanced perceptions of "the world as threatening" and a correspondingly strong desire to reduce this threat (and the fear it induces) through increased militancy toward the perceived source of threat—the conflict out-group. In fact, today perceived threat, fear, and anxiety are considered to be

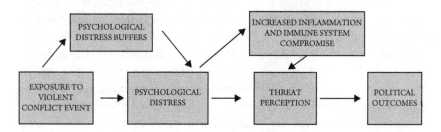

Figure 11.1:
A chain model of exposure to terrorism and its political outcomes.

the single best group-level predictors of exclusionism (Canetti-Nisim, Ariely, & Halperin, 2008; Canetti-Nisim et al., 2009), intolerance (Quillian 1995), and militarism (Bonanno & Jost, 2006). These attitudes are particularly prevalent immediately after the occurrence of major terror attacks (Huddy et al., 2002, 2005).

As shown in Figure 11.1, psychological distress plays an important role in political decision making and should be incorporated in models drawing upon political psychology. In this vein, this *Stress-Based Model of Political Extremism* goes a long way toward explaining the violent nonconciliatory policies often supported by populations suffering under the fear and threat of violence and conflict. Unfortunately, this model leads us to postulate that ongoing violence engenders more violence—by increasing the psychological distress of civilian populations, threat perceptions are (often disproportionately) magnified, leading to increased support for hostile action designed to marginalize or eliminate the perceived threat presented by the out-group. Psychological distress, resulting from exposure to terrorism, exacerbates threat perceptions, which in turn invoke political outcomes such as political exclusionism or support for militarism.

In fact, studies show a high positive correlation between fear and delegitimization of the other—an extremely negative social categorization of a group (or groups) to the effect of excluding it from humanity as such, and from the limits of acceptable norms and/or values (Bar-Tal, 1990; Halperin, et al., 2007). This correlation demonstrates the potentially destructive effects of spiraling levels of intergroup fear, mistrust, and threat to conflict situations. Stress buffers have a potentially important role to play in exacerbating or mitigating political extremism in this context. Overcoming this cycle of threat and violence also requires the rebuilding of trust between societies in conflict. This long process must include the acknowledgment of losses of those affected by conflict-related events on both sides, a rethinking of the collective conflict memory of both societies, and a restoration of hope for a nonviolent future between the parties.

THE NEED FOR RIGOROUS RESEARCH IN CONFLICT ZONES

Today, citizens in countries around the world live in conflict zones, experiencing near constant threat and exposure to violent conflict events—in Israel, the Palestinian Authority, Ireland, Sudan, Eritrea, Chechnya, Afghanistan, Iraq, to name only a few (Uppsala Conflict Data Program, 2012). Resolving enduring conflicts is therefore a first-order global challenge. As many of these countries possess democratic governments, who are inevitably swayed by the political beliefs and actions of the masses, this widespread, problematic phenomenon necessitates a comprehensive theoretical analysis of its ramifications on the political behavior of civilian populations.

In this chapter we use the Israeli-Palestinian conflict as a natural laboratory for the examination of psychological-political reactions to living in a violent and blooded war zone. We suggest a general stress-based model that represents a psychological-political process that might explain the terror-exposed population's political reactions toward reconciliation. However, in order to apply the model suggested in this chapter, rigorous empirical research on and in conflict zones is critical, and inevitable, for the deeper understanding of the conditions under which civilian conflict-affected populations live and how these conditions affect their psychological and physical well-being (Canetti et al., 2012; Haer & Becher, 2012). These investigations are needed to evaluate the mechanisms underlying processes of both militarism and attempts at conflict resolution. Furthermore, such examination can serve as a basis for therapy and intervention programs for citizens in conflict zones and enhancing individual and communal resilience under situations of conflict. However, given the complicated nature of conflict zones, it is clear that research in these regions poses a great challenge, almost as much as the global challenge of ending long-lasting conflicts.

In addition to the inherent problem of researchers placing themselves at extreme risk by operating in dangerous places, where violence is not necessarily limited to soldiers on a battlefield, during periods of active conflict, several ethical issues and methodological concerns arise when designing a study in conflict zones. First, ethical concerns center on the necessity that researchers do not create any additional harm to those living in conflict. For example, awareness of potential drawbacks from participatory methods, often requiring the gathering of large groups of people is very important (Goodhand, 2000). In certain environments, large gatherings may be the target of combatant attacks and/or propaganda efforts by militants. In addition, conducting research while ignoring the needs of the local community may be opportunistic, and ancillary care measures should be considered when appropriate. When engaging in studies of sensitive issues including mental health and personal attitudes, and when working with protected populations such as children and those displaced by conflict, researchers should protect the confidentiality of their participants and be especially mindful of issues involving coercion.

Methodological concerns may also follow from the functional limitations of many conflict settings. Finding adequate local research staff and people with appropriate research skills may be difficult. Another potential problem for researchers in conflict zones is obtaining sufficient samples. Large-scale representative samples often rely on sampling frames from a local census, population register, or area maps; however, these sources should be used with caution as they each have limitations. Another concern is the sampling method. When there is a lack of appropriate data, for example, the data are not available or up-to-date, a nonproportional sampling procedure, such as the "snow-ball" method, becomes favorable (Haer & Becher, 2012; Ramano, 2006), leading to problems with the generalization of the results to the entire population. Too often, researchers rely on comfortable sampling methods such as the snowball sample and student samples that lack identification rigidity. These methods lead to major generalization issues and can make misleading conclusions and call into question the plausibility of collecting unbiased, representative data in conflict zones.

However, notwithstanding key challenges for researchers working in conflict zones, and counter to claims in the peace and conflict scholarship (e.g., Cohen & Arieli, 2011; Romano, 2006; Tessler & Jamal, 2006), we argue that systematic rigorous empirical research in conflict zones is not only feasible but also of the utmost importance to deepening our understanding of human behavior under conditions of continuous existential threat and uncertainty. For example, two recent studies (Canetti et al., forthcoming) conducted were methodologically designed to allow for power analysis by combining two separate studies designed to analyze the political-psychological responses to conflict-related violence. Specifically, these two studies were designed to evaluate the impact of political efficacy and threat perception on psychological distress. The first study used 15 large representative samples collected during the years of the Al-Aqsa Intifada and since in Israel and the Palestinian Territories, generating a series of systematic quantitative data. The second study was a panel study that used the rigorous design of a natural experiment, allowing for cautious interpretations of causality. The construction of the two studies represents a meticulous implementation of rigorous research criteria, with high internal and external validity, despite the inherent difficulties in conducting studies in conflict-prone areas during conflict. Additionally, the longitudinal long-term design implemented in this study increases its contribution to the literature. Indeed, scholars of conflicts tend to study conflict at one particular time point; yet, due to the rapidly changing nature of conflicts, studies conducted during a single point in time naturally have limitations in terms of their long-term external validity. The unique research design presented here bridges these divides, contributing to important theoretic debates in the study of conflict, such as the importance of psychological distress buffers to citizens in conflict or the impact of psychological distress on threat perceptions, and providing the most complete and compelling study of psychological consequences of exposure to political violence to date.

In a second study (Canetti, Longo, & Hite, 2011), the authors used a quasi experimental design with real world events that serve as manipulation, to study the question of whether violence leads to obedience or rebellion. Particularly, the authors examined whether checkpoints make Palestinians more likely to support peace and reconciliation, or violence against Israel. To answer this question, the authors exploited a natural experiment based on a policy intervention prompted by the "Jenin First Initiative" in May–June 2009 to introduce easements in several checkpoints in the West Bank. This project was experimental in that the authors sampled similar villages, some beside a checkpoint slated for easement (treatment), and others beside a checkpoint that remain (control), before and after the intervention. As this easement was orthogonal to Palestinian attitudes, the authors pursued a difference-in-difference design to ascertain the effect of the policy. As a robustness check, the authors tested these findings against an independent panel study conducted between 2007 and 2009. The easement of the checkpoint made people less likely to support violence against Israel or the militant Islamist group, Hamas.

Thus, while the difficulty and complexity surrounding systematic research efforts in conflict zones, specifically survey research, is well documented (Romano, 2006), we argue (as do other researchers such as Haer & Becher, 2012) that solid quantitative research during periods of conflict is nevertheless possible. Recent field studies (Canetti et al., 2009, 2010, 2011, 2012), funded by the National Institutes of Health, supported a large-scale effort that used telephone survey methods and in-person interviews to obtain a representative sample that contributed to high external validity of this quantitative study. Qualitative methods, though not without their limits, can also be important to providing an in-depth view of the local community and its reactions to conflict events. Without such research, our understanding of conflict zones will be neglecting an important component—the time period of actual conflict. Research focusing solely on preconflict and postconflict studies or on nonsystematic materials cannot adequately explain central psychopolitical mechanisms, such as the linkages between psychological distress, threat perceptions, and political actions as discussed in this chapter, and it is thus critically important that field researchers continue to strive for rigorous quantitative methodological standards in research in active conflict zones.

CONCLUSION

It is clear that prolonged exposure to conflict causes chronic stress in civilian populations that in turn triggers skewed threat perceptions that affect political attitudes. In this chapter we have set out the basic infrastructure for understanding the effects of threat perceptions on political outcomes, such as extremism, exclusionism, and willingness to compromise for peace, in the face of ongoing conflict, and the continuous sense of existential insecurity and psychological distress it causes. We proposed a theory that allows for an analysis of the psychological origins of the desire to limit people's rights and liberties and engage in militant action against a conflict enemy. We therefore argue that personal exposure to political violence that results in psychological distress can affect political worldviews by increasing subjective threat perceptions, and fear within civilian populations.

Rigorously exploring such political outcomes as a result of a stress-based model is critical in the setting of protracted conflict. By understanding the political consequences of exposure to terrorism through psychopolitical mechanisms, we can shed light on the psychological barriers that too often stymie peacemaking efforts and contribute to the deterioration of intractable conflicts around the globe. For example, reducing stress symptoms following exposure to terrorism can be aided by proper treatment, political messaging, and public mental health interventions (Hobfoll et al., 2007), which may in turn help reduce the negative effects of exposure to terrorism on support for political exclusionism. More sinisterly, these findings also suggest that political leaders may use fear messaging for political ends (Landau et al., 2004). What's more, as new forms of terrorism such as cyber-terrorism become ever more present in conflicts, it is important to continue to explore the unique effects of these new forms of intergroup violence on the distress, threat and political attitudes of civilian populations (Canetti et al., forthcoming). These ramifications further highlight the importance of conducting rigorous quantitative and qualitative research in active conflict zones and of considering psychological processes when attempting to understand and address the challenges that terrorism poses to the maintenance of democracy.

AUTHOR'S NOTE

The authors would like to acknowledge the invaluable assistance garnered throughout the drafting of this article. This line of research was made possible by grants from NIMH (R01MH073687), the Ohio Board of Regents to Stevan E. Hobfoll and to Daphna Canetti, the Institute for Social and Policy Studies and the Macmillan Center at Yale University. Brian Hall's contribution to this chapter was supported by NIMH Psychiatric Epidemiology training grant T32MH014592–35 (PI: Zandi). Correspondence concerning this article should be addressed to Daphna Canetti at dcanetti@poli.haifa.ac.il

REFERENCES

American Psychiatric Association. *Diagnostic and statistical manual of mental disorders (DSM).* Retrieved from http://web.archive.org/web/20070630225823/http://dsmivtr.org/index.cfm

Bar-Tal, D. (1990). Causes and consequences of delegitimization: Models of conflict and ethnocentrism. *Journal of Social Issues, 46,* 65–81.

Bar-Tal, D. (2000). From intractable conflict through conflict resolution to reconciliation: Psychological analysis. *Political Psychology, 21,* 351–365.

Bar-Tal, D. (2001). Why does fear override hope in societies engulfed by intractable conflict, as it does in the Israeli society? *Political Psychology, 22,* 601–627.

Bar-Tal, D., Raviv, A., Raviv, A., & Dgani-Hirsh, A. (2009a). The influence of the ethos of conflict on Israeli Jews interpretation of Jewish–Palestinian encounters. *Journal of Conflict Resolution, 53*(2), 94–118.

Bar-Tal, D., Chernyak-Hai, L., Schori, N., & Gundar, A. (2009b). A sense of self-perceived collective victimhood in intractable conflicts. *International Red Cross Review, 91,* 229–277.

Berinsky, A., Crenshaw, M., & Mendelberg, T. (2004). Review of David O. Sears, Leonie Huddy, and Robert Jervis, eds. Oxford handbook of political psychology. *Political Psychology, 25*(6), 969–983.

Besser, A., Neria, Y., & Haynes, M. (2009). Adult attachment, perceived stress, and PTSD among civilians continuously exposed to terrorism in southern Israel. *Personality and Individual Differences, 47,* 851–857.

Bleich, A., Gelkopf, M., & Solomon, Z. (2003). Exposure to terrorism, stress-related mental health symptoms, and coping behaviors among a nationally representative sample in Israel. *Journal of the American Medical Association, 290,* 612–620.

Bonanno, G. A., & Jost. J. T. (2006). Conservative shift among high-exposure survivors of the September 11th terrorist attacks. *Basic and Applied Social Psychology, 28*(4), 311–323.

Campbell, A., Gurin, G., & Miller, W. E. (1954). *The voter decides.* Evanston, IL: Row Peterson.

Canetti, D., Galea, S., Hall, J. B., Robert J. J., Palmieri, A. P., & Hobfoll, E. S. (2010). Exposure to prolonged socio-political conflict and the risk of PTSD and depression among Palestinians. *Psychiatry—Interpersonal and Biological Processes, 73*(3), 219–232.

Canetti, D., Longo, M., & Hite, N. (2011, July 9). A checkpoint effect? Evidence from a natural experiment on travel restrictions in the West Bank. Paper presented at the annual meeting of the ISPP 34th Annual Scientific Meeting, Bilgi University, Istanbul, Turkey.

Canetti, D., Muldoon, O., Rapoport, C., Hirsch-Hoefler, S., Hobfoll, S., Johnson, R. J., & Lowe, R. (2012, July). An exposure effect? Evidence from studies on violence, troubles, and terrorism in the Middle East and Northern Ireland. Paper presented at the 35th Annual Meeting of ISPP 2012, Chicago, IL.

Canetti, D., Navot, D., Vashdi, D., Lavi, I., Hobfoll, E. S., & Longo, M. (2011, July 9). Can political efficacy protect citizens' psychological well-being in situations of political violence? Evidence from a natural experiment on war and terrorism. Paper presented at the ISPP 34th Annual Scientific Meeting, Bilgi University, Istanbul, Turkey.

Canetti, D., Russ, E., Luborsky, J., & Hobfoll, S. (2012). The influence of chronic terrorism and war-related threat on immune disregulation and inflammation. Paper presented at the 35th Annual Meeting of ISPP 2012, Chicago, IL.

Canetti-Nisim, D., Ariely, G., & Halperin. E. (2008). Life, Pocketbook, or Culture: The role of perceived security threats in promoting exclusionist political attitudes toward minorities in Israel. *Political Research Quarterly, 61*(1), 90–103.

Canetti-Nisim, D., Halperin, E., Sharvit, K., & Hobfoll, S. E. (2009). A new stress-based model of political extremism: Personal exposure to terrorism, psychological distress, and exclusionist political attitudes. *Journal of Conflict Resolution, 53*(3), 363–389.

CBS NEWS. (2009). In Gaza, Hamas struggles to restore order. Retrieved from http://www.cbsnews.com/stories/2009/01/19/world/main4734072.shtml?source=related_story

Cohen, N., & Arieli, T. (2011). Field research in conflict environments: Methodological challenges and snowball sampling. *Journal of Peace Research, 48*(4), 423–435.

Dekel, R., & Nuttman-Shwartz, O. (2009). Posttraumatic stress and growth: The contribution of cognitive appraisal and sense of belonging to the country. *Health & Social Work, 34*(2), 87–96.

Duckitt, J., & Fisher, K. (2003). The impact of social threat on worldview and ideological attitudes. *Political Psychology, 24,* 199–222.

Espenshade, T. J., & Hampstead. K. (1996). Contemporary American attitudes toward U.S. immigration. *International Migration Review, 30*(2), 535–571.

Esses, V. M., Dovidio, J. F., Jackson, L. M., & Armstrong, T. L. (2001). The immigration dilemma: The role of perceived group competition, ethnic prejudice, and national identity. *Journal of Social Issues, 57*(3), 389–412.

Galea, S. J., Ahern, H., Resnick, D., Kilpatrick, M., Bucuvalas, J. G., & Vlahov, D. (2002). Psychological sequelae of the September 11 terrorist attacks in New York City. *New England Journal of Medicine, 346,* 982–987.

Galea, S., Vlahov, D., Resnick, H., Ahern, J., Susser. E., Gold, J. ... Kilpatrick, D. (2003). Trends of probable post-traumatic stress disorder in New York City after the September 11 terrorist attacks. *American Journal of Epidemiology, 158,* 514–524.

Gidengil, E. (1990). Centres and peripheries: The political culture of dependency. *Canadian Review of Sociology and Anthropology, 27,* 23–48.

Goodhand, J. (2000). Research in conflict zones: Ethics and accountability. *Forced Migration Review, 8*(4), 12–16.

Gordon, C., & Arian, A. (2001). Threat and decision making. *Journal of Conflict Resolution*, 45(2), 197–215.

Gottmann, J. (1980). Spatial partitioning and the politician's wisdom. *International Political Science*, 1(4), 432–455.

Gray, J. A. (1987). *The psychology of fear and stress* (2nd ed.). Cambridge, UK: Cambridge University Press.

Haer, R., & Becher, I. (2012). A methodological note on quantitative field research in conflict zones: Get your hands dirt. *International Journal of Social Research Methodology*, 15(1), 1–13.

Hall, B. J., Hobfoll, S. E., Canetti-Nisim, D., Johnson, R., & Galea, S. (2009). The defensive nature of benefit finding during ongoing terrorism: An examination of a national sample of Israeli Jews. *Journal of Social and Clinical Psychology*, 28, 993–1021.

Hallis, D., & Slone, M. (1999). Coping strategies and locus of control as mediating variables in the relation between exposure to political life events and psychological adjustment in Israeli children. *International Journal of Stress Management*, 6, 105–123.

Halperin, E., Canetti-Nisim, D., & Pedahzur, A. (2007). Threatened by the uncontrollable: Psychological and socio-economic antecedents of social distance towards labor migrants in Israel. *International Journal of Intercultural Relations*, 31, 459–478.

Hobfoll, S. E. (1988). *The ecology of stress*. New York, NY: Hemisphere.

Hobfoll, S. E. (1989). Conservation of resources: A new attempt at conceptualizing stress. *American Psychologist*, 44, 513–524.

Hobfoll, S. E. (2001). The influence of culture, community, and the nested-self in the stress process: Advancing conservation of resources theory. *Applied Psychology: An International Review*, 50, 337–421.

Hobfoll, S. E., Canetti, D., Hall, B. J., Brom, D., Palmieri, P. A., Johnson, R. J., . . . Galea, S. (2011). Are community studies of psychological trauma's impact accurate? A study among Jews and Palestinians. *Psychological Assessment*, 23(3), 599–605.

Hobfoll, S. E., Canetti-Nisim, D., & Johnson, R. J. (2006). Exposure to terrorism, stress-related mental health symptoms, and defensive coping among a nationally representative sample in Israel. *Journal of Consulting and Clinical Psychology*, 74, 207–218.

Hobfoll, S. E., Canetti-Nisim, D., Johnson, R. J., Palmieri, P. A., Varley, J. D., & Galea, S. (2008). The association of exposure, risk, and resiliency factors with PTSD among Jews and Arabs exposed to repeated acts of terrorism in Israel. *Journal of Traumatic Stress*, 21, 9–21.

Hobfoll, S. E., Hall, B. J., Canetti-Nisim, D., Galea, S., Johnson, R. J., & Palmieri, P. (2007). Refining our understanding of traumatic growth in the face of terrorism: Moving from meaning cognitions to doing what is meaningful. *Applied Psychology: An International Journal*, 56, 345–366.

Hobfoll, S. E., Palmieri, P. A., Johnson, R. J., Canetti-Nisim, D., Hall, B. J., & Galea, S. (2009). Trajectories of resilience, resistance and distress during ongoing terrorism: The case of Jews and Arabs in Israel. *Journal of Consulting and Clinical Psychology*, 77, 138–148.

Huddy, L., & Feldman, S. (2011). Americans respond politically to 9/11: Understanding the impact of the terrorist attacks and their aftermath. *American Psychologist*, 66, 455–467.

Huddy, L., Feldman, S., Capelos, T., & Provost, C. (2002). The consequences of terrorism: Disentangling the effects of personal and national threat. *Political Psychology*, 23, 485–509.

Huddy, L., Feldman, S., Taber, C., & Lahav, G. (2005). Threat, anxiety, and support of antiterrorism policies. *American Journal of Political Science*, 49(3), 610–625.

Israeli Ministry of Foreign Affairs (2013). Victims of Palestinian Violence and Terrorism since September 2000. Retrieved on February 17, 2013, from http://www.mfa.gov.il/MFA/

Terrorism-+Obstacle+to+Peace/Palestinian+terror+since+2000/Victims+of+Palestinian+Violence+and+Terrorism+sinc.htm

Janoff-Bulman, R. (1992). *Shattered assumptions: Towards a new psychology of trauma*. New York, NY: Free Press.

Jost, J. T., & Amodio, D. M. (2012). Political ideology as motivated social cognition: Behavioral and neuroscientific evidence. *Motivation and Emotion, 36*, 55–64.

Kaplan, Z., Matar, M. A., Kamin, R., Sadan, T., & Cohen, H. (2005). Stress-related response after 3 years of exposure to terror in Israel: Are ideological–religious factors associated with resilience. *Journal of Clinical Psychiatry, 66*, 1146–1154.

Landau, M. J., Solomon, S., Greenberg, J., Cohen, F., Pyszczynski, T., Arndt, J., . . . Cook. A. (2004). Deliver us from evil: The effects of mortality salience and reminders of 9/11 on support for President George W. Bush. *Personality and Social Psychology Bulletin, 4*(30), 1136–1150.

Lane, R. E. (1959). *Political life: Why and how people get involved in politics*. New York, NY: The Free Press.

Laor, N., Yanay-Shani, A., Wolmer, L., & Khoury, O. (2010). A trauma-like model of political extremism: Psycho-political fault lines in Israel. *Annals of the New York Academy of Sciences, 1208*, 24–31.

Lavi, I., Canetti, D., Sharvit, K., Bar-Tal, D., & Hobfoll, S. E. (2012). Protected by ethos in a protracted conflict? A comparative study among Israelis and Palestinians in the West Bank, Gaza, and East Jerusalem. *Journal of Conflict Resolution*. Advance online publication.

Lazarus, R. S., & Folkman, S. (1984). *Stress, appraisal, and coping*. New York, NY: Springer.

Legge, J. S. (1996). Antiforeign sentiment in Germany: Power theory versus symbolic explanations of prejudice. *The Journal of Politics, 58*(2), 516–527.

Lerner, J. S., Gonzalez, R. M., Small, D. A., & Fischoff, B. (2003). Effects of fear and anger on perceived risks of terrorism: A national field experiment. *Political Science, 14*(2), 144–150.

Levine, R. A., & Campbell, D. T. (1972). *Ethnocentrism, theories of conflict, ethnic attitudes, and group behavior*. New York, NY: Wiley.

Lewitus, G. M., Cohen, H., & Schwartz, M. (2008). Reducing post-traumatic anxiety by immunization. *Brain, Behavior, and Immunity, 22*, 1108–1114.

Maoz, I., & McCauley, C. (2005). Psychological correlates of support for compromise: A polling study of Jewish-Israeli attitudes toward solutions to the Israeli-Palestinian conflict. *Political Psychology, 26*, 791–807.

Miguel-Tobal, J. J., Cano-Vindel, A., Gonzalez-Ordi, H., Iruarrizaga, I., Rudenstine, S., Vlahov, D., & Galea, S. (2006). PTSD and depression after the Madrid March 11 train bombings. *Journal of Traumatic Stress, 19*(1), 69–80.

Ohman, A. (1993). Fear and anxiety as emotional phenomena: Clinical phenomenology, evolutionary perspectives, and information processing mechanisms. In M. Lewis & J. M. Haviland (Eds.), *Handbook of emotions* (pp. 511–536). New York, NY: Guilford Press.

Punamaki, R. L. (1996). Can ideological commitment protect children's psycho-social well-being in political violence? *Child Development, 67*, 55–69.

Quillian, L. (1995). Prejudice as a response to perceived group threat: Population compositions and anti-immigrant and racial prejudice in Europe. *American Sociological Review, 60*, 586–611.

Riek, B. M., Mania, E. W., & Gaertner, S. L. (2006). Intergroup threat and outgroup attitudes: A meta-analytic review. *Personality and Social Psychology Review, 10*(4), 336–353.

Romano, D. (2006). Conducting research in the Middle East's conflict zones. *PS: Political Science and Politics, 39*(3), 439–441.

Roseman, I. J. (1984). Cognitive determinants of emotions: A structural theory. In P. Shaver (Ed.), *Review of personality and social psychology* (Vol. 5, pp. 11–36). Berkeley, CA: Sage.

Ross, L., & Nisbett, R. (1991). *The person and the situation. Perspectives of social psychology.* New York, NY: McGraw-Hill.

Rubin, G. J., Brewin, C. R., Greenberg, N., Hughes, J. H., Simpson, J., & Wessely, S. (2007). Enduring consequences of terrorism: Seven-month follow-up survey of reactions to the bombings in London on July 7, 2005. *The British Journal of Psychiatry, 190,* 350–356.

Sampson, R. J., Morenoff, J. D., & Earls. F. (1999). Beyond social capital: Spatial dynamics of collective efficacy for children. *American Sociological Review, 64,* 633–660.

Schlenger, W. E., Caddell, J. M., Ebert, L., Jordan, B. K., Rourke, K. M., Wilson, D., ... Kulka, R. A. (2002). Psychological reactions to terrorist attacks: Findings from the National Study of Americans' Reactions to September 11. *Journal of the American Medical Association, 288,* 581–588.

Schuster, M, A., Stein, B. D., Jaycox, L. H., Collins, R. L., Marshall, G. N., Elliott, M. N., ... Berry, S. H. (2001). A national survey of stress reactions after the September 11, 2001 terrorist attacks. *New England Journal of Medicine, 345,* 1507–1512.

Segerstrom, S. C., & Miller, G. E. (2004). Psychological stress and the human immune system: A meta-analytic study of 30 years of inquiry. *Psychology Bulletin, 130,* 601–630.

Shalev, A. Y., & Freedman, S. (2005). PTSD following terrorist attacks: A prospective evaluation. *American Journal of Psychiatry, 162,* 1188–1191.

Shechner, T., Slone, M., & Bialik, G. (2007). Does political ideology moderate stress? The special case of soldiers conducting forced evacuations. *Journal of Orthopsychiatry, 77,* 189–198.

Sherif, M. (1966). *In common predicament.* Boston, MA: Houghton Mifflin.

Silver, R. C., Holman, A. E., McIntosh, D. N., Poulin, M., & Gil-Rivas, V. (2002). Nationwide longitudinal study of psychological responses to September 11. *Journal of the American Medical Association, 288,* 1235–1244.

Sniderman, P. M., Hagendoorn, L., & Prior, M. (2004). Predisposing factors and situational triggers: Exclusionary reactions to immigrant minorities. *American Political Science Review, 98,* 35–49.

Solomon, Z., & Berger, R. (2005). Coping with the aftermath of terror: Resilience of ZAKA body handlers. *Journal of Aggression, Maltreatment & Trauma, 10,* 593–604.

Stephan, W. G., & Stephan, C. W. (2000). An integrated threat theory of prejudice. In S. Oskamp (Ed.), *Claremont Symposium on Applied Social Psychology* (pp. 23–46). Hillsdale, NJ: Erlbaum.

Stephan, W. G., Ybarra, O., Martınez, C. M., Schwarzwald, J., & Tur-Kaspa, M. (1998). Prejudice toward immigration to Spain and Israel: An integrated threat theory analysis. *Journal of Cross-Cultural Psychology, 29,* 559–576.

Tajfel, H., & Turner, J. C. (1979). An integrative theory of intergroup conflict. In W. G. Austin & S. Worchel (Eds.), *The social psychology of intergroup relations* (pp. 33–47). Monterey, CA: Brooks/Cole.

Tessler, M., & Jamal, A. (2006). Political attitude research in the Arab world: Emerging Opportunities. *PS: Political Science & Politics, 39*(3), 433–437.

Uppsala Universitet (2012). UCDP conflict encyclopedia. Department of Peace and Conflict Research, Uppsala Universitet. Retrieved from http://www.pcr.uu.se/research

Wolin, S. (2004). *Politics and vision: Continuity and innovation in Western political thought.* Princeton, NJ: Princeton University Press

CHAPTER 12

Political Psychology of the Death Terror

ABDOLHOSSEIN ABDOLLAHI

Many people believe that mental processes such as judgment and decision making involve a rational process unaffected by emotion (Damasio, 1994; Hastie & Dawes, 2010). For example, when one wants to buy a new car, one may consider various makes and models, compare their positive and negative features, and finally pick one that fits well with one's preference. Similarly, most people think that when they vote for a candidate in a presidential election, they put feelings aside and use all the available information to make a rational decision. In the same vein, most of us may believe that politicians are a group of smart people who possess the unique talent of making the best judgments and decisions under tough situations. However, psychologists and other behavioral scientists have shown that this is not always true. That is, sometimes we make decisions based on our gut feelings, or more technically by our intuitions (Kahneman, 2003; Kihlstrom, 1993; Zajonc, 1980).

Some experts have gone even further in postulating that more than 95 percent of our mental lives are governed by our unconscious cognitions and emotions (Lakoff, 2002) and that even politicians and politically oriented individuals are no exception in this regard (Westen, 2007). In this chapter, *terror management theory* (TMT, Greenberg, Pyszczynski, & Solomon, 1986; Pyszczynski, Greenberg, & Solomon, 1999) is used as a framework in exploring these dynamics. TMT is a social psychological theory, which posits that the leading psychological construct underlying human social behavior is a unique fundamental human emotion called mortality fear. TMT represents an existential psychological approach emphasizing the significance of death terror as a grand *unconscious* emotion occupying our mental lives and controlling the way we interact with our social world. There are certain parallels between TMT and certain motivation and emotion researchers (e.g., Izard, 1991; Tomkins, 1984), who consider emotions as motivational systems energizing and directing behavior. Indeed, TMT assumes that the reminders of death and their associated fear of mortality act as a grand motivational system to shape and direct human social behavior in an unconscious manner. Therefore, in the current analysis, the idea of death terror as an unconscious motive/emotion will be introduced.

Emotions (conscious and unconscious) play a crucial role in human cognition. They shape and direct our attitudes, goals, judgment, and decisions (Berridge & Winkielman, 2003; Lerner & Keltner, 2000; Schwarz, 1990; Winkielman & Berridge, 2004, Zajonc, 1980). They also influence our behavior; that is, the way we act in our environment (Baumeister, DeWall, Vohs, & Zhang, 2007). Indeed, at a macro level, certain incidental or anticipated emotions, such as fear or joy, can affect our political thinking and behavior as well (Westen, 2007). More elaborately, Westen (2007) maintains that our political decisions stem from our emotion and not necessarily from our rationality. For example, he writes that Democrats may predictably lose in politics just because they are rationalists. On the other hand, Republicans manipulate their audience's emotions, which are deeply connected with their core values. And, people usually make their major decisions based on their emotionsa

More specifically, in this chapter, the role of the death terror as a unique unconscious human emotion in influencing political preferences, attitudes, and behavior is considered. As mentioned above, TMT is used to explain a wide range of social, cognitive, and behavioral variables including political views, judgments, and decisions. To this end, a sample of the relevant TMT-related research findings obtained from two Western and Eastern countries (i.e., Iran and the United States) is presented. However, to set the stage for discussing the critical effect of death terror on political issues in the context of TMT, a brief overview of the definition, functions, and conscious and unconscious types of emotion is in order.

EMOTIONS: DEFINITION, FUNCTIONS AND TYPES OF EXPRESSION

Although most psychologists agree that core psychological emotions/processes influence many aspects of human behavior, they tend to disagree on their definition and purpose (Izard, 2007). However, for our purpose, an encompassing definition put forward by Keltner and Gross (1999, p. 468) efficiently represents the concept of emotion:

> [An emotion is an] episodic, relatively short-term, biologically based patterns of perception, experience, physiology, action, and communication that occur in response to specific physical and social challenges and opportunities.

According to this characterization, emotions are *biopsychosocial* entities designed to help human beings react to and cope with the immediate demands of the environment. As such, the definition invokes the important point of the function of emotions and portrays them as adaptive biological, cognitive, behavioral, and communicational responses to the social world.

The role and function of emotions in daily life vary across psychological disciplines. On the one hand, there are behaviorists (e.g., Skinner, 1953, 1957) who maintain that emotions exert less of an impact on human behavior. That is, they are simply thought to be a set of epiphenomenal and unobservable personal experiences, which must be factored out in a scientific analysis of behavior. On the other hand, drawing on Darwin's description of emotions (Darwin, 1872), the proponents of the newly established *evolutionary psychology* (e.g., Buss, 2012) as well as other psychologists (e.g., Ekman, 1993) maintain that emotions are universal adaptations evolved to be at the service of human survival and reproduction. For example, in a situation of threat and danger, such as being threatened by a hungry lion in a forest, one is motivated to escape to save one's life. In this model, fear is the central emotion directing behavior to ensure survival.

Relevant to our discussion of emotions is the importance of classifying their various expression types. The idea of emotions as conscious experiences has been widely demonstrated within psychological science (Clore, 1994; Davidson & Ekman, 1994; LeDoux, 1994). Most psychologists assume that emotions are conscious phenomena. This idea is justifiable in the sense that one main component of every emotion is its feeling dimension which must be absolutely conscious. For instance, one cannot experience fear without being aware of the feeling of fear. However, more than a century ago, Sigmund Freud invoked the notion of unconscious emotions stemming from the dynamic suppression of the pleasure and aggression instincts. Moreover, in light of new developments in cognitive psychology and neuroscience, the notion of an *unconscious emotion* is gradually being welcomed into the field. It is now well documented that cognitive processes and operations such as perception, memory, learning, and decision making have an implicit and unconscious component (Bargh & Chartrand, 1999; Dijksterhuis, Bos, Nordgren, & van Baaren, 2006; Freud, 1920; Kihlstrom, 1996; Lewicki, 1986; Marcel, 1983; Merikle & Reingold, 1990; Reber, 1967; Roediger & McDermott, 1990). For example, Reber (1967) demonstrated that subjects perceiving letter strings manipulated by complex rules, could categorize new stimulus patterns in a totally unconscious fashion. Similarly, Dijksterhuis, Bos, Nordgren, and van Baaren (2006) showed that complex decisions, as opposed to simple ones, are more optimal if made unconsciously.

Robert Zajonc (1980) was one of the first psychological scientists who empirically investigated and documented the existence of unconscious characteristics of emotions. Zajonc theorized that we can experience an emotion without being aware of its antecedents and causes. For example, Zajonc (1968) and Kunst-Wilson and Zajonc (1980) showed that when participants were exposed to subliminally perceived stimuli, they tended to like them more. This means that the mere exposure to the stimuli has unconsciously triggered a positive emotion or affect in their participants. Similarly, Winkielman and Berridge (2003, 2004) reported a number of studies in which participants were subliminally presented with various emotion-eliciting stimuli (e.g., angry versus happy faces) and then were required to engage in a specific behavior (e.g., drinking a beverage). The findings obtained from these experiments indicated that when participants were presented with a happy face, they tended to drink more, which suggests a relationship between affect and behavior. Based on these and other findings, it can be inferred that emotions (e.g., fear) and affective states may have both conscious and unconscious components. This brief digression presents a framework for understanding how mortality salience, or the fear of death, may impact political thinking and behavior.

DEATH TERROR AS AN UNCONSCIOUS MOTIVE

We frequently encounter situations (implicitly and explicitly) where the fear of death is primed. For example, upon switching on a television news channel, it is likely that you will hear about various cases of societal violence and/or about natural/man-made disasters. The issue of mortality is ubiquitous and permeates most aspects of living. At a scientific level, the first scientist who theorized extensively about the effect of death anxiety on human thinking was Ernest Becker, an American cultural anthropologist who presumed that human civilization is a direct product of our ability to know we would eventually die (Becker, 1973, 1975). As is evident, this "malignant insight" leads to debilitating anxiety or terror, because we all possess a self-preservation instinct. To defend against this inevitability, humans create cultures by which they are able to ward off death reminders. According to Becker (1973), whose ideas in this regard have been experimentally investigated and confirmed by TMT researchers, cultures provide us with a set of constructed beliefs or worldviews about reality that are shared among members of our group. Cultures imbue our world with meaning, order, and predictability—all of which serve as vehicles for allaying one's sense of mortality. By remaining dedicated and committed to these cultural worldviews, people are able to attain a sense of purpose and efficacy, which in turn wards off reminders of death. Self-esteem allows people to feel valuable in a meaningful universe (Solomon, Greenberg, & Pyszczynski, 1991). To briefly summarize Becker's position, cultural worldviews and self-esteem act as two central anxiety buffers against the fear of mortality.

However, according to Becker, a person's cultural worldviews are vulnerable to increased fragility and potential breakdown. That is, they run the potential of being threatened by other competing ideologies, which results in a state of dissonance. For example, the members of a group who believe in a tree as their god may come across another competing culture that entirely rejects this notion, and sees these beliefs as heretical. This resulting inconsistency in belief structures may contribute to a sense of existential terror in each group, where competing worldviews are seen as potentially threatening. According to, TMT, one way to restore a sense of meaning and legitimacy of one's worldviews is to denigrate the competing group and delegitimize its' views and group members (Becker, 1973). This process leads to cultural clashes and political conflicts (Pyszczynski et al., 2006). This has been investigated by TMT researchers across the globe. A handful of experimental studies have documented the role of death terror in shaping or even determining political attitudes. These are summarized next.

TERROR MANAGEMENT THEORY

Following Becker's (1973, 1975) work in this area, TMT researchers have provided some empirical evidence for the effects of mortality salience on behavior. For instance, Rosenblatt, Greenberg, Solomon, Pyszczynski, and Lyon (1989) found that participant judges exposed to death reminders (primed through writing a text on their possible physical death) were more likely to set higher bonds for a woman accused of prostitution. In a related experiment using the same procedure to activate death reminders, these researchers found that the death-informed student participants holding negative attitudes toward prostitution revealed a similar response pattern. Finally, in a third experiment, these authors demonstrated that mortality salience led their participants to take a positive attitude toward a national hero who espoused their own cultural values. As can be seen from these findings, the mere unconscious activation of death reminders move people into a cognitive state of subscribing to their cultural norms.

In such TMT experiments, participants are aware of the task designed to make their mortality salient. However, through distraction, their cognitive systems push the death reminders into the unconscious. In other studies, researchers have shown that it is possible to achieve the same experimental goal by subliminally presenting participants with death-related stimuli. For instance, Arndt, Greenberg, Pyszczynski, and Solomon (1997) subliminally exposed their experimental and control participants to the words *death* and *field,* respectively. Then, each participant was asked to form an impression of a foreign student who had written a positive (or negative) essay about the United States. Results indicated that death-informed students were more in favor of the foreign students who held a favorable attitude toward the United States. It should further be noted that TMT findings have been replicated in many cultures throughout the world.

TMT provides a very nice framework for understanding how terrorism fears may impact political process. As mentioned, a considerable portion of TMT research has been allocated to studying political attitudes and behaviors. In virtually all of the studies, participants exposed to mortality salience have demonstrated attitudes and behavioral tendencies congruent with their relevant cultural worldviews. Simply put, political thinking is extremely sensitive to reminders about death. From this point on, the chapter will focus on an exclusive group of findings from some cultures indicating that, contrary to our beliefs, death reminders play a substantial role in shaping political processes.

DEATH REMINDERS AND POLITICAL ATTITUDES ACROSS CULTURES

To test whether TMT principles could be replicated in a Middle Eastern country, Pyszczynski et al. (2006) conducted an experiment with the Iranian undergraduate students who wrote about either their death or their dental pain. Participants were then given a questionnaire supposedly filled out by another student, who held either a negative or positive attitude toward the United States and its allies, and was sufficiently motivated to get involved in martyrdom operations against these countries. Next are two sample items from the questionnaire:

1. "What do you feel to be the most pressing world issue? Showing the world that death in the name of Allah will bring an end to the imperialism practiced in the West."
2. "Do you have a life motto? One should treat all other true believers as brothers; everyone else should be considered enemies of Allah."

On the second questionnaire, participants responded to the same set of questions, but this time "another student" supported less harsh attitudes toward the United States (the anti-martyrdom condition). Two sample items are as follows:

1. "What do you feel to be the most pressing world issue? Convincing others in the world that Islam is a peaceful religion and that Allah loves all men. The world must know that not all Muslims are motivated by the hatred and misguided beliefs that have led to many needless deaths in the name of Allah."
2. "Do you have a life motto? One should treat other humans with respect and care, no matter what racial, ethnic, or religious background."

All participants then responded to a scale that measured their attitudes toward the persons who completed the first and second questionnaires. The results revealed that under the mortality salience condition, those in the pro-martyrdom operation condition were more likely to favor the participant who espoused pro-martyrdom operations, compared with those in the anti-martyrdom condition. Moreover, these participants were more willing to get involved in martyrdom operation against America and its allies. This conclusion was derived from the participants' responses to an item probing the degree to which they would consider joining a martyrdom operation.

These findings indicate that mortality salience has a strong impact on how we evaluate and react to our enemies. They also show how malleable and context dependent these opinions/reactions may be. This is a good place to allude to the observation that attitudes are highly responsive to features of the environment or how we are primed by what we are exposed to, internally or externally (Schwarz, 1999). In the Pyszczynski et al. study (2006), we see that the participants taking part in a within-subject experiment quickly changed their responses to the presented items based on which questionnaires (martyrdom-supporting or martyrdom-opposing) they received. This is important to note because it carries a significant message which may be illuminating to anyone interested in political psychology and international peace: that is, it would be hard for people to hold an attitude for long, no matter what the direction or valence of the attitude is. Fortunately, TMT researchers (e.g., Rothschild, Abdollahi, & Pyszczynski, 2009) have been exploring ways to curb the dark side of the death reminders activation. This is good news for people dedicated to international peace. A relevant study is discussed later in the chapter.

Pyszczynski and colleagues (2006, Study 2) conducted a parallel experiment in the United States to see if American conservative and liberal college students would reveal the same response pattern as observed in the Iranian sample. Here, the main hypothesis was that if Americans perceive themselves as a nation devoted to uprooting evil, then under mortality salience, they would support using extreme military measures against "enemies." To test this hypothesis, the American politically conservative and liberal college students were reminded of death, 9/11 attacks on the World Trade Center and the Pentagon, or an intense physical state. They then responded to the following items:

1. It is entirely appropriate to engage in preemptive attacks on countries (e.g., Iran, Syria, North Korea) that may pose a threat to the United States in the future, even if there is no evidence they are planning to attack us right now.
2. If necessary, the United States should use nuclear weapons to defend our interests at home and abroad.
3. If necessary, the United States should use chemical weapons to defend our interests at home and abroad.
4. If we could capture or kill Osama bin Laden we should do it, even if thousands of civilians are injured or killed in the process.
5. The Patriot Act should be strengthened, even if we have to relinquish personal freedoms to make our country more secure.

The results showed that the death-informed politically conservative, but not liberal, participants were more supportive of the U.S. military following extreme measures in the Middle East. They also were more willing to see the Patriot Act implemented by the U.S. government. What about the use of nuclear/chemical weapons?

As is evident from these findings, thoughts of death directed both Iranians and Americans to support the harming of people from the other ("enemy") country. More generally, these findings suggest that political attitudes and decisions seem to be shaped by a psychological motivation to avoid death. Now a socially responsible reader may raise the question of whether there is a way to get rid of the influence of death reminders on our thinking and behavior. Results indicate this may be so.

For example, Abdollahi, Henthorn, and Pyszczynski (2009) were interested to see if conformity with in-group members would attenuate aggression against outgroups. In this study, after being primed with mortality salience (and dental pain salience), Iranian participants were presented with three "pieces of information" about martyrdom-seeking operations. Participants in one condition read that: "A recent survey indicates that nearly 75 percent of people believe that using martyrdom-seeking operations against enemies *is* an ideal way of defending Islam and Iran." This statement made clear that the majority of the Iranian society members support martyrdom operations.

In another condition of the study, another group of participants read that: "A recent survey indicates that nearly 75 percent of people believe that using martyrdom-seeking operations against enemies *might not be* an ideal way of defending Islam and Iran." This statement made clear that the majority of the society members do not support martyrdom operations. Still in another third condition, participants read that: "Using martyrdom-seeking operations against enemies is an ideal way of defending Islam and Iran."

Results revealed that when other members of the society did not support martyrdom operations, the effects of mortality salience as found in the study by Pyszczynski et al. (2006, Study1), was reversed. That is, compared with the other two conditions, participants were less likely to agree with the item stating that the majority of their compatriots supported such actions. The findings are consistent with the major social-psychological theories (Asch, 1951; Festinger, 1954; Goethals & Nelson, 1973) indicating that people tend to compare their beliefs, attitudes, values, feelings, and behaviors with similar others. Overall, it is plausible to conclude that the death reminders effects are prone to enormous variability.

There is evidence to suggest that the negative effects of mortality salience may be controlled through such existential vehicles as religion. Religion turns out to play a significant role in shielding the death anxiety (Templer, 1970). Indeed, TMT suggests that religion, as a fundamental part of any culture, acts as a grand buffer against thoughts of mortality (Vail et al., 2010). Similarly, Norenzayan and Hanson (2006) found that death reminders increased their religious participants' beliefs in supernatural agents. Rothschild, Abdollahi and Pyszczynski (2009), in two experiments carried out in Iran and the United States, found that the religious compassionate values could mitigate the negative effects of mortality salience. In the Iranian study, following the induction of mortality salience, participants were presented with three Islamic values in the form of statements adapted from the Holy Koran. The statements, which were labeled as "Islamic Values," were as follows:

1. The Holy Koran [4:36] says: do good to parents, kinsfolk, orphans, those in need, neighbors who are near, neighbors who are strangers, the companion by your side, the wayfarer (you meet) and what your right hands possess.
2. The Holy Koran, Ghasas (77) says: do goodness to others because Allah loves those who do good.
3. Mohammad, Allah's messenger says: be kind to others.

In another condition, the participants read three statements described as "General Values." You can see them below:

1. People in general believe that one should do good to others (e.g., parents, relatives, strangers, etc.).
2. Do goodness to others because people love those who do good.
3. People in general believe that it is good to be kind to others.

Finally, all participants completed a questionnaire assessing their attitudes towards the United States and its European allies (e.g., "The U.S. and its European allies' presence in the Middle East is threatening to our Islamic being. We should fight against them," or "We cannot trust the U.S. and its European allies; they are our enemies."). The results confirmed the core study hypothesis: that is, those who had read the statements taken from the Holy Koran, tended to show *less* hostile attitudes. This indicates that religion can powerfully block the aggressive tendencies caused by mortality salience.

Rothschild, Abdollahi, and Pyszczynski (2009) ran two other similar studies with American students and found that under mortality salience and after being exposed to some compassionate statements (e.g., "Be kind and compassionate to one another, forgiving each other, just as Christ forgave you."—Ephesians 4:32; "Do not judge, or you too will be judged. For in the same way you judge others, you will be judged, and with the measure you use, it will be measured to you."—Matthew 7:1–2) from the Bible, they reported lower support for extreme military interventions. A take-home message from this body of research is that to prevent wars and strengthen international peace, the world nations and their governments must simply promote their shared religious values and emphasize their common humanities. Finally, there is research from the Middle East suggesting that experiencing severe trauma and subsequently manifesting post-traumatic stress disorder (PTSD) was associated with an inability to engage anxiety buffers. For example, Abdollahi, Pyszczynski, Maxfield, and Luszczynska (2011) introduced the anxiety-buffer disruption theory (ABDT) according to which confrontations with trauma breaks down the anxiety-buffer system consisting of cultural worldviews and self-esteem. Consequently, the individual goes into a state of recurrent bouts of anxiety and terror. For example, after a devastating earthquake in Zarand, a city in the southeast of Iran, a pool of the affected residents took part in a study investigating the effects of trauma on terror management processes. Using the Dissociative Experiences Scale II (DES-II, Carlson & Putnam, 1993), the researchers divided the participants into those with high and low dissociation. As a PTSD precursor, dissociation is an abnormal mental condition characterized by such symptoms as memory and identity problems (Carlosn & Putnam, 1993). Participants then responded to questions about their deaths, earthquakes, or dental pain. Finally, their attitudes regarding the earthquake-related foreign aid were assessed. The following are two sample items: "If foreigners (e.g., Westerners) help us in these hard earthquake conditions, they won't do it in a nonconditional way," and "Help coming from other countries (e.g., Westerners) cannot be substantial. Instead of action, they just talk." Results of the study revealed that people with a high level of dissociation had a less negative attitude toward foreign aid. That is, upon being hit by a severe life-threatening trauma such as an earthquake, people suffering from a high degree of dissociation will likely be unable to use the normal terror management defense system that has been designed to devalue alternative realities, people from other cultures, etc. Now after elaborating on a group of TMT-related studies conducted in Iran, let us turn to some findings derived from similar research carried out in the United States.

DEATH REMINDERS AND PREFERENCE FOR CHARISMATIC LEADERS

If you find yourself in a dangerous life-threatening situation and are asked to state your preference for a charismatic, task-oriented, or relationship-oriented leader, whom would you pick? In an interesting study, Cohen, Solomon, Maxfield, Pyszczynski, and Greenberg (2004) primed mortality salience in an American college student sample (by asking them to write about their own deaths), and then required them to indicate their preferences for a hypothetical charismatic, task-oriented, or relationship-oriented presidential candidate. Results indicate that these participants were more in favor of the charismatic leader, and then explained these data in the context of TMT. Specifically, they noted that when people experience psychological distress (such as being exposed to death reminders), they gravitate to such leaders because these leaders seem to be extremely committed to their core cultural values and provide them with a high sense of self-worth. This is a stunning example of how our judgments and choices are implicitly directed by deeper existential concerns.

Similarly, before the 2004 presidential election in which George Bush, John Kerry, and Ralph Nader ran for president, Cohen, Ogilvie, Solomon, Greenberg, and Pyszczynski (2005) exposed an undergraduate sample (registered voters) to either a mortality salience or TV salience condition. Then the participants were asked to specify their preferred candidate. Findings indicate that while President Bush was the preferred choice for the mortality salience condition, John Kerry was preferred among those exposed to Television. One explanation for this is that, particularly during his reelection campaign, George Bush frequently referred to the 9/11 attacks against the United States and thus was more active in priming mortality salience among the public. Landau and colleagues (2004) conducted a similar study, and found the same effect. That is, compared with control participants, the mortality-primed liberal and conservative participants were found to be much more in favor of George Bush and his policies in Iraq.

In a similar vein, Weise et al. (2008) demonstrated that there is a direct relationship between one's attachment style and his or her support for liberal or conservative presidential candidates. More specifically, these researchers first primed participants with mortality salience and another aversive state (i.e., dental pain), and then presented them with a series of questions including: "How much do you like George W. Bush [John Kerry]?" "To what extent do you have confidence in George W. Bush [John Kerry] as a leader?" "How much do you trust George W. Bush [John Kerry]?" As would be expected, compared with the less securely attached participants, those with a secure type of attachment were more willing to support the liberal presidential candidate. This observation points to the idea that secure attachment is associated with such liberal values as tolerance and that under mortality salience, securely-attached individuals tend to cling to these values. Overall, these findings are intriguing in the sense that they reveal the role of both personality (i.e., individual differences) factors and environmental events in political judgments, decisions, and preferences. They also point to the fact that it is difficult to predict the outcome of political events such as the U.S. presidential election. Some argue that many voters usually make their minds before going to the polls, although according to this study, a combination of the activated death reminders coupled with a specific kind of attachment style (i.e., secure, anxious-avoidant, and avoidant) lead to different political preferences. These studies suggest that the American people are responsive to the unconscious activation of death reminders and their subsequent effects on political attitudes.

CONCLUSION

In this chapter, first drawing on Ernest Becker's notions and TMT researcher's findings, I set forth the notion that terror surrounding one's own mortality as a fundamental human concern is an unconscious motive or emotion deeply influencing our social cognition and behavior. Then I focused on a set of studies confirming TMT assumptions, including the role of culture and self-esteem in directing our social cognition and behavior. Finally, I described a collection of TMT-based empirical work showing that our political thoughts and behavior are largely driven by the motivation to avoid death reminders. Studies conducted in the United States and Iran established the main part of the chapter. A wide range of TMT-related research on such topics as American presidential elections, preference for charismatic leaders, martyrdom, social consensus, peace, and trauma were covered.

In conclusion, an emphasis on the applied aspects of the interaction between an existential threat such as death terror and political judgment and decision-making is in order. As described above, the effects of death reminders on social-political thinking and behavior are context-dependent. By controlling some contexts, stimuli, or situations, it could be possible to block the negative influence of death reminders. For example, by systematically promoting the compassionate values that are at the core of virtually all religions, all human societies can hopefully keep the ubiquitous worries about our mortality probability at bay and be able to live together in peace.

REFERENCES

Abdollahi, A., Henthorn, C., & Pyszczynski, T. (2009). Experimental peace psychology: Priming consensus mitigates aggression against outgroups under mortality salience. *Behavioral Sciences of Terrorism and Political Aggression*, 2(1), 30–37.

Abdollahi, A., Pyszczynski, T., Maxfield, M., & Luszczynska, A. (2011). Posttraumatic stress reactions as a disruption in anxiety-buffer functioning: Dissociation and responses to mortality salience as predictors of severity of posttraumatic symptoms. *Psychological Trauma: Theory, Research, and Practice*, 3(4), 329–341.

Arndt, J., Greenberg, J., Pyszczynski, T., & Solomon, S. (1997). Subliminal exposure to death-related stimuli increases defense of the cultural worldview. *Psychological Science*, 8, 379–385.

Asch, S. E. (1951). Effects of group pressure upon the modification and distortion of judgment. In H. Guetzkow (Ed.), *Groups, leadership, and men* (pp.177–190). New York, NY: Guilford Press.

Bargh, J. A., & Chartrand, T. L. (1999). The unbearable automaticity of being. *American Psychologist, 54*, 462–479.

Baumeister, R. F., Vohs, K. D., DeWall, C. N., & Zhang, L. (2007). How emotion shapes behavior: Feedback, anticipation, and reflection, rather than direct causation. *Personality and Social Psychology Review, 11*, 167–203.

Becker, E. (1973). *The denial of death*. New York, NY: Simon & Schuster.

Becker, E. (1975). *Escape from evil*. New York, NY: Free Press.

Berridge, K. C., & Winkielman, P. (2003). What is an unconscious emotion: The case for unconscious "liking." *Cognition and Emotion, 17*, 181–211.

Buss, D. M. (2012). *Evolutionary psychology: The new science of the mind* (4th ed.). Boston: Pearson/Allyn & Bacon.

Carlson, E. B., & Putnam, F. W. (1993). An update on the Dissociative Experiences Scale. *Dissociation: Progress in the Dissociative Disorders, 6*, 16–27.

Clore, G. L. (1994). Why emotions are never unconscious. In P. Ekman and R. J. Davidson (Eds.), *The nature of emotion: Fundamental questions* (pp. 285–290). Oxford: Oxford University Press.

Cohen, F., Ogilvie, D. M., Solomon, S., Greenberg, J., & Pyszczynski, T. (2005). American roulette: The effect of reminders of death on support for George W. Bush in the 2004 presidential election. *Analyses of Social Issues and Public Policy, 5*, 177–187.

Cohen, F., Solomon, S., Maxfield, M., Pyszczynski, T., & Greenberg, J. (2004). Fatal attraction: The effects of mortality salience on evaluations of charismatic, task-oriented, and relationship oriented leaders. *Psychological Science, 15*, 846–851.

Damasio, A. (1994). *Descartes' error: Emotions, reason, and the human brain*. New York, NY: Avon Books.

Darwin, C. (1872). *The expression of the emotions in man and animals*. London, UK: Murray.

Davidson, R. J., & Ekman, P. (1994). Afterword: How are emotions distinguished from moods, temperament, and other related affective constructs? In P. Ekman, & R. J. Davidson (Eds.). *The nature of emotion: Fundamental questions* (p. 95). Oxford: Oxford University Press.

Dijksterhuis, A., Bos, M. W., Nordgren, L. F., & van Baaren, R. B. (2006). Complex choices better made unconsciously? *Science, 313*, 760–761.

Ekman, P. (1993). Facial expression and emotion. *American Psychologist, 48*, 384–392.

Festinger, L. (1954). A theory of social comparison processes, *Human Relations 7*, 117–140.

Freud, S. (1920). *Beyond the pleasure principle*. London, UK: International Psycho-Analytical Press.

Goethals, G. R., & Nelson, R. (1973). Similarity in the influence process: The belief-value distinction. *Journal of Personality and Social Psychology, 25*, 117–122.

Greenberg, J., Pyszczynski, T., & Solomon, S. (1986). The causes and consequences of a need for self-esteem: A terror management theory. In R. F. Baumeister (Ed.), *Public self and private self* (pp. 189–212). New York, NY: Springer-Verlag.

Hastie, R., & Dawes, R. (2010). *Rational choice in an uncertain world: The psychology of judgment and decision making*. Thousand Oaks, CA: Sage Publications.

Izard, C. E. (1991). *The psychology of emotions*. New York, NY: Plenum Press.

Izard, C. E. (2007). Basic emotions, natural kinds, emotion schemas and a new paradigm. *Perspectives in Psychological Science. 2*, 260–280.

Kahneman, D. (2003). A perspective on judgment and choice: Mapping bounded rationality. *American Psychologist, 58*(9), 697–720.

Keltner, D., & Gross, J. J. (1999). Functional accounts of emotion. *Cognition and Emotion,* 13, 467–480.

Kihlstrom, J. F. (1996). The trauma-memory argument and recovered memory therapy. In K. Pezdek & W. P. Banks (Eds.), *The recovered memory/false memory debate* (pp. 297–311). San Diego, CA: Academic Press, Inc.

Kihlstrom, J.F. (1993). The continuum of consciousness. *Consciousness & Cognition,* 2, 334–354.

Kunst-Wilson, W., & Zajonc, R. (1980). Affective discrimination of stimuli that cannot be recognized. *Science,* 207(4430), 557–558.

Lakoff, G. (2002). *Moral politics: How liberals and conservatives think.* Chicago, IL: The University of Chicago Press.

Landau, M. J., Solomon, S., Greenberg, J., Cohen, F., Pyszczynski, T., Arndt, J., ... Cook, A. (2004). Deliver us from evil: The effects of mortality salience and reminders of 9/11 on support for President George W. Bush. *Personality and Social Psychology Bulletin,* 30, 1136–1150.

LeDoux, J. E. (1994). Emotion, memory and the brain. *Scientific American,* 270(6), 32–39.

Lerner, J. S., & Keltner, D. (2000). Beyond valence: Toward a model of emotion-specific influences on judgment and choice. *Cognition and Emotion,* 14(4), 473–493.

Lewicki, P. (1986). *Nonconscious social information processing.* New York, NY: Academic Press.

Marcel, A. (1983). Conscious and unconscious perception: Experiments on visual masking and word recognition. *Cognitive Psychology,* 15, 197–237.

Merikle, P. M., & Reingold, E. M. (1990). Recognition and lexical decision without detection: Unconscious perception? *Journal of Experimental Psychology: Human Perception & Performance,* 16, 574–583.

Norenzayan, A., & Hansen, I. G. (2006). Belief in supernatural agents in the face of death. *Personality and Social Psychology Bulletin,* 32, 174–187.

Pyszczynski, T., Abdollahi, A., Solomon, S., Greenberg, J., Cohen, F., & Weise, D. (2006). Mortality salience, martyrdom, and military might: The Great Satan versus the Axis of Evil. *Personality and Social Psychology Bulletin,* 32, 525–537.

Pyszczynski, T., Greenberg, J., & Solomon, S. (1999). A dual-process model of defense against conscious and unconscious death-related thoughts: An extension of terror management theory. *Psychological Review,* 106, 835–845.

Reber, A. S. (1967). Implicit learning of artificial grammars. *Journal of Verbal Learning & Verbal Behavior,* 6, 855–863.

Roediger, H. L., & McDermott, K. B. (1990). Implicit memory in normal human subjects. In F. Boller & J. Graffman (Eds.), *Handbook of Neuropsychology* (vol. 8, pp. 63–131). Amsterdam, the Netherlands: Elsevier.

Rosenblatt, A., Greenberg, J., Solomon, S., Pyszczynski, T., & Lyon, D. (1989). Evidence for terror management theory, I: The effects of mortality salience on reactions to those who violate or uphold cultural values. *Journal of Personality and Social Psychology,* 57, 681–690.

Rothschild, Z. K., Abdollahi, A., & Pyszczynski, T. (2009). Does peace have a prayer? The effect of mortality salience, compassionate values, and religious fundamentalism on hostility toward outgroups. *Journal of Experimental Social Psychology,* 45, 816–827.

Schwarz, N. (1990). Feelings as information: Informational and motivational function of affective states. In E. T. Higgins & R. M. Sorrentino (Eds.), *Handbook of motivation and cognition: Foundations of social behavior* (Vol. 2, pp. 527–561). New York, NY: Guilford Press.

Schwarz, N. (1999). Self-reports: How the questions shape the answers. *American Psychologist,* 54, 93–105.

Skinner, B. F. (1953). *Science and human behavior*. New York, NY: Macmillan.

Skinner, B. F. (1957). *Verbal behavior*. New York, NY: Appleton-Century-Crofts.

Solomon, S., Greenberg, J., & Pyszczynski, T. (1991). Terror management theory of self-esteem. In C. R. Snyder & D. Forsyth (Eds.), *Handbook of social and clinical psychology: The health perspective* (pp. 21–40). New York, NY: Pergamon Press.

Templer, D. I. (1970). Death anxiety in religiously very involved persons. *Psychological Reports, 31,* 361–362.

Tomkins, S. S. (1984). Affect theory. In K. R. Scherer & P. Ekman (Eds.), *Approaches to emotion* (pp. 163–196). Hillsdale, NJ: Erlbaum.

Vail, K. E., Rothschild, Z. K., Weise, D., Solomon, S., Pyszczynski, T., & Greenberg, J. (2010). A terror management analysis of the psychological functions of religion. *Personality and Social Psychology Review, 14,* 84–94.

Weise, D. R., Pyszczynski, T., Cox, C. R., Arndt, J., Greenberg, J., Solomon, S., & Kosloff, S. (2008). Interpersonal politics: The role of terror management and attachment processes in shaping political preferences. *Psychological Science, 19,* 448–455.

Westen, D. (2007). *The political brain: The role of emotion in deciding the fate of the nation.* New York, NY: Public Affairs Books.

Winkielman, P., & Berridge, K. C. (2004). Unconscious emotion. *Current Directions in Psychological Science, 13,* 120–123.

Zajonc, R. B. (1968). The attutidinal effects of mere exposure. *Journal of Personality & Social Psychology,* Monograph Supplement 9(2, Pt. 2).

Zajonc, R. B. (1980). Feeling and thinking: Preferences need no inferences. *American Psychologist, 35,* 151–175.

CHAPTER 13

Risk Perception, Fear, and Its Consequences Following the 2004 Madrid and 2005 London Bombings

MARIE-HELEN MARAS

INTRODUCTION

Terrorist threats are evaluated in terms of risk. Risk concerns the calculation of the magnitude of harm (its adverse impact) and the likelihood of harm (its probability of occurring) (Adams, 1999; Harvard Law Review Association, 2002). Even if the likelihood of a terrorist attack is minimal, the risk of terrorism may still classified as high when the potential magnitude of devastation it may cause is significant. Rational-choice economic models portray individuals as rational actors that process information and are capable of making informed predictions about the probability of future events (Becker, 1968). However, other perspectives challenge the notion that an individual's risk perception is simply a product of objective information (e.g., Kahneman, Slovic, & Tversky, 1982; Kahneman & Tversky, 1973). Certain personal (e.g., demographics), structural (e.g., experience with terrorism), and situational factors (e.g., expected loss, catastrophic potential and beliefs in cause) can influence the public's perception of terrorism. Risk perception involves a subjective judgment, anticipating the likelihood and consequences of a future event, particularly one that requires a quick response to ensure protection. This subjective assessment is derived from psychological uncertainty and is based on an individual's mental attitude and state of mind (Slovic, 1987; Slovic, Finucane, Peters, & MacGregor, 2002). Heuristics allows us to process a large amount of information quickly and intuitively, but often at the cost of sound judgments (i.e., conclusions we would not have drawn given unlimited time).

According to economic theory of regulation, the demand for government action corresponds to the perceived risk to be regulated (Harvard Law Review Association, 2002). Typically, the public's perception of risk is considered politically more important than mathematical reality as regulations and laws regarding national security stem from their judgments about the probabilities associated with terrorism (Bannister, 2005; Jolls, Sunstein, & Thaler, 1998). Thus, policy makers are influenced by public demand for and hence also the supply of regulation. It is, consequently, important to look at the underlying mechanisms involved in risk perception as a means for understanding how public attention and support may lead to the creation of policies and laws for certain issues but not others.

Cognitive psychologists and policy researchers have investigated the underlying mechanisms that govern risk perception (Kasperson et al., 2000; Slovic, 1987). Research has shown that psychological reactions to terrorism play a fundamental role in understanding public support for counterterrorism measures (Huddy, Feldman, Taber, & Lahav, 2005). As the magnitude of harm and perceived risk of terrorism grows, the public demands increase and prompt government action. Thus, an examination of how individuals perceive threats to their own personal safety may elucidate explanations for public-supported, government employment of expansive counterterrorism measures that violate human rights. Framing this study requires a two-prong analysis. First, it assesses the actual risk of terrorism in conjunction with the public and governmental perception of this risk. To do so, it considers certain heuristics (or rules of thumb) commonly employed by individuals, such as the availability heuristic, probability neglect, and prospect theory, when evaluating risks. Second, it explores the role of their risk evaluation as it pertains to individuals' tolerance or support for measures that restrict a suspect's human rights.

Availability Heuristic

Individuals' calculations of probabilities are beset with cognitive fallacies (Harvard Law Review Association, 2002). One of the most common fallacies or source of bias is known as the availability heuristic. The availability heuristic makes "some risks seem especially likely to come to fruition whether or not they actually" will (Sunstein, 2005, p. 35). Individuals employ the availability heuristic whenever they estimate the frequency or probability of an event by the ease with which those instances could be brought to mind (Slovic, Fischhoff, & Lichtenstein, 2000b; Tversky & Kahneman, 1982a).

The introduction of laws to counter terrorist threats may themselves promote availability. That is, if a measure responds to the problems associated with terrorism, individuals may come to see those problems as readily available (Sunstein, 2006).[1] Consider, for example, antisocial behavior displayed in public. When the phrase "antisocial behavior" was introduced into the law and order discourse of the U.K. government, it "acquired a burgeoning life of its own in the public arena assisted by an increased volume of legislation" (Burney, 2005, p. 3). Specifically, the

1. Here, parallels were drawn with Sunstein's research on climate change.

U.K. government made a small problem larger when antisocial behavior became incorporated into a major policy, and as a result, people were made aware of its occurrence in their surroundings and frequently reported it as a major public safety issue (Tonry, 2004).

Even discussions of low-probability threats may increase the judged (or perceived) probability of that threat regardless of what the evidence indicates (Slovic, Fischhoff, & Lichtenstein, 2000b). For the public, the media constitutes a primary source of information concerning social problems and political discourse on how to deal with terrorist threats, thereby shaping perception of risk (Crelinsten, 2002). When news media predominantly presents sensational crimes, individuals are much more likely to inflate the risk of crime (Callanan, 2005). Studies have shown that the media's emphasis on certain crimes leads the public to believe that such crimes are more likely to be committed. For example, Singer and Endreny (1993) noted how the reporting of a terrorist incident involving U.S. citizens in Greece led to a major decline in the numbers of U.S. citizens prepared to travel to Europe. A similar situation was observed in the aftermath of the London bombings on July 7, 2005, in which suicide bombers (Shehzad Tanweer, Mohammad Sidique Khan, Jermaine Lindsay, and Hasib Hussain) detonated explosives on three separate subways and a bus. As a result of this media attention, Britain's Office of National Statistics (ONS) found that travel to and tourism in 2005 for London was adversely impacted (BBC, 2006).

Availability is also affected by the frequency of the occurrence of events. On March 11, 2004, bombs were detonated by terrorists with mobile phones on four commuter trains in Madrid. In the weeks following the Madrid bombings, the mass media focused its attention almost exclusively on the threat of terrorism and the governments' responses to it. In doing so, the mass media reinforced the availability of the attacks themselves and increased perceived risk. Politicians and the media refer to these bombings and vulnerabilities on countless occasions as a way of emphasizing "the reality of seemingly distant threats and the need to incur significant costs to counteract them" (Sunstein, 2006, p. 206). This was evident in the aftermath of the London bombings, when the British Prime Minister, Tony Blair, stated that the "rules of the game [for dealing with terrorists] had changed" and that existing restrictions by human rights law prevented Britain from effectively dealing with the terrorist threat (Economist, 2005).

Repeated news stories direct public attention toward particular risk problems, thus increasing familiarity with them (Kasperson, 2000). Familiarity affects how individuals think because it can affect the availability of instances (Sunstein, 2005). Accordingly, individuals' consider an event likely to happen because it is easy to recall. A risk that is familiar (available) will be seen as more serious than one that is unfamiliar. Salience can further affect how individuals think about risks. For example, the impact of seeing a house burning down either in person or on the television will impact on individuals' perception of risk than will reading about a fire in a local newspaper because humans typically process information visually (Sunstein, 2006;

Table 13.1. TERRORIST ATTACKS IN SPAIN

Group Type	Attacks	Deaths	Injured
Islamic extremist	1	191	1841
Secular/political/anarchist	251	10	272
Total	252	201	2113

Source: Data obtained from the Worldwide Incidents Tracking System of the National Counterterrorism Center.

Tversky & Kahneman, 1982b). Availability, which is produced by "a particularly vivid case or new finding that receives considerable media attention," plays a major role in the public's perception of that risk (Loewenstein & Mather, 1990, p. 155, cited in Sunstein, 2005, p. 38). Rare but high-consequence events, such as the Madrid and London bombings, tend to be more vividly remembered, thus making individuals likely to overestimate these risks. Accordingly, highly visible or salient events are easy to recall and are likely to be overestimated in perceived frequency.

Terrorist attacks by Islamic extremists in Europe are extremely rare events. However, even though the probability is low, individuals may subjectively consider the risk of terrorism as great because the consequences of an attack are usually extremely severe. Consider various events in Spain and the United Kingdom in 2004 and 2005, respectively. According to information retrieved from the Worldwide Incidents Tracking System database of the National Counterterrorism Center (see Table 13.1), 251 terrorist attacks were conducted in 2004 by secular/political/anarchist groups resulting in 10 dead and 272 injured. On March 11, 2004, in a single incident involving multiple coordinated bombings on Madrid's public transportation system, 191 individuals were killed and 1841 were injured. Before the attacks, unemployment was considered the top problem of Spain (Centro de Investigaciones Sociologicas, 2003; Dannenbaum, 2011). However, this changed after the bombings in Madrid. In a poll conducted after the attacks, terrorism was considered the most serious problem facing Spain (Opina, 2004; Dannenbaum, 2011). Likewise, in June 2004, a German Marshall Fund poll (2004) revealed that 97 percent of respondents believed that "international terrorism would be an important or extremely important threat to Spain over the next decade" (cited in Dannenbaum, 2011, p. 344).

Moreover, information retrieved from the Worldwide Incidents Tracking System database of the National Counterterrorism Center (see Table 13.2) in 2005 revealed that 111 terrorist attacks were conducted in the United Kingdom by secular/political/anarchist groups, which resulted in 7 deaths and 189 people injured. On July 7, 2005, in a single coordinated suicide bombing on London's public transportation system, 52 individuals were killed and over 700 were injured. In the aftermath of the bombings, a July survey conducted by the Pew Research Center's Global Attitudes Project (2005) revealed that 70 percent of those surveyed in Great Britain expressed worry about Islamic extremism within their countries. In another

Table 13.2. TERRORIST ATTACKS IN UNITED KINGDOM

Group Type	Attacks	Deaths	Injured
Christian extremist	1	0	0
Islamic extremist	5	52	703
Secular/political/anarchist	111	7	189
Total	117	58	892

Source: Data obtained from the Worldwide Incidents Tracking System of the National Counterterrorism Center.

survey, which was conducted by Ipsos MORI (2005) between July 18, 2005, and July 20, 2005, terrorism was considered the "most serious threat to the future well-being of the world" (Q1). Furthermore, on July 23, 2005, over 75 percent of those surveyed believed that there would be future acts of terrorism (Angus Reid Global Scan, 2005). Despite the low number of terrorist attacks, on the whole, citizens of these countries believe that a terrorist attack from Islamic terrorists was imminent.

Several other studies conducted after the Madrid and London bombings rendered similar results: individuals perceived the risk of terrorism to be great following an attack (e.g., Davis & Silver, 2004; Gerber & Neeley, 2005; Larsen, Brun, Øgaard, & Selstad, 2011). The availability heuristic can, therefore, produce an inaccurate assessment of probability (Sunstein, 2005). By focusing on one or two incidents, the public's perception of the risk of these incidents is likely to be substantially exaggerated as a result of increased publicity. The mass media covers rare or dramatic events selectively, thus distorting the public's perception of risks. The result of disproportionate coverage contributes to individuals' assessment for common and often serious health ailments, such as heart disease, cancer, diabetes, etc., as low risk, while perceiving uncommon acts of terrorism as a great risk.

Research has shown that levels of individuals' perceived risks were "linked to willingness to support aggressive anti-terrorist policies" (Huddy et al., 2005, pp. 593–608, cited in Jenkin, 2006, p. 3). A study conducted by Gerber and Neeley (2005) revealed that individuals increased perceived risks of a threat were positively related to support for the regulation of that threat, even when the costs of this regulation, whether economic and/or social (restrictions on civil liberties) were considered significant. A case in point is the U.K. Prevention of Terrorism Act of 2005. This act gives the U.K. home secretary the power to issue control orders (which range from restrictions on communications to house arrest) that severely restrict the liberty of individuals suspected of terrorism without any need for a trial prior to their imposition (Zedner, 2005). Before the implementation of this act, Tony Blair defended the proposed law by stating that Britain is under threat by several hundred individuals plotting terrorist attacks within its borders and that expansive security and police powers were needed to combat them (Daily Mail, 2005). A poll conducted after the London bombings showed public support for this measure and, more generally, for expansive police powers. Specifically, an ICM/BBC survey conducted in 2005 revealed that the majority of those surveyed believed that governments should have extraordinary powers to, for example, detain or deport terrorists (Rubin, 2010).

Other research, such as that conducted by Davis and Silver (2004), similarly found that individuals' increased perceived risk of a threat was positively related to a willingness to restrict civil liberties. Public opinion polls conducted in the United Kingdom in 2005 by Johnson and Gearty (2007) found that four of every five individuals supported a number of counterterrorism measures implemented and the restrictions of rights that resulted from these measures. In fact, the Home Office, which published a report in 2010 based on a review of existing studies on the perceptions of counterterrorism measures in the United Kingdom, showed support overall among the general population for existing rights-invasive counterterrorism measures (Defence Science and Technology Laboratory, 2010).

Probability Neglect

When incidents are both salient and emotionally gripping, individuals tend not to think about probability at all (Sunstein, 2005). Any event that generates strong emotions leads individuals to focus on the devastation level, "rather than on the probability that the outcome will occur" (Sunstein, 2003, p. 121). This type of processing is known as probability neglect. The word "terrorism" evokes images of impending and personal disaster in individuals even when they are unlikely to become victims (Sunstein, 2005). For example, Shapiro (2006) reported that people in Kansas were concerned that they would be the next victims of al-Qaeda following the 9/11 attacks in New York.

Governments often express uncertainty in their ability to determine the level of threat regarding if, when, and under what conditions a terrorist attack will occur. Consequently, probability neglect contributes to the public's perception that the government will be ineffective in providing security (Sunstein, 2005). Additionally, governments' promotion and use of the public's beliefs and assumptions about risk and fear (i.e., that they are all vulnerable as actual or potential victims in need of protection) to achieve certain goals solidify inaccurate conclusions about terrorism (Altheide, 2006a; Garland, 2001). Accordingly, the language used—the rhetoric strategy—to communicate to the masses can be used to invoke fear or to create unease regarding a policy issue.

Rhetoric is used first to persuade an audience that the issue raised is paramount and then to convince them to adopt their conclusions (Carawan, 1998). Reflective strategy is a type of rhetoric in which government officials use discourse first to assert their legitimacy and then press for action (Leeway, 1991). One way legitimacy is established is by using the distinction between *us* (friend) and *them* (enemy) in political discourse. The calls for unity, the existence of a collective *we* or *us*, not only mobilize the masses in support of political power to combat *them* but also serve to justify or legitimate this power despite the means (the measures) used by authorities to achieve the end (combating the threat). This dichotomous view of the world divides individuals (and even nations) into those who are with and those who are against terrorists. The government (the counterterrorist in this case) uses this polarizing discourse to vehemently oppose the terrorist, who is presented as inhumane and barbaric (Leeway, 1991). The calls for unity and action against the "others" may therefore serve as a means to suppress dissent and reduce the scope for democratic debate.

In the aftermath of the London bombings, Tony Blair had stated that the debate on recent counterterrorism measures "is not an argument about whether we respect civil liberties or not; but whose take priority. It is not about choosing hard line policies over an individual's human rights. It's about which human rights prevail" (Guardian, 2006, para. 57). He further noted, this "means not disrespecting civil liberties but re-assessing what respect for them means today and placing a far higher priority, in what is a conflict of rights, on the rights of those who keep the law rather than break it" (Guardian, 2006, para. 103). In line with this argument, British public opinion polls have shown that many of those surveyed support the suspension of human rights for those suspected of terrorism-related offenses (Pantazis & Pemberton, 2012).

The broad scope of the powers afforded to governments to deal with situations such as the Madrid and London bombings, however, are linked to the belief that the adopted measures do "not affect ordinary law which applies to ordinary decent folk, i.e., to ourselves" and are instead "directed against a clear enemy of 'others' namely the terrorists" (Gross, 2001, p. 44). Dworkin (2002) asserts that "the trade-off is not between *our* liberty and *our* security in times of threat, but between *our* security and *their* liberty"; by the term *their*, Dworkin means "the freedoms of small suspect groups, like adult male Muslims" (cited in Ignatieff, 2005, p. 32). For instance, many of the restrictions on liberty resulting from U.S. authorities' responses to the 9/11 attacks were limited to noncitizens, such as the indefinite detention of terrorist suspects and enemy combatants in Guantanamo Bay (Sunstein, 2005). Yet what happens when citizens of a nation or member state are responsible for terrorist attacks? Consider the United Kingdom, where the attacks in London on July 7, 2005, were perpetrated by its own citizens. After these bombings, Britain acknowledged that it had allowed the al-Qaeda hydra to grow inside its own society relatively undetected (Phillips, 2006).[2] The recognition of the existence of homegrown terrorists led to the rapid revision of the assumption that terrorists affiliated with al-Qaeda and those inspired by al-Qaeda's cause were noncitizens. Accordingly, this distinction is not limited to citizens and noncitizens but is more generally applicable to the distinction between *us* (ordinary, law-abiding citizens) and a clearly defined set of others, *them* (such as terrorists).

---

2. After 7/7, British officials estimated that there were approximately 16,000 British Muslims either actively engaged in or in support of al-Qaeda's cause.

The measures governments implement against *them* are accepted on the assumption that these restrictions do not and will not apply to *us*. That is, by selectively targeting a clearly defined set of "others," these measures assure citizens that their own civil liberties are not in jeopardy. The limited target of such measures also makes them easier for the majority to accept because they are not sacrificing their own civil liberties (Cole, 2002). The distinction between *us* and *them* also results in a greater willingness to afford governments the use of exceptionally broad powers in the face of crises. As Gross (2003) argues, the "clearer distinction between *us* and *them* and the greater the threat *they* pose to *us*" (emphasis added), the greater the scope of the powers assumed by the government and tolerated by the public (p. 1037). The abridgments of *their* rights are justified, therefore, when the threat of terrorism appears to endanger *our* security (Ignatieff, 2005). And yet, as Cole (2002/2003) observes, the argument that only the rights of *others* are targeted, and as such, *we* "need not worry, is in an important sense illusory," for what governments do to *others* "today provides a precedent for what can and will be done to" *us* tomorrow (The Illusory Double Standard section, para. 1).

Apart from the rhetoric used, the media's portrayal of terrorism also affects the impact of the threat and individuals' perception of it. Through media such as television, the "effects of terrorism extend well beyond its immediate victims and physical destruction" including a broader target population (Crenshaw, 1986; Long, 1990; Wardlaw, 1982; cited in Huddy et al., 2005, p. 593). Through the process of risk amplification, which increases public fear of risks, the adverse consequences of a dramatic, horrific event (like the Madrid and London bombings) can extend beyond the direct damages to victims (loss of life) and property. Indeed, fear, crime, terrorism, and victimization are (or can be) experienced vicariously through the mass media by the public (Altheide, 2006b). The psychological effect that terrorist attacks have on individuals far removed from the incident itself is known as the multiplier effect (Falkenrath, 2001).

The medium through which the psychological effects (evoking a sense of horror, fear, indignity, and vulnerability in individuals removed from the incident) of terrorism are transmitted is typically a news source, such as television (Falkenrath, 2001). Once this information is retrieved, particularly through a visual communiqué, individuals discuss their fear and concern with one another. Next, public widespread fear and concern renews and increases media attention and the cycle of awareness about risks continues as each dramatic event is covered (Sunstein, 2006). Consider the killing of the toddler James Bulger by two other children in the England and the disappearance of Madeleine McCain on May 3, 2007, from Prais Da Luz, Portugal, while she was on vacation with her parents. These highly publicized events helped shape the impression that these tragedies "could happen to every child" (Furedi, 1997, p. 24). High volumes of information can thus mobilize latent fears about a particular risk and enlarge the extent to which particular failures or consequences of events can be imagined (Kasperson, 2000). The nature of these events engenders public outrage and a call for action (in terms of legislation) on the part of the government.

The coverage of homegrown terrorist threats provokes similar reactions by the public and government. The London bombings, despite initial claims that they were directed under the leadership of Osama bin Laden, were actually perpetrated by a cell of radicalized young men who, inspired by al-Qaeda, decided to express their faith by engaging in these suicide attacks. The investigations of the perpetrators of these bombings "forced counter-terrorist chiefs to tear up their intelligence assessments of potential terrorists," because none of the individuals responsible for the attacks fit their existing threat profiles (O'Neill & McGrory, 2005, cited in Rai, 2006, p. 157). This attack demonstrated how Europe faces a threat beyond al-Qaeda and related Islamic terrorists groups. As Vidino (2006) stated, "Europe is growing its own terrorists, through the radicalization of the Muslim community within Europe, thus creating the 'new face of al-Qaeda in Europe'" (p. 359).

The attacks on Madrid and London illustrated this point by revealing homegrown terrorists, who were inspired by al-Qaeda's cause, rather than directed by (or directly linked with) them. As Furedi (2007) stressed, a threat that can be found anywhere in a community acquires a "ubiquitous and menacing character. Its very proximity to people's everyday lives serves as a reminder that the enemy is at home" (p. 95). By stressing the existence of an omnipresent enemy within the community with nothing to fear and nothing to lose, governments and the media are making matters worse by creating the impression that there is no defense against this kind of threat, thus causing widespread panic and fear.

Probability neglect has several implications for law and policy, particularly in the context of counterterrorism. If probabilities are neglected, especially when emotions are engaged, then excessive public concern will be given to specific low-probability risks (Sunstein, 2005). Probability neglect also leads individuals "to focus on the worst case, even if it is highly improbable" (Sunstein, 2005, p. 35), such as the child murder and child disappearance events. This heuristic helps explain excessive reactions to low-probability risks of harm. When probability neglect is at work, the public's attention is focused on the bad outcome itself, and they are inattentive to the fact that it is unlikely to occur.

Another example of probability neglect was observed in the elections in Spain following the Madrid bombings. The elections took place during an intense and emotional period, that is, only three days after the bombings in 2004 (Vazquez, Perez-Sales, & Matt, 2006). The terrorists responsible for the Madrid bombings sought to influence the elections (Indridason, 2008). Indeed, Jamal Zougam (who was found guilty for his involvement in the bombings) verified this by asking, "Who won the election?" following his arrest on March 15, 2004. In Spain, the public believed that they were targeted because of their involvement in the Iraq war. Consequently, Spaniards favored José Zapatero and his Socialist Party after the attack, whereas before the attack, the incumbent Popular Party was ahead in the polls (Chari, 2004; Powell, 2004; Torcal & Rico, 2004). Zapatero had promised to remove Spanish troops from Iraq.

The fact that terrorism can influence decisions, such as the Madrid elections, has serious consequences. Terrorists engage in attacks to gain concessions from the targeted government. In the case of the Madrid bombings, one of the reasons why the terrorists engaged in this attack was to get Spain to remove its troops from Iraq. The demands of the terrorist in this case, as well as in other past incidents (e.g., the American military's withdrawal from Lebanon after the suicide attacks of the terrorist group Hezbollah in 1983), were met and sent the message that "terrorism works" (Dershowitz, 2002).

It can be deduced that heuristics used by individuals would be similarly used by both government and law enforcement officials. Thus, when the public shows unusually strong reactions to low-probability harms due to their use of probability neglect, even a democratic government would fall victim to illogical conclusions. In the context of terrorism, especially after the Madrid and London bombings, it seems that governmental response to probability neglect (whether it is their own, the public's, or a combination of both), resulted in unjustified or even counterproductive regulations, as was the case for the European Union.

Specifically, prior to the Madrid bombings, the following measures were severely criticized as being unjustified: "passenger name record" (PNR) checks on all flights in and out of the European Union (whereby the personal information of passengers is recorded, stored and transferred to authorities in the United States upon request); the use of IDs, visas, and passports with biometric identifiers (e.g., digital fingerprints and retinal scans), whose information is stored on a central database; and the Data Retention Directive (Directive 2006/24/EC), which mandates the blanket retention of data on all European Union citizens. In fact, on March 9, 2004, the European Parliament (2004) declared that any form of mass surveillance was unwarranted, which actually included all of the aforementioned targeted measures. However, in the wake of the 2004 Madrid bombings this view changed. Specifically, the European Council's statement in the *Declaration on Combating Terrorism* (adopted on March 25, 2004), on the urgency and necessity to adopt measures such as biometric IDs and wide retention of communications data to counter terrorism attests to this. The necessity of these measures was reiterated on July 13, 2005, in the Council of the European Union's *Declaration on the EU Response to the London bombings*.

Moreover, when the public uses probability neglect to ascertain the risk of terrorism, the resulting increased anxiety prompts government and law enforcement's responses, such as increased surveillance, which further serves to amplify public reactions. Studies have also shown that increased stress levels have been observed in communities following terrorist attacks (Bleich, Gelkopf, & Solomon, 2003; Schuster et al., 2001). In London, a study by Rubin et al. (2005) revealed stress and anxiety among respondents in London 11 to 13 days after the 2005 attacks. Similar increased stress levels were observed in parallel studies conducted in Spain (Miguel-Tobal, Cano-Vindel, Iruarrizaga, González, & Galea, 2004; Vazquez, Perez-Sales, & Matt, 2006). Heightened anxiety about the threat of terrorism may partly explain the tolerance (lack of dissent) or public support for the expansion of surveillance powers.

The psychological effects of anxiety are politically important because they lead to an overestimation of risk and risk-averse behavior (Huddy et al., 2005; Lerner & Keltner, 2001). Therefore, terrorism can lead to public demand for legal interventions that might not reduce the risks at stake and might even make the situation worse. This was observed in United Kingdom with the passage of the Terrorism Act of 2006 in the aftermath of the Madrid and London bombings. This act, among other things, criminalized the distribution of terrorist publications; the encouragement of terrorism (both direct and indirect); acts taken in preparation of terrorist attacks; and the attainment or provision of terrorist training.

Another notable and controversial part of this law was the extension of precharge detention of terror suspects. In the United Kingdom, a 28-day period of precharge detention of a suspected terrorist is currently in effect, having been extended from 14 days. The length of precharge detention has been justified on the grounds that postarrest evidence gathering in connection with the terrorism offense usually takes a considerable amount of time and resources (Home Office, 2011). The 2006 act initially sought to extend precharge detention for up to 90 days, but despite overwhelming support for the longer detention according to a poll conducted by YouGov during deliberation (Economist, 2008; Guardian, 2006), a last-minute compromise of 28 days was made (Smith, 2007).

Yet, the current 28-day period and the previous 14-day detention have only rarely been used by authorities (Peck, 2005). According to U.K. Home Office Minister Hazel Blears, between January 20, 2004, and September 4, 2005, a total of 357 people were arrested under the Terrorism Act of 2000, of whom 36 had been held for more than 7 days (Hansard, 2005) and 321 (of 357) suspects were charged in less than 8 days. To date, only 11 individuals have been held for over 14 days precharge detention—9 were arrested in Operation Overt (the "transatlantic airline plot" in 2006), one in a Manchester-based arrest in 2006 and one in Operation Seagram (the London Haymarket and Glasgow airport attacks in 2007). Six of these 11 people were held for the maximum 27 or 28 days: three were charged and three were released without charge (Home Office, 2011). Thus, the extension of precharge detention from 14 to 28 days seems to exceed that which is ordinarily useful for law enforcement purposes.

While this practice may be effective in preventing terrorists from engaging in future crimes by incapacitating them (albeit temporarily), it is only so if those detained are actually terrorists. Even if it is in principle justifiable to attempt to incapacitate highrisk individuals in order to enhance security, the use of extended precharge detention (a form of preventive detention) as a means of preventing someone from potentially committing a crime is indefensible. As a preemptive measure, extended precharge detention (beyond that which is necessary) legitimates the substantial curtailment of human rights, such as liberty, at earlier points in time than those of the ordinary criminal justice process, before the requirement of *mens rea*, much less *actus reus*, have been established. In summary, a threat of terrorism, particularly an imminent one can, therefore, lead the public and governmental officials to demand the implementation of such a rights-invasive measure.

Prospect Theory

Prospect theory is used to accentuate a number of anomalies in individuals' reactions to risks (Kahneman & Tversky, 1979; Sunstein, 2002). This theory emphasizes the public's and governments' aversion to significant harms that have a low probability of occurring (Sunstein, 2005). Prospect theory predicts an overreaction to small probabilities of catastrophic outcomes. That is, it suggests that individuals will seek regulation to prevent grave but highly unlikely harms from occurring. For example, individuals typically overestimate the dangerousness of air travel and underestimate the dangerousness of automobile racing and bungee jumping. Therefore, by focusing on these aspects of the theory, it may be possible to understand certain forms of risk regulation, which show an exaggerated response to low-probability harms (Noll & Krier, 1990). Although this theory can be taken as a form of probability neglect, it "does not set out any special role for emotions . . . and it does not predict that people will react in any special way to emotionally gripping risks" (unlike probability neglect) (Sunstein, 2003, p. 123). While availability or vividness biases may be one explanation for why individuals overestimate low-probability events and underestimate high-probability events, in prospect theory "it is proposed that over weighting of low probability events occurs regardless" (Jackson, Allum, & Gaskell, 2004, p. 5).

Overestimation may be explained through individuals' loss aversion (an aspect of prospect theory)—their dislike of losses from the status quo (Sunstein, 2005). Specifically, individuals are "far more willing to tolerate familiar risks than unfamiliar ones, even if they are statistically equivalent" (Slovic, Fischhoff, & Lichtenstein, 2000a, pp. 137–143, cited in Sunstein, 2005, p. 43). Research has shown that the number of individuals who have died from worldwide terrorism is not much greater than the number of individuals who have drowned in their bathtubs in the United States (Mueller, 2005). Moreover, since 2001, "fewer people have been killed in America by international terrorism than have drowned in toilets or have died from bee stings" (Mueller, 2006, cited in Furedi, 2007, p. 158). When loss-aversion is at work, individuals' fear the former risk more than the latter even though they are (approximately) statistically equivalent.

Consider another example, a comparison between terrorist attacks and automobile travel. Traffic accidents (familiar risk) represent a much greater risk than terrorism (unfamiliar risk). To put things into perspective, the following examples were used by Adams (2005): the total death toll in the Madrid bombings (191 people) represents approximately the number of individuals killed in Spain about every 12 or 13 days in traffic accidents, whereas the total death toll in the London bombings is approximately equivalent to 6 days of traffic fatalities in the United Kingdom, where on average 9 individuals die and over 800 are injured daily. While the risk of death is greater when traveling by automobile, far more individuals are afraid of terrorist attacks than of driving or being driven in automobiles. Individuals, therefore, show a disproportionate fear to risks that are unfamiliar.

Research has shown that individuals desire a sense of control in the face of uncertainty and danger (Brown & Siegel, 1988; Woods, 2007). Because of this, individuals tend to show disproportionate fear of risks that are involuntary or hard to control. Adams argued that individuals react strongly to terrorist attacks because harm is intentional and not accidental (Adams, 2005, p. 4). For example, individuals are less likely to tolerate malignly imposed risks, which include crimes such as rape, mugging, and murder (Adams, 2005; see also, more generally, Adams, 1999). The same could be said about terrorism.

By contrast, individuals are more tolerant of voluntary risks such as smoking or playing extreme sports (e.g., mountain-climbing). Individuals are also more tolerant of risks they can control, such as driving their own vehicles. Accordingly, individuals are less tolerant of risks they cannot control such as using public transport systems. That is, while individuals may voluntarily board airplanes, "buses and trains, the popular reaction to crashes in which passengers are passive victims, suggests that the public demand a higher standard of safety in circumstances in which people voluntarily hand over control of their safety to pilots, or to a bus or train driver" (Adams, 2005, p. 3). Public transport, however, is safer than automobile travel. While the risk of death is greater when traveling by automobile, far more individuals are afraid of flying than of driving or being driven in an automobile (Bannister, 2005). Despite the Madrid and London bombings, public transport is still an extremely safe form of travel (Litman, 2005). Specifically, studies have shown that the "traffic fatality rate per passenger-kilometer is less than one-tenth that of automobile travel" (Litman, 2005, p. 2).

In governmental application of loss aversion (a central tenet of prospect theory), the focus is on the losses introduced by a particular risk while simultaneously downplaying the benefits foregone as a result of implementing risk-reducing measures (Sunstein, 2005). Public fear might produce unjustified intrusions on human rights resulting from individuals' use of probability neglect in their assessment of the threat. When individuals are fearful of a particular risk, they will seek or tolerate incursions into their human rights that could not have been justified if their fear was logically reasoned (Sunstein, 2005). Individuals' use of the availability heuristic increases their perceived risk of a threat. Studies have shown heightened terrorism risk perception is linked to the public's willingness to support right-invasive measures (e.g., Davis & Silver, 2004; Gerber & Neeley, 2005; Huddy et al., 2005; Jenkin, 2006). Thus, individuals' use of the three underlying sources of error—the availability heuristic, probability neglect, and prospect theory—may well explain public support for and/or tolerance of legally unjustified measures to combat terrorism.

Citizens place their trust in governments to protect them from current terrorist threats and possible future attacks. Yet, as has been shown in this chapter, individuals willingly and complacently relinquish civil liberties to their governments believing that this sacrifice makes them safer (Bloss, 2007; Romero, 2003). By focusing on the evil and spectacle of terrorism, a danger arises "of distorting rational analysis not only about the probability of terrorism" (Sunstein, 2005, as cited in Ramraj, 2005, p. 107), but also about "the best way to prevent it and limit its harms" (Sunstein, 2003, pp. 121–136, cited in Roach, 2006, p. 2167).

CONCLUDING REMARKS

The Madrid and London bombings brought about a significant change both in European conceptions of the threat posed by Islamic terrorists and concerning the suitability of measures with which to respond to this threat. Specifically, the European Union implemented measures mandating the blanket surveillance and registration of the population, which were, prior to the attacks on Madrid and London, considered indefensible. Fear of terrorism may offer an explanation as to the change in perception on the appropriateness of measures with which to respond to these attacks, as well as the public's and governments' perception of the risk of terrorism.

Statistics show that the probability of a terrorist attack occurring is quite low. However, the impact of a terrorist attack is significant. It is the extent of the impact of a terrorist attack that causes the risk of terrorism to be considered high. Individuals, when thinking about risks, tend to rely on certain heuristics; namely, the availability heuristic, probability neglect, and prospect theory. Collectively, these heuristics govern how individuals view and assess risk.

Sunstein (2005) argues that as the magnitude of the terrorist threat grows, governments' arguments for intruding on human rights also increases. Especially if the risk is great (whether real or perceived), governments might, for example, allow law enforcement and intelligence agencies to engage in practices that would not have been permitted under normal circumstances. Since misjudgment of risk frequently leads to poor decision making, the public can easily be swayed into thinking that expansive measures that curb civil liberties will automatically work. With daily reminders of terrorism through the media (especially online news) and governments' repetition and emphasis of the gravity of the threat, the fear of terrorism is not expected to diminish anytime soon. As Schneier (2006) argues, when individuals do not understand risk, they make bad security tradeoffs, often resulting in measures that violate human rights.

REFERENCES

Adams, J. (1999). *Risk*. London, UK: UCL
Adams, J. (2005). What kills you matters, not numbers. *The Social Affairs Unit*. Retrieved from http://www.socialaffairsunit.org.uk/blog/archives/000512.php

Altheide, D. L. (2006a). The mass media, crime, and terrorism. *Journal of International Criminal Justice, 4*, 982–997.

Altheide, D. L. (2006b). Terrorism and the politics of fear. *Cultural Studies & Critical Methodologies, 6*, 415–438.

Angus Reid Global Scan. (2005, July 23). Britons anticipate more terrorist attacks. *Angus Reid Public Opinion*. Retrieved from http://www.angus-reid.com/polls/16897/britons_anticipate_more_terrorist_attacks/

Bannister, F. (2005). The panoptic state: Privacy, surveillance and the balance of risk. *Information Polity, 10*(1/2), 65–78.

Becker, G. S. (1968). Crime and punishment: An economic approach. *Journal of Political Economy, 76*(2), 169–217.

Bleich, A., Gelkopf, M., & Solomon, Z. (2003). Exposure to terrorism, stress-related mental health symptoms, and coping behaviors among a nationally representative sample in Israel. *JAMA, 290*(5), 612–620.

Bloss, W. (2007). Escalating U.S. police surveillance after 9/11: An examination of causes and effects. *Surveillance and Society, 4*(3), 208–228.

Brown, J. D., & Siegel, J. M. (1988). Attributions for negative life events and depression: The role of perceived control. *Journal of Personality and Social Psychology, 54*(2), 316–322.

Burney, E. (2005). *Making bad people behave: Anti-social behaviour, politics, and policy*. Devon, UK: Willan.

Callanan, V. J. (2005). *Feeding the fear of crime: Crime-related media and support for three strikes*. New York, NY: LFB Scholarly Publishing LLC.

Carawan, E. (1998). *Rhetoric and the law of Draco*. Oxford, UK: Clarendon.

Centro de Investigaciones Sociologicas (CIS). (2003, December). Barometro de Diciembre, *Estudio no. 2.548*. Retrieved from http://www.cis.es/cis/export/sites/default/-Archivos/Marginales/2540_2559/2548/Es2548.pdf

Chari, R. S. (2004). The 2004 Spanish election: Terrorism as a catalyst for change? *West European Politics, 27*(5), 954–963.

Cole, D. (2002). Enemy aliens. *Stanford Law Review, 54*(5), 953–1004.

Cole, D. (2002/2003, December/January). Their liberties, our security. *Boston Review, 27*(6). Retrieved from http://bostonreview.net/BR27.6/cole.html

Council Directive (EC). (2006). Directive 2006/24/EC of March 15, 2006 on the retention of data generated or processed in connection with the provision of publicly available electronic communications services or of public communications networks and amending Directive 2002/58/EC [2006] OJ L105/54.

Council of the European Union. (2005). Declaration on the EU response to the London bombing. Retrieved from http://www.libertysecurity.org/IMG/pdf/JHA_Council_13_July_2005.pdf

Crelinsten, R. D. (2002). Analysing terrorism and counter-terrorism: A communication model. *Terrorism and Political Violence, 14*(2), 77–122.

Crenshaw, M. (1986). The psychology of political terrorism. In M. G. Hermann (Ed.), *Political psychology: Contemporary problems and issues* (pp. 379–413). New York, NY: Jossey-Bass.

Dannenbaum, T. (2011). Bombs, ballots, and coercion: The Madrid bombings, electoral politics, and terrorist strategy. *Security Studies, 20*(3), 303–349.

Davis, D. W., & Silver, B. D. (2004). Civil liberties vs. security: Public opinion in the context of the terrorist attacks on America. *American Journal of Political Science, 48*(1), 28–46.

Defence Science and Technology Laboratory (DSTL). (2010) *What perceptions do the UK public have concerning the impact of counterterrorism legislation implemented since 2000?* London, UK: Home Office.

Dershowitz, A. M. (2002). *Why terrorism works: Understanding the threat, responding to the challenge*. New Haven, CT: Yale University Press.

Detention without charge. (2008, May 29). *The Economist*. Retrieved from http://www.economist.com/node/11455036

Dworkin, R. (2002). The threat to patriotism. In C. Calhoun, P. Price, & A. Timmer (Eds.), *Understanding September 11* (pp. 273–284). New York, NY: New Press.

European Council. (2004). Declaration on combating terrorism. Retrieved from http://www.consilium.europa.eu/uedocs/cmsUpload/DECL-25.3.pdf

European Parliament. (2004, March 9). European Parliament Resolution on the First Report on the implementation of the Data Protection Directive (95/46/EC). COM(2003) 265. *Europa*. Retrieved from http://www.europarl.europa.eu/omk/sipade3?SAME_LEVEL=1&LEVEL=5&NAV=S&LSTDOC=Y&DETAIL=&PUBREF=-//EP//TEXT+TA+P5-TA-2004-0141+0+D OC+XML+V0//EN

Falkenrath, R. (2001). Analytic models and policy prescription: Understanding recent innovation in U.S. counterterrorism. *Studies in Conflict and Terrorism*, 24(3), 159–181.

Furedi, F. (1997). *Culture of fear: Risk-taking and the morality of low expectation*. London, UK: Cassell, London.

Furedi, F. (2007). *Invitation to terror: The expanding empire of the unknown*. New York, NY: Continuum.

Garland, D. (2001). *The culture of control: Crime and social order in contemporary society*. Chicago: University of Chicago Press.

Gerber, B. J., & Neeley, G. W. (2005). Perceived risk and citizen preferences for government management of routine hazards. *Policy Studies Journal*, 33(3), 395–419.

German Marshall Fund. (2004, June 6–26). *Polling the nations*. Retrieved from http://poll.orspub.com

Gross, O. (2001). Cutting down trees: Law-making under the shadow of great calamities. In R. J. Daniels, P. Macklem, & K. Roach (Eds.), *The security of freedom: Essays on Canada's anti-terrorism bill* (pp. 39–61). Toronto, Canada: University of Toronto Press.

Gross, O. (2003). Chaos and rules: Should responses to violent crises always be constitutional? *The Yale Law Journal*, 112(5), 1011–1134.

Hansard. (2005, October 12). HC vol 437 col 501W. Retrieved from http://www.publications.parliament.uk/pa/cm200506/cmhansrd/vo051012/text/51012w07.htm#51012w07.html_spnew1

Harvard Law Review Association. (2002). Responding to terrorism: Crime, punishment, and war. *Harvard Law Review*, 115(2), 1217–1238.

Huddy, L., Feldman, S., Taber, C., & Lahav, G. (2005). Threat, anxiety, and support of anti-terrorism policies. *American Journal of Political Science*, 49(3), 593–608.

Hundreds' planning terror attack in UK. (2005, February 28). *Daily Mail*. Retrieved from http://www.dailymail.co.uk/news/article-339506/Hundreds-planning-terror-attack-UK.html

Ignatieff, M. (2005). *The lesser evil: Political ethics in the age of terror*. Edinburgh, Scotland: Edinburgh University Press.

Indridason, I. H. (2008). Does terrorism influence domestic politics? Coalition formation and terrorist incidents. *Journal of Peace Research*, 45(2), 241–259.

Ipsos MORI. (2005). London bombings survey. Retrieved from http://www.ipsos-mori.com/researchpublications/researcharchive/496/London-Bombings-Survey.aspx

Jackson, J., Allum, N., & Gaskell, G. (2004). *Perceptions of risk in cyberspace*. Cyber Trust & Crime Prevention project. London School of Economics and Politics. Retrieved from http://www.berr.gov.uk/files/file15284.pdf

Jenkin, C. M. (2006). Risk perception and terrorism: Applying the psychometric paradigm. *Homeland Security Affairs*, 2(2), 1–14.

Johnson, M., & Gearty, C. (2007). Civil Liberties and the Challenge of Terrorism. In A. Park, J. Curtice, K. Thomson, M. Philips & M. Johnson (Eds.), *British social attitudes: Perspectives on a changing society* (pp. 143–174). London, UK: Sage.

Jolls, C., Sunstein, C. R., & Thaler, R. (1998). A behavioral approach to law and economics. *Stanford Law Review*, 50(5), 1471–1550.

Kahneman, D., Slovic, P., & Tversky, A. (Eds). (1982). *Judgment under uncertainty: Heuristics and biases*. New York, NY: Cambridge University Press.

Kahneman, D., & Tversky, A. (1973). On the psychology of prediction. *Psychological Review*, 80(4), 237–251.

Kahneman, D., & Tversky, A. (1979). Prospect theory: An analysis of decision under risk. *Econometrica*, 47, 263–291.

Kasperson, R. E., Renn, O., Slovic, P., Brown, H. S., Emel, J., Goble, R., Kasperson, J. X., & Ratick, S. (2000). The social amplification of risk: A conceptual framework. In P. Slovic (Ed.), *The perception of risk* (pp. 232–245). London, UK: Earthscan.

Larsen, S., Brun, W., Øgaard, T., & Selstad, L. (2011). Effects of sudden and dramatic events on travel desire and risk judgments. *Scandinavian Journal of Hospitality and Tourism*, 11(3), 268–285.

Leeway, R. W. (1991). *The rhetoric of terrorism and counterterrorism*. New York, NY: Greenwood.

Lerner, J. S., & Keltner, D. (2001). Fear, anger and risk. *Journal of Personality of Social Psychology*, 81(1), 146–159.

Litman, T. (2005). Terrorism, transit, and public safety: Evaluating the risks. *Victoria Transport Policy Institute*. Retrieved from http://www.vtpi.org/transitrisk.pdf

Loewenstein, G., & Mather, J. (1990). Dynamic processes in risk perception. *Journal of Risk and Uncertainty*, 3, 155–175.

London bombs take toll on tourism. (2006, January 11). *BBC News*. Retrieved from http://news.bbc.co.uk/2/hi/business/4602564.stm

Long, D. E. (1990). *The anatomy of terrorism*. New York, NY: Free Press.

Miguel-Tobal, J. J., Cano-Vindel, A., Iruarrizaga, I., González, H., & Galea, S. (2004). Consecuencias psicológicas de los atentados del 11-M en Madrid. Planteamiento general de los estudios y resultados en la población general. *Ansiedad y Estrés*, 10, 163–179.

Mueller, J. (2006). *Overblown: How politicians and the terrorism industry inflate national security threat and why we believe them*. New York, NY: Free Press.

Mueller, J. (2005). Simplicity and spook: Terrorism and the dynamics of threat exaggeration. *International Studies Perspectives*, 6, 208–234.

Noll, R., & Krier, J. (1990). Some implications of cognitive psychology for risk regulation. *Journal of Legal Studies*, 19(2), 749–760.

O'Neill, S., & McGrory, D. (2005). Detectives draw up new brief in hunt for radicals. *The Times*. Retrieved from http://www.timesonline.co.uk/tol/news/uk/article782897.ece

Opina. (2004, March 22). Resultados Pulsómetro. Retrieved from http://www.opina.es/

Pantazis, C., & Pemberton, S. (2012). Reconfiguring security and liberty: Political discourses and public opinion in the new century. *British Journal of Criminology*, 52, 651–667.

Peck, M. (2005, October 20). The Terrorism Bill 2005–2006. HC Library Research Paper 05/66, 39. Retrieved from http://www.parliament.uk/commons/lib/research/rp2005/rp05-066.pdf

Pew Research Center. (2005, July 14). Islamic extremism: Common concern for Muslim and Western publics. *Pew Global Attitudes Project*. Retrieved from http://pewglobal.org/2005/07/14/islamic-extremism-common-concern-for-muslim-and-western-publics/

Phillips, M. (2006). *Londonistan: How Britain is creating a terror state within*. London, UK: Gibson Square.

Powell, C. (2004). Did terrorism sway Spain's election? *Current History, 103*(676), 376–382.

Prime minister's speech on criminal justice reform. (2006, June 23). *The Guardian*. Retrieved from http://www.guardian.co.uk/politics/2006/jun/23/immigration-policy.ukcrime1

Rai, M. (2006). *7/7: The London bombings, Islam, and the Iraq war*. London, UK: Pluto.

Ramraj, V. V. (2005). Terrorism, risk perception and judicial review. In V. V. Ramraj, M. Hor, & K. Roach (Eds.), *Global anti-terrorism law and policy* (pp. 107–126). Cambridge, UK: Cambridge.

Roach, K. (2006). Must we trade rights for security? The choice between smart, harsh, or proportionate security strategies in Canada and Britain. *Cardozo Law Review, 27*(5), 2151–2221.

Romero, A. (2003). Living in fear: How the U.S. government's war on terror impacts American lives. In C. Brown (Ed.), *Lost liberties: Ashcroft and the assault on personal freedom* (pp. 112–131). New York, NY: The New Press.

Rubin, G. (2010). Balancing fear: Why counter-terror legislation was blocked after the Oklahoma City and London bombings. *Historia Actual Online, 22*, 125–142.

Rubin, G. J., Brewin, C. R., Greenberg, N., Hughes, J. H., Simpson, J., & Wessely, S. (2005). Psychological and behavioral reactions to the bombings in London on July 7, 2005: A cross sectional survey of a representative sample of Londoners. *British Medical Journal, 331*(7517), 606–611.

Rubin, G. J., Brewin, C. R., Greenberg, N., Hughes, J. H., Simpson, J., & Wessely, S. (2007). Enduring consequences of terrorism: 7-month follow-up survey of reactions to the bombings in London on July 7, 2005. *British Journal of Psychiatry, 190*, 350–356.

Schneier, B. (2006). *Beyond fear: Thinking sensibly about security in an uncertain world*. New York, NY: Springer.

Schuster, M. A., Stein, B. D., Jaycox, L. H., Collins, R. L., Marshall, G. N., Elliot, M. N., ... Berry, S. H. (2001). A national survey of stress reactions after the September 11, 2001, terrorist attacks. *New England Journal of Medicine, 345*, 1507–1512.

Shapiro, L. (2006). Remembering September 11th: The role of retention interval and rehearsal on flashbulb and event memory. *Memory, 14*(2), 129–147.

Singer, E., & Endreny, P. (1993). *Reporting on risk: How the mass media portrays accidents, diseases, disasters and other hazards*. New York, NY: Russell Sage Foundation.

Slovic, P. (1987). Perception of risk. *Science, 236*, 280–285.

Slovic, P., Finucane, M., Peters, E., & MacGregor, D. G. (2002). The affect heuristic. In T. Gilovich, D. Griffin, & D. Kahneman (Eds.), *Intuitive judgment: Heuristics and biases* (pp. 397–420). New York, NY: Cambridge University Press

Slovic, P., Fischhoff, B., & Lichtenstein, S. (2000a). Facts and fears: Understanding perceived risk. In P. Slovic (Ed.), *The perception of risk* (pp. 137–153). London, UK: Earthscan.

Slovic, P., Fischhoff, B., & Lichtenstein, S. (2000b). Rating the risks. In P. Slovic (Ed.), *The perception of risk* (pp. 104–120). London, UK: Earthscan.

Smith, A. (2007). Balancing liberty and security? A legal analysis of United Kingdom anti-terrorist legislation. *European Journal of Criminal Policy Research, 13*(1/2), 73–83.

Sunstein, C. R. (2002). Probability neglect: Emotions, worst cases, and law. *The Yale Law Journal, 112*(1), 61–107.

Sunstein, C. R. (2003). Terrorism and probability neglect. *Journal of Risk and Uncertainty, 26*(2), 121–136.

Sunstein, C. R. (2005). *Laws of fear: Beyond the precautionary principle*. Cambridge, UK: Cambridge University Press.

Sunstein, C. R. (2006). The availability heuristic, intuitive cost-benefit analysis, and climate change. *Climatic Change, 77*(1–2), 195–210.

Terrorism Act 2006. (2009, January 19). *The Guardian*. Retrieved from http://www.guardian.co.uk/commentisfree/libertycentral/2009/jan/19/terrorism-act-2006

Tonry, M. (2004). *Punishment and politics*. Cullompton, UK: Willan.

Torcal, M., & Rico, G. (2004). The Spanish general election. *South European Society and Politics, 9*(3), 107–121.

Tversky, A., & Kahneman, D. (1982a). Availability: A heuristic for judging frequency and probability. In D. Kahneman, P. Slovic & A. Tversky (Eds.), *Judgment under uncertainty: Heuristics and biases* (pp. 163–178). Cambridge, UK: Cambridge University Press.

Tversky, A., & Kahneman, D. (1982b). Judgments under uncertainty. In D. Kahneman, P. Slovic & A. Tversky (Eds.), *Judgment under uncertainty: Heuristics and biases* (pp. 3–20). Cambridge, UK: Cambridge University Press.

U.K. Home Office. (2011, January). *Review of counter-terrorism and security powers: Review findings and recommendations*. Retrieved from http://www.homeoffice.gov.uk/publications/counter-terrorism/review-of-ct-security-powers/review-findings-and-rec?view=Binary

Vazquez, C., Perez-Sales, P., & Matt, G. (2006). Post-traumatic stress following the March 11, 2004 terrorist attacks in a Madrid community sample: A cautionary note about the measurement of psychological trauma. *The Spanish Journal of Psychology, 9*(1), 61–74.

Vidino, L. (2006). *Al-Qaeda in Europe: The new battleground of international jihad*. New York, NY: Prometheus.

Wardlaw, G. (1982). *Political terrorism*. Cambridge, UK: Cambridge University Press.

Watch your mouth. (2005, August 12). *The Economist*. Retrieved from http://www.economist.com/node/4284380

Woods, J. (2007). What we talk about when we talk about terrorism: Elite press coverage of terrorism risk from 1997 to 2005. *The Harvard International Journal of Press/Politics, 12*(3), 3–20.

Zedner, L. (2005). Securing liberty in the face of terror: Reflections from criminal justice. *Journal of Law and Society, 32*(4), 507–533.

CHAPTER 14

Rallying Without Fear: Political Consequences of Terror in a High-Trust Society

DAG WOLLEBÆK, KARI STEEN-JOHNSEN,
BERNARD ENJOLRAS, GURO ØDEGÅRD

In this chapter, we examine the relationship between terror, fear, and institutional trust in the context of a high- trust society, based on the case of Norway. On July 22, 2011, Norway was struck by a violent terror attack. A car bomb was detonated outside the central government offices, killing 8, and another 69, mostly teenagers, were brutally massacred at a Labor Party youth camp at Utøya outside Oslo. The perpetrator, a 32-year-old right-wing extremist, had aimed his attack at the governing party in Norway, claiming in court that it had betrayed the Norwegian people by supporting and implementing multiculturalist policies.

Previous studies suggest that terror events may create a rallying effect around the government, which is expressed in increased institutional trust (Chanley, 2002; Gaines, 2002; Perrin & Smolek, 2009). This rallying effect has been explained by a mechanism where terror leads to a perception of fear, which in turn creates a need to rely on the protective capacity of the authorities (Sinclair & LoCicero, 2010). However, it might be assumed that how this mechanism operates depends on the preestablished relationship between the people and their government and that low- and high-trust societies may react differently when exposed to terror. Norway presents a particular case in the international context, since it has consistently been one of the highest-ranking countries in cross-national surveys measuring interpersonal and institutional trust over the past 30 years (Catterberg & Moreno, 2005). A particular type of relationship might be envisioned between fear and trust in Norwegian society, given the long-standing trust relationship between the people and societal institutions. Indeed, the reactions to the tragedy of 7/22 among the Norwegian population were contrary to what might have been expected, in the sense that they were only somewhat characterized by fear or anger. Following the call made by the prime minister on the eve of the attacks to respond to terror with "more openness, more democracy," peaceful mass mobilizations were organized throughout the country to show sympathy for the victims and to stand up for core values of Norwegian society. Thus, what came to be termed the "Rose Marches" were characterized more by serenity and containment than by anger and fear.

A population-representative survey that was carried out shortly after the attacks corroborated this impression. It showed relatively little concern about future terrorist attacks and a great deal of confidence in the government's ability to prevent new ones (Wollebaek, Enjolras, Steen-Johnsen, & Ødegård, 2012). However, as time passed and new information emerged concerning the actions of core institutions before and during the attacks, collective grief gradually gave way to an emerging criticism against lax security measures, unpreparedness, and slow police efforts. The increasingly vocal criticism of the efforts of central public institutions may have pushed public opinion in the direction of placing less trust in the abilities of the government to protect against future attacks, and possibly a stronger sense of fear.

Many of the key contributions in studies of the relationship of fear and trust in government are linked to the 9/11 events in the United States. While these contributions serve as a natural reference point for our discussions in this chapter, we would like to underscore that we are not attempting a case comparison between the United States after 9/11 and Norway after 7/22. Existing research points to a number of contextual factors that may influence rallying dynamics, among them the characteristics of the event itself (Perrin & Smolek, 2009), the response of the government (Gaines, 2002; Skocpol, 2002), and media coverage (Prior, 2002), and controlling for this range of factors would be impossible based on the data that we possess. Instead, what we seek to achieve is an examination of the specific mechanism linking (or not linking) fear and institutional trust within the context of a high-trust society. We make use of individual survey data on fear and trust that were collected during the spring of 2011, in August 2011 directly following the terror events, and in May 2012. The panel structure of these data allows us to assess how interpersonal and institutional trust developed during the first year following the events, and also how these forms of trust are influenced by and in turn influence levels of fear in the population.

PAST RESEARCH

Over the past decade, a growing literature has sought to examine the consequences of terrorism at individual, group and societal levels. At the individual level, terror has been shown to have an impact on behavior and emotions (Lavanco, Romano, & Milio, 2008), as well as on cognitive perceptions and beliefs (Eidelson & Plummer, 2005). Fear and perceptions of threat can be considered key factors in creating individual responses to terror events (Chanley, 2002; Huddy, Feldman, & Weber, 2007; Lerner, Gonzalez, Small, & Fischhoff, 2003). As suggested by Huddy et al.

(2007, p. 486), fear has the potential of creating some degree of "cognitive shutdown," implying phenomena such as increased ethnocentrism and xenophobia, closed-mindedness and the rejection of challenging beliefs, as well as intolerance and a willingness to forego civil liberties. Fear may also trigger the need to seek the support of authority figures (Huddy, Feldman, Capelos, & Provost, 2002: Sinclair & LoCicero, 2010). The literature on the political and societal consequences of terror follows this line of thought when focusing on fear as a triggering factor for institutional trust, and for changing policy preferences (Chanley, 2002; Sinclair & LoCicero, 2010). The argument made is that when faced with a perceived personal or national threat, people will tend to place their trust in the government and to give it a mandate to take all of the measures necessary to prevent future acts of terror. For example, Huddy et al. (2002) demonstrated a link between perceived national threat and support for national and domestic security policies. They also showed that following 9/11, perceived future terrorist threat was linked to increased support for the war in Afghanistan and for increased surveillance targeting Arab immigrants.

However, the rallying effect of terror may rely on different sets of mechanisms, depending on the context. Norway constitutes a very different context from the countries that have previously fallen victim to large scale terror, such as the United States, Great Britain, and Spain. Trust in Norwegian government institutions was much higher before the attacks than in any of the aforementioned countries, to the extent that Norway could even be characterized as a "state-friendly society," with strong ideological proximity between state and civil society (Kuhnle & Selle, 1992). One consequence of this "state-friendliness" is that the relationship between interpersonal (or horizontal) and institutional (or vertical) trust is stronger in the Nordic countries than elsewhere in Europe. Those who trust other people (who constitute the overwhelming majority) tend to trust core institutions as well (Wollebæk, 2011). In very broad terms, the state is not a threat or an opponent in normal situations, or something to turn to for support in times of crises when society fails, but rather an extension of society.

The type of terrorist attack that struck on 7/22 differed from 9/11 on many counts, as did the responses of the U.S. and Norwegian governments. While the events of 9/11 were perceived as being a war against the United States, the 7/22 events were quickly framed as a war against the core values of Norwegian society, such as openness and democracy. In the following days and weeks, this perspective was strongly backed and reinforced by civil initiatives and engagement, as expressed in the Rose Marches.

Thus, in the Norwegian context, it might be hypothesized that the mechanism behind the observed rallying effect was one of reconfirming the existing institutional trust and the values embedded in it, rather than a fear-driven search for protection. In order to test this hypothesis, we first examine the levels of fear in the Norwegian population, and how they developed between August 2011 and May 2012. We then look at the development of institutional trust during the period ranging from before the attacks to 1 year after. Finally, we test the relationship between institutional trust and fear levels by looking at how they are related across the three points in time: before, directly after, and 1 year after the terror events. Can changes in the trust in government be explained by elevated levels of fear, or is the order the other way around in this case, supporting the notion that high trust in government at the outset has a prophylactic effect on the perceived threat of terror?

METHOD

The data on which the analyses below are based consist of a three-wave web survey carried out in April 2011, August 2011, and May 2012. The samples were drawn from Taylor Nelson Sofres (TNS) Gallup's web panel, comprising 62,000 individuals. The panel is designed to be representative of the 93 percent of the Norwegian population with Internet access (SSB, 2011) in terms of geography, gender, and age.

The data collection was funded by the Norwegian Research Council as part of the project "Social Media and the Public Sphere." The first wave of data collection was undertaken in March/April 2011, some months before the terror attacks, and focused on social media usage, civic engagement, and trust. The first wave consisted of three parts: a sample representative of the Internet population aged 16 and over (N = 1127); a sample representative of the population of active social media users (Facebook more than once a week or Twitter at least once a week) (N = 4183); and an extra sample of individuals aged between 16 and 24 (N = 427). The second wave was undertaken between August 12 and August 17, 2011, and was designed to capture the role of social media and other types of media in the weeks after the terrorist attacks, as well as possible attitudinal and value changes in the population as a result of the terror. The August data consisted of two sections: (1) a separate population sample (N = 931) and (2) re-interviews of 2252 of active social media users who were interviewed during the first wave in April. The third survey wave was carried out in May 2012 and consists of two parts: a sample representative of the population (N = 1017) and new interviews with 2747 of the active social media users who were interviewed in either the first or the second wave; 1655 individuals responded to all three waves. The two-fold strategy combining panel data and independent, cross-sectional population surveys allows us to study both if and how the attitudes and behavior of individuals with different characteristics have changed, as well as changes in overall levels in the population as a whole without the limitation of studying only social media users as well as the potentially distorting impact of panel attrition.

The response rates of the population samples, defined as the percentage of contacts made resulting in valid responses, were 48 percent in the first and second waves and 40 percent in the third wave. The twofold strategy combining panel data and three independent, cross-sectional population surveys allow us to study both changes in the population as a whole, and how individuals changed their attitudes and behavior in the aftermath of the act of terrorism.

The central variables used in the analysis are based on internationally established measures of fear and trust intended to capture perceived national and personal threat (Huddy et al., 2002; Lewis, 2000), while institutional trust is measured through an additive index of 5-point Likert scales of trust in six specified institutions. The institutions are municipality, Parliament, government, the courts, the police and public administration (Cronbach's α = .88 at t1, .89 at t2, .88 at t3).

RESULTS

Fear and Trust in Norway After 7/22

Fear

To what extent did the terror attacks usher in a new era of fear in Norwegian society? Table 14.1 displays levels of personal and national concern about terror attacks a few weeks after 7/22 (August 2011) and 9 months later (May 2012), as well as the respondents' assessment of whether Norway as a society was characterized by more or less fear following the atrocities. The figures indicate a somewhat heightened sense of watchfulness in the wake of the July 22 attacks. A substantial proportion of the population—45 percent—claimed that Norwegian society was characterized by a little more fear a few weeks after the terrorist attacks. However, only 3 percent argued that there was "a lot more" fear, and more than half said that it was about the same or less. Nine months later, the proportion reporting more fear had declined slightly, from 48 to 44 percent. Panel responses show that many respondents have shifted—in both directions—between the alternatives "the same as before" and "slightly more." And 30 percent of those responding "as before" in August 2011 responded "a little more" 9 months later; 34 percent of those responding "a little more" in August 2011 responded "the same as before" 9 months later. The consensus seems to be that a weak sense of uncertainty that was not present before has indeed crept into the population, but that widespread, outright fear did not transpire.

With respect to the possibility of future attacks, people were remarkably optimistic right after the attacks. Seventeen percent were "somewhat concerned" about the possibility of new attacks in Norway in the near future. Only 2.5 percent were "very concerned." The overwhelming majority—80 percent—were "not very concerned" or "not concerned at all." Nine months later, those who were somewhat or very concerned constituted a quarter rather than a fifth of the population—a modest, but significant increase. Analysis of panel data (GLM repeated measures) confirm small but significant changes—a slight increase ($p \leq .05$) with regard to national concern, a slight decrease ($p \leq .05$) with regard to personal concern and a more marked decrease ($p \leq .01$) in the confidence in the authorities' ability to prevent new terrorist attacks.

Table 14.1. FEAR AFTER 7/22

If you compare Norway today with the situation before the July 22 attacks, would you say that society is more or less characterized by fear?

	Aug. 11	May 12
A lot more	3%	4%
A little more	45%	40%
The same as before	47%	46%
A little less	5%	6%
A lot less	.7%	1%

NATIONAL CONCERN: How concerned are you about the possibility there will be more terror attacks in Norway in the near future?

	Aug. 11	May 12
Very concerned	3%	4%
Somewhat concerned	17%	21%
Not very concerned	62%	60%
Not concerned at all	18%	15%

PERSONAL CONCERN: To what extent are you concerned that future terrorist attacks will harm you, your family or your friends?

	Aug. 11	May 12
Very concerned	3%	4%
Somewhat concerned	16%	14%
Not very concerned	61%	66%
Not concerned at all	20%	17%

GOVERNMENT PREVENT: How confident are you that the authorities will be able to prevent new, major terrorist attacks?

	Aug. 11	May 12
Very high confidence	9%	2%
Quite high confidence	40%	39%
Neither/nor	32%	33%
Little confidence	15%	21%
No confidence	4%	5%
	N (avg) = 928	N (avg) = 1010

In international comparison, however, the levels of national concern are low. After the Oklahoma City bombing in 1995 (Lewis, 2000), which in some respects is comparable to the Oslo bombing/Utøya massacre, 38 percent of Americans were "very concerned" and 40 percent "somewhat concerned."

In the Norwegian data, personal worry about falling victim to a terrorist attack is at approximately the same level as the more abstract fear of terrorism on Norwegian soil. Nineteen percent were very or somewhat concerned and figures remained stable from August to May. The corresponding rate after the Oklahoma City bombing was 25 percent—much lower than the abstract fear of terrorism. The higher concrete/abstract fear ratio in Norway could be due to the fact that the atrocities were aimed directly and explicitly at children and youth. The fear and emotion connected with losing children and youth is particularly strong and probably evokes strong identification in the population. Nonetheless, this fear of terror victimization was not widespread—81 percent were not very concerned or not concerned at all.

The Norwegian respondents expressed a great deal of faith in the authorities' ability to prevent new attacks. Data show that 49 percent had "some" or "very high" trust that new attacks could be avoided, while only 19 percent had little or no trust. However, figures had dropped somewhat to 41 percent by May the year after, with only 2 percent professing very high trust in the government's preventive abilities. Eventually, criticism against the authorities' actions before and during the attacks became gradually more vocal. The government's inability to carry out basic preventive countermeasures against terrorism, such as sealing off the street where the main government building is located from general public access, was increasingly criticized, as was the lack of coordination, efficiency, and rapid response of the police force on the day of the attacks. This emerging debate, which was starting to become heated in the spring of 2012, no doubt weakened the public's confidence in the authorities' ability to prevent terror.

The levels in May 2012 approximate, but are still somewhat higher than, the levels in the responses of the American population after the Oklahoma attacks, where the proportion with "a great deal" or "some" confidence in the government's ability to avert new attacks varied between 33 percent and 37 percent in different polls (Lewis, 2000). Forty-five percent of the American population responded to a Gallup poll that the authorities would not be able to prevent new terrorist attacks.

We conducted General Linear Models (GLM) repeated measure analyses to evaluate whether outset levels (between-subject effects) or change between the two observation points (within-subject effects) differed within population subgroups (see Table 13.3 in the Appendix for F values and significance tests). In line with past research (Perrin & Smolek, 2009), we found that fear levels were higher among women than men but that women also professed a stronger belief in the ability of the authorities to prevent new attacks. Those with higher education expressed less fear and a stronger belief in the authorities' abilities than those with lower levels of education. The development between the two observation points was the same for both sexes and all education levels.

However, there are generational differences with regard to how fear levels have developed in the interim since the attacks.

Figure 14.1 shows marginal estimates of national and personal concern by age group. The estimates are based on a GLM repeated measures analysis of the second and third waves of the panel data, with controls for gender, education and party identification. Both variables have been treated as continuous scales and recoded to run from 0 to 100 to ease interpretation.

The analysis shows that when it comes to perceptions of both national and personal threats, young people have become more anxious. The figure shows an increase on both scales among those below the age of 25, while levels are stable among those older than 25. With regard to national threat, young people are still somewhat less concerned than those above the age of 45, but youth fear levels

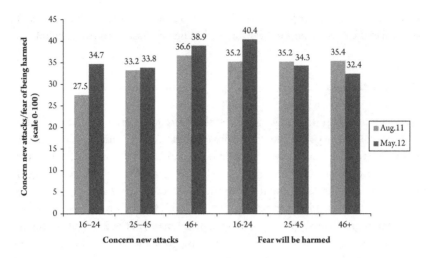

Figure 14.1:
Fear by age group (GLM repeated measures analysis).
Note: Concern about new attacks, estimated marginal means by age groups (GLM-analysis). Significance of within-subject effects time * age <.01 for both scales, meaning that fear levels have developed differently according to age. Control variables: gender, education, and party identification. Party identification is a categorical variable based on responses to the question of whether respondent identified themselves as supporters of the eight major Norwegian parties, an "other" category, or whether they did not identify with any party.

have risen substantially in the months following the attacks to match the levels of 25- to 45-year-olds. With regard to personal threat, young people now stand out with substantially higher fear levels than the population in general. Expressed in percentages, 43 percent of panel respondents below 25 now report more fear on a combined measure of national and personal threat, and 20 percent report less fear. Among those above the age of 25, fear levels are stable, with 24 percent reporting higher fear and the same proportion reporting lower fear (N = 1519).

These findings indicate that the shock of the attacks may have left a stronger and more lasting impression on young people. This is likely due to a combination of two factors. First, as the terror targeted participants at a youth camp, young people are more likely to identify with the victims, and fear that they or their peers may be at risk. Second, as the literature on socialization and generation effects states (Mannheim, 1952), watershed events may leave a stronger and more lasting imprint on adolescents than on adults; they are at pivotal, impressionable points in life at which core beliefs and value systems are not firmly established. If this is the case, which will only be confirmed or disproved some years from now, "generation Utøya"—a label sometimes applied to teenagers and young adults in Norway today—may carry with them the baggage of heightened alertness into adulthood.

In sum, there were only weak indications that the terror was a harbinger of a new culture of fear just after the attacks. In the following months, however, national concern rose somewhat, accompanied by (or maybe, as we shall see, caused by) an emerging distrust in the government's ability to effectively deal with terrorism. In particular, the terror seems to have made a lasting impression on young people.

Trust in Institutions

As discussed in the introduction, terrorist attacks frequently result in the population rallying around the government and core institutions. According to some authors, this is due to an elevated sense of fear in the population, which leads them to turn to the state for protection. The increase in levels of fear observed, however slight in international comparison, could lead to similar effects in Norway.

On the other hand, the initially high trust levels in Norway in relation to government might create other types of dynamics. One hypothesis might be that the terror attacks would lead to a breakdown in trust, given the fact that the government had not been able to protect the population against the attack. As pointed out by Chanley (2002), one important determinant of the people's trust in government is whether they perceive the government to be efficient in achieving its goals. In supporting this hypothesis, it might be pointed out that in time, the post 7/22 debate shifted from praise of solid political leadership after the attacks toward a decisively more critical stance toward the actions of that same leadership and other institutions prior to and during the terror. The responses show that people felt less confident that the government could effectively protect them against terror 10 months after the attacks than they did just after terror had struck.

An alternative hypothesis would be that the initial high trust in government might be mobilized and reinforced by the events of terror. If this is the case, institutional trust levels should remain high or even increase in the aftermath of the events. The initial political and public responses to the attacks make such a dynamic likely. In a pivotal statement made shortly after the attacks, the prime minister called for "more democracy and openness" in response to terrorism. Appeals such as this helped raise awareness that terror seeks to destroy trust, participation, and openness, and they spurred a national mobilization in defense of these values.

Using our data, we are able to examine how institutional trust levels changed directly following the attack, and how they developed in the 10-month period that followed. Table 14.2 shows levels of institutional trust before and after the attacks in separate population samples and the panel. The items are 5-point Likert scales ranging from no trust to very high trust (in institutions). We have recoded all items to run from 0 to 100 to ease interpretation.

Table 14.2 shows that trust in institutions rose substantially in the wake of the tragedy, and remained at a higher level than they were pre-July 22, even 10 months after the attacks (see also Wollebæk, Enjolras, Steen-Johnsen, & Odegaard, 2012, for a more in-depth discussion of results). Confidence in all institutions was significantly higher in May 2012 than it was the year before. The increase in support directly after the attacks was greatest when it came to political institutions—the Government and

Table 14.2. INSTITUTIONAL TRUST

Institutional trust	Population Samples: Comparisons of Means (*t* Tests)						Panel: GLM Repeated Measures (Pairwise Comparisons With Bonferroni Correction)					
	April 2011	August 2011	May 2012	t1-t2	t2-t3	t1-t3	April 2011	August 2011	May 2012	t1-t2	t2-t3	t1-t3
Municipal authorities	53.4	59.5	56.7	++	--	++	53.1	59.2	55.7	++	--	++
Parliament	55.8	65.1	60.3	++	--	++	54.3	63.5	59.6	++	--	++
Courts	70.9	76.2	76.5	++	n.s	++	70.9	75.0	76.0	++	n.s.	++
Government	53.5	64.6	58.9	++	--	++	52.3	63.6	59.7	++	--	++
Police	71.7	75.2	74.7	++	n.s.	++	71.4	74.5	72.7	++	-	++
Public administration	56.1	60.9	59.6	++	n.s.	++	55.5	60.9	57.5	++	--	++

Note: ++ Significant and positive at 99% level, + significant and positive at 95% level, – significant and negative at 95% level, -- significant and negative at 99% level.

the Parliament—for which scores normalized somewhat between August 2011 and May 2012. There was also increased trust in law enforcement and the judicial system, referring to the courts and the police, with no apparent decline in the months after the attacks. The increased trust in the police even 10 months after the attacks was remarkable considering the very high outset levels of trust and the increasingly outspoken criticism of the actions by the police during the attacks.

The substantial increase in institutional trust was paralleled by both higher interpersonal trust and a strengthened sense of community in the aftermath of 7/22 (not shown in the table). Levels of generalized trust rose from 6.2 to 6.9 between April and August 2011 on the standard 10-point scale juxtaposing "most people can be trusted" with "you can't be careful enough." In May 2012, levels were still significantly higher than they were prior to the attacks (at 6.5). Trust in those living in the local municipality, other Norwegians, people of different nationalities and people of other religions were all significantly higher 10 months after the atrocities than they were some months before the attacks, even though the figures had also normalized from even higher levels just after terror had struck. Trust in people of another religion increased more than any other trust form after the attacks. In April 2011, 46 percent trusted people of another religion "quite a lot" or "completely." In August, 56 percent expressed the same view. In May 2012, the proportion was still higher than prior to the attacks, at 55 percent. All percentages refer to the independent population samples. A possible cause for the increased trust in people of other nationalities and religions could be an effect of the atrocities being committed by a Christian, ethnic Norwegian when most people were much more wary of the prospect of Islamist terrorism.

In other words, there were weak indications of the "cognitive shutdown," including xenophobia and distrust, described as a common reaction to terror by Huddy et al. (2007). As many as 79 percent of the respondents said that Norway was characterized by more "community and togetherness" after the attacks, while 1 percent supported the opposite view. Even 10 months after the attacks, 63 percent still felt the sense of community and togetherness was strengthened, while only 2 percent felt it was weakened. Again, the sentiment was most pronounced among young people. Among those between the ages of 16 and 24, 88 percent responded that there was more community and togetherness just after the attacks, dropping to 75 percent in May 2012.

Altogether, the findings clearly show that values such as trust and national community were strengthened rather than weakened in the aftermath of 7/22, and that this effect had not fully dissipated almost a year later. This sentiment of togetherness, community and trust concurred alongside rallying around government institutions and a moderate elevation of fear levels.

Rallying with or without fear

The causes of this rallying effect remain unclear thus far. One interpretation is that elevated fear causes citizens to turn to the state for protection. This mechanism has been demonstrated in other contexts, most notably in post 9/11 United States (Sinclair & LoCicero, 2010). If this is the case, we would expect those who are most concerned about future terrorism to increase their trust in government the most. They would also become more willing to forego civil liberties.

An alternative interpretation would call attention to the fact that Norway constitutes a very different institutional setting; it is a country with a deeply rooted culture of state-friendliness and high institutional trust. This benevolent view of public institutions could work to strengthen the population's belief in the ability of public authorities to prevent new attacks. A positive view of the state occurs in combination with a culture of high interpersonal trust, where people tend to expect the best from others. The combination of both has had a prophylactic effect against widespread fear and concern. In this perspective, the rallying effect occurs as the state is considered to be extensions, or even carriers, of the core values of national community. Thus, the prevalent sentiment of togetherness evident in state-friendly Norway after July 22 included government institutions as well as fellow citizens. If this is the case, we would expect high trust in institutions to lead to a firm belief in the institutions' preventive capabilities, which, in combination with high generalized trust, would thwart fear.

Below, we test these two alternative accounts using Structural Equation Modeling (SEM) techniques. We start out by examining the first hypothesized dynamics, namely the notion that fear leads to increased institutional trust and the acceptance of foregoing civil liberties. With regard to the latter, the surveys allow us to examine changes in the acceptance of the surveillance of internet communication to prevent serious crime. This is a particularly salient question with regard to the terror committed on 7/22, as the perpetrator actively used the Internet and social media to gather information and communicate with people sharing his views. More vigilant surveillance of electronic communication could reduce the risk of extremist terrorism, but would also restrict individual freedom. The question posed juxtaposes two opposing statements on a 0–10 scale, namely "Government surveillance of Internet communication is necessary to prevent serious crime" (0) vs. "The Internet should be as free as possible from government surveillance" (10). The data show that public support for such measures did increase after the attacks. Before the attacks, the mean score on the index in the population sample was 4.96, in August 2011, the score was 4.76, and in May 2012, the mean value was 4.56. The change from April 2011 to May 2012 is significant at the 99 percent level.

The results of the SEM analysis are presented in Figure 14.2. The figure renders little support to the argument that the increased institutional trust is a result of fear. Rather, those who were least concerned about the possibility of a new terrorist attack on Norwegian soil directly after the attacks reported the greatest increase in institutional trust (standardized coefficient –.07, significant at 99 percent level). The stability coefficient for institutional trust is very high, at .77 and .76, indicating no sudden shift in who trusts the government before

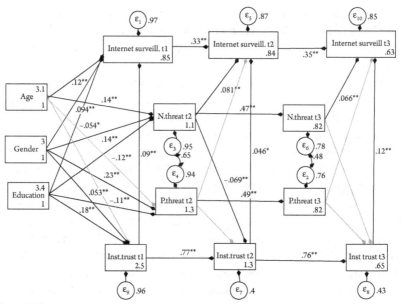

Figure 14.2:
Fear rallying model. SEM analysis.

Note: *Significant at 95% level, **significant at 99% level. Analysis based on panel respondents responding to all three surveys (N = 1612). t1 = April 2011, t2 = August 2011, t3 = May 2012. N.threat = National Threat. P.Threat = Personal Threat. Inst.trust = Institutional Trust. Insignificant coefficients are not printed and arrows are drawn in gray. Internet surveillance: Government surveillance of Internet communication is necessary to prevent serious crime (0) vs. the Internet should be as free as possible from government surveillance (10).

and after July 22. We do, however, find that perceived national (but not personal) threat is linked to increased acceptance of Internet surveillance at all three observation points. There is also a clear tendency toward those having the most trust in the government being the most willing to accept such surveillance. Although the increased trust in government does not appear to be driven by fear as such, fear of new attacks does seem to play a role in the acceptance of curbing individual liberties to prevent crime.

Figure 14.3 shows an SEM analysis of the second account discussed here. The results support the notion that high trust levels prior to 7/22 contributed to curbing fear after the attacks. High trust in institutions before the attacks strongly influenced the belief in the government's ability to prevent new atrocities after terror had struck. This belief is in turn significantly related to lower perceived national and personal threats. Institutional trust at t2 also predicts continued belief in the government's ability to prevent terror at t3. Furthermore, generalized trust also plays a role, both independently and in conjunction with institutional trust. Trust in other people is strongly related to trust in institutions—as mentioned, this relationship is stronger in the "state-friendly" Nordic countries than in most other countries—which contributes to the positive dynamics described earlier. Furthermore, levels of generalized trust prior to the attacks also predicted perceived threats on both a

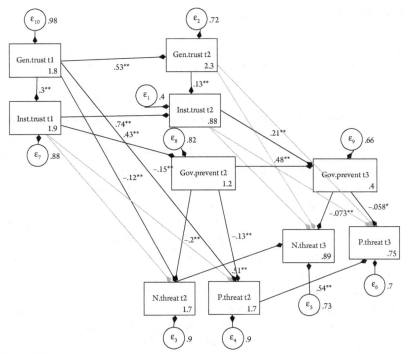

Figure 14.3:
The prophylactic effect of trust on fear.

Note: *Significant at 95% level, **significant at 99% level. Age, gender, and education included in model but removed from diagram to improve readability. Analysis based on panel respondents responding to all three surveys (N = 1612). t1 = April 2011, t2 = August 2011, t3 = May 2012. N.threat = National Threat, 4-point Likert scale. P.Threat = Personal Threat, 4-point Likert scale. Gov.prevent = Government will be able to prevent future attacks. Inst.trust = Institutional Trust. Institutional trust is a six-item additive index of trust in municipality, Parliament, government, the courts, the police, and public administration. Cronbach's α = .88 at t1, .89 at t2, .88 at t3. Insignificant coefficients are not printed and arrows are drawn in gray. Internet surveillance: Government surveillance of Internet communication is necessary to prevent serious crime (0) vs. the Internet should be as free as possible from government surveillance (10).

national and personal level post-7/22, independently of the relationship to institutional trust. Fear therefore seems to have been curbed by both the deep-rooted belief in the good intentions of others, as well as trust in the ability of the authorities to prevent future attacks.

In summary, the rallying behind public institutions that occurred in the wake of the terror attacks of 7/22 cannot be attributed to fear. Rather, those who express the strongest sense of fear after the attacks trusted public institutions (and other people) less to begin with. We found no evidence that this group increased their trust in institutions more than others; rather, the analysis pointed weakly in the opposite direction. Their concern seems to be at least partially connected to their lack of belief in the government's ability to protect them. In contrast, both strong generalized and institutional trust seem to have contributed to curbing the emergence of a culture of fear after the attacks.

DISCUSSION AND CONCLUSION

In this chapter, we have used the case of Norway to examine rallying effects in a high-trust society that is exposed to terror. In particular, we wanted to look at the relationship between fear and institutional trust within such a context. What we found contrasted with findings in a range of other studies: in the Norwegian case, increased institutional trust did not occur as a result of fear. On the contrary, high levels of institutional and interpersonal trust served as a prophylactic that stymied fear. The observed increase in institutional trust after 7/22 should therefore be interpreted as a re-mobilization of existing trust relationships affirming a sentiment of national togetherness, which also includes the public institutions. We have termed this dynamic "rallying without fear."

Even though this dynamic differs from the mechanisms that have been described in relation to the 9/11 terror attacks, we would still like to suggest that some shared lines of reasoning might be applied across cases. Following Chanley (2002), a major reason behind rallying is that the attention of the people shifts from domestic affairs to issues of homeland security, in a process in which the nation pulls together when faced with an external threat. This pulling together indicates an increased sense of belonging to some sort of "we" constituted by the nation. The factors that underpin this pulling together are a sense of fear *and* the belief that government can establish measures to provide protection against terror (Chanley, 2002; Sinclair & LoCicero, 2010). As pointed out in the Norwegian case, the sense of pulling together as a "we" is a crucial element of the Norwegian rallying process. In comparison with the situation after 9/11, however, there are two differences that need to be underscored: first, that pulling together was not primarily driven by fear, and second, that this was not a process of the people looking to the government for support, but rather a process of mobilization that spanned across the government and the people, which were conceived of as part of the same community. Thus, to understand the Norwegian rallying process, it is crucial to take its character of being a "state-friendly society" into account, in which the state is viewed as being part of society, rather than as a fully external entity.

However, even in this trusting and "state-friendly" context, the virtuous cycle is not perpetual and may be broken. As shown in our analysis in Figure 14.3, it largely hinges on the confidence in the protective capacities of core institutions. The belief that government will be able to prevent future attacks plays a crucial role in influencing perceived national and personal threats. If this belief is weakened, the prophylactic effect of institutional trust on fear may dissipate.

A pivotal point in the public debate occurred with the report issued by the 7/22 commission delivered in August 2012. The committee was designated to evaluate the actions of the political leadership, the police, the intelligence service, the emergency health care system, and the military before and during the attacks. The report was damning, especially with regard to the first three institutions. It concluded that the bomb attack against the central government building could have been avoided if only the security measures that had been agreed on had been sufficiently implemented, that the intelligence service could have picked up on the trails left by the perpetrator and that lives could have been saved had the police response been quicker and more efficient. The findings of the report clearly showed that the authorities did not sufficiently acknowledge the risk of terror, and left little reason to place a great deal of trust in their protective capabilities.

Although the commission was careful to point out that the open and trusting society was not to blame for what happened, but rather the failure to implement already passed plans, laws and measures into concrete action, the report still led to a degree of national introspection regarding the flipside of this trust culture: an unprotected society, low risk awareness, and naivety. The degree to which this will lead to a drop in institutional trust, and subsequently fear, in the long run, will depend on resolute action on the part of the authorities to rectify the misjudgments and shortcomings pointed out by the report. The first public reactions indicated confidence in the authorities' ability to reform; when the leading newspaper *Verdens Gang* called for the resignation of the prime minister in its editorial on August 14, 2012, polls showed that *Verdens Gang*'s demand was supported by only one in five voters (Granbo & Lydersen, 2012; Risa, 2012).

Another indication that the virtuous cycle may at one point be broken is found in the responses of the youth. Several indicators in our data indicate that the atrocities have been experienced in a magnified way by adolescents and young adults, who are still in their formative years. They express a greater sense of togetherness and community, but also stronger and growing concern and fear. Previous research has shown that terror attacks leave a more lasting impression on the value orientations of the young than among older generations (Sander & Putnam, 2010). The upshot of the 7/22 attacks may be the emergence of an understandably more apprehensive generation. This has not as yet impacted their trust in government in either direction, but the future direction of the relationship between institutional trust and fear in this generation is difficult to predict.

The nature of the terror that struck on 7/22—a solo terrorist apprehended directly after the attacks—may have made it easier to avoid a widespread sentiment of fear than would be the case in a situation characterized by a more continual threat, such as the one posed by al-Qaida in the United States after 9/11. Nonetheless, an "end of innocence"-effect of the atrocities on a nation that has been largely shielded from these types of events could have been expected, with increasing fear and distrust as likely consequences. Our results indicate a trust culture that has proved to be more robust and resilient than one might have feared. In the first 10 months after the attacks, the structures of interpersonal and institutional trust have become reinforced rather than weakened. However, the shifts in the ongoing public debate and the orientations of the young indicate that the final legacy of 7/22 is yet to be determined.

REFERENCES

Catterberg, G. & Moreno, A. (2005). The individual bases of political trust: Trends in new and established democracies. *International Journal of Public Opinion Research, 18*(1), 31–48.

Chanley, V. A. (2002). Trust in government in the aftermath of 9/11: Determinants and consequences. *Political Psychology, 23*(3), 469–481.

Eidelson, R. J., & Plummer, M. D. (2005). Self and nation: A comparison of Americans' beliefs before and after 9/11. *Peace and Conflict: Journal of Peace Psychology, 11*(2), 153–175.

Gaines, B. (2002). Where's the rally? Approval and trust of the President, Cabinet, Congress, and Government since September 11. *Political Science & Politics, 35*(3), 530–536.

Granbo, K., & Lydersen, T. (2012, August 14 2012). 7 av 10 vil ikke at Stoltenberg går [7 in 10 do not want Stoltenberg to go]. Retrieved from http://www.nrk.no/nyheter/norge/1.8281748

Huddy, L., Feldman, S., Capelos, T., & Provost, C. (2002). The consequences of terrorism: disentangling the effects of personal and national threat. *Political Psychology, 23*(3), 485–509.

Huddy, L., Feldman, S., & Weber, C. (2007). The political consequences of perceived threat and felt insecurity. *The Annals of the American Academy of Political and Social Science, 614*, 131–153.

Kuhnle, S., & Selle, P. (1992). Government and voluntary organizations: A relational perspective. In S. Kuhnle & P. Selle (Eds.), *Government and voluntary organizations* (pp. 1–33). Aldershot, UK: Avebury.

Lavanco, G., Romano, F., & Milio, A. (2008). Terrorism's fear: Perceived personal and national threats. *World Academy of Science, Engineering and Technology, 40*, 413–416.

Lerner, J. S., Gonzalez, R. M., Small, D. A., & Fischhoff, B. (2003). Effects of fear and anger on perceived risks of terrorism: A national field experiment. *Psychological Science, 14*(2), 144–150.

Lewis, C. W. (2000). The terror that failed: Public opinion in the aftermath of the bombing in Oklahoma City. *Public Administration Review, 60*(3), 201–210.

Mannheim, K. (1952). The problem of generation. [Das Problem der Generationen]. In P. Kecskemeti (Ed.), *Essays on the sociology of knowledge (pp.* 276–323). London, UK: Routledge & Kegan Paul.

Perrin, A. J., & Smolek, S. J. (2009). Who trusts? Race, gender and the September 11 rally effect among young adults. *Social Science Research, 38*(1), 134–145.

Prior, M. (2002). Political knowledge after September 11. *Political Science & Politics, 35*(3), 523–529.

Risa, E. (2012, August 14 2012). Bare en av fem mener Stoltenberg må gå [Only one in five thinks Stoltenberg should go], *Stavanger Aftenblad*. Retrieved from http://www.aftenbladet.no/nyheter/terror/Bare-n-av-fem-mener-Stoltenberg-ma-ga-3013728.html

Sander, T. H., & Putnam, R. D. (2010). Still bowling alone? The post-9/11 split. *Journal of Democracy, 21*(1), 9–16.

Sinclair, J., & LoCicero, A. (2010). Do fears of terrorism predict trust in government? *Journal of Aggression, Conflict and Peace Research, 2*(1), 57–67.

Skocpol, T. (2002). Will 9/11 and the War on Terror revitalize American civic democracy? *Political Science & Politics, 35*(3), 537–540.

SSB. (2011). IKT-bruk i husholdningene, 2. kvartal 2011 [Household use of ICT, 2nd quarter 2011]. Oslo, Norway: Statistisk Sentralbyrå [Central Bureau of Statistics].

Wollebæk, D. (2011). Norge og Nordens sosiale kapital i europeisk kontekst. In D. Wollebæk & S. B. Segaard (Eds.), *Sosial kapital i Norge* (pp. 51–77). Oslo, Norway: Cappelen Damm.

Wollebaek, D., Enjolras, B., Steen-Johnsen, K., & Ødegård, G. (2012). After Utøya—how a high trust society reacts to terror. *Political Science & Politics, 45*(1), 32–37.

APPENDIX

Table 14.3. GLM REPEATED MEASURES ANALYSIS OF BELIEF THAT GOVERNMENT WILL PREVENT FUTURE ATTACKS, PERCEIVED NATIONAL THREAT AND PERSONAL THREAT

	df	Government Will Prevent				National Threat				Personal Threat			
		Between-Subjects Effects		Within-Subjects Effects		Between-Subjects Effects		Within-Subjects Effects		Between-Subjects Effects		Within-Subjects Effects	
		F	Sig.	F	Sig.	F	Sig.	F	Sig.	F	Sig.	F	Sig.
Age (15–24, 25–49, 50+ y)	2	1.497	.224	1.558	.211	12.149	.000	4.469	.012	2.084	.125	7.384	.001
Gender	1	4.966	.026	1.135	.287	35.103	.000	1.295	.255	114.552	.000	2.356	.125
Education (primary, secondary, some university/college, long university/college)	3	4.950	.002	.724	.538	10.539	.000	1.290	.276	7.291	.000	.709	.547
Party identification (10 different parties, including "do not identify with any party")	9	18.969	.000	2.480	.008	1.317	.223	2.884	.002	.678	.729	2.093	.027

Note: All dependent variables were recoded to run from 0–100. Full results with parameter estimates available on request.

PART THREE

CHAPTER 15
The Politics of Terrorism Fears
RICHARD JACKSON

As other chapters in this volume and a great many studies have noted, the public fear of terrorism has remained at significant and elevated levels in a number of Western countries, but particularly the United States, for more than a decade since 9/11 (Celikpala & Ozturk, 2012). In itself, this provides a compelling reason to seek to understand the nature, causes, and effects of terrorism fear in contemporary society, particularly its collective effects on political structures and processes. However, in attempting to understand both the psychological dynamics and political consequences of contemporary terrorism fear, it is important to note that, in the first instance, individual fears do not occur in a vacuum and thus cannot be understood in isolation. Rather, they always take place in a specific social context (Daase & Kessler, 2007) and are in many ways constructed intersubjectively through interaction with the surrounding society and its cultural and political structures. At the very least, individual fears are interpreted and experienced within a specific social milieu characterized by collective norms, narratives, and discourses, which subsequently shapes their expression and character. Individual fears are also vulnerable to the influence of powerful social actors like the media and the actions of politicians and other kinds of opinion leaders. For example, an individual's particular fear of crime or antisocial behavior in Britain or America today cannot be fully understood in isolation from the broader culture of fear and frequent moral panics that have characterized Western society in the past few decades (Furedi, 2002; Glassner, 1999).

Second, it is important to note that social fears and moral panics, particularly in relation to acts of political violence and terrorism, are nothing new (Campbell, 1998; Carr, 2007; Mueller, 2005). In other words, political fear, including the fear of terrorism, has both a specific genealogy and a broader social history (Robin 2004). The history of fear forms an important part of the context shaping society's understandings of, and responses to, contemporary fears. That is, the ways in which society has framed, understood, and responded to particular kinds of fears in the past provides a set of interpretive frames, narratives, norms, cultural grammars, and repertoires of strategic action for understanding and responding to new fears as they arise in the present. Historical responses to the fear of violent anarchists, communists, the dangers of illegal drugs, rogue states, and weapons of mass destruction, for example, provide a ready-made set of interpretive frames and strategic responses, which can then be reflexively enacted to deal with new fears that arise (Campbell, 1998; Mueller, 2005; Robin, 2004). In short, social fears are not the result of objective evaluation, nor are they natural or inevitable. Rather, from an almost limitless array of potential threats and dangers in the world, the fears of a particular society at a given moment in time are contingent on a complex and dynamic set of cultural, political, and historical factors and preexisting conditions.

Third, social fears are never without important social and political consequences. As alluded to, not only does the response to social fear construct or reify specific frames, narratives, norms, and action repertoires—that is, social fears in the present form part of the process of constructing durable social structures, which then constrain and enable responses and actions in the future—but social fears can also provide opportunities for certain kinds of actors to pursue their agendas (Jackson, 2007; Mueller, 2006). At a material level, for example, the private security industry can directly profit from the manipulation and intensification of widespread fear of crime and insecurity. On the other hand, the political authorities can benefit from increased levels of approval, depending on how they are perceived to have dealt with sources of fear. In other words, social fears are experienced in the context of ongoing political struggles and competing interests, and play a key role in those political struggles; from this vantage point, they possess an inherent political dimension.

In this chapter, I attempt to provide a necessarily brief analysis of the politics of terrorism fear in Western societies in the period since 9/11. I begin by examining the cultural-political context in which 9/11 occurred and some of the ways in which this context shaped the resulting social fear and moral panic about the terrorism threat. Next, I briefly explore how the fear of terrorism became embedded and normalized in daily life through processes of cultural and discursive sedimentation, the spread of securitization and risk management practices, the consolidation of a "terrorism industry," and incorporation into the institutions of law and politics. The final section of the chapter examines the way in which terrorism fears can be, and frequently have been, exploited and manipulated for particular material and political interests. In the conclusion, I discuss the puzzling gap between the public's fear of terrorism and the actual risk of falling victim to terrorism, and explore what this tells us about the social construction of fear and the inherently political nature of terrorism fear. Although much of the analysis presented here refers to the politics of terrorism fears in American society particularly, as a growing number of studies suggest, very similar processes, although not always as intense, have nonetheless characterized many other Western countries (De Castella et al., 2009; Lee Koo, 2005).

THE CONTEXT OF CONTEMPORARY TERRORISM FEAR

The contemporary politics of terrorism fear cannot be fully understood in isolation from the social and political conditions within which it emerged and developed. It is important, therefore, to briefly outline the context of the 9/11 attacks and the genealogy of contemporary narratives and understandings of the terrorist threat. These two factors—existing social and political structures, and established understandings and narratives about terrorism—are central to understanding both the character and the high levels of terrorism fear in society and the kinds of security responses they have provoked by the authorities (Jackson, 2011).

As a number of studies demonstrate, the social context in which the 9/11 attacks occurred was characterized by, first, a pervasive and robust "culture of fear," particularly in relation to violent crime and other perceived threats to social order, such as illegal drugs, teenage mothers, road rage, Internet sex crimes, killer kids, cancer-causing cell phones, and so on (Furedi, 2002; Glassner, 1999). Second, sociologists had noted that Western societies were characterized by an evolving risk culture rooted in precautionary thinking (Beck, 1992), most visible in the spread of health and safety practices and the zero risk attitudes of public institutions, for example. Third, American society in particular had long been characterized by a minority but nonetheless significant conspiracy culture that reflected a range of broader ontological insecurities, such as distrust of big government and economic insecurity (Hofstadter, 1964; Knight, 2002; West & Sanders 2003). Popular conspiracy theories about the Kennedy assassination, the moon landing, the United Nations, Area 51, and others are examples of this persistent conspiracy culture. Fourth, American society had been characterized by regular moral panics over a disparate array of threats and dangers (Shafir & Schairer, 2012). For example, prominent political moral panics focusing on seemingly dangerous categories of people have included: the various "red scares" of the frontier confrontations with Native Americans, the Palmer Raids, and McCarthyism in the 1950s; the "brown scare" of German citizens during the two world wars; and the "yellow scare" of Japanese Americans in World War II that led to the incarceration of thousands of innocent Japanese people in concentration camps (Campbell, 1998).

More specific to the subject of this chapter, there had been a number of prior moral panics and social fears surrounding the threat of terrorist violence, which had socially and institutionally established a core set of interpretive frames, narratives, and programmatic responses to the perceived threat. For example, the wave of anarchist violence at the turn of the twentieth century had resulted in widespread fears surrounding the "infernal machines" of terrorism (Campbell, 1998; Carr, 2007). In the 1960s and 1970s, fears of communist terrorists were routinely expressed, particularly in relation to the conflicts in Vietnam and Latin America and the cold war more broadly (Winkler, 2006). Later, the Reagan administration declared the first "war on terrorism" and stated that it believed terrorism to be a major threat to modern civilization itself (Gold-Biss, 1994; Jackson, 2006; Wills, 2003). The result was that by the late 1980s, polls showed that a large majority of Americans believed that terrorism was one of the most serious security issues facing the nation, despite the fact that less than a dozen people had died at the hands of terrorists in America over the previous decade (Zulaika & Douglass, 1996). In other words, by the early 1990s, terrorism was already well established in anthropological terms as a modern cultural taboo—an object of fear, loathing, and censure—and American society existed in something of an ontological condition of "waiting for terror" (Zulaika & Douglass). This condition was reinforced by several high-profile terrorist attacks during the following decade, such as the first World Trade Center attack in 1993, the Tokyo sarin gas attack in 1995, the Oklahoma City terrorist attack in 1995, and the East African embassy bombings in 1998.

One of the main effects of these prior social fears and the responses they generated was the establishment in society of a whole series of norms, metaphors, narratives, and discourses—a kind of "deep cultural grammar" (Johnson, 2008; Katzenstein, 2003)—for interpreting and responding to the dangers posed by terrorism and political violence. Such beliefs were normalized and embedded in society through the media and entertainment culture, public political speech, academic research, and security practices, among others. By the time of the 9/11 attacks, therefore, it was widely accepted that not only was the whole world threatened by unpredictable terrorist violence, but there was a "new terrorism," which was driven by religious fanaticism, aimed at maximum casualties and destruction, would readily employ weapons of mass destruction, and which threatened the entire way of life of Western societies (Burnett & Whyte, 2005; Spencer, 2006; Winkler, 2006). At a more detailed level, terrorism was widely understood as a form of exceptional modern "evil" (Aune, 2003) practiced by psychologically deviant and deeply cruel individuals, who operated in hidden networks across the world and exploited the vulnerabilities of modern society. Terrorism, in other words, was understood as an unpredictable, potentially catastrophic threat by individuals and groups who could not be reasoned with. Metaphorically, it was viewed as a kind of deadly disease—a cancer and a scourge. Within the context of this preexisting cultural understanding of the dangers of terrorism, the 9/11 attacks and the way they were portrayed and represented by the media, the authorities and security experts, among others, appeared to confirm these preexisting fears and thus had the effect of reinforcing them.

From this perspective, it is therefore unsurprising that the terrorist attacks, particularly following media saturation of the horrific images for many months afterward, functioned to activate and intensify the whole raft of collective memories, fears, anxieties, and discourses about the dangers of terrorism, political violence, and insecurity. Variously, terrorism fear found expression in publically voiced concerns about the imminent possibility of further attacks, the threat of full-scale war by terrorists, invasion and infiltration by terrorists and other undesirables, the probability of attacks with weapons of mass destruction, the potential collapse of American society and the economy, conspiracy theories of U.S. government involvement in the attacks, terrorist infiltration into all aspects of U.S. society, and other similar narratives (Lustick, 2006; Mueller, 2006). As time went on, wider fears of the Islamicization of American society and cultural conflict with the Islamic world at a global level also developed and spread.

In short, from this perspective, the high levels of terrorism fear immediately following the 9/11 attacks are unsurprising. Not only were the attacks objectively horrific and rupturing of American self-understandings, but they also appeared to objectify existing social understandings of the terrorism threat, while at the same time activating and drawing on collective memories of previous social fears and moral panics. However, to understand why terrorism fears remained elevated and highly salient for a whole decade following the events, we also need to understand how they became embedded in social structures and institutions—in other words, how they were normalized.

THE NORMALIZATION OF TERRORISM FEAR

Partly, but not solely, as a consequence of the 9/11 attacks and the way in which the existing history and context served to amplify and intensify fears and anxieties about terrorism, terrorism fear became normalized across society in a number of specific ways. By "normalized," I mean that it became widely accepted and viewed as no more than commonsense among the public to fear terrorism at an ontological level, to adjust personal behavior to reduce risk and prepare for terrorist events, and to accept often intrusive security measures in everyday life as a necessary cost for security against terrorism. The widespread acceptance by the public of new security measures at airports or public sporting events is one small example of the normalization of terrorism fear.

First, following the 9/11 attacks there was a cultural and discursive burgeoning followed by a rapid sedimentation of the core narratives, metaphors, and discourses surrounding the terrorist threat across society. This can be seen in the tens of thousands of novels, films, television shows, comic books, video games, plays, websites, blogs, jokes, cartoons, artistic exhibitions, poetry, popular songs, children's books, and other texts that portrayed and reiterated scenarios of fanatical terrorists attacking Western cities with weapons of mass destruction or otherwise threatening massive destruction and loss of innocent life (Croft, 2006; Spigel, 2004). In addition to the entertainment industry, the news media played a particularly important role in reminding Americans almost daily about the dangers and threats posed by terrorism in America and around the world in its countless stories and reports, editorials, documentaries, interviews, and books relating to terrorism (Altheide, 2002, 2006; Chermak, 2003; Kaufmann, 2004). Related to this, soon after 9/11 the American retail sector launched numerous products designed to protect consumers from terrorism, such as home weapons-of-mass-destruction decontamination kits, parachutes for high-rise office workers, radiation detection kits, and the like. It also exploited terrorism fear as a means of advertising products, such as the call for patriotic unity and consumerism as a way of resisting terrorism (Croft, 2006; Heller, 2005; Silberstein, 2002). Other cultural institutions and social practices, including churches and religious bodies, comedy, tattoos, art, literature, email, and everyday conversation, were also important processes through which terrorism fear was reproduced, embedded, and normalized in American and Western societies.

Second, terrorism fear was normalized and consolidated through the widespread use of securitization and risk management practices which spread across many sectors of society, and which have since become an ingrained part of American (and Western) life and culture (Amoore & De Goede, 2005, 2008; Coaffee, O'Hare, & Hawkesworth 2009). For example, in addition to the security measures that are now accepted as normal and legitimate on public transport, at public events, in official public buildings, on university campuses, and in areas of life like banking, immigration and telecommunications, terrorism fear has become part of everyday life in America through the Department of Homeland Security (DHS) Threat Level Warnings (and its replacement system after January 2011) reported daily by the media, the Traveler Redress Inquiry Program (TRIPS) program, the trucker's Eyes of the Road program, Federal Emergency Management Agency publications such as the *Are You Ready?* booklet, and a great many more federal and local initiatives designed to enlist the public's help in security management. Similar public threat warning systems, community surveillance and reporting programs, and public information campaigns have been instituted and normalized in Australia, the United Kingdom, Canada, and elsewhere (Kampmark, 2004; Lee Koo, 2005). These daily reminders and public involvement in costly programs to detect and deal with terrorist threats functioned to normalize terrorism fear and maintain its salience for ordinary people.

Third, terrorism fear was normalized through the enactment of new legal measures and the institutionalization of counterterrorism agencies and procedures, including: the establishment of major new government departments like DHS that were specifically tasked with countering the terrorism threat; the enactment of new legislation such as the PATRIOT Acts; the adoption of a whole range of new security doctrines, action plans, strategic plans, surveillance and reporting programs, official reports, memos, operating procedures, and the like, all of which were designed to understand, deal with, and counter the perceived terrorist threat; and the reorganization and reform of the security services, policing, the military, the justice system, immigration, and the like to include counterterrorism measures as an important part of their remit (Croft, 2006; Jackson, 2011). Accompanying these institutionalized practices and measures, a whole language or discourse of the terrorism threat was articulated and consolidated (Jackson, 2005), which soon dominated the public language of political debate and speech-making in the institutions of government, the language and activities of lobby groups and advisory think tanks, academic institutions, and media experts. As before, this discourse expressed terrorism fear through narratives which emphasized the potentially catastrophic threat posed by terrorists, the unpredictability and ubiquity of terrorism, and the necessity of constant vigilance in detecting terrorist activity. In other words, through these myriad daily practices and activities, and their accompanying narratives and common understandings, these new laws, security practices, and institutions embodied terrorism fear, giving it a concrete external "reality" and a broad sense of legitimacy, thereby normalizing it.

A fourth important set of practices and institutions that functioned to normalize terrorism fear involves memorialization, or the collective remembering and commemoration of events and lives lost, particularly the 9/11 attacks and the War on Terror casualties in Iraq and Afghanistan. In virtually every town and city across America, in the media, and on nationally prescribed days, many of the core narratives and accepted understandings of the terrorism threat are rearticulated and collectively reenacted through public ceremonies in visual reminders like public monuments, or in works of art, collectables, photographic books and exhibitions, songs, poems, and the like. In many ways, these acts and processes of remembrance have functioned to construct "9/11" and its associated narratives in particular, as another "foundational myth" of American national identity, similar to the War of Independence and Civil War myths and to Pearl Harbor myths (Croft, 2006; Hughes, 2003; Silberstein, 2002). In terms of terrorism fears, they functioned to reinscribe accepted responses to social fears and threats, as well as play an important role in constantly reminding the public—or psychologically priming them—about the mortal dangers posed by terrorism.

Finally, terrorism fear has been normalized in part through the emergence and consolidation of a powerful "terrorism industry" (Lustick, 2006; Mueller, 2006). This refers to the large number of different actors involved in all aspects of counterterrorism, such as military contractors who supply weapons and services to the military, DHS, Federal Bureau of Investigation (FBI), and other state security institutions; private security companies that supply screening and investigative services, and a range of physical protection services; pharmaceutical firms that supply vaccines and decontamination kits in preparation for bioterrorism; information technology companies that provide data-mining software and services; and many other related actors. One study identified some 1271 government bodies and 1931 private contractor companies working on aspects of counterterrorism in the United States, employing nearly a million people and costing the taxpayer tens of billions of dollars annually (Pilkington, 2010). Similar terrorism industries have arisen in other Western countries such as the United Kingdom, Australia, Canada, and the European Union. The establishment of this industry and its integration into the national economy and political structures form an important part of the normalization of terrorism fear, not least through the millions of people employed in it.

In sum, these myriad social practices, processes, and institutions function to give expression to, and externalize terrorism fear, thus providing it with a concrete external reality and a sense of legitimacy. After all, so much activity and such large investment in human and material resources would not be made unless the danger was "real" and the fear fully justified. As such, these social practices wed terrorism fear to the daily activities of Americans, normalize it as an unquestioned part of everyday life, and incorporate it into the broader life patterns of society. In this way, terrorism fear becomes part of a shared understanding of the new "reality" in which potentially catastrophic terrorism is an ever-present threat. Merging with existing cultural understandings about related threats and dangers, terrorism fear becomes part of a collective "grid of intelligibility" (Milliken, 1999) through which to interpret new sources of fear and danger and decide on strategic responses. Importantly, terrorism fear is sustained in part by the way in which these social processes and activities simultaneously activate and alleviate fear in a continuous, self-reinforcing cycle. That is, they function to remind people of the threat, while also reassuring them of the security measures taken to protect them.

THE POLITICS OF TERRORISM FEAR

It is within this broader context—a preexisting history of social fears and established responses to them, and the spread and normalization of terrorism fear in everyday life—that the politics of terrorism fear operates. There are two important elements in the politics of terrorism fear.

First, in the process of normalizing terrorism fear and response across society, security and military institutions like the DHS, the Central Intelligence Agency, the FBI, and other similar organizations have come to acquire or reinforce a concrete set of material interests linked to the perpetuation and maintenance of terrorism fear (Mueller, 2006). That is, terrorism fear has become part of the political structure. A similar process occurred during the cold war in relation to fears of communism. For example, more than 180,000 employees in DHS now have careers in counterterrorism that depend on the continued widespread acceptance of the terrorist threat and the subsequent ongoing social commitment of resources to its control. Agencies like the military, DHS, and the CIA, moreover, now depend on counterterrorism for large parts of their annual budgets, as well as the increased prestige, recognition, and room to maneuver that goes along with taking responsibility for dealing with a serious threat like terrorism. Beyond this, as mentioned, other actors in the "terrorism industry," such as military contractors, private security companies, pharmaceutical firms ,and the like, now have direct material interests in terrorism fear.

In short, the normalization of terrorism fear has led to a situation where economic and security actors now have direct and ongoing financial, material, and nonmaterial interests in the maintenance of terrorism fear, and there is a large and powerful sector of the economy invested in providing services and materials for dealing with the threat it poses. The effect on the political system therefore is the creation of inbuilt material incentives and political-economic pressures to maintain jobs, careers, and profit levels for companies and their shareholders. In a political system where lobbyists and pressure groups play a key role in setting policy, the effect is to bring terrorism fear right to the heart of lobbying, media campaigning, and electoral and legislative politics. Thus, not only would it be difficult in terms of the widely accepted discourse and commonsense about the nature of the ongoing terrorist threat (i.e., existing social structures), but it would also be difficult in terms of economic and institutional structures (the political-economic system that has grown up around dealing with terrorism fear) for political leaders to downplay or reassure the public about the terrorist threat. The system and its structures are thus now part of the processes that maintain terrorism fear.

In addition, not unlike similar processes that occurred during the Cold War, the development of material interests in terrorism fear extends beyond the United States to encompass other international actors who have since developed their own embedded material and political interests in its maintenance (Keen, 2006). For example, states like the United Kingdom and Australia have also normalized and institutionalized terrorism threat narratives and embedded it within their security procurement programs, national security practices, and electoral and legislative politics (Kampmark, 2004; Lawrence, 2006; Lee Koo, 2005). A great many other countries and regions, particularly those of strategic interest to the United States, have also benefitted directly from U.S. military training and assistance programs, counterterrorism cooperation, and economic and political support (Keen, 2006; Keenan, 2010; Smith, 2010). Such support can create an incentive structure for states, particularly those that are weak or poor, in which the maintenance of a certain level of terrorism fear results in important military and security support. In other words, the political economy of terrorism fear has globalized beyond America and taken on some of the characteristics of the earlier Cold War system in which the fear of communism created a series of dependent material and political relationships.

In addition to the systemic pressures exerted by the political economy of terrorism fear, a second important element is the extent to which heightened social fears and moral panics present political elites with an opportunity—and a powerful temptation—to directly exploit social fear for political purposes and gains (Goodin, 2006; Jackson, 2007; Kassimeris, 2007). In the first place, as a growing number of studies demonstrate, using terrorism fear can be a successful and effective way for political leaders to "sell" policies and programs to the wider public (De Castella, McGarty, & Musgrove, 2009; McCulloch, 2004; McDonald & Merefield, 2010; Winkler, 2006). More specifically, in America, the United Kingdom, and elsewhere, terrorist fears have been exploited in pursuit of a range of often ideologically driven political projects, such as National Missile Defence, broader military rearmament, and expansion, establishing a military presence in new regions, promoting regime change, legitimizing the doctrine of preemptive war, controlling strategic sources of oil, and so on (Buckley & Singh, 2006; Callinicos, 2003; Colás & Saull, 2006; Mahajan, 2003). At the domestic level, terrorism fear has been used by political elites to try and justify and legitimize a wide range of projects, often only tangentially connected to terrorism, such as cutting welfare programs, increasing social surveillance, reducing and controlling immigration, banning opposition groups, promoting minority integration and multiculturalism, and many others.

More prosaically, terrorism fear can be readily used by political elites as a means of limiting and constraining broader forms of political dissent and opposition (Kassimeris, 2007), particularly for groups that are perceived as threatening to dominant economic or political interests. For example, terrorism fear has been used as a key strategy by agribusiness lobbyists and the FBI in the United States for suppressing and delegitimizing animal rights and environmental protest groups (Sorenson, 2009). More broadly, a recent study has argued that terrorism fear has been exploited by political elites in a variety of contexts as a form of counterrevolution or the ideologically articulated attempt to roll back legal and social advances, particularly for vulnerable groups (Shafir & Schairer, 2012). Certainly, in a number of states facing serious domestic opposition, including Russia, China, India, Zimbabwe, and many others, terrorism fear has been exploited as a means of suppressing and restricting oppositional political activity.

Related to this, terrorism fear can also function (or be used instrumentally) to distract the public from more complex and pressing social ills (Glassner, 1999; Woods, 2011), thereby inhibiting transformative or counter-hegemonic pressures. Actually, some fears are better than others for this purpose, because some fears— such as the fear of being without health care or meaningful employment—are not amenable to quick-fix solutions and carry the risk of policy failure. Terrorism fear, on the other hand, is ubiquitous, catastrophic, and fairly opaque, particularly to the degree that it relies on state control of secret information and a public imagination fuelled by disaster entertainment. There is also little risk that the authorities will be seen to fail; every subsequent terrorist attack can be readily construed as a vindication of previous official warnings. As a consequence, more pressing and complex social ills and threats to individual and social security, such as crime, gun control, urban poverty, lack of health insurance, and unsafe workplace conditions, among many others, can be neglected while the government invests vast human and material resources in security and counterterrorism.

Some of the specific narrative techniques which political elites have employed over the past decade for stoking terrorism fears include, among others, exaggeration and overinflation of the terrorist threat; continuous repetition in public debate and the media of the purported dangers posed by terrorism; treating isolated incidents as longer-term and more pervasive trends; misdirection and false correlations between factors, such as the purported links between illegal drugs or animal rights activism and terrorism; employing precautionary, capability-based reasoning and emphasizing the possible rather than the probable; knowledge subjugation of contradictory perspectives and facts; treating terrorism as an external and unpredictable risk rather than a political conflict; and employing alarmist and dehumanizing metaphors and cultural narratives, such as terrorism as cancer, poison, scourge, and a form of evil (Daase & Kessler, 2007; Glassner, 2004; Jackson, 2005, 2012; Steuter & Wills, 2010).

Moreover, terrorism fear is an ideal tool for elite exploitation, in part because the securitization process is inherently depoliticizing. That is, declaring terrorism to be an issue of national security transforms it from an issue of normal political debate to an exceptional problem placed in the hands of experts and security technicians. Political opponents who object to the adoption of particular measures can be easily accused of endangering the nation by their opposition, and therefore as unpatriotic. In other words, terrorism fear provides an ideal means of exerting "rhetorical coercion" (Krebs & Jackson, 2007) or "representational force" (Mattern, 2001) against opponents of government policies and measures. Additionally, research suggests that fear produces several social effects that are advantageous to political elites. For example, it makes people more willing to exchange civil liberties for security and more willing to spend government resources on homeland security (Ridout et al., 2008). It also activates authoritarian tendencies, deference to leaders, in-group identification and "rally-around-the-flag" effects, intolerance for dissent, and increased patriotism (Pyszczynski, 2004; Woods, 2011).

However, beyond some of these direct instrumental uses of terrorism fear by political elites, the politics of fear has another fundamental political function, namely, constructing and sustaining a sense of collective identity. It is basic psychology that groups unify in the face of external danger. For sizeable and diverse collectivities such as states, the existence of abiding and multiple exogenous threats is indispensable for bolstering the unity of the "imagined community" (Anderson, 1983). From this perspective, security threats do not necessarily exist independently of states; rather, states deliberately construct and exploit them for the purposes of disciplining the domestic sphere and sustaining national unity. Creating and maintaining an ever-present "discourse of danger"—maintaining terrorism fear, in this case—is therefore, one of the constitutive functions of foreign policy, designed to enforce inside/outside, self/other boundaries and thereby construct or "write" collective identity (Campbell, 1998; Pyszczynski, 2004). More broadly, terrorism fear can be used by elites to "hail" core identity narratives (Jackson & McDonald, 2009), a practice noted in America, Australia, and the United Kingdom in particular.

In a related sense, elites believe that fear can act as a tool of political renewal by providing an alternative sense of purpose and establishing a foundation for the national interest (Robin, 2004). This is one reason why the political manipulation and exploitation of fear has such a long genealogy; from the "red scares" of the American frontier to McCarthyism and the post-9/11 war on terror, political fear has been deployed by elites to provide meaning and purpose, often during periods of destabilizing social transformation. Creating a new national project based on a socially constructed fear of an alien "other" (such as terrorists) is, moreover, much easier than attempting to define a positive moral vision for society—especially in an era defined by the "end of ideology," "risk society," and an accompanying elite crisis of confidence. Importantly, this means that in addition to a political economy of terrorism fear, there is also a moral economy of terrorism fear: it is self-legitimating and provides collective purpose and direction during moments of self-doubt, such as that created by the 9/11 attacks. From this perspective, the current period of terrorism fear, like its predecessor, the Cold War, functions as "a project of political and cultural reconstruction" for the body politic (Robin, 2004, p. 37).

In sum, the past decade has witnessed political leaders in a variety of countries exploiting terrorism fear directly or opportunistically in a number of different ways and for a variety of purposes. The root of this politics of terrorism fears lies in its systemic political-economic basis, as well as the wilful actions of political elites. Importantly, in the final analysis, an important consequence of terrorism fear—and social fear more broadly—is to perpetuate elite rule and established social hierarchies by reifying existing power structures and controlling domestic challenges (Oliverio, 1997; Robin, 2004).

CONCLUSION

It was always highly likely that the 9/11 attacks would lead to the intensification and spread of terrorism fear and be responded to with militarism abroad and securitization at home (Jackson, 2011). This is because, in addition to the objective psychological effects of the attacks themselves, the existing cultural context and social structures made it unlikely to be experienced and interpreted in any other way. From this perspective, it was also always likely that political leaders would respond with a "War on Terror" and take the opportunity to exploit the public's fears for political gain. However, this is not meant to imply that such a response was predetermined or inevitable. Societies—and political leaders—always face choices about what dangers will be treated as security threats, and how they will interpret and respond to such threats and the fears they generate; structures, even powerful social and economic ones, do not entirely trump the agency of actors.

Unfortunately, the politics of terrorism fear in the decade since 9/11 has resulted in what many judge to be unnecessary overreaction (Mueller, 2005, 2006), particularly in relation to the actual risk posed by terrorism, and a series of highly destructive effects and costs (Cole, 2007; Jackson et al., 2011). For example, apart from the direct human costs of the hundreds of thousands of people killed and injured in wars and military interventions in Iraq, Afghanistan, Pakistan, Yemen, and elsewhere, terrorism fears have led to the expenditure of trillions of dollars, often wastefully and certainly representing incalculable opportunity costs in relation to healthcare, education, development assistance, road safety, and many other socially progressive projects. It has also resulted in the demonstrable erosion of international human rights law, the spread of practices such as extrajudicial killing, extraordinary rendition, torture and political repression, and legal changes that have restricted habeas corpus, limited free speech, and undermined constitutionally protected rights (Foot, 2005; Greenberg, 2006; Mayer, 2005; Snow, 2003). Socially, it has led to a rise in hate crimes, widespread and growing Islamophobia, the destruction of intercommunal trust and social capital, and the construction of "suspect communities" (Fekete, 2004; Hillyard, 1993; Woods, 2011). Arguably, and more broadly, it has also resulted in the increased militarization of society and foreign policy, the greater securitization of social life, the concentration of power in the executive, and the perpetuation of a state of exception in which norm violation is tolerated. More broadly, the normalization of terrorism fear could be argued to have undermined democratic deliberation, as fear is inherently antithetical to democratic participation (Goodin, 2006; Robin 2004).

In addition to noting the numerous negative consequences of the politics of terrorism fear, there are three important conclusions to be drawn from the analysis presented in this chapter. First, social fears, including terrorism fear, are socially constructed in a dynamic and self-reinforcing social system. This is not to deny that fears are not rooted in real-world dangers and experiences, but simply to note that what a society fears at a given moment may not necessarily represent objective conditions of significant danger. Instead, it may be the result of a combination of historically established social structures, an isolated but nonetheless precipitating event, the role of the media and other social actors, and the deliberate actions of political leaders. For example, it is well known that in the 1990s, fear of crime increased in America at the same time as reported crime levels decreased, in part because at the same time that crime levels declined, media coverage of crime disproportionally increased (Glassner, 2004; Mueller, 2005). Similarly, as a growing number of scholars assert, levels of terrorism fear in Western societies are far out of proportion to the risks of dying at the hands of terrorism, regardless of which method or approach is used to measure the level of risk (Jackson et al., 2011; Lustick, 2006; Mueller, 2006). As Mueller (2005, p. 220) notes, "Outside of 2001, fewer people have died in America from international terrorism than have drowned in toilets." Comparatively, we might also note the ways in which handguns have resulted in consistently significant levels of fatalities in America over many decades (more than a million since 1965), but have never resulted in a moral panic or elevated fears of gun ownership, particularly in comparison to the current terrorism moral panic (Shafir & Schairer, 2012). The simple fact is that a great many other things—heart disease, auto accidents, suicide, domestic violence, legal medicines, and even bathtubs—are more likely to kill Western citizens than a terrorist attack.

Second, social fears are deeply political, and we cannot hope to understand them fully outside of the social and political context in which they arise, the material and political interests they often generate, and the ways in which they can be, and often are exploited and manipulated for various ends. In particular, the different ways in which terrorism fears have played out over the past ten years of war on terror has been highly politicized, with, as noted, a great many often deleterious political and social effects.

Finally, this chapter reminds us that political leaders play a central role in mediating, managing and constructing social fears, not least because of the symbolic social position they occupy. Particularly in times of perceived social crisis, society looks to political leaders for interpretive frames, guidance, assurance, and policy programs that can deal with the perceived threat. Although highly constrained by the existing social structures and history of dealing with previous social fears, they nonetheless retain the necessary agency to choose a path that will either help to moderate and reduce fear, or stoke and manipulate it further for political gain.

In short, in seeking to understand terrorism fear we cannot go past the role of politics and political leaders.

REFERENCES

Altheide, D. (2002). *Creating fear: News and the construction of crisis*. Hawthorne, NY: Walter de Gruyter.
Altheide, D. (2006). *Terrorism and the politics of fear*. Lanham, MD: Alta Mira Press.
Amoore, L., & De Goede, M. (2005). Governance, risk and data surveillance in the War on Terror. *Crime, Law and Social Change, 43*, 149–173.
Amoore, L., & de Goede, M. (2008). *Risk and the War on Terror*. London, UK: Routledge.
Anderson, B. (1983). *Imagined communities: Reflections on the spread of nationalism*. London, UK: Verso.
Aune, J. (2003). The argument from evil in the rhetoric of reaction. *Rhetoric & Public Affairs, 6*(3), 518–522.
Beck, U. (1992). *Risk society: Towards a new modernity*. London, UK: Sage.
Buckley, M., & Singh, R., Eds. (2006). *The Bush Doctrine and the War on Terrorism: Global responses, global consequences*. London, UK: Routledge.
Burnett, J., & Whyte, D. (2005). Embedded expertise and the new terrorism. *Journal for Crime, Conflict and the Media, 1*(4), 1–18.
Callinicos, A. (2003). *The new Mandarins of American power*. Cambridge, UK: Polity Press.
Campbell, D. (1998). *Writing security: United States foreign policy and the politics of identity*, Revised edition. Manchester, UK: Manchester University Press.
Carr, M. (2007). *The infernal machine: A history of terrorism*. New York: Free Press.
Celikpala, M., & Ozturk, D. (2012). The only thing we have to fear: Post 9/11 institutionalization of in-security. *Uluslararasi Iliskiler, 8*(32), 49–65.
Chermak, S. (2003). Marketing fear: Representing terrorism after September 11. *Journal for Crime, Conflict and the Media, 1*(1), 5–22.
Coaffee, J., O'Hare, P., & Hawkesworth, M. (2009). The visibility of (in)security: The aesthetics of planning urban defences against terrorism. *Security Dialogue, 40*(4–5), 489–511.
Colás, A., & Saull, R., Eds. (2006). *The War on Terrorism and the American empire after the Cold War*. London, UK: Routledge.
Cole, D. (2007). *Less safe, less free: Why we are losing the War on Terror*. New York, NY/London, UK: The New Press.
Croft, S. (2006). *Culture, crisis and America's War on Terror*. Cambridge, UK: Cambridge University Press.
Daase, C., & Kessler, O. (2007). Knowns and unknowns in the "War on Terror": uncertainty- and the construction of danger. *Security Dialogue, 38*(4), 411–434.
De Castella, K., McGarty, C., & Musgrove, L. (2009). Fear appeals in political rhetoric about terrorism: An analysis of speeches by Australian Prime Minister Howard. *Political Psychology, 30*(1), 1–26.
Fekete, L. (2004). Anti-Muslim racism and the European security state. *Race & Class, 46*(1), 3–29.
Foot, R. (2005). Collateral damage: Human rights consequences of counter-terrorist action in the Asia-Pacific. *International Affairs, 81*(2), 411–425.
Furedi, F. (2002). *Culture of fear: Risk-taking and the morality of low expectation*, Revised Edition. London, UK: Continuum.
Glassner, B. (1999). *The culture of fear: Why Americans are afraid of the wrong things*. New York, NY: Basic Books.

Glassner, B. (2004). Narrative techniques of fear mongering/ *Social Research, 71*(4), 819–826.
Gold-Biss, M. (1994). *The discourse on terrorism: Political violence and Subcommittee on Security and Terrorism 1981–1986*, New York, NY: Peter Lang.
Goodin, R. (2006). *What's wrong with terrorism?* Cambridge, UK: Polity Press.
Greenberg, K., Ed. (2006). *The torture debate in America*. Cambridge, UK: Cambridge University Press.
Heller, D., Ed. (2005). *The selling of 9/11: How a national tragedy became a commodity*. Basingstoke, UK: Palgrave.
Hofstadter, R. (1964). The paranoid style in American politics. *Harpers Magazine*, November.
Hillyard, P. (1993). *Suspect community: People's experience of the prevention of terrorism acts in Britain*. London, UK: Pluto.
Hughes, R. (2003). *Myths America lives by*. Urbana and Chicago, IL: University of Illinois Press.
Jackson, R. (2005). *Writing the war on terrorism: Language, politics and counterterrorism*. Manchester, UK: Manchester University Press.
Jackson, R. (2006). Genealogy, ideology, and counter-terrorism: Writing wars on terrorism from Ronald Reagan to George W. Bush Jr. *Studies in Language & Capitalism, 1*, 163–193.
Jackson, R. (2007). Playing the politics of fear: Writing the terrorist threat in the War on Terrorism. In G. Kassimeris, Ed. *Playing politics with terrorism: A user's guide* (pp. 176–202). New York, NY: Columbia University Press.
Jackson, R. (2011). Culture, identity and hegemony: continuity and (the lack of) change in US counter-terrorism policy from Bush to Obama. *International Politics, 48*(2/3), 390–411.
Jackson, R., Jarvis, L., Gunning, J., & Breen Smyth, M. (2011). *Terrorism: A critical introduction*. Basingstoke, UK: Palgrave Macmillan.
Jackson, R., & McDonald, M. (2009). Constructivism, US foreign policy and the "War on Terrorism." In I. Parmar, L. Miller, & M. Ledwidge, Eds. *New directions in US foreign policy* (pp. 18–31). London, UK: Routledge.
Johnson, H. (2008). Ritual, strategy and deep culture in the Chechen National Movement. *Critical Studies on Terrorism, 1*(3), 321–342.
Kampmark, B. (2004). How to read an anti-terrorist kit: LOFA and its implications for Australian identity and security. *Journal of Intercultural Studies, 25*(3), 287–301.
Kassimeris, G., Ed. (2007). *Playing politics with terrorism: A user's guide*. New York, NY: Columbia University Press.
Katzenstein, P. (2003). Same war-different views: Germany, Japan and counter-terrorism. *International Organization, 57*(4), 731–760.
Kaufmann, C. (2004). Threat inflation and the failure of the marketplace of ideas. *International Security, 29*(1), 5–48.
Keen, D. (2006). War without end? Magic, propaganda and the hidden functions of counter-terror. *Journal of International Development, 18*, 87–104.
Keenan, J. (2010). Africa unsecured? The role of the global War on Terror in securing US imperial interests in Africa. *Critical Studies on Terrorism, 3*(1), 27–47.
Knight, P., Ed. (2002). *Conspiracy nation: The politics of paranoia in postwar America*. New York, NY: New York University Press, 2002.
Krebs, R., & Jackson, P. (2007). Twisting tongues and twisting arms: The power of political rhetoric. *European Journal of International Relations, 13*(1), 35–66.
Lawrence, C. (2006). *Fear and politics*, Carlton North, UK: Scribe.
Lee Koo, K. (2005). Terror Australis: Security, Australia and the "War on Terror." *Borderlands e-Journal, 4*(1).
Lustick, I. (2006). *Trapped in the War on Terror*. Philadelphia, PA: University of Pennsylvania Press.
Mahajan, R. (2003). *Full spectrum dominance: U.S. Power in Iraq and beyond*. New York, NY: Seven Stories Press.

Mattern, J. (2001). The power politics of identity. *European Journal of International Relations*, 7(3), 349–397.

Mayer, J. (2005). Outsourcing torture: The secret history of America's "extraordinary rendition" program. *The New Yorker*, February 14, 2005. Retrieved from http://www.newyorker.com/archive/2005/02/14/050214fa_fact6

McCulloch, J. (2004). National (in)security politics in Australia: Fear and the federal election. *Alternative Law Journal*, 29(2), 87–91.

McDonald, M., & Merefield, M. (2010). How was Howard's war possible? Winning the war of position over Iraq. *Australian Journal of International Affairs*, 64(2), 186–204.

Milliken, J. (1999). The study of discourse in international relations: A critique of research and methods. *European Journal of International Relations*, 5(2), 225–254.

Mueller, J. (2005). Simplicity and spook: Terrorism and the dynamics of threat exaggeration. *International Studies Perspectives*, 6, 208–234.

Mueller, J. (2006). *Overblown: How politicians and the terrorism industry inflate national security threats and why we believe them.* New York, NY: The Free Press.

Oliverio, A. (1997). The state of injustice: The politics of terrorism and the production of order. *International Journal of Comparative Sociology*, 38(1–2), 48–63.

Pilkington, E. (2010). America's secret army: How the "War on Terror" created a new industry. *The Guardian*, July 20, 2010. Retrieved from http://www.guardian.co.uk/world/2010/jul/19/us-spies-triple-since-2001

Pyszczynski, T. (2004). What are we so afraid of? A Terror Management Theory perspective on the politics of fear. *Social Research*, 71(4), 827–848.

Ridout, T., Grosse, A., & Appleton, A. (2008). News media use and American's perceptions of global threat. *British Journal of Political Science*, 38, 575–593.

Robin, C. (2004). *Fear: The history of a political idea*. Oxford, UK: Oxford University Press.

Shafir, G., & Schairer, C. (2012). The War on Terror as political moral panic. In G. Shafir, E. Meade, & W. Aceves, Eds. *Lessons and legacies of the War on Terror: From moral panics to permanent war.* Abingdon, UK: Routledge.

Silberstein, S. (2002). *War of words: Language, politics and 9/11*. London, UK: Routledge.

Smith, M., Ed. (2010). *Securing Africa: Post 9-/11 discourses on terrorism*. Aldershot, UK: Ashgate.

Snow, N. (2003). *Information war: American propaganda, free speech and opinion control since 9-11.* New York, NY: Seven Stories Press.

Sorenson, J. (2009). Constructing terrorists: Propaganda about animal rights. *Critical Studies on Terrorism*, 2(2), 237–256.

Spencer, A. (2006). Questioning the concept of "new terrorism." *Peace, Conflict & Development*, 8, 1–33.

Spigel, L. (2004). Entertainment wars: Television culture after 9/11. *American Quarterly*, 56(2), 235–270.

Steuter, E., & Wills, D. (2010). "The vermin have struck again": Dehumanizing the enemy in post 9/11 media representations. *Media, War & Conflict*, 3(2), 152–167.

West, H., & Sanders, T. (2003) *Transparency and conspiracy: Ethnographies of suspicion in the new world order*. Durham, NC: Duke University Press.

Woods, J. (2011). The 9/11 effect: Towards a social science of the terrorist Threat. *The Social Science Journal*, 48, 213–233.

Wills, D. (2003). *The first war on terrorism: Counter-terrorism policy during the Reagan Administration.* Lanham, MD: Rowman & Littlefield.

Winkler, C. (2006). *In the name of terrorism: Presidents on political violence in the post-World War II Era.* Albany, NY: State University of New York Press.

Zulaika, J., & Douglass, W. (1996). *Terror and taboo: The follies, fables, and faces of terrorism.* London, UK: Routledge.

CHAPTER 16
Constructing Psychological Terror Post 9/11

DAVID L. ALTHEIDE

This chapter examines how mass media reports about crime and terrorism in the United States, especially domestic terrorism threats, have been purposefully managed by police agencies to promote fear and support for heightened surveillance to protect citizens from risks. I argue that terrorism fears and what I will discuss as a "discourse of fear" were grounded in decades of mass media propaganda about "fear of crime," and that political discourse after 9/11 promoted the politics of fear. My comments are informed by three books that have examined the impact of mass media messages about fear, crime, and terrorism on mass psychology and public policy: *Creating Fear: News and the Construction of Crisis* (Altheide, 2002), *Terrorism and the Politics of Fear* (Altheide, 2006), and *Terror Post-9/11 and the Media* (Altheide, 2009).

These works argue that (1) the use of the word *fear* has increased in news reports and popular culture; (2) this increase is due to the widespread use of an organizational entertainment format for selecting, organizing and presenting information; (3) this widespread use of fear reflects a pervasive "discourse of fear," or the pervasive communication, symbolic awareness, and expectation that danger and risk are a central feature of everyday life; (4) this discourse links emotions of everyday life to organizational control and surveillance; (5) political leaders rely on the politics of fear, which refers to the promotion and use of audience beliefs and assumptions about danger, risk and fear in order to achieve certain goals; and (6) the propaganda of fear has promoted terrorism as a world condition, and this has significantly altered social institutions and public life. These points will be illustrated with a discussion of how decades of crime news enabled politicians to enact draconian laws and policies that promoted more social control and surveillance, while promising to protect citizens.

Fear is part of our everyday discourse, even though we enjoy unprecedented levels of health, safety, and life expectancy. Popular culture's promotion of fear of crime and violence preceded the preoccupation with threats of terrorism. Entertaining news or "infotainment" promotes fear as a way to connect emotionally with audiences. Crime reporting, especially about violent attacks and homicides, promotes fear in audiences, and dominates local newscasts and newspapers in the United States, even though the crime rate has fallen for nearly two decades. Television shows stress violence and danger. News reports are merging with television "reality programs" and crime dramas "ripped from the front pages," which in turn provide templates for looking at everyday life (Cavender, 2004; Fishman & Cavender, 1998).

Stories of assaults and kidnappings that dominate headlines—even when false or greatly distorted—make it difficult for frightened citizens to believe that families and relatives are more dangerous to children than strangers and that schools are one of the safest places in American society. Repetitious news reports that make connections between fear, children, schools, and suspected assailants who fit stereotypes are easy to accept even when they are false. Katheryn Russell's (1998) study of 67 publicized racially tinged hoaxes between 1987 and 1996 documents how story tellers frame their accounts in social identities that are legitimated by numerous reports and stereotypes of marginalized groups (e.g., racial minorities). For example, in 1990 a George Washington University student falsely reported that another student had been raped by two black men with "particularly bad body odor," in order to "highlight the problems of safety for women."

Emotions and Media Logic

The mass media and popular culture cultivate the emotions of fear, anger, dread, and revenge by making events and issues personally relevant or threatening. The mass media operate with media logic, or the way in which the grammar, syntax, and symbolic representations are discursively organized to present simple narratives that connect with basic cultural meanings (Altheide & Snow, 1979). Advertisers have long recognized that striking a "responsive chord" in audiences is key to the communication process (Ewen & Ewen, 1992; Jackall & Hirota, 2000; Schwartz, 1973). The mass media construct, frame, and amplify fear through entertainment formats and programming that define situations for various audiences. This developed through two processes: First, there was competition for the news market: News organizations adapted and expanded popular culture's entertainment formula to attract readers and viewers—sex, fear, and humor were consistent with an emerging media logic that made newswork more predictable. Guided by this media logic, newsworkers would seek out events and topics that could be easily framed as fearful and, therefore, very relevant to viewers. News sources and managers of news events, including politicians, quickly learned how to frame and cast their favorite topics in ways that could be presented in entertaining ways, including fear, victimization, crisis, etc.

Fear is a dominant emotion that has been cultivated as part of an entertainment format by the mass media and popular culture. The long-time association of fear with crime news was strengthened with numerous news reports about drug wars, random violence, and, particularly, threats to children. Such reports continued regardless of actual crime trends, and over time constituted a discourse of fear, which may be defined as the pervasive communication, symbolic awareness, and expectation that danger and risk are a central feature of the everyday life. Officials and other news sources recognized the importance of fear for media logic and began to adjust messages and frame issues that would resonate fear and urgency. Mass-mediated citizens gradually permitted officials to take action that would control the source of fear (e.g., criminals, terrorists). Officials became more adept at fashioning policies and programs (e.g., mandatory life sentences) (Grimes, 2007) based on an emerging politics of fear.

Public perceptions of problems and issues (the texts they construct from experience) incorporate definitions, scenarios, and language from news reports (Altheide & Snow, 1991; Bennett, 1988; Comstock, 1980; DeFleur & Ball-Rokeach., 1982; Ericson, 1995; Ferraro, 1995; Snow, 1983). Emphasizing fear, danger, and threat strikes a powerful chord that can encourage audiences to support programs and policies to curtail crime as well as terrorism.

> "Because the media often distort crime by over representing more severe, intentional, and gruesome incidents, the public overestimates its frequency and often misperceives reality." (Heath & Gilbert., 1996 p. 371)

Audiences are told dramatic institutional narratives about fear and threats to their lives and social order. News narratives promote challenges to institutional forces that are dedicated to protecting us. The strongest attacks are against individual criminals that harm us and government agencies that fail to protect us from individual threats. These narratives are captured in reports about crimes that are presumed to be more or less motivated by drugs and/or greed (Surette, 1998). There has been an increase in such narratives since the late 1990s, but this has increased since the 9/11 attacks. Ericson (2007) argued that neoliberal governments, in particular, promoted insecurity and risk directly and indirectly by offering programs and policies to protect citizens, mainly from crime, but also terrorists—internal and external, with an emphasis on surveillance, including the use of television programs such as "real crime programs," to encourage citizen awareness and participation in surviving numerous threats. Such programming serves to transform routine harms and inconveniences into broader threats that are consistent with the discourse of victimization and abuse. One consequence was to heighten citizen-audience fears, but another was to increase criminalization by adding more rules and potential violations (i.e., disobeying more security personnel and rules; some violent acts that occur in schools have been recast as acts of terror). Since 9/11, we see more crimes cast as versions of terrorism in which victims are said to be terrorized.

Fear and crisis were other ways to capture news attention within the new bounds of media logic. When it came to crime, television news could connect with viewers emotionally by stressing individual cases of heroism or deviance/crime because these were easier to cover visually and could be tailored to simple cultural narratives about good/evil, strength/weakness, etc. (Cavender, 2004; Cavender & Bond-Maupin, 1993; Surette, 1998). Moreover, the crime news focuses on individual crimes of violence, often threatening children. Social conditions, including differential police enforcement against poor and minorities, are seldom presented. Less common are reports about corporate/business crime and state crime. Thus, over time, news comes to be defined as "crime news," and other political and civic information receives less coverage and public interest declines in the noncrime aspects of social life. This is best illustrated with crime news that dominates "local news" coverage in the United States (Surette, 1998), as well as the United Kingdom and more Italian news as well (Forti & Bertolino, 2004).

The world of popular culture and news stressing crime and victimization promotes the pervasive awareness of "victimage" that is easily cultivated by officials who respond to terrorist acts. Victims abound in American life. Victims are but the personal side of crisis; a crisis is where victims reside (Chermak, 1995; Chiricos, Eschholz, & Gertz, 1997; Dubber, 2002; Ferraro, 1995; Warr, 1987). A personal crisis may affect "one victim," but more generally "crisis" refers to "social crisis," involving numerous people. All take place in a time of fear. All of this requires that citizens have information and constant reminders of the pitfalls and hazards of life, whether potential or realized (Ericson & Haggerty, 1997). News reports, talk shows, news magazine shows, and a host of police and "reality crime dramas" seem to proclaim that everybody is a victim of something, even though they may not know it. The notion that "life is hard" and that things do not always work out the way we would like seems to be lost on popular culture audiences who clamor for "justice," "revenge," and, of course, redemption, often in the form of monetary rewards. And it is not just in the United States. Prominent personalities in other countries seem to celebrate victimhood.

> It is in the USA that victimhood is most developed as an institution in its own right... .
> Victimhood is one of the central categories of the culture of abuse... Celebrities vie with one another to confess in graphic detail the painful abuse they suffered as children. The highly acclaimed BBC interview with Princess Diana symbolized this era of the victim (Furedi, 1997, p. 95).

The propaganda of fear that has pervaded the United States is actually a continuation of several decades of crime control, and ultimately social control. Much of this has been systematically communicated through the mass media entertainment formats. And a staple of that format is fear. These programs have been fairly consistent, especially the dominant narrative: *There is danger everywhere and it looks like crime (e.g., drugs, gangs, random killings, domestic violence, child abuse, etc.).* Formal *agents of social control (FASC) can save you, but they have to contend with courts and "technicalities" (e.g., illegal search and seizure, entrapment, and related civil rights). Still, trust them/us.*

The focus on fear and danger is good for business. While businesses cashed in on the threats from terrorism after 9/11, fear of crime laid a solid foundation for merchandising numerous products ranging from alarm systems and personal protection (e.g., mace, electronic tasers) to carrying firearms. Most states in the United States permit "open carrying" of firearms, which means that the weapon can be openly displayed, but only recently have many states permitted "concealed carrying"—packing concealed guns under clothing, in purses, etc. Indeed, in Arizona it is legal to carry a concealed weapon without attending a class for instruction. And arms sales have skyrocketed since 9/11. The mass media messages promote the psychology of fear and victimage, and the sense of imminent danger pervades much of everyday life. More recently, clothing designers have tapped the market for fashionable clothing for the millions of customers carrying concealed weapons.

> Woolrich, a 182-year-old clothing company, describes its new chino pants as an elegant and sturdy fashion statement, with a clean profile and fabric that provides comfort and flexibility. And they are great for hiding a handgun.
>
> The company has added a second pocket behind the traditional front pocket for a weapon. Or, for those who prefer to pack their gun in a holster, it can be tucked inside the stretchable waistband. The back pockets are also designed to help hide accessories, like a knife and a flashlight.
>
> The chinos, which cost $65, are not for commandos, but rather, the company says, for the fashion-aware gun owner. And Woolrich has competition. Several clothing companies are following suit, building businesses around the sharp rise in people with permits to carry concealed weapons... [A vice-president of a clothing manufacturer stated]. The latest styles, by contrast, are called "concealed carry" or "covert fashion."
>
> "What we've tried to do is create a collection of garments that allows the end user to have stylish lifestyle apparel but have features in the garment that enable them to carry a weapon and draw the weapon quickly."(Richtel, 2012, p. A1)

The 9/11 attacks added to this everyday fear.
The discourse of fear was more than just "hating the enemy." It was also about consuming things, keeping up appearances, and staying strong, not repeating prior mistakes of "cutting and running," and "supporting our troops," honoring "fallen heroes," and not letting others "sacrifice in vain." And then more consuming, but as audiences, rather than critical publics trying to iron out the numerous contradictions of market strategies and gaining the good life with widely recognized stealth and deceit by government officials. The propaganda trades on audience members' beliefs, attitudes, and experiences with various sources of fear, including crime, but mainly it trades on mass media reports about threat and danger that have pervaded news and entertainment fare for decades.

Terrorism, Fear, and Popular Culture

Victimization was linked to terrorism in order to promote more fear and gain compliance with government directives, but such propaganda efforts are not easily sustained, at least not for an educated and critically thinking minority of citizens. This disenchantment with government explanations, identification of clear propaganda ploys—ranging from exaggeration to distortion to lies—began to raise many doubts among citizens. Such doubts were supported and shaped by narratives produced through alternative media.

Extensive study of news reports and entertainment programs suggests that fear expanded greatly and moved from being an emotion to a communication style. The word itself increased by several hundred percent in news reports from the mid 1980s to the late 1990s (Altheide, 2002). Fear came to be closely linked with crime, drugs, gangs, immigrants, and, after the horrendous "Columbine" school shootings, fear became even more closely linked with schools and children. This was part of the context for the attacks of 9/11, which were quickly folded into it, except the language quickly shifted from crime to "war." The playing to fear continued into 2008, when President Bush argued that the House of Representatives should reauthorize the administration's national security act also known as the Patriot Act that permitted blanket communication surveillance, without even the most perfunctory checking with a special court that was created three decades ago under the Foreign Intelligence Surveillance Act. According to Mr. Bush, if this authorization was not extended:

> "At this moment," he said, "somewhere in the world terrorists are planning new attacks on our country. Their goal is to bring destruction to our shores that will make Sept. 11 pale by comparison." (Lichtblau, 2008)

The expanded domestic surveillance program was initiated without congressional or legal approval; agents of the regime simply went to major communications companies (e.g., AT&T), and asked them to provide the government access. Virtually all complied, and when this became known several years later, clients of the communications magnates filed multi-billion dollar lawsuits. Granting amnesty and protecting the communications industries from lawsuits was a key part of the legislation. Thus, fear not only exacted a civil liberties cost, it could also penalize giant conglomerates billions of dollars.

The biggest impact of terrorism and fear was on the mass media and culture. The attacks of 9/11 came to be associated with many "threatening" or important matters. For example, NBC's "Morning Show" added a segment, "Money 911," that dispensed advice about investing and saving. Many things changed and became more normalized and accepted, including pervasive threat, state intervention, and surveillance, and the protests against civil liberties violations became more common, and therefore more a part of the "news and communication routine," the surrounding environment of fighting terrorism. Terrorism meanings sanction any activity that is purported to help eliminate this fear. In the United States, this has included extended propaganda campaigns, gross violations of civil liberties, including kidnapping, torture, imprisonment without due process (i.e., habeas corpus), massive wiretapping of U.S. citizens' telephone calls and emails, drug testing, profiling—racial, religious, ethnic—, as well as journalistic investigations and reporting. Moreover, most of these have been "normalized" and accepted as the "status quo" in terms of mass communication.

The major impact of the discourse of fear is to promote a sense of disorder and a belief that "things are out of control." Ferraro (1995) suggests that fear reproduces itself or becomes a self-fulfilling prophecy. Social life can become more hostile when social actors define their situations as "fearful" and engage in speech communities through the discourse of fear. And people come to share an identity as competent "fear realists" as family members, friends, neighbors, and colleagues socially construct their effective environments with fear. Behavior becomes constrained, community activism may focus more on "block watch" programs and quasi-vigilantism, and we continue to avoid "downtowns," and many parts of our social world because of "what everyone knows." In short, the discourse of fear incorporates crime reflexively; the agents, targets, and character of fear are constituted through the processes that communicate fear.

Social control and security efforts rely on the participation of the controlled. Frightened people are more compliant. Consider the airport security ritual where passengers stand in line, take off shoes, open their belongings, and when summoned, even submit to physical "wandings" and pat downs by workers. The ritual that is enacted, such as standing in line, holding one's arms out for search, opening up luggage for inspection, precedes getting cleared to proceed, to be selected for inclusion, for being passed, for being allowed to enter the aircraft for one's journey. The potential passengers participate in order to be selected, but they must give up something, they must demonstrate compliance, indeed, passivity, as they pass through the portal of security, the electronic device(s) that scan their bodies for metal and other substances. (These might include "x-ray" photographs of bodies, visually stripping them of clothing.) I suggest that this is tantamount to the supplication of religious rituals, including presenting one's body for inspection. But there are also offerings, giving up one's personal things. One of the most extreme examples followed the announcement that British authorities had arrested several dozen people involved in a plot to blow up international airliners. The explosives would be provided by various liquids carried on board by separate individuals, who would then mix the explosive brew in flight. Almost immediately, liquids, gels, and many personal items were banned from being taken on board. Tens of thousands of items were thrown away or confiscated at the door of security portals during the next few days. While many people resisted the efforts by consuming such things as water, wine, and whiskey, most willingly dropped the offerings in trash bins or gave them to airport employees. Airport trash workers reported that it was like Christmas! Several travelers who were interviewed indicated that they did not mind at all if this would keep them safe.

9/11 and Expansion of Terrorism and Propaganda

The terrorist attacks on the United States on September 11, 2001, were strategically used by officials to justify various domestic and international actions in order to "protect us," including two wars, expanded domestic surveillance, suspension of many civil liberties, torture of suspected terrorists, and kidnapping of foreign citizens (also known as extreme rendition) (Altheide, 2006). Patriotism was rampant, critical questions were rare for several years, and those concerned about civil liberties violations were referred to as "privacy advocates." This discourse was extended to the drug war, as noted, but it was also applied to immigration threats, which were framed as potential terrorists. This was all consistent with the politics of fear. Such actions were symbolically communicated through a propaganda campaign in which (1) fear supported consumption as a meaningful way for audiences to sustain an identity of substance and character; (2) the absence of a clear target for reprisals contributed to the construction of broad symbolic enemies and goals; and (3) the fight against terrorism was also celebrated through the construction of "heroes" and support of "troops," whose stories were told as part of the emotional bonding of war, family and community. The presidential campaigns of 2004 and 2008 stressed vulnerability, plotting enemies, and the need for strong leadership to protect us.

Propaganda plays to fear (Altheide & Johnson, 1980; Jackall, 1994; Kellner, 2004; Lasswell, Speier, & Lerner, 1979). The Iraq War propaganda illustrates a process that linked giving and spending to patriotism, domestic control, and a major foreign policy shift following the terrorist attacks on September 11, 2001 (9/11) (Altheide, 2006). Analysis of news reports and advertisements suggests that popular culture and mass media depictions of fear, patriotism, consumption, and victimization contributed to the emergence of a "national identity" and collective action that was fostered by elite decision-makers' propaganda and the military-media complex (Altheide, 1999). Numerous replays of the "falling towers" transformed buildings into icons of "the terrorist threat" that morphed into the endless "war on terrorism," a battle against a world condition and not a specific country, group, or tactic. Global policing that would justify a "first strike" against sovereign governments was socially constructed as commensurate with personal caring and a national identity.

Now 9/11 is used throughout the world, but especially North America, as a symbolic vessel that is only partly full; it contains some basic meanings (e.g., crashing airliners into buildings), but it is a space for the interpretation of new events and for any speaker (or writer) to associate themselves (or their project) with some unspecified values and concerns. To share 9/11 integrates and legitimizes individual behavior, social policies, and institutional practices. Searching information bases shows that the phrase "9/11" is invoked in a kind of global unity but mainly as either a justification or an excuse for certain policies and practices. Terrorism oozes from this phrase, but mainly it is the reaction and rationale for more social control and wariness of threats from a seemingly endless source of "others," typically immigrants. These uses of 9/11 may be as diverse as the European Union trying to forge a common military force (beyond

NATO), to Middle Eastern countries proposing and tempering policies of defending-against-terrorism that closely resemble attacking old threats with new language.

The terrorism narrative has not changed with a new president, Barack Obama. While President George W. Bush stressed terrorism throughout his terms in office, Obama has not really changed the rhetoric, although for several months his administration essentially stopped referring to the "war on terrorism" in favor or other euphemisms. Seven years after the 9/11 attacks, in a speech to West Point military cadets Bush reiterated the connection between 9/11 and the "terrible attack in Mumbai" "last month," adding that his successor (Barack Obama) should continue. He stated: "In the years ahead, our nation must continue developing the capabilities to take the fight to our enemies across the world ... we must stay on the offensive" (Savage, 2008).

During his acceptance speech for the Nobel Peace Prize, President Obama invoked the time-worn phrase of a "just war" to justify U.S. military incursions, and then added his commitment to not only believing in "evil" in the world, but to stridently opposing it, just as his campaign-nemesis, George W. Bush, had done. This included linking the drug war with terrorism.

The drug war and ongoing concerns with crime contributed to the expansion of fear with terrorism. Messages demonizing Osama bin Laden, his Taliban supporters, and "Islamic extremists" linked these suspects with the destructive clout of illegal drugs and especially drug lords. News reports and advertisements joined drug use with terrorism and helped shift "drugs" from criminal activity to unpatriotic action. As the destructive acts were defined as "war" rather than "attacks," it became apparent that the propaganda about one war would replicate the other war. By this I refer to the demonization of drugs/terrorists, the call for harsh measures against both, and the unanimity—especially among news media—that force was the best weapon (*Dallas Morning News*, March 14, 2002, KO487, reprinted in the *Arizona Republic*, March 14, 2002, p. A8). A $10 million ad campaign promoted the message from President Bush, "If you quit drugs, you join the first against terror in America."

The expanding definition of terrorism promoted the view that terrorism was a condition of the world, a war without end that would require fundamental changes in civil liberties and governmental control, including intrusive spying on numerous Muslim groups to find likely domestic terrorists, and to conduct proactive "sting" operations to demonstrate their guilt.

FBI terrorist sting operations suggest that Superman's adaptable archenemy Lex Luthor had it right when he said, "The more fear you make, the more loot you take." The audience's fear of terrorism is cultivated with entertaining popular culture and mass media reports about terrorism threats. Pew opinion surveys show that terrorism continues to be one of the United States' top three priorities—much higher than reducing crime, providing health insurance, or protecting the environment (Pew Research Center, 2004). Sting operations help with the programming. Stings have become popular in the United States over the last 35 years or so as the FBI became more oriented to popular culture and media logic. Improved and smaller audio and video recording technology has helped provide "evidence" for legal proceedings as well as news and other entertainment shows. Expanded surveillance is now part of everyday life and entertainment. Audiences nurtured with decades of fear of crime and now, terrorism, are also familiar with the sting genre of reality television shows such as "To Catch a Predator."

The FBI has become skilled at recording the planning, carrying out, and prevention of would-be terrorist acts. The general approach is to assist people who make verbal threats to actually do something more "operational" (their word). According to a report by the Center for Human Rights and Global Justice at New York University, Muslim "home grown terrorists" would be good recruits for dramatic presentations of fear and threat:

> Since September 11, 2001, the U.S. government has targeted Muslims in the United States by sending paid, untrained informants into mosques and Muslim Communities. This practice has led to the prosecution of more than 200 individuals in terrorism-related cases. The government has touted these cases as successes in the so-called war against terrorism... . "The government played a significant role in instigating and devising the three plots featured in this Report—plots the government then 'foiled' and charged the defendants with," according to the study. "The defendants in these cases were all convicted and are facing prison sentences of 25 years to life" (Center for Human Rights and Global Justice, 2011 p. 2; Klasfield, 2011).

The FBI's extensive efforts to surveil, encourage, and ensnare culpable participants were captured in a Pulitzer Prize–winning report that documented egregious tactics (see http://www.ap.org/media-center/nypd/investigation):

> AP's investigation has revealed that the NYPD dispatched undercover officers into minority neighborhoods as part of a human mapping program. Police also used informants, known as "mosque crawlers," to monitor sermons, even when there was no evidence of wrongdoing.
>
> The AP also determined that police subjected entire neighborhoods to surveillance and scrutiny, often because of the ethnicity of the residents, not because of any accusations of crimes. Hundreds of mosques and Muslim student groups were investigated and dozens were infiltrated. Many of these operations were built with help from the CIA, which is prohibited from spying on Americans but was instrumental in transforming the NYPD's intelligence unit after 9/11.

These reports helped launch a congressional investigation, although the New York City police department declined to end them.

Another FBI terror-episode played out in November 2010 featuring Mohamed Osman Mohamud, a 19-year-old jihadist in Portland, Oregon. After being alerted by his parents, FBI surveillance identified suspicious discussions with potential enemies in Pakistan, and then devoted months in bringing their scripted procedures and undercover roles into play. The aim was not to stop Mr. Mohamud or bring charges against him; there was already probable cause to detain and arrest when he took initial steps toward committing a terrorist act to harm people. Like many foiled plots, this case received media attention, complete with video of the aftermath of the arrest, along with audio transcriptions of conversations with informants. The FBI produced a dramatic performance of a bomb threat for media publicity purposes and to promote a sense of imminent danger and fear. The federal agents provided the knowledge, means, technology, organization, and money for rent and to purchase bomb supplies. Network anchors wondered how many more domestic terrorists were out there, and citizens who were interviewed stressed how grateful they were to be protected from such threats.

Of course, not all agents agree that "chasing ghosts" is the best use of scarce resources that were previously committed to criminal investigations of "corrupt politicians, bank robbers, drug dealers, and financial scammers." One agent told a reporter:

> "Look, obviously terrorism is important, but it's not why I joined the FBI and you have to wonder what we're missing—people are getting away with things we would have been all over 10 years ago," said a veteran agent.
>
> (Shiffman, 2011).

The language of terrorism has become more prominent in the crime-fighting agenda as well. Pittsburgh police chief Nate Harper referred to the arrests of several "Original Gangster" (OG) members as "home-grown terrorists."

> "They terrorized the neighborhoods with gunfire, with the homicides that were committed in the Manchester area and the North Side area," he said. "There are still remnants out there, but this is a takedown of the most violent OG members (Lord, 2011).

TERRORISM AS A CONDITION

The mass media emphasis on international as well as domestic terrorism—along with the rituals of the "security theater" at airports and numerous public events—promoted the idea that the "world had changed since 9/11" and that terrorism was not just a tactic by an enemy, but rather, terrorism was a condition of the world. It would not go away; it could not be defeated; it would always be with us.

Casting terrorism as a condition of the world not only led to an expanded use and application of the word "terrorism" to a wide range of activities, it also contributed to associating terrorism more closely with victims and victimization. The emphasis of the coverage of 9/11 was on the commonality of the victims rather than the cause or the rationale for the attacks.

The psychology of fear of terrorism was reinforced by the numerous countries that supported the proposition that terrorism is a condition. Numerous "internal" conflicts and revolutionary movements were classified as "terrorism," and any government that opposed them would, presumably, be joining the United States in its fight against global terrorism. Within a matter of days countries dealing with revolutionary movements in their own borders, (e.g., Colombia, Peru and Israel) vowed to join the United States in its fight against terrorism (Bennett, 2001). Placing virtually all "opposition" forces in the terrorist camp was consistent with the military-media script of pervasive fear and opposition. The serious opposition that disappeared with the end of the Cold War was reconstituted worldwide as "global terrorism."

TERRORISM, THE RISK SOCIETY, AND THE BANALITY OF EVIL

The prevalence of fear in public discourse contributed to stances and reactive social policies that promote state control and surveillance. The banality of evil has been transformed by the role of media logic and the news cycle in our information system. The mass media and journalism are changing according to the economic and risk assessment rationality that governs much of social life. Risk assessment is based on applying knowledge about how to reduce unfavorable results.

Fear is a key element of creating "the risk society," organized around communication oriented to policing, control, and prevention of risks (Ericson & Haggerty, 1997; Staples, 2000). A constitutive feature of this emerging order is a blanket reminder of fear. While fear is commonly associated with crime, I suggest that fear provides a discursive framework of expectation and meaning within which crime and related "problems" are expressed. Media practices and major news sources (e.g., law enforcement agencies) have cooperatively produced an organizational "machine," fueled by entertainment and selective use of news sources, that simultaneously connects people to their effective environments even as it generates entertainment-oriented profits (Altheide, 1997). As one law enforcement official stated about Arizona's televised "crime stoppers" dramatizations, "If you can have a little entertainment and get your man, too, that's great." Fear of crime has become one of the common meanings in our mass society; we increasingly share understandings about what to fear and how to avoid it. The consequences are felt in numerous ways but particularly in accelerated negative perceptions about public order and even our built environment (Ellin, 1997) (e.g., the streets are not safe, strangers are dangerous, the state must provide more control and surveillance).

The sources of public information still shout about terrorism, but they have added global warming and, more recently, immigration threats—a portrait of our shores and borders being overrun by aliens, who not only enter here illegally, but according to many websites that discuss Hispanics, also plan to take over the United States. The specter of citizenship rights is apparent. But it is just not the United States that is reacting strongly to immigrants. Headlines, websites, and blogs circle the globe denouncing immigrants and advocating for "our citizens." The refrain is familiar: Crime, drugs, disease, and, since 2007, the economic downturn are used to justify more extreme measures. Scandinavia and virtually the entire European

Union are altering immigration policies, including checking identification papers and deporting illegal immigrants.

CONCLUSION

Crime, terrorism, and other sources of fear are well established in decades of popular culture, including the proactive treatments by formal agents of social control to intervene through enticing—and entrapping—scenarios (Skoll, 2010). The situation gets defined as threatening; a terrorist world is limitless in risk. Whatever it takes to reduce or eliminate risk is warranted. When the "bust" "comes down," as the media lingo often has it, it is entertaining, reinforcing of strong action as well as confirming stereotypes about external as well as internal threats. The dramatic actions play well in media reports, audiences think they work and are being protected, and the nexus of social control and entertainment is strengthened. Thus, recent actions against "home grown" terrorists are embedded in the communicative order underlying the policies of everyday life.

Fear limits our intellectual and moral capacities, it turns us against others, it changes our behavior and perspective, and makes us vulnerable to those who would control us in order to promote their own agendas. The politics of fear simply translates these "concerns" into preventative action; claims are made that the "bad situation" can be fixed through more control. This is true regardless if the hot issue is crime, illegal drugs, immigration, or international conflict. In most cases, the control is focused on regulating individuals rather than broader social issues, such as poverty and oppressive foreign relations, that have contributed to the problem. More recently, however, the work linking fear to the politics of fear has become far more sophisticated; the recent war on terrorism, for example, rests on important changes that have occurred in our culture and social institutions, and owes less to cunning individuals, who simply ride these cultural changes.

Risk communication about terrorism is now institutionalized as many domestic crimes, including school shootings have been recast as "terrorist," and horrendous attacks on civilian populations, such as the 2008 Israeli invasion of Gaza, are justified as a battle against terrorism (Altheide, 2009). Communications framed by the terrorism discourse dominates U.S. domestic and international perspectives some 12 years after the 9/11 attacks in the United States. Indeed, more risk communication calls for more domestic control and scrutiny even though there is scant evidence of systematic "legitimate terror" threats against the United States. More risk communication is designed to keep U.S. citizens focused on terrorism-related surveillance. When few attacks come from foreigners, we are instructed to be wary of our own citizens who might turn against us.

Risk communication merges handily with the discourse and the politics of fear. All have become more prevalent since the 9/11 attacks on the United States. More information is gleaned, and boundaries separating private and public behavior are routinely crossed, just as corporate and governmental interests—including control and "safety"—are breached. Surveillance and more information gathering, mining, interpolating, and combining are a big part of the focus on risk communication. Marx's (1988) brilliant analysis of the growth of surveillance monitoring, often by undercover operations, laid the conceptual groundwork (e.g., Foucault, 1979) for additional insights into the use of various technologies that have been investigated by Staples (2000) Lyon (2003), and others, including more recent work by Monahan (Monahan, 2006a, 2006b; Monahan & Palmer, 2009).

The risk of terrorism, like all risks, calls for measured responses grounded in an understanding about limits, and particularly intended and unintended consequences. How we define new risks is often contingent on previous risks, but when the mass media emphasize a context of fear and imminent danger, the ante is raised and politicians are likely to play the fear card in order to justify measures. Terrorism tops risk discourse and in its application has elevated public perceptions about the plausibility of other risks. Certain applications of risk communication reflect a control narrative with important underlying assumptions about social order. Regulating or policing selected individuals as members of certain groups is central. A risk discourse grounded in fear of the future has become more prevalent; particularly fear of uncertain interactions and involvements with "others" either as foreigners, criminals or terrorists. We acquire knowledge about our present-future and know just enough about the constitutive process of human agency, with all its fickleness, hubris, and excess in an increasingly contingent social, political, and natural environment. An expanding awareness of our role in making futures, along with the hubris that we *might* be able to somewhat control (and survive) technological applications—from dams to poison emitting engines to microchips to nuclear power—opens up a can of doubt and despair about the unsustainable future. What if, we ask? What are the odds, the chances? The answer is not pursued, but instead we seek insurance, prevention, caution, warning, and a million forms of monitoring and surveillance. Social control agents tell audiences about this; we communicate, ever so carefully and selectively, what there is to be concerned about—some pollution, nicotine, illegal drugs, crime, illegal immigrants, and terrorism. And we gather more information, more detailed data about nature, the body, always seeking to see more detail, as though "more data" will provide the security, or at least, the knowledge-tricks that will help us. Fighting the dominant exemplar of fear, such as terrorism, trumps all else, even evil! (Altheide, 2009). We monitor and we discipline and punish; but above all, we tell mass-mediated stories framed by symbolic manipulators of a society in control and out of control, infused with the discourse of fear.

REFERENCES

Altheide, D. L. (1997). The news media, the problem frame, and the production of fear. *The Sociological Quarterly*, 38, 646–668.

Altheide, D. L. (1999). The military-media complex. *Newsletter of the Sociology of Culture, 13*(3), 1 ff.
Altheide, D. L. (2002). *Creating fear: News and the construction of crisis.* New York, NY: Aldine de Gruyter.
Altheide, D. L. (2006). *Terrorism and the politics of fear.* Lanham, MD: Alta Mira Press.
Altheide, D. L. (2009). *Terror post 9/11 and the media.* New York, NY: Peter Lang.
Altheide, D. L., & Johnson, J. M. (1980). *Bureaucratic propaganda.* Boston, MA: Allyn and Bacon.
Altheide, D. L., & Snow, R. P. (1979). *Media logic.* Beverly Hills, CA: Sage.
Altheide, D. L., & Snow, R. P. (1991). *Media worlds in the postjournalism era.* Hawthorne, NY: Aldine de Gruyter.
Bennett, J. (2001, September 16, 2001). Israel wants cease-fire to precede truce talks. *The New York Times,* p. 1.
Bennett, W. L. (1988). *News: The politics of illusion* (2nd ed.). New York, NY: Longman.
Cavender, G. (2004). In search of community on reality TV: America's most wanted and survivor. In S. a. D. J. Holmes (Ed.), *Understanding reality* (pp. 154–172). London, NY: Routledge.
Cavender, G., & Bond-Maupin, L. (1993). Fear and loathing on reality television: An analysis of America's most wanted and unsolved mysteries. *Sociological Quarterly, 63*(3), 23–30.
Center for Human Rights and Global Justice. (2011). *Targeted and entrapped: Manufacturing the "homegrown threat" in the United States.* New York, NY: NYU School of Law.
Chermak, S. (1995). *Victims in the news: Crime and the American news media.* Boulder, CO: Westview Press.
Chiricos, T., Eschholz, S., & Gertz, M. (1997). Crime, news and fear of crime: Toward an identification of audience effects. *Social Problems, 44*(3), 342–357.
Comstock, G. (1980). *Television in America.* Beverly Hills, CA: Sage.
DeFleur, M. L., & Ball-Rokeach., S. (1982). *Theories of mass communication.* (4th ed.). New York, NY: Longman.
Dubber, M. D. (2002). *Victims in the war on crime: The use and abuse of victims' rights.* New York, NY: New York University Press.
Ellin, N. (1997). *Architecture of fear.* New York, NY: Princeton Architectural Press.
Ericson, R. V. (2007). *Crime, risk and uncertainty.* London, UK: Polity Press.
Ericson, R. V. (Ed.). (1995). *Crime and the media.* Brookfield, VT: Dartmouth University Press.
Ericson, R. V., & Haggerty, K. D. (1997). *Policing the risk society.* Toronto, Canada: University of Toronto Press.
Ewen, S., & Ewen, E. (1992). *Channels of desire: Mass images and the shaping of American consciousness.* Minneapolis, MN: University of Minnesota Press.
Ferraro, K. F. (1995). *Fear of crime: Interpreting victimization risk.* Albany, NY: State University of New York Press.
Fishman, M., & Cavender, G. (1998). *Entertaining crime: Television reality programs.* New York, NY: Aldine de Gruyter.
Forti, G., & Bertolino, M. (Eds.). (2004). *Le televisione del crimine.* Milano, Italy: Vita E Pensiero.
Foucault, M. (1979). *Discipline and punish: The birth of the prison.* New York, NY: Vintage Books.
Furedi, F. (1997). *Culture of fear: Risk-taking and the morality of low expectation.* London: Cassell.
Grimes, J. N. (2007). *Crime, media, and public policy: Striking out ten years later.* Unpublished Ph.D., Arizona State University, Tempe.

Heath, L., & Gilbert., K. (1996). Mass media and fear of crime. *American Behavioral Scientist*, 39, 379–386.

Jackall, R. (Ed.). (1994). *Propaganda*. New York, NY: New York University Press.

Jackall, R., & Hirota, J. M. (2000). *Image makers: Advertising, public relations, and the ethos of advocacy*. Chicago, IL/London, UK: University of Chicago Press.

Kellner, D. (2004). Media propaganda and spectacle in the war on Iraq: A critique of U.S. broadcasting networks. *Cultural Studies & Critical Methodologies*, 4(3), 329–338.

Klasfeld, A. (2011). Terror stings breed entrapment, study say. *Courthouse News*. Retrieved from http://www.courthousenews.com/2011/05/20/36745.htm

Lasswell, H. D., Speier, H., & Lerner, D. (1979). *Propaganda and communication in world history*. Honolulu, HI: Published for the East-West Center by the University Press of Hawaii.

Lichtblau, E. (2008, February 14, 2008). Eavesdropping law is likely to lapse. *The New York Times*, p. 25. Retrieved from http://www.nytimes.com/2008/02/14/washington/14fisa.html?_r=1&th&emc=th&oref=slogin

Lord, R. (2011, March 4, 2011). North side of takedown; 29 gang members from Manchester indicted for drug and gun crimes. *Pittsburgh Post-Gazette*, pp. B-1. Retrieved from http://www.lexisnexis.com.ezproxy1.lib.asu.edu/hottopics/lnacademic/?

Lyon, D. (2003). Technology vs "terrorism": Circuits of city surveillance since September 11th. *International Journal of Urban and Regional Research*, 27(3), 666–678.

Marx, G. T. (1988). *Undercover: Police surveillance in America*. Berkeley, CA: University of California Press.

Monahan, T. (2006a). Securing the homeland: Torture, preparedness, and the right to let die. *Social Justice*, 33(1), 95–105.

Monahan, T. (2006b). *Surveillance and security: Technological politics and power in everyday life*. New York, NY: Routledge.

Monahan, T., & Palmer, N. A. (2009). The emerging politics of DHS fusion centers. *Security Dialogue*, 40(6), 617–636,.

Pew Research Center. (2004). A year after Iraq war mistrust of America in Europe ever higher, Muslim anger persists. The Pew Research Center for the People and the Press. http://people-press.org/reports/display.php3?ReportID=206

Richtel, M. (2012, April 24, 2012). New fashion wrinkle: Stylishly hiding the gun. *The New York Times*, p. A1. Retrieved from http://www.nytimes.com/2012/04/24/us/fashion-statement-is-clear-the-gun-isnt.html?_r=1

Russell, K. K. (1998). *The color of crime: Racial hoaxes, white fear, black protectionism, police harassment, and other macroaggressions*. New York. NY: New York University Press.

Savage, C. (2008). Bush warns Pakistan as he defends military strategy. *The New York Times*, p. A10.

Schwartz, T. (1973). *The responsive chord* (1st ed.). Garden City, NY: Anchor Press.

Shiffman, J. (2011, May 8, 201). Philly's terrorist watch: An exclusive look inside the squads at work in the region. *The Philadelphia Inquirer* p. A01. Retrieved from http://www.lexisnexis.com.ezproxy1.lib.asu.edu/hottopics/lnacademic/?

Skoll, G. R. (2010). *Social theory of fear (open access): Terror, torture, and death in a post-capitalist world*. New York, NY: Macmillan.

Snow, R. P. (1983). *Creating media culture*. Beverly Hills, CA: Sage.

Staples, W. G. (2000). *Everyday surveillance: Vigilance and visibility in postmodern life*. Lanham, MD/Oxford, UK: Rowman & Littlefield.

Surette, R. (1998). *Media, crime and criminal justice: Images and realities* (2nd ed.). Belmont, CA: West/Wadsworth.

Warr, M. (1987). Fear of victimization and sensitivity to risk. *Journal of Quantitative Criminology*, 3(1 Mar), 29–46.

CHAPTER 17
Why Is It So Difficult to Evaluate the Political Impact of Terrorism?
AMI-JACQUES RAPIN

The rapid increase of studies devoted to terrorism during the last decade has enriched the field of knowledge and given rise to new ways of thinking. Particularly, the development of quantitative approaches in measuring terrorism is a significant trend. We will refer to a few examples that take diverse factors into consideration in order to illustrate the diversity of the variables taken into account.

Berrebi and Ostwald (2011) established a relationship between natural catastrophes and terrorism in 146 countries during the period from 1970 to 2007, which demonstrated an association between the frequency of terrorism with that of natural calamities. Nitsch and Schumacher (2004) noticed a reduction in bilateral commerce volume in countries affected by terrorism while looking into 217 countries and territories, over the period from 1948 to 1997. Freytag and colleagues (2011) subsequently conducted a study on 110 countries during the period between 1971 and 2007 and concluded that economic underdevelopment was conducive to terrorism. In doing so, they questioned the dominant idea that terrorism was not a result of unfavorable socioeconomic conditions. Qvortrup (2012, p. 514) confirmed that in Western Europe manifestations of domestic terrorism were "inversely correlated with consensus mechanisms" during the period from 1985 to 2010. Investigating in the same region, Indridason (2008) examined the influence of terrorism on the formation of coalition governments during the period from 1950 to 2006 and concluded that the main political parties under threat responded by creating stable coalitions. Gassebner and colleagues (2008) scrutinized 800 elections in 115 countries from 1968 to 2002 and found that terrorist attacks increased the likelihood of cabinet changes after elections.

Although the purpose of this study is not to deny the significance of the hypotheses and arguments advanced in the quantitative research, it is important to note that its authors quantify "terrorism" by resorting to databases with questionable reliability. This problem is as old as the creation of the very first databases on terrorism

(Fowler, 1981), and unfortunately, it has not been solved adequately since then. Schmid (2004), holds similar views after analyzing the content of eight databases frequently consulted by researchers on terrorism:

> When the working definitions of various databases are considered, considerable differences are found as to what constitutes terrorism. Some databases include guerrilla activities, others attacks against military personnel in peacetime. [...] Not only do the working definitions of what constitutes terrorism differ, but when the actual entries into the databases are examined, even entries that do not fit into the respective working definition are sometimes found. (p. 52-53)

Collecting data with insufficient quality is, in effect, an inherent weakness in the quantification of terrorism. In short, these databases do not allow for the measurement of a specific phenomenon like terrorism, but catalogue a wide range of politically motivated violence, from wholly military operations (e.g., attacks by Liberation Tigers of Tamil Eelam on Sri Lankan army camps), to minor acts of vandalism (e.g., the burning of two cars at a Mercedes dealer company on the outskirts of Zurich). We should add that ambiguous interpretations sometimes label insignificant events as terrorist attacks. This is the case when the Global Terrorism Database (www.start.umd.edu/gtd/) provides the following information: "Two rockets [in reality fireworks that only resulted in a broken window] were fired at the international congress center in Davos, Switzerland, where the World Economic Forum was scheduled for January 27–February 1, 2000."

To some extent we could say that all these forms of political violence create fear. However, it is also clear that the scale of violence has a direct influence on the level of fear experienced in different situations. What does it imply? It implies that "terrorist incidents" produce a wide range of psychological reactions—from inconsequential to severe. The main point here is that not all forms of political violence are equal in their psychological impact. Unfortunately, the indiscriminate use of the words "terrorism" and "terror" eliminates nuances precisely where we need to make distinctions among different degrees of emotional reaction (Rapin, 2011).

The heterogeneity of the data obviously limits the scope of comparative analyses that address the "terrorism" variable as a function of "terrorist incidents" frequency. For the comparison to make sense, the "structure of terrorist events" should remain, on the whole, constant (Frey et al., 2007, p. 2); that is, the type of events should not, to an inordinate degree, vary in order to not create confusion between acts of vandalism, military operations, and terrorist attacks. One way to get around the problem inherent in the heterogeneity of data consists of reprocessing the same to improve their usefulness in studying the impact of terrorist attacks. Llussa and Tavares (2011) proceeded along those lines by stating that the number of attacks carried out against civilians, and the number of victims, were determining factors when it comes to the economic impact resulted from the violence. These results are interesting since they reinforce the idea that different types of violence have different impacts depending on its intensity and scope. These results are also interesting because they suggest that the concept of terrorism covers a broad range of fear-inducing situations.

Focusing on a very high number of countries (168 and 187, according to the variables considered), the study carried out by Llussa and Tavares (2011) is problematic, however, because of a bias in the identification of events to be considered. The databases related to terrorism are created from official sources or the media. Therefore, the quality of official sources varies greatly from one country to another—without forgetting that the counting of terrorist acts is dependent on political considerations (LaFree et al., 2011, p. 5)—and that the media coverage of political acts of violence is, most definitely, not uniform on the global scale. Under these conditions, there is scarcely any doubt that an imbalance exists between regions for which the slightest incident gives rise to their inclusion in the databases and other regions that make up veritable gray zones of political violence (e.g., there were only 30 incidents in Congo-Kinshasa, from 1998 to 2006 in the Global Terrorism Database, even though the period was characterized by the unleashing of violent acts, the greatest part of which correspond to the criteria established for the coding of terrorist acts).

The advantage of quantitative approaches increases when the scale of analysis grows smaller, for the simple reason that the data relative to political acts of violence tend to become homogenous. This homogenization can be achieved by limiting the study to a national case, a specific type of operations (e.g., hostages taking, suicide attacks), or a specific campaign of violence. Studies devoted to the psychological sequelae of violence in a population, or to its economic impact, have thus produced significant results after the suicide bombing campaigns in Israel, the 9/11 attacks in the United States, and those on March 11, 2004, in Madrid, and on July 7, 2005, in London. On the other hand, the problem regarding the consequences of this type of violence, in relation to political process, remains more uncertain since the empirical studies devoted to the same are less numerous and more ambiguous in their results.

The problem can be approached from two different angles that we will take into consideration. First, to what extent do the authors of this violence succeed in having an impact on the political process or, more precisely, to what extent does the anxiety generated by the violence contribute to the achievement of goals pursued by those who carry out the attacks? Second, to what extent is the response by officials to the violence a source of anxiety that affects the political process?

The first question has been at the center of reflection on terrorism since the 1930s. However, this has generally been done in the absence of sound empirical support, until recently. To simplify the issue, one has to look at the alternative questions: does terrorism work or not? Expanding on the work of Berrebi and Klor (2008), Gould and Klor (2010) responded to that question in the affirmative. To understand the issue involved in the question, it is, basically speaking, necessary to summarize it. Berrebi and Klor revealed the ideological polarization of the Israeli electorate upon establishing an increase in votes for right-wing parties in localities that have been affected by terrorism. Gould and Klor's research confirmed this trend but added that attacks also affected the right-wing party's platform, while causing it to gravitate toward the left. That is to say, it moved toward a more conciliatory position in relation to the issue of territorial concessions. It turns out, from all of this, that terrorism—at least "in small doses"—would be an effective political tool, to the extent that "it creates domestic political pressure from the targeted electorate" (Gould & Klor, 2010, pp. 1507–1508).

Without getting into the methodological issues raised by this research (see Hlavac, 2010; Munayyer, 2009), it is important to point out a weakness in the argument: not having really defined the goal assigned to the attacks by those who have perpetrated them, it is difficult to conclude that "terrorism is an effective strategy for achieving political goals" (Gould & Klor, 2010, p. 1507). In reality, Gould and Klor demonstrated that terrorist attacks committed in Israel exercised an influence on the political process, but not that terrorists truly had the specific intention of strengthening the electoral weight of right-wing parties, and of modifying their platform.

Previously, Abrahms (2006) arrived at a totally opposite conclusion when attempting to determine the terrorists' ability to achieve their goals. Attributing 42 policy objectives to 28 terrorist organizations (some of the groups pursue several goals), Abrahms reported a success rate of only 7 percent. According to the author, the marginal successes of terrorists are the result of the limited nature of their policy objectives and of their choice of not targeting civilians, while the strategy of groups that assume maximalist objectives and target civilians is doomed to failure.

Abrahm's reasoning is also subject to discussion, inasmuch as his conclusion that "terrorism does not work" is, to a great extent, predetermined by restrictions that are brought to bear in relation to the object of his analysis. Other than the consideration of an overly narrow list of groups, which only partially accounts for the phenomenon (see Rose & Murphy, 2007), the main problem lies in the definition of goals. Excluding intermediate objectives (e.g., to gain international attention) and tactical and operational objectives, the author only focuses on the final political objective of each organization (i.e., the clausewitzian *Zweck*). The latter is elsewhere identified through the information database supplied by Rand Corporation and the Federation of American Scientists Directory of Terrorist Organizations, and not through that which has resulted from an analysis of the strategic orientations of the groups concerned. Thus, the objective of the Aum Shinrikyo sect is "to establish a utopian society in Japan," and that of the Revolutionary Nuclei and the November 17 group is "to establish Marxism in Greece" (Abrahms, 2006, pp. 49–50). Such objectives could not be immediately achieved by terrorist attacks, as numerous as they might have been. Therefore, by themselves they were not able to explain the recourse to violence, as carried out by the groups under consideration. In this case, it was precisely the intermediate, operational, and tactical objectives that allow us to conceive of such an explanation.

It is important to not confuse the actual effects of terrorist attacks and the ultimate political aims of the groups that commit them, with the immediate function attributed to the violence for which it is carried out. An overly instrumental perspective does not sufficiently take into account the complexity of the motivations of the authors of the attacks, and in particular, the fact that the majority of the attacks consist of a double component: reactive and proactive. To simplify matters, we should say that the reactive component originates from the perception of a political environment judged to be oppressive, which is supposed to justify a response or recourse to retaliatory actions. The proactive component is inscribed inside of a perspective that is more strategic inasmuch as the use of violence is aimed at accomplishing a goal (the clausewitzian *Ziel*) and consists of subjecting others to the will of the author of the attack. The respective weight of these two components can greatly vary from one terrorist attack to another; it is often difficult to identify, in a precise manner, the goal (or multiple goals) pursued by the authors of the attacks, like in the case of the 9/11, Madrid, and London attacks.

The psychological impact of a terrorist attack does not depend upon its proactive or reactive components. It is true, however, that in the case of a proactive attack, the fear is mobilized as an instrument for breaking the will of the opponent, while in a reactive attack the fear is a mere byproduct of an act of retaliation. The aims and means of political violence can be understood only through an analysis combining an examination of the attacker's intentions, the role a particular attack plays in the framework of a more global strategy, and the relation between the action's intended objective and its psychological impact on the public (Rapin, 2011).

In one way or another, it would be appropriate to integrate a criterion relative to the reactive and proactive components of violence into the databases in order to better distinguish the role attributed to the attacks by those who commit them. Along the same lines, it would be just as important that these databases integrate the context of conflict inside of which attacks are inscribed (Schmid, 2004, p. 68). Some actors participate in a larger repertoire of violent activities, while others emerge out of the circumstances of social tensions and political polarization. Finally, there are others who, to a large extent, are dissociated from actual conflict. The meaning of the violence and the aggressive behaviors through which it manifests are not independent from the diverse conflictual configurations that imply that an attack carried out by the Taliban in Afghanistan is not, exactly speaking, the same phenomenon as the mass murder perpetrated by Anders Behring Breivik in Norway.

Some other example will illustrate our previous considerations. The reactive component of violence predominated in the Sarin gas attacks that were perpetrated by the *Aum Shinrikyo* sect in Matsumoto on June 27, 1994, and in the Tokyo subway on March 20, 1995. These attacks are inscribed inside of the logic of the apocalyptical Shoko Ashara prophecies; but their immediate motivation resided in the belief that the sect and its guru were victims of persecution on the part of the authorities. At the beginning of 1994, Asahara had indicated to his disciples that the sect's facilities were the objects of biological and chemical attacks (Shimazono, 1995, p. 402).

Recourse to extreme violence originated from sectarian radicalization and a "spiral of paranoia" (Reader, 2002, p. 167), whose sole conflictual dimension resided in Shoko Asahara's idiosyncratic tendencies that were directed at conceiving a principle that consisted of a fight to the death between his millenarist organization and its enemies. The case of the Revolutionary Nuclei and the November 17 group is different. The proactive component of the violence was dominant, with attacks aimed at exacerbating sociopolitical tensions, so that conditions for a prerevolutionary situation could be created. To express it differently, the two groups practiced what anarchists called "propaganda of the deed" and the Red Brigade's "armed propaganda," a strategy that Mario Moretti (2010) summed up while asserting that "we wanted to be the catalyst of a certain process, and not only its protagonists" (p. 277).

The last example has brought a marked interest that shows up in the specialized literature. It allows us to ask, with a particular kind of acuity, about the political impact of terrorist attacks. This obviously has to do with the attacks in Madrid during 2004. These attacks are both reactive and proactive. The reactive component, in all likelihood, played a significant role in acting out; it consisted of carrying out retaliation against the "Crusaders" who had attacked Muslim countries as well as potential revenge because of the arrest of extremists that previously took place out in Spain (Alonso, 2010, p. 214). But all the attention has been concentrated on the proactive component of the attacks, which consisted of putting a stop to military intervention by the West, and more specifically, of achieving the withdrawal of Spanish troops from Iraq and Afghanistan.

There is hardly any doubt today that the attacks in Madrid on March 11, 2004, have had an influence on the results of the elections that took place 3 days later, which overturned José Maria Aznar's right-wing government (Montalvo, 2011). The socialist party's victory, whose electoral platform anticipated the withdrawal of Spanish troops from Iraq, and the announcement of the same by the new prime minister, José Luis Rodriguez Zapatero, added a new dimension to the Madrid terrorist attacks. Did not the chain of events demonstrate that terrorism could work? That is what was indicated in the critique by Rose and Murphy (2007), which was a response to Abrahm's thesis (2004), according to which attacks targeted at civilians do not allow for the granting of concessions from political authorities. There are good reasons, however, to make qualitative statements about this interpretation.

In the first place, it is because the perpetrators of the attacks did not act with a plan to specifically influence the result of the elections, nor to bring about the victory of Spain's socialist party (Reinares, 2010, p. 97). In the second place, it is because the electoral defeat of the government party was not so much the direct consequence of the attacks, but the result of poor crisis management. That is, the government's obstinacy when it came to blaming the ETA for the attacks was perceived as an attempt to manipulate public opinion for electoral purposes (Fominaya, 2011). In the third place, it is because the new Spanish government did not give in to the demands of the attackers when it withdrew troops from Iraq, but fulfilled an electoral promise that had been made prior to the attacks, which, moreover, was accompanied by the announcement that it would strengthen the Spanish military presence in Afghanistan.

Dannenbaum (2011) is correct when he asserts that the Madrid attacks affected the political process, not "through effective terrorist strategy but via an unpredictable and serendipitous (from the terrorist perspective) chain of circumstances" (p. 348). We should add that the authors of the attacks seemingly attempted to adapt themselves to the evolution of events as they clarified their demands and made their conditions tougher after the elections (Reinares, 2010, pp. 98–99). In that regard, it is important to not overestimate the proactive component of these attacks. The main motivation of the perpetrators apparently did not fall within the province of the electoral defeat of the government party, nor did it have anything to do with the withdrawal of Spanish troops from Iraq. This is what the preparation of new attacks and the establishment of an unrealistic 24-hour deadline for the withdrawal of the same from Iraq and Afghanistan, as outlined in the April 3, 2004, communiqué, tend to suggest.

Actually, the events in Madrid demonstrate the fact that the political impact of a terrorist attack does not originate only from the act itself, but also, and above all, from the reactions of society and the state. The first of those reactions are relatively easy to measure through the use of interviews and questionnaires. On the other hand, the reactions of the state in part fall outside of the scope of empirical studies, especially when it comes to two areas of importance. The first is concerned with the psychological impact of violence on political authorities. The second, with the interactions between political authorities and the bureaucracy that centers its activity around security (police, secret service, army), following an attack. Each of these areas is important if one is attempting to determine the ability of authorities to exploit, in a Machiavellian way, violence in their political communication strategy. So that these authorities are truly able to exploit the anxiety generated by an attack for political ends, it is necessary that they themselves are not subject to the same type of anxiety that affects the population (which seems likely, but which has not been demonstrated empirically). It is also necessary for them to fully master the parameters relative to the threat that confronts them, and therefore, for the security services bureaucracy to offer them a clear, intelligible perspective on that threat (which seems unlikely, but which has not been demonstrated empirically, either).

The psychological impact of terrorist attacks on government authorities constitutes one of the gaps in our knowledge about terrorism. Nijdam and colleagues (2010) are among the few writers who have dealt with this issue as they attempted to evaluate the psychological reactions of twelve Dutch politicians who were placed under police protection after they received death threats. Even if their study is not all that conclusive (the authors only note that symptoms of posttraumatic stress disorder occurred in some individuals) and does not focus on the direct impact of violence, nor specifically on the members of a government executive body, it does point to a path to be followed for future research that will have to be innovative so that their protocols can be adapted to a category of subjects that is difficult to access.

For the time being, one can, however, harbor a reasonable belief that the political authorities are not "terrorized" by terrorist acts: they are confronted by a threat they are trying to manage in a rational way (Goodin, 2006, p. 197). Surely, the choice of terminology is one of the most important problems in the field of terrorism studies. We choose here to define terror as an intense paralyzing fear, assuming that when anxiety reaches an acute level, it significantly impairs the subject's ability to deal with a threatening situation. The resilience of government authorities is probably supported by their activities and individual experiences, the terrorist threat being nothing more than a source of anxiety among numerous other sources of stress which are inherent in their political responsibilities. If regular exposure to risks lessens the subject's sensitivity in relation to the same (Yechiam et al., 2005, p. 437), it is highly possible that the psychological consequences of violent acts affect government officials less than the citizens. This, however, needs to be empirically verified.

It is nonetheless true that the authorities' psychological reactions cannot be totally independent of the nature, intensity, and frequency of attacks. The majority of terrorist incidents creates little confusion in those who have to politically manage them; but certain incidents bring about emotional reactions of the largest scale. That was the case when a "veritable hysteria of fears and phantoms" (Leitenberg, 2009, p. 103) reigned in the heart of the American government at the time of the anthrax attacks. The narrative of the incidents offered by Mayer (2008, pp. 2–6) caused a startling contrast between the composure with which Vice President Dick Cheney managed 9/11 and the climate of paranoia that reigned a few weeks later at the center of the government at the time of the "Amerithrax" crisis. Contrary to what was feared, Dick Cheney was not a victim of anthrax. On the other hand, he was apparently one of the victims of the "culture of fear" that he himself had contributed to by establishing bio-terrorism as a high-priority threat. The vice president had, since the 1980s, been familiar with doomsday scenarios that might confront the United States but was particularly impressed by a simulation of a bio-terrorist attack (code name "Dark Winter") in June of 2001 (Guillemin, 2006, p. 249).

Whether or not one is in agreement with the conclusions of Furedi (2002), Altheide (2006), and Mueller (2006), there is hardly any doubt about the existence of a culture of fear. It has two complementary dimensions. One of these originated from the dissociation between the perception of the risk and the real risk of suffering damages (Jackson, Jarvis, Gunning, & Smyth, 2011, p. 143). It is a matter of cognitive bias, the neglect of probability bias (Sunstein, 2003). The other has to do with the uncertain, indiscernible nature of the threat. The real issue resides in the deliberate exploitation of terrorism by authorities in order to feed this culture of fear: to what extent is the terrorist threat actually manipulated for political ends? The elements of a response to this question are located inside of an opaque area of the decision process that, to a very great extent, eludes any observation of the interactions between security services bureaucracies and political authorities.

The most significant political impact that resulted from the major attacks that took place at the beginning of the 21st century was seen in the strengthening of security organizations. In different proportions, the United States and the European countries have increased their budgets and anti-terrorist staffs, while at the same time remodeling the architecture of their security systems according to the principle of placing institutions concerned with security issues inside of a network ("comprehensive security" or "networked security"). In that regard, the case of Spain is totally representative of this trend. Although the Spanish State had accumulated experience in the fight against the ETA, the Madrid attacks constituted the beginning of a comprehensive restructuring of the security system. Because of legislation that followed the attacks, the number of anti-terrorist personnel was increased by 35 percent and budgets that were directly tied in to security increased by 48 percent. At the same time, a plan to fight terrorism (*Plan Operativo de Lucha Contra Terrorismo*) was drawn up by a new body (*Comité Ejecutivo para el Mando Unificado*), which assumed the responsibility of coordinating security measures (Reinares, 2009).

These new measures originated from an intervention carried out by political authorities, which the Minister of the Interior, José Antonio Alonso, reported to the deputies of the Spanish Parliament on May 24, 2004. The recently elected socialist government asked security professionals if they had sufficient resources and personnel in order to respond to the threat of the "new international terrorism" (Reinares, 2009, p. 370). As if it should have been, the bureaucracy's response was that resources should be increased and security organizations strengthened. In other words, the political authorities were confronted with a new challenge whose exact nature they were unable to comprehend; they entrusted the task of management to competent sectors of the bureaucratic system that responded to this priority, while justifying the increase of their influence at the center of the state organization.

The problem is that security organizations do not know what the terrorist threat exactly consists of. They certainly have factual information at their disposal—which is more or less exact—that relates to specific groups and individuals; but this information is not sufficient when it comes to describing this protean and partially undefined threat called "terrorism." As noted by Deflem (2004, p. 86) about the FBI, security organizations define terrorism "in vague and general terms" so that the goals and methods involved in the fight against terrorism can fit inside the framework of their customary activities. The result is that terrorism ceases to be a specific category of political violence and ends up merging with every other form of political violence.

Since the terrorist threat is uncertain, its ability to generate anxiety increases. This sort of anxiety is not directly linked to violence, but to the discourse on terrorism. In other words, the misperception (or the approximate perception) of terrorism give rise to a psychological tension in relation to the identification of the threat.

The vagueness of the definition of "terrorism" is likewise a response to a considerable difficulty that is inherent in the political authorities' orders. They order their security bureaucracies to not only respond to the existing threat that certain organizations present, but also to be on the lookout for new threats. This requirement of anticipating threats introduces confusion about what is an actual threat as opposed to a potential risk which contributes even more to making the idea of a "terrorist threat" vague. Such confusion clearly appears in relation to the use of weapons of mass destruction by non-state actors, an area in which a divorce between reality and alarmist words relative to the use of those kinds of weapons has been established (Leitenberg, 2009, p. 106).

In short, the "culture of fear" or "moral panic" (Rothe & Muzzatti, 2004) is not just a construct of political authorities and the media. It is the product of a complex process that has a foundation (of very real attacks), which is then developed on the basis of a double kind of uncertainty. The first uncertainty comes about when political authorities require security service officials to be specific about the nature of a poorly defined terrorist threat. The second uncertainty is an extension of the first, insofar as the officials maintain the uncertainty of the threat for several reasons. First, it is because they do not really have a definition for terrorism—rather, it is lost inside of the wider category of political violence. As a result, they are prompted to anticipate potential terrorist acts and therefore confuse the risk, threat, and effective preparation for an attack. Finally, it is because the logic of the bureaucratic functioning of these agencies requires them to increase their influence in order to justify their existence.

The majority of security organization officials only does its work and acts in complete good faith as it tries to respond to the expectations of political authorities. In other words, they are not engaged in a conspiracy aimed to shape the behavior of individuals by increasing their level of anxiety. However, the role they play in the creation of representations of terrorism contribute to the anxiety-provoking dimension of the phenomenon. In a routine kind of way, they will have a tendency to overestimate a threat so that no one will be able to reproach them for underestimating it. Sometimes, in an exacerbated manner, they come up with doomsday scenarios that could result from the use of weapons of mass destruction. The case of the "Amerithrax" crisis is certainly extreme, as it is exceptional. Nevertheless, it reveals the influence that representations of terrorism have on the perception of the threat by political authorities, an influence that, most likely is exercised with less magnitude, under the most ordinary circumstances. The Amerithrax case is actually even more disturbing since the attacks came from inside the security system. The FBI (Department of Justice, 2010, p. 38) attributed them to a bio-terrorism expert who was been motivated by the risk of failure when it comes to his work, which has been focused on the development of an anthrax vaccine. The Report of the Expert Behavioral Analysis Panel is even a bit more specific as it indicated that one of Dr. Ivin's motivations was to demonstrate the reality of the threat presented by anthrax, and to re-train his laboratory team, which was in charge of fighting against the potential threat (White et al., 2010, p. 9–10).

For the reasons just put forth, it is very difficult to distinguish anxiety-provoking factors directly tied in with a terrorist attack from those that are related to representations that are more or less based on a threat. These two kinds of factors simultaneously accumulate in different proportions, depending on the circumstances, and work to influence the political process, without it always being possible to determine if authorities are reacting to a real and immediate, uncertain or potential, or imaginary or contrived danger.

CONCLUSION

One might consider four elements of response to the question that is presented as the title of this contribution. In the first place, the political impact of terrorism is difficult to precisely define because the category of violence under consideration remains partially undefined. It is a problem which affects quantitative approaches that use databases that list a vast registry of politically motivated violent acts. By adding data that lack homogeneity, these studies deliver conclusions that are overly general and contribute to keeping a misunderstanding about just what terrorism is exactly.

In the second place, ambiguity permeates the debate regarding terrorism's effectiveness. While trying to determine whether terrorism works, researchers have frequently confused the actual effect of attacks with their proactive component, while at the same time ignoring their reactive component. Therefore, the actual political impact of violent acts, the purpose assigned to them by those who resort to them, and their immediate motivations are three things that are more or less different, and it is important to keep them separate.

In the third place, we still lack solid empirical knowledge regarding the psychological impact of attacks on political authorities. Nevertheless, that is one of the main factors that would allow one to specify what kinds of violent acts are more likely to have an effect on the same, and consequently, to create confusion and interfere with the decision process.

In the fourth place, the uncertainty and confusion that terrorist attacks cause are not just the result of acts of violence per se. Each attack is interpreted as an index of a threat that is important to identify and suppress. Therefore, the interpretive framework that the "terrorist threat," such as it is defined,—and more specifically, such as it remains undefined,—offers itself is permeated by uncertainty and contributes to the development of the confusion it should dispel.

REFERENCES

Abrahms, M. (2006). Why terrorism does not work. *International Security*, 31, 42–78.
Alonso, R. (2010). Radicalisation and recruitment among jihadist terrorists in Spain. In M. Randstorp (Ed.), *Understanding violent radicalisation* (pp. 207–230). London, UK: Routledge,.

Altheide, D. (2006). *Terrorism and the politics of fear*. Lanham, MD: Alta Mira Press.

Berrebi, C., & Klor, E. F. (2008). Are voters sensitive to terrorism? Direct evidence from the Israeli electorate. *American Political Science Review, 102*, 279–301.

Berrebi, C., & Ostwald, J. (2011). Earthquakes, hurricanes, and terrorism: Do natural disasters incite terror? *Public Choice, 149*, 383–403.

Dannenbaum, T. (2011). Bombs, ballots, and coercion: The Madrid bombings, electoral politics, and terrorist strategy. *Security Studies, 20*, 303–349.

Deflem, M. (2004). Social control and the policing of terrorism: Foundations for a sociology of counterterrorism. *The American Sociologist, 35*, 75–92.

Department of Justice (2010). *Amerithrax investigative summary*. Washington, DC: United States Department of Justice.

Fominaya, C. F. (2011). The Madrid bombings and popular protest: misinformation, counter- information, mobilisation and elections after "11-M." *Contemporary Social Science, 6*, 289–307.

Fowler, W. W. (1981). *Terrorism data bases: A comparison of missions, methods, and systems*. Santa Monica, CA: Rand Corporation.

Frey, B. S., Luechinger, S., & Stutzer, A. (2007). Calculating tragedy: Assessing the costs of terrorism. *Journal of Economic Surveys, 21*, 1–24.

Freytag, A., Krüger, J. J., Meierrieks, D., & Schneider, F. (2011). The origins of terrorism: Cross-country estimates of socio-economic determinants of terrorism. *European Journal of Political Economy, 27*, 5–16.

Furedi, F. (2002). *Culture of fear: Risk-taking and the morality of low expectation*. London, UK: Continuum.

Gassebner, M., Jong-A-Pin, R., & Mierau, J. O. (2008). Terrorism and electoral accountability: One strike, you're out! *Economics Letters, 100*, 126–129.

Goodin, R. (2006). *What's wrong with terrorism*. Cambridge, UK: Polity.

Gould, E. D., & Klor, E. F. (2010). Does terrorism work? *The Quarterly Journal of Economics, 125*, 1459–1510.

Guillemin, J. (2006). Terrorism and dispelling the myth of a panic prone public. *Journal of Public Health, 27*, 246–249.

Haunstrup Qvortrup, M. (2012). Terrorism and political science. *The British Journal of Politics and International Relations, 14*, 503–517.

Hlavac, M. (2010). Comment on Claude Berrebi and Esteban F. Klor: "Are voters sensitive to terrorism? Direct evidence from the Israeli electorate." Retrieved from http://papers.ssrn.com/sol3/papers.cfm?abstract_id=1690344

Indridason, I. H. (2008). Does terrorism influence domestic politics? Coalition formation and terrorist incidents. *Journal of Peace Research, 45*, 241–259.

Jackson, R., Jarvis, L., Gunning, J., & Smyth, M. B. (2011). *Terrorism. A critical introduction*. New York, NY: Palgrave Macmillan.

LaFree, G., Dugan, L., Fogg, H. V., & Scott, J. (2011). *Building a global terrorism database*, Darby. PA: Diane Publishing.

Leitenberg, M. (2009). The self-fulfilling prophecy of bioterrorism. *Nonproliferation Review, 16*, 95–109.

Llussa, F., & Tavares, J. (2011). Which terror at which cost? On the economic consequences of terrorist attacks. *Economic Letters, 110*, 52–55.

Mayer, J. (2008). *The dark side: The inside story of how the war on terror turned into a war on American ideals*. New York, NY: Doubleday.

Moretti, M. (2010). *Brigatte rosse*. Paris: Amsterdam Ed.

Montalvo, J. G. (2011). Voting after the bombings: A natural experiment on the effect of terrorist attacks on democratic elections. *The Review of Economics and Statistics, 93*, 1146–1154.

Mueller, J. (2006). *Overblown*. New York, NY: Free Press.
Munayyer, Y. (2009). Paper on "Does terrorism work?" flawed. Retrieved from http://blog.thejerusalemfund.org/2009/12/paper-on-does-terrorism-work-flawed.html
Nijdam, M. J., Gersons, B. P., & Olff, M. (2010). Dutch politicians' coping with terrorist threat. *The British Journal of Psychiatry, 197*, 328–329.
Nitsch, V., & Schumacher, D. (2004). Terrorism and international trade: An empirical investigation. *European Journal of Political Economy, 20*, 423–433.
Rapin, A. J. (2011). What is terrorism? *Behavioral Sciences of Terrorism and Political Aggression, 3*, 161–175.
Reader, I. (2002). Spectres and shadows: Aum Shinrikyo and the road to Meggido. In J. Kaplan (Ed.), *Millenial violence. Past, present, and future* (pp. 147–186). London, UK: Frank Cass.
Reinares, F. (2009). After the Madrid bombings: Internal security reforms and prevention of global terrorism in Spain. *Studies in Conflict & Terrorism, 32*, 367–388.
Reinares, F. (2010). The Madrid bombings and global jihadism. *Survival, 52*, 83–104.
Rose, M., & Murphy, R. (2007). Does terrorism ever work? Madrid train bombings. *International Security, 32*, 185–189.
Rothe, D., & Muzzatti, S. L. (2004). Enemies everywhere: Terrorism, moral panic, and US civil society. *Critical Criminology, 12*, 327–350.
Schmid, A. (2004). Statistics on terrorism: The challenge of measuring trends in global terrorism. *Forum on Crime and Society, 4*, 49–69.
Shimazono, S. (1995). In the wake of Aum. The formation and transformation of a universe of belief. *Japanese Journal of Religious Studies, 22*, 381–415.
Sunstein, C. R. (2003). Terrorism and probability neglect. *The Journal of Risk and Uncertainty, 26*, 121–136.
White, J. C., Shouten, R., Lamberti, J. S., Johnson, S. C., Holstege, C., Everett, A., ... Saathoff, G. (2010). *Amerithrax case: Expert behavioral analysis panel*. Vienna, VA: Research Strategies Network.
Yechiam, E., Barron, G., & Erev, I. (2005). The role of personal experience in contributing to different patterns of response to rare terrorist attacks. *Journal of Conflict Resolution, 49*, 430–439.

NOTES ON CONTRIBUTORS

THE EDITORS

Samuel Justin Sinclair is assistant professor at Harvard Medical School and director of research at the Psychological Evaluation and Research Laboratory (*The PEaRL*), Department of Psychiatry, Massachusetts General Hospital. He is founder and past-president of the Society for Terrorism Research and co-founder and co-editor-in-chief of the academic journal *Behavioral Sciences of Terrorism and Political Aggression*. He has co-written/edited several volumes on terrorism, including *Creating Young Martyrs* (Praeger Security International, 2008), *Interdisciplinary Analyses of Terrorism and Political Aggression* (Cambridge Scholars Publishing, 2010), *The Psychology of Terrorism Fears* (Oxford University Press, 2012), and *Contemporary Debates on Terrorism* (Routledge Publishers, 2012). Additionally, he has published numerous papers in the areas of terrorism, aggression, violence, psychological assessment, and psychometrics and continues to have active research programs in these areas. Dr. Sinclair is also the past recipient of the Association for Threat Assessment Professional's (ATAP) Dr. Chris Hatcher Memorial Scholarship Award (2007).

Daniel Antonius is assistant professor and director of forensic research in the Department of Psychiatry at University at Buffalo School of Medicine and Biomedical Sciences. He also holds the title adjunct assistant professor at the New York University School of Medicine and is a forensic psychologist with the Erie County Forensic Mental Health Services. He is president-elect of Protect New York and past governing board member of the Society for Terrorism Research. He has published in the areas of terrorism, aggression, violence, mental illness, psychological assessment, and psychometrics. He is the co-founder and co-editor-in-chief of the journal *Behavioral Sciences of Terrorism and Political Aggression*, and he is co-editor of the book *Interdisciplinary Analyses of Terrorism and Political Aggression* (Cambridge Scholars Publishing, 2010) and co-author of the book *The Psychology of Terrorism Fears* (Oxford University Press, 2012). Dr. Antonius has received awards from the International Society for Research on Aggression, American Psychological Foundation, and the Association for Threat Assessment Professionals.

THE CONTRIBUTORS

Abdolhossein Abdollahi is a professor of psychology teaching at various national and international universities. Dr. Abdollahi's primary research interests are social cognition, trauma, memory, and social embodiment. His more specific interest is Terror Management Theory (TMT). He has published papers in many peer-reviewed psychological journals, including *Journal of Personality and Social Psychology*, *Personality and Social Psychology Bulletin*, *Journal of Experimental Social Psychology*, *Current Directions in Psychological Science*, *Psychological Trauma: Theory, Research, Practice, and Policy*, and *Behavioral Sciences of Terrorism and Political Aggression*. He is also on the editorial boards of *Journal of Social Psychology*, *Journal of Social, Evolutionary, and Cultural Psychology*, and *Behavioral Sciences of Terrorism and Political Aggression*.

David Altheide is emeritus regents' professor on the faculty of Justice and Social Inquiry in the School of Social Transformation at Arizona State University, where he taught for 37 years. His work has focused on the role of mass media and information technology in social control. His most recent book is *Terror Post 9/11 and the Media* (Lang, 2009). Dr. Altheide received the Cooley Award three times, given to the outstanding book in symbolic interaction, from the Society for the Study of Symbolic Interaction: in 2007 for *Terrorism and the Politics of Fear* (AltaMira Press, 2006), in 2004 for *Creating Fear: News and the Construction of Crisis* (Aldine Transaction, 2002), and in 1986 for *Media Power* (SAGE Publications, 1985). Dr. Altheide received the 2005 George Herbert Mead Award for lifetime contributions from the Society for the Study of Symbolic Interaction, and the society's Mentor Achievement Award in 2007.

Anne (Azza) Aly is an ECR fellow in the Department of Social Science and International Relations of the Faculty of Humanities at Curtin University, Australia. Her research spans responses to terrorism, countering violent extremism and radicalization, and counterterrorism. She has an interest in how governments and societies respond to terrorism and the impacts of these responses. Anne is the author of *Terrorism and Global Security: Historical and Contemporary Perspectives* (Palgrave Macmillan, 2011). She has also contributed over 40 publications in books, journals, and conference proceedings on various themes including the fear of terrorism, counter terrorism, radicalization, and constructions of terrorism. In 2011, Anne was inducted into the inaugural Western Australia Women's Hall of Fame in recognition of her work and contributions to the study of terrorism and its responses.

Adam Beavers is a master's student at San Diego State University. His interests include topics in social psychology such as impression formation, stereotypes, prejudice, and discrimination. He has studied issues of sexual orientation, gender, and race/ethnicity.

Daphna Canetti has authored over 80 journal articles and book chapters. She is an associate professor and faculty chair of the MA program in Democracy Studies at the School of Political Science, University of Haifa. Her research focuses on the impact of war and violence on individuals, specifically on adults in the Middle East. She is using controlled randomized field experiments, spatial analysis, and experimental surveys for her biopolitical research of immunity and inflammation resulting from exposure to war and terrorism. Her work is supported by the National Institute of Mental Health, National Science Foundation, Binational Science Foundation, and other foundations. Recently, she was a Fulbright fellow at the Helen Kellogg Institute for International Studies, Notre Dame University, and a Rice Family Foundation visiting professor at the Council on Middle East Studies, the MacMillan Center, and the Department of Political Science, Yale University.

Virginia Chanley is a senior methodologist and research analyst at the U.S. Government Accountability Office in Washington, D.C., and she teaches courses in research methods and program evaluation at George Mason University in Arlington and Fairfax, Virginia. She has published research on U.S. public trust in government, U.S. public opinion on the role of the U.S. internationally, political tolerance, and political accountability.

Krista De Castella is a graduate student in clinical psychology and visiting researcher at Stanford University. Her main interests lie at the intersection of social psychology and affective science with a specific focus on fear and motivation in political, clinical, and educational contexts.

Dietrich Dörner is professor and the director of the Institute for Theoretical Psychology at the Otto-Friedrich Universität Bamberg, Germany. His main research interests are the study of complex problem solving and the modeling of psychological processes. He developed the autonomous agent PSI, which is a computer-simulated theory on the interaction of motivation, emotion, and cognition. He won the Leibnitz Price, the highest award in science in Germany, for his research. His books *The Logic of Failure* (Basic Books, 1997) and *Bauplan für eine Seele* [Blueprint for a Soul] (Rowohlt Tb, 2001) have been bestsellers.

Bernard Enjolras is research director at the Institute for Social Research in Oslo, Norway, and director of the Research Center on Civil Society and Voluntary Sector at the ISF. He holds a Ph.D. in sociology from the University of Québec in Montréal (Canada) and a Ph.D. in economics from the University of Paris I. Panthéon-Sorbonne, France. He is editor-in-chief of *Voluntas International Journal of Voluntary and Nonprofit Organizations*. His fields of research are civil society, voluntary organizations, public policies, governance, and social media and the public sphere.

Alexandra N. Foust graduated summa cum laude from University of North Florida in 2012 with a BA/BA in psychology and international studies. In August 2012, she began the M.Ed. program at Vanderbilt University in International Education Policy and Management. As a member of C. Dominik Güss' research team, she is currently working on a cross-cultural investigation of creativity, with a primary focus on data she collected in Guatemala.

Shana Kushner Gadarian is an assistant professor of political science, Maxwell School, Syracuse University. Her primary research interests are in American politics, political psychology, political communication, and experimental methods. The interest that motivates her research is how the political media environment influences how Americans seek political information and form opinions. In particular, she is interested in how citizens learn and form attitudes when politics is threatening, whether threats come from terrorism, public health outbreaks, or media and elite rhetoric. Her research has been funded by the National Science Foundation, Robert Wood Johnson Foundation, Princeton Policy Research Institute for the Region, and the Bobst Center for Peace and Justice. Her work has been published in the *Journal of Politics, Perspectives on Politics, Political Psychology* and volumes on experimental methods and immigration attitudes.

C. Dominik Güss is associate professor at the Psychology Department, University of North Florida, and research fellow of the Humboldt Foundation, Germany. His main research areas are suicide terrorism and cross-cultural studies on dynamic decision making and complex problem solving funded by the National Science Foundation. His research on suicide terrorism has been published in the *Journal for the Theory of Social Psychology, Behavioral Sciences of Terrorism and Political Aggression*, and in chapters in the edited book *Global Community: Global Security*.

Brian J. Hall is a clinical psychologist and NIMH T32 postdoctoral fellow in psychiatric epidemiology at the Johns Hopkins Bloomberg School of Public Health. Dr. Hall's research is focused on the social determinants of health, evaluating the association between social resources and health, and determining the effects of multiple forms of stress and adversity, particularly among vulnerable populations, within low- and middle-income contexts globally.

Stevan Hobfoll has authored and edited 11 books and one novel, including *Traumatic Stress* (Plenum Press, 1995) and *Stress, Culture and Community* (Springer, 1998), and over 200 journal articles and book chapters. He is the Judd and Marjorie Weinberg presidential professor and chair of the Department of Behavioral Sciences at Rush Medical College in Chicago. He was a member of the Disaster Mental Health Subcommittee of the United States National Biodefense Science Board (NBSB). His recent work on mass casualty intervention was designated as one of the most influential contributions to psychiatry.

Richard Jackson is deputy director of the National Centre for Peace and Conflict Studies, University of Otago, New Zealand. He is the editor-in-chief of the journal *Critical Studies on Terrorism* and the author or editor of eight books on terrorism, political violence, and conflict resolution, including *Contemporary Debates on Terrorism* (with Samuel Justin Sinclair; Routledge, 2012), *Terrorism: A Critical Introduction* (with Lee Jarvis, Jeroen Gunning, and Marie Breen Smyth; Palgrave Macmillan, 2011), *Contemporary State Terrorism: Theory and Cases* (with Eamon Murphy and Scott Poynting; Routledge, 2010), *Conflict Resolution in the Twenty-first Century: Principles, Methods and Approaches* (with Jacob Bercovitch; Michigan

University Press, 2009), and *Critical Terrorism Studies: A New Research Agenda* (with Marie Breen Smyth and Jeroen Gunning; Routledge, 2009).

Katarzyna Jaśko received her Ph.D. in psychology in 2011. She works in the Institute of Psychology at Jagiellonian University, Kraków, Poland. Her recent research has focused on the relation between group identification and acceptance of social inequalities among members of disadvantaged groups. She is also interested in political system legitimacy.

Małgorzata Kossowska is a full professor, working at the Institute of Psychology at Jagiellonian University, Kraków, Poland. Her areas of interest include cognitive and motivational underpinnings of social and political beliefs, cognitive rigidity, and its relationships with problem solving and decision making. She has published articles on psychological determinants on political beliefs, political conservatism, and strategies of social problem solving, among others, in *Political Psychology, Personality and Individual Differences, British Journal of Psychology,* and *European Journal of Social Psychology*.

Marie-Helen Maras is an assistant professor of Criminal Justice at the State University of New York and an adjunct assistant professor at New York University. She holds a D.Phil. in law and an M.Phil. in criminology and criminal justice from the University of Oxford.

Craig McGarty is professor of social and political psychology and director of research collaboration at Murdoch University in Western Australia. He is well known for his research on the categorization process in social psychology and on the processes of stereotype formation and change. He is also heavily involved in research on group-based emotions including collective guilt and on public opinion and collective action.

Rachel Monaghan is a senior lecturer in criminology at the University of Ulster. She is the author (with Colin Knox) of *Informal Justice in Divided Societies: Northern Ireland and South Africa* (Palgrave MacMillan, 2002) and has been researching political violence in Northern Ireland since 1998. She has published a number of articles on the subjects of paramilitary "punishments," loyalist violence, and counterterrorism measures in Northern Ireland in the *International Criminal Justice Review, Space and Polity, Terrorism and Political Violence,* and *Journal of Conflict Studies*. She is an associate editor for the journal *Behavioral Sciences of Terrorism and Political Aggression* and is on the editorial board for *Studies in Conflict and Terrorism*.

Guro Ødegård is a senior researcher at the Institute for Social Research. Her research interests include civil society, voluntary organizations and political participation, with a particular emphasis on youth and ethnic minorities.

Carmit Rapaport is a postdoctoral fellow in political psychology at the School of Political Science, University of Haifa. She received her Ph.D. from the Technion–Israel Institute of Technology. Her research focuses on the social and behavioral aspects of disasters, social and national resilience, and political-psychological mechanisms underlying terrorism and political violence.

Ami-Jacques Rapin is a tenured senior lecturer in history at the University of Lausanne, Switzerland. He has also served as a consultant for an international organization in Southeast Asia.

Melody Sadler is assistant professor of psychology at San Diego State University. Her interests include topics in social and quantitative psychology. Her research has examined the emotional and cognitive underpinnings of prejudice based on race/ethnicity, mental health status, gender, and sexual orientation.

Maciek Sekerdej is a lecturer and researcher at the Institute of Psychology, Jagiellonian University, Kraków, Poland. His research interests cover principally the areas of intergroup relations, prejudice, stereotyping, and nationalism. He has published articles on anti-Semitism, nationality stereotypes, and psychology of religion. He is also a co-author of the book *Image of the Other: Polish Attitudes Towards Ukrainians* (VDM Verlag Dr. Müller, 2008). Currently, he is involved in the research on the group processes in the framework of Relational Models Theory and theories of embodiment. He is a member of European Association of Experimental Social Psychology and International Society of Political Psychology.

George E. Shambaugh is associate professor of international affairs and government at Georgetown University. He holds a joint appointment in the School of Foreign Service and Department of Government and served as chairman of the Department of Government from 2005 through 2012. He is the author of *States, Firms, and Power: Successful Sanctions in US Foreign Policy* (SUNY Press, 1999), co-author of *The Art of Policymaking: Tools, Techniques, and Processes in the Modern Executive Branch* (Longman, 2003), co-editor of *Anarchy and the Environment: The International Relations of Common Pool Resources* (SUNY Press, 1999), and co-editor of *Taking Sides: Clashing Views on Controversial Issues in U.S. Foreign Policy* (McGraw Hill, 2010).

Kari Steen-Johnsen is a senior researcher at the Institute for Social Research in Oslo, Norway. She is a sociologist, and her research centers on changes in civil society and voluntary organizations. Her previously published works include articles on local communities, organizational change, and the impact of digitalization on social capital.

Michael J. Stevens is a professor at Illinois State University, where he was named outstanding university researcher. He holds an honorary doctorate and professorship at The Lucian Blaga University in Romania. He is an APA fellow and past-president of its Division of International Psychology, and has published and presented extensively on the psychology of terrorism.

Ryan Stolier is a graduate student in social psychology at San Diego State University. His research interests broadly concern mentalization, threat inference, and emotions in stereotyping and prejudice. His research involves computerized study designs and uses implicit, neuroimaging, and physiological measures.

Carly Wayne completed her M.A. in government-diplomacy and conflict studies in 2010 at IDC Herzliya in Israel. Her current research interests focus on analyzing the psychological processes such as emotions, cognitive and motivational processes, and ideology that hinder optimal political decision making in situations of conflict at both the elite and mass levels. Currently, she is working on a study analyzing the link between accountability and motivation to regulate emotion in conflict decision making and a book analyzing the disjointed group decision-making processes (a phenomenon termed "polythink") that can lead to suboptimal foreign policy decisions by governments.

Bradley M. Weisz is a psychology master's student at San Diego State University. His interests include topics in social and political psychology. His research has examined how politicized framings of controversial legislation can impact people's political motivation, particularly for those who have social identities that may be threatened by the legislation.

Geoffrey Wetherell is a Ph.D. student in the experimental psychology program at DePaul University. His research examines political psychology, moral convictions, and how moral and political belief systems relate to the desire for existential meaning.

Dag Wollebæk is a senior researcher at the Institute for Social Research in Oslo, Norway. He holds a Ph.D. in comparative politics from the University of Bergen, Norway. His previously published work includes articles on social capital, voluntary organizations, and social media. In recent years, he has focused on the study of trust in local context as well as the consequences of terror for trust and civic engagement. Among his recent publications is "After Utøya: How a High Trust Society Reacts to Terror," published in *Political Science & Politics* (2012) (together with Bernard Enjolras, Kari Steen-Johnsen, and Guro Ødegård).

INDEX

ABC poll, Afghans, 115, 116–117
ABC/*Washington Post*, 5, 13
Abdollahi, Abdolhossein, 213–223, 314
Abdulmutallab, Umar, 158
Abu Ghraib, 98, 102
ACNielsen Global Consumer Opinion Survey, 158, 159
action tendencies, 126
actus reus, 237
Adams, Gerry, 148
affect, undifferentiated emotion, 126
affect heuristic, threat response, 60
affective intelligence theory, 59–60, 64
affective modulation, term, 163
affiliation need, 108, 109f
affiliative tendencies, fear, 111–112
Afghanistan, 98, 102, 113, 204, 273
    fear after suicide attack, 113
    military interventions, 278
    suicide terrorism and policy implications, 114–117
    Taliban as enemies of, 110
Afghanistan war, xv, 12, 16, 57, 63, 67, 85, 168, 273
aggression, fear response, 110–111
airport security, 12, 126, 131, 157, 167–168, 173, 271, 289, 293
Al-Aqsa Intifada, 206
Al-Jazeera web site, 97
Al Kadhimiya Mosque, Shiite pilgrims, 111
Al-Maliki, Nouri
    policy decisions, 116f, 120, 121
    suicide terrorism, 119
al-Muhajir, Abu Hamza, AQI leader, 119
Alonso, José Antonio, 307
Al Qaeda, 86, 103, 158, 175, 176, 180, 233, 235, 261

Al-Qaeda in Iraq (AQI), 118–119
Altheide, David L., 283–296, 314
Aly, Anne (Azza), 156–169, 314
Aly–Balnaves metric of fear, 158
American National Election Studies (ANES), public trust, 4, 5f, 6, 8
Amerithrax crisis, 306, 308
anger. *See also* emotions
    antiterrorism policy, 129–130
    political engagement, 56–58
anger-mongering, 133
anthrax, 306
anticipated effort, appraisals, 128
antisocial behavior, 228
Anti-terrorism Bill 2004, Australia, 162
Anti-Terrorism Bill 2005, Australia, 163
antiterrorism policies. *See also* counterterrorism policies
    effects of 9/11 on public views of, 10–13
    public opinion and responses to terrorism, 14–16
antiterrorism support
    anger, 129–130
    fear, 130
    sadness, 131
Antonius, Daniel, xv–xxiii, 313
anxiety-buffer disruption theory (ABDT), 221
appraisals, prompting emotions, 127, 128
appraisal tendency theory, 64
    emotion, 128
    emotions, 56–57
    risk perception, 61
appraisal theory, xx
    fear, 92
    opinion-based groups, 62
    stress, 203

Arab Americans, 57
Arabs, surveillance and immigration, 10
Area 51, 269
Are You Ready? (booklet), 272
armed propaganda, 304
Asahara, Shoko, 303, 304
Assassination, Ambassador Stevens, xv–xvi
Associated Press, 97
attachment theory, xvi, 54, 64
attentional activity, appraisals, 128
attributions, prompting emotions, 127–128
attribution theory, terrorism policy, xx, 127–128
Aum Shinrikyo, 302, 303
Australia, xvii, 156–157, 168–169
    Bali bombings, 156
    collective identity, 277
    counterterrorism measures, 162–163
    fearing terror, 163–164
    fear of losing civil liberties, 165–166
    fear of terrorism, 160–163
    feeling insecurity, 167–168
    images of terrorism, xx
    National Security Public Information Campaign, 157
    National Terrorism Public Alert System, 158
    political fear, 164–165
    security programs, 275
    terrorism industry, 273
    terrorist threat and public perception, 157–160
Australian Election Study, 158
Australian Security Intelligence Organisation Legislation, 162
authoritarians, ideology, 177–179
automobile travel, comparing to terrorist bombings, 238–239
availability, risk, 229
availability heuristic, risk probability, 228–232
Aviation Transport Security Bill 2003, Australia, 162
Aviation Transport Security Bill 2007, Australia, 162
Aznar, José Maria, 304

Bali bombings, 156, 167
Beavers, Adam, 125–133, 314
Becker, Ernest, 216, 223

Belfast/Good Friday Agreement, 139, 151
Beltway Sniper, Washington D.C., 113
Bible, 221
bin Laden, Osama, xix, 73–74, 101, 102, 158, 291
    death by U.S. CIA, 173, 174
    speeches, 95, 97–98
bio-terrorism, 306, 308
bipartisan support, terrorism, 24
Blair, Tony, xix, 102, 231
    aftermath of London bombings, 233
    fear appeals, 92, 93
    fear content in speeches, 94f
    "rules of the game," 229
    speeches, 95, 98–101
Blears, Hazel, 237
Blum, Scott, 20, 25, 47
Breivik, Anders Behring, 303
brown scare, German citizens, 269
Bulger, James, 234
Bush, George W., xviii, xix, xxii
    approval ratings, 182
    counterterrorism, 22
    fear appeals, 92, 93
    fear content in speeches, 94f
    mass media and terrorism, 70–71
    mortality salience, 222
    National Security Strategy, 77
    policies and threat perception, 10, 12–13
    public perceptions of administration, 28
    speeches, 95–97
    terrorism narrative, 291
    terrorism threat and public support, 20
    threat perceptions, 21
    trust in government, 45, 63, 67, 69
    USA PATRIOT Act, 55, 219, 272, 288

Canada, terrorism industry, 273
Canetti, Daphna, 193–208, 314–315
Carroll, Stephen, 148
Carter, Jimmy, 4, 9
casualties
    military conflicts, 22–23
    U.S. policy in Iraq, 38t, 39t
    war in Iraq, 29
Catholicism, Poland, 180–181
CBS/New York Times, 5, 80
Center for Human Rights and Global Justice, 292

Central Intelligence Agency (CIA), 173, 174, 274
certainty, appraisals, 128
certainty need, 108, 109f
Chanley, Virginia, 3–17, 315
charismatic leaders, death reminders and preference for, 222–223
Chechnya, 204
Cheney, Dick, 306
China, 276
Christians, 62
Christmas Day 2009, failed terrorist attempt, 158–159
Churchill, Winston, 86
civil liberties
  fear of losing, 165–166
  security, 267
civil rights legislation, 6
Civil Rights Network, 165
Civil War myths, 273
Club de Madrid Series on Democracy and Terrorism, 165
CNN/ORC International survey, 13
CNN surveys, 5
CNN/*USA Today*/Gallup Polls, 93
Cognitive Calculus Model, 56, 64
cognitive closure, need for, 63
cognitive evaluation, threat perception, 199
cold war, 269, 275, 277, 294
collective level, threat perception, 200
Columbine school shootings, 288
combatants, image of terrorists, 175
Commonwealth Games, Melbourne, 159
communication
  risk, and politics of fear, 295–296
  speeches by leaders, 97–102
  surveillance program, 288
  terrorism news, 69–71
competence needs, 108, 109f
concealed weapons, focus on fear, 287
confirmatory perception, fear of terrorism, 112
conflict, ethos of, 198–199
conflict zones, need for research in, 204–207
Conservation of Resources (COR) theory, xxi, 197, 203
conservativism, political, 62–63
conspiracy theories, 269
Continuity IRA, Northern Ireland, 141, 148, 149
controllable attributions, 127
Cost of the Troubles Study, Northern Ireland, 147
counterterrorism, 21
  probability neglect, 235
  procedures for terrorism fear, 272–273
  support and perceived risk, 228
counterterrorism policies
  Australia, 162–163
  Northern Ireland, 141–143
  survey, 26t, 28
  war in Iraq, 44
Coyle, Raymond, 150
Creating Fear: News and the Construction of Crisis, Altheide, 283
credibility, trust in government, 24–25
crime narrative
  alternative, 102–103
  elements of, 89–91
  fear campaigns, 87
  popular culture, 283–284
  terrorism as, 86–87
Crusaders, 304
culture of fear, 269, 308
cultures
  death reminders and political attitudes, 217–221
  mortality, 216
Customs Legislation (2006), Australia, 162
cynicism, decline in trust, 6

Darwin, emotion, 215
Data Retention Directive, 236
death terror
  death reminders and preference for charismatic leaders, 222–223
  terror management theory (TMT), 217
  unconscious emotion, 213, 216
De Castella, Krista, 85–103, 315
Declaration on Combating Terrorism, European Council, 236
deep cultural grammar, 270
Democratic Unionist Party (DUP), Northern Ireland, 140, 151
Democrats
  political information, 71
  terrorism images, 79f
  terrorism information, 68
  terrorism news, 69–71, 76, 80
  terrorism news lab experiment, 72

INDEX [323]

Democrats (*Cont.*)
    torture and terrorists, 12–13
    trust and president, 11
Department of Homeland Security (DHS), 16, 273, 274
    formation of, 9–10
    new Department of, 156
    Secretary Ridge, 0 xvii
    threat advisory, 69
    Threat Level Warnings, 272
Derry Journal, 150
discourse of danger, 277
discourse of fear, 283, 287, 289
Dissociative Experiences Scale II (DES–II), 221
doctrine of preemptive war, 275
doing the right thing, 28, 45
Dörner, Dietrich, 107–121, 315
doublespeak, 88
dovish foreign policy, terrorism, 77, 79*f*, 131
dread risk, perception, 174
drone attacks, Obama, 16
drug war, 291
dual process theory, 59, 64

Eastern African embassy bombings, 270
economy
    terrorism, *xvi–xvii*
    trust in government, 7
education, trust in government, 7
Egypt, 113, 114
electoral politics
    Israel, 301–302
    Madrid bombings and, 235–236, 304–305
    terrorism and counterterrorism policies, 23
emotional response, terrorism, *xvii*
emotions
    affect as undifferentiated, 126
    anger, 56–58, 129–130
    antiterrorism policy support, 129–131
    anxiety and fear, 54–56
    appraisals, 127, 128
    attributions, 127–128
    biopsychological entities, 214
    concept, 214
    death terror as unconscious emotion, 213
    evolutionary psychology, 215
    expression types, 215
    fear, 108–110, 130

    human cognition, 214
    mass media and popular culture, 284–287
    negative emotionality in Poland, 183–185
    political action, 53–54
    PSI-theory, 108–110
    role and function in daily life, 215
    sadness, 131
    stress-based model, *xx–xxi*
    terrorism policy preferences, 132–133
    unconscious characteristics, 215–216
    voting behavior, 59, 60
employment, 276
end of innocence, 261
enemies of freedom, 88
England, *xvii*. *See also* London
Enjolras, Bernard, 246–263, 315
Eritrea, 204
ethnocentric utilitarian perspective, 64
    anger, 58
    opinion-based groups, 63
Europe, 240
European Council, Declaration on Combating Terrorism, 236
European Social Survey, 172
European Union, 236, 290
    Declaration on the EU Response to the London Bombings, 236
    terrorism industry, 273
    terrorist threats, 171–172
    trust in, 182
evolutionary psychology, *xvi*
    emotion, 215
    public opinion and responses to terrorism, 14–16
    terrorism and trust in government, 13
evolutionary theory, *xviii*
existential needs, 108, 109*f*
Eyes of the Road, Trucker program, 272

familiarity, risk, 229–230
fear. *See also* Northern Ireland; psychological terror; terrorism fear
    age group, in Norway, 253*f*
    Aly–Balnaves metric of, 158
    antiterrorism policy, 130
    appraisal theory, 92
    behavioral consequences of, 110–113
    emotions and popular culture, 284–287
    human emotion regulation, 108–110
    impact of Troubles on health and, 147

losing civil liberties, 165–166
mortality, 213–214
negative emotionality in Poland, 183–185
Northern Ireland, 143–147
Norway after 7/22/11, 250–254, 251t
past research of, and threat perceptions, 247–249
political, 164–165
popular culture promoting, 283–284
probability neglect, 239
propaganda, 286–287
suicide bombings, 109f, 111f
terrorism, and political outcomes, 199–201
terrorism, fear and popular culture, 288–289
terrorism in Australia, 160–164
threat perception and, 201–204
fear appeals
alternative to, 102–103
differences between speakers and over time, 101–102
evidence for, 91–93, 95
speeches by George W. Bush, 95–97
speeches by Osama bin Laden, 97–98
speeches by Tony Blair, 99–101
fear-mongering, 133
fear rallying model, Norway, 258f
Federal Bureau of Investigation (FBI), 273, 274, 291, 292, 308
Federal Emergency Management Agency, 272
Federation of American Scientists Directory of Terrorist Organizations, 302
financial costs. U.S. policy in Iraq, 40t, 41t
Finland, 172
Firearms, personal protection, 287
flight response, fear, 110, 111
Flitton, Daniel, 158–159
Foreign Intelligence Surveillance Act, 288
Foust, Alexandra N., 107–121, 315
fundamentalist ideology, 100

Gadarian, Shana Kushner, 67–83, 316
Gaza, 194, 202, 295
gender
anxiety, 56
government retaliation against terrorism, 53
political engagement, 62

trust and terrorist threat to personal security, 34
General Linear Models (GLM), 253
General Social Survey (2008), 77
generation Utoya, Norway, 253
George Washington University, 284
German citizens, brown scare, 269
German Marshall Fund poll, 230
Global Attitudes Project, Pew Research Center, 230
Global Terrorism Database, 157, 300, 301
Global War on Terror, 27
Gonzalez, Paloma, 20, 25, 47
government retaliation
after 9/11 attacks, 52
moral justifications for aggression, 52–53
Great Society programs, 6
Greece, 302
grid of intelligibility, 274
group identity, threat perception, 179–180
group level, threat perception, 200
Guantanamo, 98, 102, 233
Gulf War of 1991, 7
Güss, C. Dominik, 107–121, 316

Hall, Brian J., 193–208, 316
Hamas, 206
Harper, Nate, 293
hawkish foreign policy, terrorism, 70–71, 77, 131
Hazelwood Integrated Primary School, Belfast, 146
health care, 7, 276
Hezbollah, 236
high-trust societies, xxi, 260–261. See also Norway
Hobbes, fear of terrorism, 162
Hobfoll, Stevan, 193–208, 316
Holy Koran, 220
homegrown terrorist threats
coverage of, 235
language of terrorism, 293
Homeland Security. See Department of Homeland Security (DHS)
hostile-world effect, xix, 52
Howard, John, 102
fear appeals, 92, 93
fear content in speeches, 94f
Hussain, Hasib, 229
Hussein, Saddam, 20, 98

ICM/BBC survey, 231–343
ideologues, image of terrorists, 175
ideology. *See also* partisanship
  ethos of conflict, 198–199
  fundamentalist, 100, 102
  Poland, 177–179
  risk society, 277
  terrorism and news messages, 68
imagined community, 277
immigration restrictions, anxiety and fear, 54–55
Independent Monitoring Commission (IMC), Northern Ireland, 140–141
Independents, terrorism news, 76, 80
India, 276
individual level, threat perception, 200
information
  news and threat perception, 68–69
  role of political, 71
institutional trust, Norway, 255t
intercoder reliability, fear appraisal, 93
intergroup emotion theory, 64
  anger, 129–130
  anger vs. fear, 57
  opinion-based groups, 62
intergroup threat, fear, 201
internal attributions, 127
Internal Revenue Service, fear of, 8
International Body on Decommissioning, Northern Ireland, 139
International Monetary Fund (IMF), Afghanistan, 115
International Terrorism Attributes of Terrorist Events (ITERATE) database, 23
Iran, *xvii*
  mortality salience, 217–218
  questionnaire, 218
Iran-Contra scandal, 4
Iraq, 98, 204
  Al-Qaeda in Iraq (AQI), 118–119
  fear, terrorism, and invasion of, 165
  fear of suicide terrorism, 117–120
  Kuwait invasion, 7
  military interventions, 278
  weapons of mass destruction, 20
Iraq war, *xv*, 12, 16, 20, 24, 57, 63, 67, 85, 273
  casualties and U.S. policy in Iraq, 38t, 39t
  financial costs and U.S. policy in Iraq, 40t, 41t
  level of threat and policy support, 44–45
  perceptions of threat, 34–35
  policy support for, 29–30, 45
  propaganda, 290
  trust in government and public support, 34–35
  United States justified in post-9/11 attack, 35, 36t, 37t
Ireland, 204. *See also* Northern Ireland
Irish Protestants, 202
Irish Republican Army (IRA). *See also* Northern Ireland
  Prevention of Terrorism Act, 142, 151
  Provisional IRA (PIRA), 140, 142, 147–149
  Real IRA and Continuity IRA, 141, 148, 149
Islam, 100, 113
Islamic extremism, 12
Islamic martyr, 112
Islamic terrorism, 180
Islamic terrorists, threat conceptions, 240
Islamic values, 220
isolationism, United States, 10
Israel, 204, 206
  electorate and terrorism, 301–302
  invasion of Gaza (2008), 295
  Jews. 202
Israeli-Palestinian conflict
  climate of violence, 193–194
  ethos of conflict, 198–199
  psychological-political process, 204–205
Israeli-Palestinian situation, *xvii*, *xx*, *xxiii*
Israelis
  climate of violence, 193–194
  international response, 52
  military force against Palestinians, 55
  psychopolitical responses, 195
  retaliatory action, 53

Jackson, Richard, 267–280, 316–317
Japanese Americans, yellow scare, 269
Jaśko, Katarzyna, 171–186, 317
Jordan, 113, 114, 194

Kaczyński, Lech, 183
Karmal, Babrak, 116
Karzai Administration

Afghanistan, 115–117
  policy decisions, 116f, 121
Kennedy assassination, 269
Kerry, John, 222
Khan, Mohammad Sidique, 229
Knowledge Networks (KN), survey, 25, 77
Koran, 100
Korean war, 22–23
Kossowska, Malgorzata, 171–186, 317
Kuwait, Iraqi invasion, 7

leader rhetoric
  differences between speakers and over time, 101–102
  emotional appeals, 102–103
  fear appeals, 91–93, 95
  fear content in speeches, 94f
  opinion polls, 93
  speeches by George W. Bush, 95–97
  speeches by Osama bin Laden, 95, 97–98
  speeches by Tony Blair, 95, 98–101
Lebanon, 114, 194
legacy of fear, xx
liberals
  terrorism images, 79f
  terrorism news, 69–71
Liberation Tigers, Tamil Eelam, 300
Libya, assassination of Ambassador Stevens, xv–xvi
Lindsay, Jetmaine, 229
London
  aftermath of bombings, 233
  government powers, 233
  homegrown terrorists, 235
  shoot to kill policy, 166
  studies after, 231
  suicide bombers, 229
  terrorism bombings in 2005, xxi, 73, 160, 163, 173, 301
  threat conceptions, 240
Los Angeles Times, 13
Lowy Institute, 159
Loyalist Volunteer Force (LVF), 141

McCain, Madeleine, 234
McCarthyism, 269, 277
McDonald, Bryan, 20, 25, 47
McFadden, Ciaran, 150
McGarty, Craig, 85–103, 317
McGuinness, Martin, 140, 148, 151

Madrid. *See also* Spain
  elections after bombing, 235–236, 304–305
  government powers, 233
  homegrown terrorists, 235
  media and availability of attacks, 229
  passenger name record (PNR), 236
  studies after, 231
  terrorist attacks of March 2004, 0xv, 173
  threat conceptions, 240
Maras, Marie-Helen, 227–240, 317
martyr, 112
martyrdom operations
  mortality salience, 220
  opinions in Iran, 218, 219
mass media
  coverage of homegrown terrorist threats, 235
  crime stoppers, 294
  Democrats and liberals rejecting terrorism news, 69–71
  emotions and popular culture, 284–287
  impact of terrorism and fear, 288–289
  information about terrorism, 67–68
  information environment and threat perception, 68–69
  laboratory experiment, 72–76
  online cues experiment, 76–80
  portrayal of terrorism, 234
  promoting crime and violence, 283–284
  reactance hypothesis, 70, 74–76
  research hypotheses, 72
  role of political information, 71
  social fears, 267
  terrorism images and fear, 79f
  terrorism news and partisanship, 80–81
  terrorism news backfiring with Democrats and liberals, 74f
Massoud, Ahmad Zia, 116
Massumi, 156, 162, 163
The Matrix (film), 164
Matthew, Richard, 20, 25, 47
mens rea, 237
MI5, British domestic security, 141
Middle East, xv, xxi, 100, 117, 219, 221
military action, anxiety and fear, 54–55
military conflicts, casualties, 22–23
military interventions, 221
Mohamud, Mohamed Osman, 292–293
Monaghan, Rachel, 139–151, 317

moon landing, 269
morality, terrorism, 16
Moretti, Mario, 304
Morgan, Roy, 158, 159
mortality
   death terror, 216
   fear, 213–214
mortality salience
   martyrdom operations, 220
   terror management theory (TMT), 161, 217
Muslims, 57, 113, 118, 119

Nader, Ralph, 222
National Counterterrorism Center, Worldwide Incidents Tracking System, 230, 230t, 231t
National Election Studies (2004), 69
national identity, emergence after 9/11, 290
National Institutes of Health, 207
nationalism, Poland, 179–180
National Missile Defense (NMD)
   doctrine of preemptive war, 275
   placement in Poland, 176
National Science Foundation Human and Social Dynamics, 20, 25
national security
   terrorism as threat to, 30, 31t, 45, 46
   trust and perceptions of terrorist threat to, 31t, 33
National Security Information Bill 2005, Australia, 162
National Security Public Information Campaign, Australia, 157
national signals, public opinions about, 24–25
National Terrorism Advisory System, 109
National Terrorism Public Alert System, Australia, 158
national threat, government and future attacks, 263t
needs, PSI-Theory, 108, 109f
negative affect, undifferentiated emotion, 126
negative emotionality, Poland, 183–185
"new age" theme, September 11, 2001 attack, 90–91, 103
New York Police Department (NYPD), 292
New York Times, 70
New York University, 292

Nixon, Richard, 4
Nobel Peace Prize, Obama, 291
normalization, terrorism fear, 271–274
North Atlantic Treaty Organization (NATO), 173, 182, 291
Northern Ireland, *xvii, xx, xxiii*
   Belfast/Good Friday Agreement, 139, 151
   continuance of "othering," 150–151
   counterterrorism measures, 141–143
   deeply divided society, 143–147
   impact of Troubles on health and fear, 147
   "other" community, 145
   othering, 142–143, 150–151
   peace walls, 145, 146, 151
   Prevention of Terrorism Act, 142, 151
   punishments, 148–149
   religious labels, 140
   Republican Action Against Drugs (RAAD), 150
   residential segregation, 144–145
   threat posed by terrorism, 140–147
   Troubles and political violence, 139–140
   violence dissident republicanism, 147–150
Northern Ireland Life and Times Survey (NILTS), 143–144
Northern Irish Catholics, 202
North Korea story, 73, 75, 82
Norway, *xvii, xxi, xxiii*
   Breivik, 303
   commission report, 260–261
   fear after 7/22/11, 250–254, 251t
   fear by age group, 253f
   fear of terrorism, 172
   fear rallying model, 258f
   government and future attacks, 263t
   July 22, 2011 terror attacks, 246–247
   rallying effects in high-trust society, 260–261
   rallying with or without fear, 256–259
   Rose Marches, 247, 248
   survey by Taylor Nelson Sofres (TNS) Gallup, 249–250
   trust in government, 254–256
Norwegian Research Council, 249

Obama, Barack, 5, 16, 47, 82, 113, 291
Office of National Statistics (ONS), Britain, 229

Oglaigh nahEireann (ONH), 148
Oklahoma City bombing, 125, 251, 252, 270
Omagh bombing in 1998, 147–148
Operation Cast Lead, 194
Operation Demetrius, 141
Operation Desert Storm, 7
Operation Overt, 237
Operation Seagram, 237
opinion-based groups, political engagement, 62–63
opinion polls, fear rhetoric, 93
Orange Order, survey, 150–151
Original Gangster (OG) members, 293
othering, Northern Ireland, 142–143, 150–151
overestimation, risk, 238
overkill response, 57

Paisley, Ian, 140
Pakistan, 113, 114, 115, 121, 278
Palestine, 114
Palestinian Authority, 204
Palestinians
  climate of violence, 193–194
  international response, 52
  Israeli support for military force against, 55
  psychopolitical responses, 195
Palestinian Territories, 194, 206
Palmer Raids, 269
Pape, Robert, 102–103
partisanship
  public opinions, 24–25
  terrorism and news messages, 68
  terrorism news, 74f, 80
  threat perception, xix, 21
  trust and terrorist threat to national security, 33
  trust in government, 11
passenger name record (PNR), Madrid, 236
Patriot Act, 55, 219, 272, 288
peace walls, Northern Ireland, 145, 146, 151
Pearl Harbor myths, 273
pentaerythritol tetranitrate (PETN), 158
Pentagon, 3, 131, 219
personal security
  terrorism as threat to, 30, 32t, 45, 46
  trust and perceptions of terrorist threat to, 32t, 33–34
personal threat, 200, 263t

persuasive communication, terrorism news, 69–71
Pew Research Center, 5, 11, 113, 230
pleasantness, appraisals, 128
Poland, xvii, xx, 63
  American National Missile Defense system (NMD), 176
  attitudes toward war on terror, 173–174
  ideology, 177–179
  nationalism, 179–180
  negative emotionality, 183–185
  perceptions of terrorism and terrorists, 174–177
  religion, 180–181
  terrorist threats, 171, 172–174
Police Service of Northern Ireland (PSNI), 148, 149
police surveillance, anxiety and fear, 54–55
policy support
  casualties in Iraq, 38t, 39t
  financial costs in Iraq, 40t, 41t
  individual characteristics, 45
  level of threat and, 44–45
  time to achieve objectives in Iraq, 42t, 43t
  trust in government and, 35, 44
  war in Iraq, 29–30
political action, emotions and, 53–54
political efficacy, 198
political engagement
  anger, 56–58
  demographic groups, 55–56
  moral outrage, 57–58
  opinion-based groups, 62–63
  risk perception, 60–62
  voting behavior, 59–60
political extremism
  psychological distress-based model, 195
  stress-based model of, 202, 204
political fear, Australia, 164–165
political ideology, xix. See also ideology
political intolerance, moral outrage, 57–58
political outcomes
  exposure to terrorism, 203f
  stress-based model, 201–204
  terrorism fears and, 199–201
political reactions, terrorism, 51, 52–53
popular culture
  crime and victimization, 286
  emotions and media logic, 284–287
  promotion of fear, 283–284
  terrorism, fear and, 288–289

Popular Party, election, 235
post-traumatic stress disorder (PTSD), 194, 196, 197, 199, 221
Poulin, Michael, 20, 25, 47
Powell, Colin, 20
Prevention of Terrorism Act, Northern Ireland, 142, 151
Princeton University, 77
probability, risk, 229
probability neglect, public stress levels, 236–237
propaganda
    9/11 and expansion of, 290–293
    fear, 286–287
prospect theory, 64
    risk, 238–240
    risk perception, 61
Provisional Irish Republican Army (PIRA), Northern Ireland, 140, 142, 147–149
PSI-Theory
    affiliation, 120
    emotions, 108–110, 120–121
    fear, 107–108
    fear-activated motivations, 115
    fear of terrorism, 112
psychological distress
    anxiety, 237
    buffers and resilience to, 197–198
    exposure to terrorism, 195–197
    political extremism, 195
    political psychology, 202–203
    prolonged exposure to violence, 194–195
psychological terror
    9/11 and expansion of terror and propaganda, 290–293
    emotions and media logic, 284–287
    terrorism, fear and popular culture, 288–289
    terrorism, risk society and banality of evil, 294–295
    terrorism as condition, 293–294
psychological well-being, political efficacy, 198
psychology
    PSI-theory, 107–108
    terrorism, *xvi*, 293–294
psychopathic criminals, image of terrorists, 175
public opinion
    partisanship, 24–25

policies to combat terrorism, 10–13
    responses to terrorism, 14–16
    United Kingdom, 232
public perceptions. *See also* threat perception
    media emphasis, 285–286
    terrorism threat, 28–29
public support, Iraq war, 34–35
punishments, Northern Ireland, 148–149

rallying effect
    Norway attacks, 246, 260–261
    terror, 248
    with or without fear, 256–259
rally-round-the-flag effect, 5, 27, 277
Rand Corporation, 302
Rapaport, Carmit, 193–208, 317
Rapin, Ami-Jacques, 299–309, 318
rationalist perspective, public assessing policies, 22
reactance, communication, 70
reactance hypothesis, terrorism news, 74–76
Reagan, Ronald, 4, 9, 269
Real IRA, Northern Ireland, 141, 148, 149
Red Brigade, 304
Red Hand Commando (RHC), 147
red scares, 269, 277
reflective strategy, rhetoric, 232–234
religion
    Poland, 180–181
    terrorism in terms of, 15–16
religious fanaticism, new terrorism, 270
religious labels
    divided Northern Ireland society, 143–147
    Northern Ireland, 140
Report of the Expert Behavioral Analysis Panel, 308
representational force, 277
Republican Action Against Drugs (RAAD), Northern Ireland, 150
Republicans
    political information, 71
    terrorism images, 79
    terrorism information, 68
    terrorism news, 76, 80
    torture and terrorists, 12–13
    trust and president, 11
residential segregation, Northern Ireland, 144–145

responsibility, appraisals, 128
Revolutionary Nuclei, 302, 304
rhetoric, reflective strategy, 232–234
rhetorical coercion, 277
Ridge, Tom, *xvii*
Right-Wing Authoritarianism (RWA), 130, 177–179
risk
  availability, 229
  availability heuristic, 228–232
  familiarity, 229–230
  management for terrorism fear, 272
  media and awareness of, 234
  probability, 229
  probability neglect, 232–238
  prospect theory, 238–240
  regulation of perceived risk, 227–228
  terrorism, 296
  terrorist threats, 227
  voluntary risk tolerance, 239
risk communication, politics of fear, 295–296
risk orientation, threat, 61–62
risk reduction, war on terror, 166
risk society, 277, 294–295
Robinson, Peter, 145, 151
Romney, Mitt, 13
Rose Marches, Norway, 247, 248
Royal Ulster Constabulary (RUC), 141
Russell, Katheryn, 284
Russia, 172, 276
Rwandan Genocide, 86

Sadler, Melody, 125–133, 318
sadness, antiterrorism policy, 131
safeguarding, fear triggering, 111
St. Andrew's Agreement, Northern Ireland, 140
security, 88
  airport, 12, 126, 131, 157, 167–168, 173, 271, 289
  airport and public events, 293
  Australia, 167–168
  comprehensive or networked, 307
  terrorism fear, 271–272
Sekerdej, Maciek, 171–186, 318
September 11, 2001 attacks, *xv*, 3
  anger response, 129–130
  expansion of terrorism and propaganda, 290–293
  fear response, 130
  leader rhetoric, 85–86
  "new age" theme, 90–91
  personal impact, 125
Shambaugh, George, 20–47, 318
shattered assumptions approach, COR theory, 203
Shiite pilgrims, Al Kadhimiya Mosque, 111
Silver, Roxane, 20, 25, 47
Sinclair, Samuel Justin, *xv–xxiii*, 313
Sinn Féin, Northern Ireland, 140, 143
Smith, Stephen, 158
social dominance orientation (SDO), ideology, 177–179
social feedback, threat perception, 179
social identity theory, 64
  anxiety and fear, 55
  group membership, 128
Social Security, trust in government, 7
Spain, *xvii*. *See also* Madrid
  fear of terrorism, 172
  Madrid bombings and elections in, 235–236, 304–305
  political impact of terrorism, 304–305, 307
  terrorist attacks, 230t
stability, attributions, 127
state of terror, 160
Steen-Johnsen, Kari, 246–263, 318
Stevens, Ambassador, assassination, *xv–xvi*
Stevens, Michael J., 51–64, 318
sting operations, FBI, 291–292
Stolier, Ryan, 125–133, 318
strategists, image of terrorists, 175
stress-based model, political consequences of exposure, 201–204
Stress-Based Model of Political Extremism, 202, 204
stress response, exposure to violence, 196
Structural Equation Modeling (SEM)
  fear rallying model, 257, 258f
  prophylactic effect of trust on fear, 258, 259f
Sudan, 204
suicide bomber, 112, 301
suicide terrorism. *See also* terrorism
  Afghanistan, 114–117
  consequences for politicians and governments, 113–114

suicide terrorism (*Cont.*)
consequences of fear for Karzai and al–Maliki decisions, 116f
definition, 107
fear, 108–110
fear effects, 109f, 111f
Iraq, 117–120
motives, 102–103
politician's fear of, 120–121
prevalence, 107
PSI-theory, 107–108
response, *xix*
suicide terrorist, 112
Surveillance Devices Bill 2004, Australia, 162
surveillance system
expanded domestic, 288
Norway, 257
risk communication, 296
terrorism fear, 272–273
voting behavior, 59, 60
survey
control variables, 27t, 30
descriptive statistics, 25
policy support for war in Iraq, 29–30
public perceptions of threat, 28–29
questions and variables, 26t, 27t
U.S. policy in Iraq, 36t, 37t, 38t, 39t, 40t, 41t, 42t, 43t
suspect communities, *xx*, *xxiii*, 142, 278
Sydney Morning Herald, 158
Syria, 194

Taliban, 110, 116, 117, 291, 303
Tanweer, Shehzad, 229
Taylor Nelson Sofres (TNS) Gallup, survey in Norway, 249–250
Telecommunications Act (2004, 2005, 2006, 2007), Australia, 162
terror. *See* death terror; psychological terror
terrorism, 157, 232. *See also* suicide terrorism
9/11 and expansion of, 290–293
climate of violence, 193–194
cognition and emotion interplay, 131–132
comparative analyses, 300–301
as a condition, 293–294
counterterrorism, 21f
crime narrative, 86–87
Democrats and liberals rejecting news, 69–71
exposure to, and psychological distress, 195–197
fear and popular culture, 288–289
fear of, in Australia, 160–164
hawkish foreign policy, 70–71
international, 86
international significance, *xvii–xviii*
narratives, 102–103
national security threat, 30, 31t
news messages, 67–68
Northern Ireland, 140–147
perceptions in Poland, 174–177
personal security threat, 30, 32t
Poland and threat of, 181–183
political reactions to, 52–53
politics, 51
psychology, *xvi*
public fears of, 168–169
public views on policies to combat, 10–13
societal implications, *xxi–xxii*
torture and terrorists, 12–13
trust in government and perceptions of threats, 30–33
understanding public opinion and responses to, 14–16
vagueness of definition of, 307–308
war narrative, 86–87
Western political rhetoric, 90
Terrorism Act of 2000, 237
Terrorism Act of 2006, 237
Terrorism and the Politics of Fear, Altheide, 283
terrorism fear
contemporary, 269–271
counterterrorism procedures, 272–273
memorialization or collective remembering, 273
normalization of, 271–274
political elites, 276
politics of, 267–268, 274–278, 279
security, 271–272
social context, 267
tool for elite exploitation, 276–277
terrorism industry, 273
terrorist attacks
anthrax, 306
Australia, 157–158
Bali bombings of 2002, 156, 167
bombing of Killyhelvin Hotel, 148

government preventing future, 263t
leader rhetoric, 85–87
Libya on September 11, 2012, xv–xvi
London 2005, 0xxi, 73, 160, 163, 173, 229, 301
Madrid in March 2004, xv, xxi, 173, 229, 301
Norway July 2012, xxi, 246
Oklahoma City bombing, 125, 251, 252
Omagh bombing in 1998, 147–148
psychological impact of, 305–307
U.S. in September 11, 2001, xv, 3, 85–86, 160, 161, 290
terrorists
homegrown threats, 235
image of, 175–176
terror management theory (TMT), xxi, xxiii, 64, 217
anger, 58
anxiety and fear, 55
human behavior, 161
mortality fear, 213–214
mortality salience, 217
nationalism, 179
opinion-based groups, 63
Terror Post-9/11 and the Media, Altheide, 283
threat perception, 0xviii
Australia, 157–160
counterterrorism, 21f
fear and, 201–204
fear of terrorism, 112–113
ideology, 74–76
Iraq war, 34–35
news influencing, 68–69
partisanship, 0xix
past research of fear and, 247–249
Poland, 174–177
public and terrorism, 28–29
trust in government, 22–25
types, 200
Tokyo sarin gas attack, 270, 303
torture, terrorists, 12–13
Towards a Democratic Process, Club de Madrid, 165
traffic accidents, comparing to terrorist bombings, 238–239
transatlantic airline plot, 237
Traveler Redress Inquiry Program (TRIPS) program, 272
The Truman Show (film), 164
trust in government, 3, 5f

American National Election Studies (ANES), 4, 5f
changes over time, 4–5
consequences of public, 8–10
counterterrorism, 21f
descriptive statistics of survey, 25
fears of terrorism, 112
focusing on the decline, 5–8
Iraq war, 34–35
Norway, 248–249, 254–256, 255t
perceptions of threat of terrorism, 30–33
Poland, 181–183
policy support, 35, 44
protection from terrorist threats, 239–240
questions, 26t, 27t
relationship of fear and, 246, 247–249
survey, 25, 27–28
terrorism and, xvi
threat and, 22–25
Turkey, 113

U.K. Prevention of Terrorism Act of 2005, 231
Ulster Defence Association (UDA), 147
Ulster Freedom Fighters (UFF), 147
Ulster Volunteer Force (UVF), 141, 147
unconscious emotion
death terror as, 213
notion of, 215
United Kingdom
anti-terrorist policies, 231
collective identity, 277
fear of terrorism, 172
public opinion polls, 232
security programs, 275
terrorism industry, 273
terrorist attacks, 231t
United Nations, 20, 182, 269
United Nations Assistance Mission to Afghanistan (UNAMA), 114–115, 117
United States
casualties and policy in Iraq, 38t, 39t
collective identity, 277
financial costs and policy in Iraq, 40t, 41t
justification in post-9/11 Iraq attack, 35, 36t, 37t
mortality salience, 218–219
popular culture and news, 286
questionnaire, 218
terrorism industry, 273
time to achieve objectives in Iraq, 42t, 43t

unknown risk, perception, 174
U.S. airline industry, terrorism, xvi–xvii
USA PATRIOT Act, 55, 219, 272, 288
U.S. Central Intelligence Agency (CIA), 173, 174, 274
US-Ireland Alliance, 146

Verdens Gang, 261
victimization, popular culture and news, 286
Vietnam, 4, 6, 22–23, 269
violent dissident republicanism, Northern Ireland, 147–150
volunteer, 112
voting behavior, political engagement, 59–60

Wag the Dog (film), 164
war narrative, 86
  alternative, 102–103
  elements of, 87–89
War of Independence, 273
War of Terror story, 80–81
War on Terror, xv, 7, 10, 16, 57, 70, 80, 278
  leader rhetoric, 85–87, 101–102
  negotiation of risk, 166
  term, 157
  using fear for consensus, 162
Washington Post, 5, 13
Watergate scandal, 4
Wave of Terror, 75, 76

Wayne, Carly, 193–208, 319
weapons of mass destruction, 20, 95–96, 271
Weisz, Bradley M., 125–133, 319
West Bank, 194, 202, 206
Wetherell, Geoffrey, 125–133, 319
Wollebaek, Dag, 246–263, 319
women. *See* gender
World Trade Center, 3, 69, 86, 219
  1993 bombing, 52
  first attack in 1993, 270
  images of, 70, 73, 131
  narrative, 103
worldview defense paradigm, terror management theory (TMT), 161
World War II, 22, 86, 144, 269
Worldwide Incidents Tracking System, National Counterterrorism Center, 230, 230t, 231t

yellow scare, Japanese Americans, 269
Yemen, 278

Zajonc, Robert, 215
Zapatero, José, 235, 304
Zimbabwe, 276
Zougam, Jamal, 235

Ødegård, Guro, 246–263, 317